ASHES OF IMMORTALITY

Widow-Burning in India

Catherine Weinberger-Thomas

TRANSLATED BY JEFFREY MEHLMAN AND DAVID GORDON WHITE

The University of Chicago Press Chicago and London

CATHERINE WEINBERGER-THOMAS is professor of Hindi at the Institut National des Langues et Civilisations Orientales, and a member of the Centre d'Études de l'Inde et de l'Asie du Sud, École des Hautes Études en Sciences Sociales, Paris. She is the author of *L'Ashram de l'amour. Le gandhisme et l'imaginaire* (1979) and editor of *L'Inde et l'imaginaire* (1988).

The University of Chicago Press, Chicago 60637
The University of Chicago Press, Ltd., London

Printed in the United States of America
08 07 06 05 04 03 02 01 00 99   1 2 3 4 5

ISBN: 0-226-88568-2 (cloth)
ISBN: 0-226-88569-0 (paper)

Originally published as *Cendres d'immortalité. La crémation des veuves en Inde.* ©
Éditions du Seuil, February 1996

Library of Congress Cataloging-in-Publication Data

Weinberger-Thomas, Catherine.
[Cendres d'immortalité. English]
Ashes of immortality : widow-burning in India / Catherine Weinberger-Thomas ; translated by Jeffrey Mehlman and David Gordon White.
p. cm.
Includes bibliographical references and index.
ISBN 0-226-88568-2 (cloth : alk. paper). — ISBN 0-226-88569-0 (paper : alk. paper)
1. Widow suicide—India. 2. Sati—India. 3. Widows—Legal statutes, laws, etc.—India. 4. Hinduism—Social aspects—India. I. Mehlman, Jeffrey. II. White, David Gordon. III. Title.
GT3370.W5613 1999
393′.9—dc21   99-37258
CIP

∞ The paper used in this publication meets the minimum requirements of the American National Standard for Information Sciences—Permanence of Paper for Printed Library Materials, ANSI Z39.48-1992.

TO THE MEMORY OF JÁNOS AND MARCSA,

WHO WOULD HAVE FOUND THEMSELVES IN IT

In India one must avoid being either a dog or a widow.

—Henri Michaux, *A Barbarian in Asia*

Now the two branches of the curve, the metaphysical and the pragmatic, were meeting; the *mors philosophica* had been accomplished: the operator, burned by the acids of his own research, had become both subject and object, both the fragile alembic and the black precipitate at its base; the experiment that he had thought to confine within the limits of the laboratory had extended itself to every human experience.

—Marguerite Yourcenar, *The Abyss*

In isolation, a puzzle piece means nothing—just an impossible question, an opaque challenge. But as soon as you have succeeded . . . in fitting it into one of its neighbours, the piece disappears, ceases to exist as a piece. The intense difficulty preceding this link-up—which the English word *puzzle* indicates so well—not only loses its *raison d'être,* it seems never to have had any reason, so obvious does the solution appear. The two pieces so miraculously conjured are henceforth one, which in its turn will be a source of error, hesitation, dismay, and expectation.

—Georges Perec, *Life, A User's Manual*

CONTENTS

ILLUSTRATIONS

ACKNOWLEDGMENTS

The research that has resulted in this book, which has combined both textual analysis and fieldwork, would not have been possible without the cooperation of all those persons who gave me their help—often under difficult circumstances. I especially have my Indian informants in mind, some of whom asked that their names not be mentioned. Yet their contributions are essential, and I am deeply indebted to each and every one of them.

First and foremost, I wish to thank Sarasvati Joshi, my Indian sister, who was tireless in providing me with every sort of precious information, and without whose assistance I could not have obtained or verified much of the material presented here. This book owes a great deal to her. I also wish to thank Henri Chambert-Loir, Roland Lardinois, and David Gordon White for the documentation they helped me to assemble and the support they offered me, as well as Abdul Sattar Khan and Dominique-Sila Khan, who greatly facilitated the final stages of my fieldwork in Rajasthan.

I also wish to thank N. K. Baj, France Bhattacharya, Françoise Cousin, Inder Dan Detha, Violette Graff, Rajendra Joshi, Komal Kothari, Nandkishor Parik, Omkar Singh, N. K. Singhi, Romila Thapar, and K. S. Ujjwal, some of whom offered me illuminating insights in the course of my interviews with them, and others of whom placed hard-to-find documents at my disposal.

Madeleine Biardeau, Catherine Clémentin-Ojha, Charles Malamoud, André Padoux, and Francis Zimmerman read the French manuscript, and this would not have been the book it is without their remarks and advice. Colette Poggi typed the first draft of the bibliography. Catharina Kasi translated the German and Dutch excerpts for me. Silvia Mancini helped me in clarifying a particularly difficult passage from a fifteenth-century Italian work. Federica Boschetti and Frédérique Lanoir in France, and Paul Hackett in the United States, helped me to resolve impossible computer-generated crises. My thanks go out to all of them. Finally, I wish to thank Maurice Olender for welcoming this book into his collection, for the French edition; and Alan Thomas, for the present American edition.

FUNEREAL PRELUDE

A Burning in Bali

It is in outer India, on the most distant marches of Hinduism, that the scene paradoxically will be set—a macabre yet dazzling scene to which the reader shall have to adjust his vision and above all his sensitivity if he is to follow us in our exploration of a cultural enigma in which blinding darkness merges with blinding light. Here, we are inviting him to embark on the discovery of extraordinary aspects of feminine life, or rather of the voluntary death of women; of certain categories of women known in India as satīs. These are women who burn themselves alive on their husbands' funeral pyres in a rite also known (erroneously, in fact) as satī.

These things shock us. They fill us with indignation and horror. Yet Indian tradition exalts them and the Hindu orthodoxy holds them to be eminently prestigious, nay, one of the defining features of its identity. It is only through our concerted attention to them, as we work our way through a maze of texts, images, and forms of worship, that the opacity of these facts will give way to transparency: like the contours of the night, they must be intuited before they can be apprehended. By way of preparing the reader for this exile from the familiar, we begin by casting him upon the shore of the exotic as we transport him to the small kingdom of Badung, in the south of Bali.

It is 1829. The witness, Pierre Dubois, is himself worth the trip. This Netherlands-Indies official, of French or Walloon extraction, has been given the assignment, in 1827, of proceeding to Bali with the sole purpose of acquiring a contingent of male slaves. The Dutch colonial army is embroiled in a war with the Javanese prince Dipanegara of Jogjakarta, and is in need of men to bolster its troop strength. All of this gives Dubois occasion to provide us with a *Légère Idée de Balie en 1830:* eight letters that are a treasure trove of information regarding trade, customs, religion, and power in these climes in which a foreigner hailing from Europe finds himself in the unwonted position of pagan most "especially while the god *Brahma* is publically exercising his office."[1]

It is the eighth of these letters that contains the description of the ritual into which we wish to initiate the reader. It is based on notes taken even as the ceremony was unfolding before Dubois's eyes; and his account was drawn up in the hours that immediately followed. The scene, still fresh in his mind, was a spectacle which no eyewitness, before or after, has ever succeeded in erasing from his memory.

"Yesterday evening," he writes to his anonymous addressee, "I left you in the great outer courtyard of a Balinese palace named *Bentjigna,* with the promise of taking you today to that part of the city of *Badong* consecrated to the celebration of funeral rites. I will in fact have you behold a rite of supreme interest, since it will involve a prince of the highest rank. . . . To begin, you must picture this as the most august and solemn of brahmine religious ceremonies . . . the entire body of ministers of the brahmanic cult . . . will be performing its pontifical duties."

We are in the very heart of the royal city. The burning ground, consecrated to that use from ancient times, is adjacent to the palace of the Pamacutans, whose dynasty has ruled over Badung since the beginning of the century. Of the three Rajahs who have shared the power, one died in 1817; and his successor has died, precisely, in 1829. Or rather, in the Balinese perspective, Gusti G'de Ngurah Pamacutan is about to join, through the funerary rites, the ranks of the gods. Among the throng of a hundred thousand spectators is Dubois, probably in the company of a young Englishman named Tomlin.[2] As the emissary of a power with which "speculative and friendly relations" have been established, the Dutchman is, in this circumstance, the guest and protégé of the deceased Rajah's youngest son, Gusti Made Oka. With as much courtesy as enthusiasm, the Balinese prince is about to unveil to his guest the mysteries of his country's great funeral ceremonies.

The cremation ground is divided into three parts. "There, to the east, is the space reserved for sovereign princes and other members of the high nobility. Here, in the middle, is the site allotted the lesser nobility. There, to the west, is the area assigned to the common people." As for the "haughty Brahmanas," their obsequies take place at a particular site, in the small market town of Intaran, of which the pontiff of Badung is the landowner. Intaran looms over the eastern end of the kingdom, inscribing in its very topography the privileged status this "divine troop" enjoys in Bali.

It is in the first section of this funeral ground—to the east, the direction of the gods—that the traditional pavilion of sun-dried bricks has been erected. Its impressive twelve-foot elevation testifies to the pomp of a ceremonial intended to reflect the exalted status of the deceased. It would be lower for men of lesser birth, and still lower for women of royal rank. In Bali as in India, all is a matter of hierarchy, and death, far from undermining social stratification, only throws it into higher relief.

This Pavilion, whose sides face the four cardinal points, is open, resting on four posts topped by a conical roof made of rough cloth. . . . In the middle of the pavilion, atop supports three feet in height, is a most skillfully sculpted (and no less magnificently decorated) wooden casket, depicting a large variety of quadruped, sometimes a *Lion,* sometimes an *Elephant,* and sometimes a *Crocodile.* For a princess, it is a white *Cow.* The quadruped before our eyes . . . is a red *Lion,* facing eastward, whose long and bristling mane resembles leaping flames.

At the time the royal coffin comes to be placed in the fire, this funerary casket with its leonine motif will serve as a vessel for the remains of the Rajah of Badung—or what is left of them, since custom dictates that they be held for months within the palace. It was necessary to await what the brahmans deemed to be the favorable day, a day marked by the convergence of every propitious sign and falling within the period of the bright lunar fortnight. In Bali, the waiting period between a person's death and his funeral could at times be considerable, with variations occurring as a function of one's status within the caste hierarchy. As the German Orientalist R. T. Friederich noted in 1849, there were corpses in Badung that had been preserved for twenty years.[3] Embalmed with spices, adorned with certain pieces of finery (for example, a gold ring with a ruby setting, placed in the mouth to ensure protection against demons), cured in the juices of their own secretions gathered together in a collecting vessel, sprinkled with lustral water and libations of various sorts, bodies would be covered with cloth, matting, and a bamboo screen. This procedure did not prevent the decomposition of the flesh. After some six months, the corpse was entirely desiccated, such that, were the cremation to be delayed any longer, there would be nothing left but a skeleton.

Well to the side and to the east of the Pavilion stands the foot of a stairway or inclined bridge which, sloping upward at an angle of 45 degrees, reaches a height of over 100 perpendicular feet. This bridge, four feet in width and consisting of Bamboo and rattan, is supported by two rows of coconut trunks . . . but since, even though that tree attains a gigantic height in *Balie,* there are nevertheless none capable of reaching the required elevation . . . it has been necessary to resort to expedients: using bamboo, rattan, and a great deal of artistry, a support mechanism has been developed which can only be classified as bold and ingenious. . . . Lastly, we can see at the top of the aforementioned bridge a level surface upon which there stands a little house, which has been rendered most attractive by its gilded, festooned, and floral decorations. As for the pillars and railings of the bridge itself, these are beautified by sprays of green leafy branches in such amazing profusion that when viewed from the outside, the various parts of the framework are nearly imperceptible.

Turning his gaze toward the south, Dubois notices a row of similar, albeit less lofty, structures. A horizontal bridge affords access to the leafy cabin from the south, whereas the principal bridge, which faces on the lion-pavilion, leads to it from the north. It is at this juncture that he notices the flaming chasms the suspended bridges overhang at their highest point of elevation. The burning pits are brick constructions consisting of circular walls three to four feet in height and approximately ten feet in diameter, topped by a row of banana trunks.

Looking in the opposite direction, he perceives the sumptuous *pondoks*, canopies of sorts reserved for members of the royal family, each attending the ceremony in the company of his principal wife and daughters. Thousands of men and women “of the plebeian caste” rush onto the square. The crowd is so dense, so compact, that the trees themselves are crawling with people.

It is eleven o’clock. The cannon booms, followed by musket shots, whilst the gongs of the *gamelan*s blend with devotional chants, forming a veritable jungle of sound. It is now that a three-story bamboo pyramid, decorated with festoons and tassels of colored paper, comes into view. Atop its upper story, the silhouettes of two women stand out against the sky. Is it its height, of approximately forty feet, that is so striking to the eye, or is it the troop of men (no less than fifty in number) who are carrying it on their shoulders? A company of footsoldiers forms its escort; this is followed by a cortege of women, a virtual procession of ritual vessels, each carried on the head of a woman. Other men bring up the rear, carrying “a very high movable ladder.”

Once it has arrived on the square, the cortege heads toward the first of the structures cum pits located to the south of the Lion Pavilion; it parades twice around this first edifice before stopping at the foot of its bridge, where the Pyramid is set down; four strapping fellows take the movable ladder and set it up against the Pyramid; they then climb this and in groups of two take in their arms the two women who were on the highest storey. They continue to carry them in their arms as they come down the ladder and then climb up the bridge, up to the little house located at the top. One of the two women is the first *Béla;* those who carried her are her father and brother, or other close relatives. The other woman is a *Manko* . . . whose duty it is to accompany the *Béla* and supervise her acts until the final moment.

Once again, silence reigns. But soon a new clamor arises: a second pyramid has made its entrance onto the square; and with it the second *bela* (which term, as will have been surmised, indicates "the woman who will burn herself alive"). This scene is repeated several times, with the same ceremonial. Curiously, Dubois fails to mention the number of women who sacrificed themselves on this day, but we know from other sources that there were seven. At last, all the *bela*s have been set in place, like so many precious objects, in the huts built "for their sake" atop the bridges. The last of these is set apart from the others: she has been led before an edifice without a bridge, with nothing but the pit before her. This woman has chosen a different death. As an alternative to fire, women are in fact free to choose a dagger with a wavy blade called a kris, which they use to pierce their breast (fig. 1).

Noon. The heat is intense: that of the pounding sun to be sure, but also the heat belching forth from the the burning pits, which are constantly being fed. Moreover, fireballs are blowing off into the air with a muted, lugubrious roar which, as Dubois notes, is admirably attuned to the occasion. But soon the crackling of the flaming firepits is drowned out by a new explosion of gunfire and noise. It is now that a pyramidal hulk, some eleven stories and more than a hundred feet in height, comes into view, towering over the highest treetops. Making its way slowly, it looks as if it were being carried by the enormous tortoise that seemingly supports it—a sheer optical illusion, for this is nothing other than the shoulders of its four hundred porters! This moving bamboo monument, grandiosely decorated with brilliantly colored silk bunting and netting, heralds our departure from this "funereal prelude" and our entry into the central part of the ceremony. The presence of the high priest, seated next to the royal coffin on the uppermost floor of the crematory tower, is a clear indication of this.

Fig. 1. The Kriss: Nawang Rum and Madukara stab themselves. Drawing by Ida Madé Tlaga. University of Leiden, Balinese Manuscript Collection (cod. or. 3390-138).

The escort has the same fantastic proportions as the mechanism itself. It is led by a large battalion, armed with pikes and muskets, and in martial array—which is tantamount to saying that its men would be stark naked were it not for the white loincloths they are wearing about their hips (which, to the Dutchman's indignation, conceal neither buttocks nor thighs) and, on their chests, a kind of red sleeveless jerkin (which only goes down to the nipples). Their heads are covered with white cloth turbans that leave the nape of the neck and the top of the scalp exposed: Balinese men are required to be shaved upon the death of their prince; their hair, as a result, has grown back so as to resemble a thick brush cut. Officers wear the same attire, save for the jerkin, which is green. Each carries a kris on his back. More naked still are the brahmans, whose throng advances between the battalion and the pyramid. They are wearing neither jerkin nor turban; however, they too are armed with the "mighty kris." The pyramid is followed by a troop of former officers and followers of the late Rajah. Bringing up the rear is a group of three to four hundred women, also carrying pots on their heads.

When it draws even with the bridge adjoining the lion pavilion, the pyramid comes to a halt. Several brahmans nimbly clamber up: these will assist the high priest in transferring the bones of the Rajah into a less precious coffin, to be fed into the flames. Greeted by salvos and preceded by the royal guard in black jerkins, the court now makes its stately entrance.

Here is the current reigning prince, surrounded by the regalia of his supreme power, who is ushered in upon a ceremonial palanquin carried on the shoulders of four prominent citizens. The royal glaive, the two diamond-studded krises, the four great pikes with golden inlay, and two huge guilded "Payons" carried by the high officers of the crown surround the royal palanquin. The Prince is clad exactly like his guard, with the exception of his jerkin, which is of yellow velvet embroidered with gold; his cloth band of embroidered silk; and, last of all, his head, which is bare.

Members of the royal family follow on foot, in blue and green jerkins. . . . Last in the procession are the officers in the service of the new Rajah. The glittering cortege halts to the west of the lion pavilion to offer its final respects to the deceased sovereign. Then it disperses, with each returning to his place. The troop of princesses, as if airborne, makes its way along the palace wall to the royal canopy. Hereafter, not a sound will interrupt the delicate and meticulous operations the brahmans will conduct under the close surveillance of the high priest (called *Pedanda Agong*). Here they are spreading bolts of new white cloth over the full length of the great bridge, while others are lowering the royal coffin to carry it atop a fine palanquin to the lion pavilion, where the same material has been unfurled. The funeral procession circles the pavilion twice, after which the long series of lustrations begins.

Surrounded by the principal officiants, the *Pedanda Agong,* who has previously been busying himself with "manipulating what was inside the coffer of bones," pours the contents of the vessels carried by the women over the scarlet lion, whose entrails presently shield the remains of the Rajah.

As he spills the aromatic fluids from each of the three hundred vessels, he intones *mantras,* ritual formulas, "so energetically that one could hear their cadence two hundred feet away." Each pot is then shattered, with half its fragments cast to the west and half to the east. Deepened by the silence, time seems to stand still in this unending sequence of gestures joined to words.

Then, all of a sudden, things appear to speed up. Now a dozen brahmans lay hold of long torches of precious wood, and running to light them at the nearest pit, bring them to the high priest, who places them beneath the lion's belly.

No sooner does the flame appear beneath the Pavilion, than the *Béla* who had occupied the pit structure farthest to the right steps out of her little house. She is clad in white, but only from her breasts down to her knees; her hair, arranged in a curious way, is adorned with flowers. Her family and the *Manko* are crouched beside the railing of the small horizontal bridge across which she slowly proceeds; they encourage her to bear up nobly under the pressure of her role; her movements and poses are those of a Tandak (dancer). A deep silence reigns on all sides—all one hears is the dark murmur of the fire-pits. After ten minutes she reaches the midpoint of her bridge, where she comes to a door. While she is standing before this door, a turtle-dove that had been attached to it by a piece of thread tied to its foot and whose tether the *Manko* has now cut, flies up into the air. At this moment, the cheers of a hundred thousand stentorian voices break out on all sides, for this signals that her self-sacrifice has met with the gods' approval.

A single circumstance may yet save the *bela:* menstruation (which is occasionally provoked by fear) would render her impure and disqualify her for this sacrifice. The *manko* consequently proceeds with a secret examination. And if such be the case, the woman returns to the world of the living without further unpleasantness.

When the cheers occasioned by the flight of the turtle-dove have abated, the *Béla* continues on her journey: now, however, she makes her way upon a plank extending to the end of her bridge . . . most of those in attendance intone funeral chants . . . the *Béla* lets down her hair, letting it flow down over her shoulders . . . her skirt has been tied up around her knees like a pair of drawers . . . once again, she takes up the movements and poses of the Tandak. . . . [H]er father passes her his kris, with which she cuts her arm and shoulder . . . using the point of the blade, she draws blood from the wounds she has inflicted on herself and stains her forehead with it. With this, she seeks to convince her family, who urge her to persevere, that she is unafraid of death . . . her voice rises in accompaniment with the pious chants she hears all around her . . . at last, she arrives at the fatal end of the plank . . . returns the kris to her father and, with her hands crossed over her chest, falls straight downward, suspended for a moment in the air before being devoured by the burning pit that awaits her, while a dozen men placed around the pit in anticipation of this moment, and armed with firewood and long bamboo poles filled with oil, throw or empty them on top of her—and while the clamorous cheers of the multitude ring out, blessing her happy fate, and a great column of black smoke, rising from the pit, shoots up into the sky.

Dubois has more than sufficient time to observe these women in their crossing of the bridge as well as of the plank: nothing in their expression or demeanor betrays the slightest fear. On the contrary, their faces reflect a perfect serenity, nay, an ecstatic anticipation. It is true that not all are equally intrepid. There are those who, having reached the final brink, "fanned by the fiery air belching up out of the pit, and envisaging the horrendous spectacle beneath their feet, hesitate to take the final step." In such cases, the *bela*'s father or brother raises the other end of the plank. Less than five minutes separate this from the next identical scene, which follows as soon as the "vociferous acclamation of the crowd" has died down.

Each little house, and each bridge and pit successively offer the spectator's eye a similar triumphal catastrophe, until the last *Béla*—with the exception of she who had wished to die of a kris-thrust to the heart. . . . [W]hen her time comes, she emerges, is surrounded by her kin, receives her father's kris with which she pierces herself perpendicularly above the left shoulder; whereupon she falls, and her father and brothers lift her to cast her, still twitching, into the blaze.

And Dubois adds: "This was not the least horrible scene in the play." Among these women, he is most touched by an old servant of the deceased Rajah: in less than four seconds she has crossed the bridge, and in three bounds has leapt into the pit.

When the coffin has been totally consumed, the court withdraws and the crowd disperses. Only a guard of brahmans and the male relations of the *bela* remain on the premises. These will wait until the following morning for the fire-pits to cool down sufficiently, and then pick through the ashes for bones not totally consumed by the flames. These bones will be placed in funerary urns—golden for the Rajah and women who had belonged to the "nobility," and silver for those descended from the "common people." The urns will be carried to a magnificent altar—that of Rajah to the east, and those of the women slightly lower and to the west. The funeral ground nonetheless continues to blaze, since people are now burning everything that had been used in the ceremony (with the exception of a few precious pieces of cloth): coffins, pyramids, matting, fabrics, and decorations.

Ten days after the obsequies, on a different site located to the east of the palace, another body of funerary observances will be celebrated with the end of ensuring the dead a happy afterlife. These rites, equally grandiose and resplendent, are characterized by a remarkable attention to "protocol" and by the exuberance of a symbol system in which each minute element reproduces, ad infinitum, the totality, the density of its meaning.

This first account ushers us into the rite of widow sacrifice. Here we have encountered it in a perspective (as viewed from Bali) in which it has been blended with indigenous elements, and projected upon a screen of monumental proportions. In fact, the "apparatus of death," that extraordinary mechanism composed of fixed and moving structures (the pavilion, crematory towers, suspended bridges, *bela*s' huts, and animal-shaped coffin), the enormous cast of thousands, and such accessories as the kris and turtledove properly belong to the funerary tradition of this region of Asia. However, while the ceremonial is different in both its pomp and its attention to detail, the rite as a social practice as well as the religious sentiment that inspires it is related, undeniably, to the body of data one finds in India. So it is that the surreal dimensions of this Balinese variant paradoxically allow us to gauge the phenomenon in its true proportions.

Dubois's letter is valuable for yet another reason: it has led us, from the outset, into a world of representations in which the indigenous point of view, far from being occulted (as in the great majority of such accounts), has been woven into the narrative texture itself. It is through the good graces of Gusti Made Oka that Dubois attends the funeral of the Rajah of Badung. It is in his company that Dubois takes notes on all he observes. It is his remarks that Dubois reports. Moreover, the Balinese prince shows himself to be quite gifted in his improvised role as cultural go-between. He intervenes indefatigably to make a point, explain, expand, and argue. His learned commentaries on the ritual shape Dubois's description and cast their light—or shadow—over the scene being shown to us. The contrast in reactions thus stands out in exemplary relief. For whereas the Dutch slave trader is shocked and deeply moved by the horrific tragedy he has viewed with nothing but regret and repugnance, the Balinese, by his own admission, derives extreme pleasure from it. He wonders and exults over it, as its pageant literally brings to life a heroic fantasy world that is, for him and all his compatriots, all too uncommon, eminently sacred, admirable, and joyous. "May the wolf gobble me down for supper if one were ever to catch me again at such a spectacle," Dubois exclaims. Whereas Gusti Made

Oka, calling on the foreigners invited to the ceremony to back him up, says: "Well then, gentlemen, are you not amazed at the resoluteness of all these *Bélas*' spirits? Not one of them flinched; every one of them *fell* so grandly. It has greatly pleased the court to see them; but now let us dine."

Dubois protests: what he has seen resembles a descent into Tartarus. These men who burn women alive have the ferocious look of devils about them. In the final analysis, all of these ceremonies have been devised, out of superstition and deceit, with the sole aim of committing fanatical murders with impunity. He nonetheless notes that for the Balinese, the souls of the *bela*s are henceforth enthroned in a world of eternal felicity. Everyone returns home with a look of uncommon gaiety imprinted on their faces. As for the families of these unfortunate women, they could not be happier: the *bela*s will now ward off any calamity that might otherwise befall them. What, exactly, are we being shown? A sinister panorama of the refined forms of violence to which the women of Bali were subjected, or an edifying tableau of the beauties of voluntary sacrifice? Dubois's *Letter* invites us (unknowingly, but vigorously) to evaluate in relative terms those cultural phenomena that seem to challenge both reason and nature.[4]

A Question of Words

The word *bela,* which entered into the Balinese and Indonesian from Old Javanese, is worthy of our attention. The term is possessed of a wide array of meanings, an obscure etymology, and a complex semantic history. Out of all its specific usages, however, there is a common notion that emerges: *bela* means to follow into death—and, by metonymy, those persons who accompany their deceased master to his celestial abode. *Bela*s are the servants of a prince who immolate themselves on the day of his funeral; *bela*s the warriors who run *amok* if their chief is defeated in battle;[5] and *bela*s the wives who are burned or krissed during the grandiose cremations reserved for members of the royal castes. With this, the lexical landscape becomes somewhat more nuanced and blurred, as it is refracted through a second term: this is *satia* (or *mesatia)*, through which the Sanskrit *satī* is readily recognizable. In its primary sense, *satī* simply means "a virtuous wife, faithful to her conjugal vow."[6] The word (whose tortured career will be uncovered in due course) comes to take on the meaning of a "wife who immolates herself on her husband's funeral pyre" through circumstances we will elucidate forthwith.

At times the terms *bela* and *satia* are so tightly intertwined as to become synonymous (in certain arenas they are employed interchangeably); in other cases they enter into a hierarchical relationship that renders them virtual antonyms. The word *satia* may be used in a technical sense to designate women who immolate themselves on their husbands' crematory fires, as opposed to a separate pit (as we saw in Dubois's *Letter*). These alone will have mingled their ashes with those of the deceased. This privilege confers upon them a greater dignity and consequently a status undeniably higher (in the symbolic order) than that of the *bela*s.[7]

But above all else what separates these two categories of women is the redundancy of death among the *satia*s, who die by the kris before being burned—by their own hand if they have the strength and courage to do so; or by that of close family members or of men assigned the task if such is not the case. The first thrust generally falls between the left asternal ribs, the next below the left shoulder blade. The serpentine dagger is plunged transversally, and up to the hilt, so as to reach the heart. The operation is not simple, nor is the kris easy to handle. Zollinger, a Swiss naturalist who had gone to the region to collect plant specimens, and who found himself caught up (against his will) in the Dutch expedition against the Rajahs of Bali, witnessed the burning of a *gusti*[8] on the neighboring island of Lombok. The widow, who was young and beautiful, had chosen such a death. Her adoptive brother asked her in a low voice whether she still consented. When she responded in the affirmative, he implored her forgiveness for the violence he was about to inflict on her, took up his kris, and landed a blow on the left side of her chest. The wound was shallow, and the woman remained standing, motionless. The man then threw down his weapon and fled the scene. Another man immediately stepped forward, showing himself to be more adroit than the last. The woman collapsed without a whimper. Her body was rolled into a pallet, which was compressed to force out all the blood. But the woman was still alive. Hereupon, the man who had struck with the greatest result stepped forward once again and finished her off with a thrust to the back, between the shoulder blades. These events transpired in 1846. Like Dubois, Zollinger noted that the native onlookers appeared to find nothing shocking in this "awful butchery."[9]

To stab oneself, and then to leap so cold-heartedly into a flaming pit: each of those acts seems so difficult to grasp in and of itself that the two combined, as our eyewitnesses state, quite defy the imagination. These are, nonetheless, the hard facts and they are closer to us in time than we might believe (the last account dates from 1903: two women immolated themselves during the cremation of the Rajah Ngurah Agung of Tabanan, in southern Bali).[10] It is also remarkable that the ritual structure seems to be in no way modified when there is a dichotomy between voluntary mutilation with the kris, and the death by fire which constitutes its conclusion (and, to be sure, its apotheosis). The *bela*s also wounded themselves with the tip of the kris, and smeared their foreheads with the blood of their wounds as a mark of their determination. But what was no more than a symbolic gesture for the *bela* became an absolute necessity for the *satia.* It is as if the solemn commitment to take one's own life had to be inscribed in the letter of the flesh in order to validate the act itself. The wounded and slashed body gave eloquent voice to the *satia*'s desire to die, or rather to be reunited with her deceased husband.

It may seem paradoxical that the emphatic and fundamentally useless gesture—of stabbing oneself prior to burning oneself—that characterized the *satia*s of Bali has no equivalent in Indian traditions of widow sacrifice. For, in the final analysis, India is the place of origin not only of the word *satia,* but probably of the custom as well; and most especially of the religious ideology that sustains it and was its source. The question then arises as to whether anything comparable to the death of these *satia*s is to be found in the wide array of self-mutilations and self-immolations that have been something of an Indian specialty.

A preliminary remark is in order here. Widow-burning is but one among a variety of forms of a funerary ceremonial that involves the voluntary death of certain categories of survivors. They sacrifice themselves (individually or en masse) in the course of the obsequies of a higher-ranking deceased person—a ruler, master, or husband. The belief underlying this body of suicidal practices (termed altruistic by Durkheim[11]) is that the deceased will enjoy the same goods and services in the beyond as he had on earth. He will need his mount and his weapons to wage war, food to assuage his hunger, and finery to set off his beauty and glory. In the same manner, he will need to be accompanied by his servants, his councillors and, finally, his wives. It is the settling of a debt—a debt of obligation and love (the two go together) binding the various parties engaged to a common master—that lies at the heart of the practice of "following in death."[12] From this standpoint, it can no longer be said that the act of the *satia* is alien to the Indian world.

Veḷevāḷi (or *veḷevāḍica*) is the term employed in the Kannada language to designate the heroic warrior (*vīra,* in Sanskrit) whose life is governed by his vocation for death.[13] The *veḷevāḷi*'s entire existence is caught up in the active devotion he shows his master, a devotion that finds expression in the term "vow of the *veḷe.*" When his master dies, he elects to follow him in death, according to the oath he has taken. In 1298–1299, Marco Polo offered the following account from "Maabar" (Malabar, the name erroneously given to the Coromandel coast in the thirteenth century):

> And know that when the king dies, and his body burns in a great fire, all those barons who were his faithful subjects . . . cast themselves into the fire and burn with the king in order to keep him company in the other world.[14]

And shortly thereafter, in the same third volume of his *Description of the World,* Polo added:

> And I declare to you yet again that in this kingdom [of Tanjore, ruled by King Maravarman Kulashekhara of the Pandya dynasty] there is still another custom: when a man has died and his body is burning, his wife casts herself into the same fire and allows herself to burn along with her baron out of love for him, saying that she wishes to go with him to the other world. And the ladies who act in this manner are widely praised by the people. And I tell you in all truth that many are the women who do as I have told, but not all of them, and that those who are fearful of dying with their husbands are greatly censured.[15]

An inscription from Halebid glorifies the suicide of Kuvara Lakshmana, a general in the army of King Vira-Ballala II of the Hoysala dynasty, who, in keeping with his oath of fealty, followed his king in death in 1220, together with his wife and warriors. He and his wife were thereby united with Garuḍa (the vehicle of the god Viṣṇu) and Lakṣmī (Viṣṇu's consort).[16]

As spectacular as it may appear, however, suicide as an act of loyalty forms but a single panel in a vast tableau, sharing the field with traditions of votive, devotional, and expiatory suicide. The beneficiary of the "murder of the self" *(ātma-hatyā)* is not one's master but rather the deity in its "terrible" aspect. This is the god Śiva, either in his *liṅga* hypostasis, or replaced by the gods Bhairava or Vīrabhadra, those lesser forms of the great god that are so omnipresent in popular devotion. This is also Durgā, a goddess diffracted into an infinite number of divine beings , whose names vary according to time, place, caste, and sectarian affiliation. Here the hero or devotee offers up his body and life to the divinity who granted him the victory or favor he requested.[17] And in order to prove his mettle he, like the *satia,* takes the rhetorical path of excess: he throws himself into a fiery pit, leaps into the void from atop a sheer cliff, flays himself alive, carves out strips of his own flesh (the eight "members" or the "nine parts"), gouges out his eyes, cuts out his tongue, slits his throat, or rips out his heart or entrails. All of these deeds are immortalized by funeral stele whose inscriptions provide descriptions of such practices (figs. 2 to 4).[18]

Figs. 2 and 3. Hero Stones *(vīrakkals)*. Safdarjang Museum, Hyderabad (private collection).

Fig. 4. Stela showing a woman cutting her throat. Safdarjang Museum, Hyderabad (private collection).

The twelfth-century C.E. *Kṛtyakalpataru* of Lakṣmīdhara offers the candidate for suicide for the love of Bhairava all the information he needs, something of a user's manual, complete with indications of the "fruits" *(phala)* gained from the sacrifice as accomplished in this or that fashion.[19] The Lawbook of Vasiṣṭha (the *Vasiṣṭha Dharma Sūtra,* probably composed between 300 and 100 B.C.E.) instructs anyone guilty of having committed the odious crime of brahmanicide to undertake an expiation whose tantric aspect has been emphasized by David Lorenzen: while invoking Yama, the god of the dead, he is to offer into the sacrificial fire eight oblations cut from his own body: hair, skin, blood, flesh, tendon, fat, bone, and marrow.[20] The parts of the human body offered in sacrifice do not all have the same flavor for the god who is consuming them, blood, flesh, and the head being the choicest portions. The *Kālikā Purāṇa,* a Śākta text believed to predate the fourteenth century C.E.,[21] provides useful detail on the subject. One learns that the goddess Kāmākhyā is satisfied for a thousand years by the sacrifice of one man and for a hundred thousand years by that of three men; that human flesh delights her consort Bhairava for three thousand years; and finally that the blood of victims offered in oblation is transformed into ambrosia on the condition that it be purified through ritual formulas:

> The [goddess] Śivā eats the head and the flesh of the sacrifice, and one should, in the course of worship, offer her the head and blood in oblation. Therefore, the wise man shall offer the various sorts of flesh in the burnt offering of food to be consumed [by the Goddess]. The practitioner should definitely not offer raw flesh in worship, with the exception of the bloodied head, because that becomes nectar.[22]

Head offerings were highly valued in southern India.[23] The hero could cut it up piece by piece, or lop it off with a sword, a sabre, or an ingenious instrument—called a *gaṇḍakattera*—designed expressly to facilitate auto-decapitation.[24] We find a description of these procedures and their complex technology of death in the writings of the Franciscan Odoric of Pordenone (1265–1331), the Dominican Jourdain de Séverac (who would become Bishop of Kollam in 1329),[25] and the Venetian merchant Nicolo di Conti (1395–1469)—who visited the Kingdom of Vijayanagar ("Bizengalia," "Bisinagar") and other Indian countries around the year 1420, shortly after the accession to the throne of Devarayya II—and whose travel narrative, *De varietate fortunae,* was written (or rather dictated) in 1448 and published in 1492:

In the city of Cambay [in Gujarat], the priests preach to the people before idols, persuading them to wish to serve the idols through some worthy act, and [assuring] them that the thing that most pleases [the idols] and for which one earns the greatest rewards in the other world is the desire to die and to seek death out of love for them. Therefore, by virtue of the great effectiveness of the priests' power of persuasion, many step resolutely forward to offer themselves, and they are immediately escorted to a platform where, after the performance of certain ceremonies, a large iron collar is placed around their necks; this is rounded on the outside, whereas the inside [which touches the skin] is fashioned like a razor. Hanging down from the front of the collar and over the chest is a chain into which, once they are seated and have lifted their legs, they place their feet. Then, as the priest intones certain words, they bravely extend their feet and, by lifting their head, detach it with a single stroke from the trunk, before the eyes of the entire population; in this way, by offering up their life in sacrifice to their idols, they are deemed saints.[26]

The *Maṇimekhalai,* the celebrated Tamil poem whose date is a matter of debate (some place it in the second century C.E., others in the medieval period), evokes these sacrifices:

Only the friends of the dead dare to tread this terrifying place surrounded by ramparts. Others never enter. Within there stands a vast temple dedicated to the black goddess who dwells in the desert. Before its door is an altar on which offerings are left. The temple is surrounded by trees, whose long branches bow under the burden of the severed heads hanging from them. These are the heads of fanatical votaries, who sacrifice themselves to the goddess.[27]

Tamil Sangam poetry (which dates from the beginning of the common era) teems with references to heroic and devotional sacrifices.[28] Through epigraphy, it is possible to place these rites in their geographical, historical, and religious contexts: they appear to have been prevalent in south India. Recorded since the Pallava period (the end of the third century C.E.), they became widespread in the thirteenth century, at which time such militant Śaivite movements as the Vīraśaivas virtually institutionalized them. The offering of one's head to Śiva became an act of faith. In 1378, King Anavema Reddi of Kondavidu (in present-day Andhra Pradesh) patronized the construction, in the courtyard of the temple of Mallikārjuna at Śrīśailam (a great center of the Vīraśaiva cult), of a stone pavilion (*Vīraśiromaṇṭapa,* the "Pavilion of Heroes' Heads") to facilitate such sacrifices. Other Śaivite communities, such as the Vīrabhadras, the Vīramuṣṭis, or the Mailāra

Vīrabhatas, embraced the practices of self-mutilation and self-sacrifice with equal fervor.[29]

Returning to the word *veḷevāḷi,* it should be noted that it has been glossed as a compound of *veḷe* and *pāli. Veḷe,* from the Sanskrit *velā,* signifies "limit, border, end" and, by extension, "time limit, period, hour." In Hindi, this commonly used word (in the form *belā*) means "time" or "appropriate moment for doing something." *Pāli* (from the Sanskrit *pāla,* "one who guards, protects, defends") designates, among other things, one who observes a vow or keeps a promise. *Veḷevāḷi* would thus have the sense of "one who carries through on a promise or vow at the proper time" (upon his master's death).[30] With this, we find that we have returned to the semantic field of the Old Javanese word *bela,* the point of departure for these linguistic digressions into which we were obliged to enter as a means of glimpsing the relationship between superficially heterogeneous elements.

Immortality: Time Reckoned

A curious feature of the iconography of the stele erected to the memory of heroes in Saurashtra illustrates, in a cryptic manner, the key notion of that future time in which the hero would be called upon to demonstrate his loyalty. On certain "hero-stones," called *pāḷiyo* in Gujarati as well as Rajasthani (the word probably means territorial "guardian"), one encounters a motif that might appear to be out of place in this funerary context: an hourglass.[31] Ancient Tamil poetry mentions an hourglass-shaped drum called a *tuṭi.*[32] At the moment the battle was joined, in which the *vīra* prepared himself to offer his life as an oblation in the sacrifice of war, this drum was played, together with other percussion instruments. The motif of the hourglass may symbolize heroic death—a shared death, for if he failed to meet his own death on the battlefield, the warrior, in killing his enemy, offered the gods a substitute for himself, an alter ego, by the mediation of which he acceded to the "path of heroes."

In India, it is the violence of his death that transforms a victim into an object of worship. The sting of this death (the fact that it occurred prematurely, or that it left its mark in the victim's flesh) appears to lie at the origin of the erection of funerary stele in a culture characterized by a marked absence of monumental funerary art (a point to which we shall return).[33] Ancient Tamil poetry illuminates this link between violence and heroic status: when the king did not die a "good death" while facing his enemies, when he had fallen in an ignominious ordinary death—the victim of the workings of Time, rather than the master of Time through a voluntary death—his body was slashed with a sword in simulation of a heroic demise. Emblazoned thus with the badge of his wounds, the warrior could present himself at the gates of Paradise.[34]

The hourglass may also be interpreted as a sectarian Śaiva symbol and a representation of the small hourglass-shaped two-headed drum called the *ḍamaru.* This drum sets the rhythm for the cosmic dance of Śiva, associated with Time and the recurrence of the cosmic cycles: Śiva-Naṭarāja ("Lord of the Dance") creates and dissolves the worlds. As an emblem of Bhairava, the "terrible" aspect of the god, it heralds the destruction of the worlds at the end of a cosmic age. A highly realistic depiction of the hourglass drum with its beaded strings may be found on a satī stone at the (ninth–tenth century C.E.) Gadag-Betgeri site, in Karnataka. The geometric form of the hourglass may also evoke the interlocking triangles that symbolize the union of Śiva and Śakti in the Śrīcakra diagram. In haṭha yoga and alchemy, two other symbol systems saturated with Tantra, the two triangles symbolize the two halves of the yogic body or the two communicating chambers of an alchemical apparatus.[35]

The hourglass may bear yet another symbolic meaning, one that remains closely connected to the duality of Time, to the tension and mystic union between death and immortality. It may be a rendering of Time as measured in an hourglass, embedded in an image of immortality. It is figured on the upper portion of such stele between the sun and moon, which throughout India together constitute a depiction of eternity (whence the formulation of the traditional wish: may this or that thing last as long as the sun and moon).[36] It is as if the promise of eternal glory depended on a pledge of voluntary death, and as if the long-awaited moment, in which he had to prove his virility and the power of his love, formed the very stuff of a hero's life—his sole end in life.

The Truth about Women

The psychological landscape that has been uncovered here, with unconditional love and absolute fidelity in the foreground, and self-sacrifice as the proof of that love and devotion in the background, is that which defines, quite precisely, the *bhāva* of the satī. *Bhāva* may be defined as one's innate disposition, one's innermost feelings, that constellation of affects that point to a particular moment in one's emotive life, but also reveal an individual's inherent nature (one's *svabhāva*). The history of the word *satī* and the semantic ridges along which its trail has been blazed point out the ways in which conjugal love was fated to cross paths with voluntary death—for women, that is, since within the context of marriage, tradition only acknowledges the love of wives for their husbands—love being a woman's duty.[37]

The word stems from the Sanskrit *as-*, "to be," which generates the present active participle *sat* (also used as a noun), of which the feminine form is *satī*. The primary sense of *sat* is thus "what is," or "what exists." Other semantic shoots came to be grafted onto this original meaning. *Sat* became associated with the idea of "goodness" or "virtue"; the *satī* is thus the chaste and faithful "virtuous wife." But *sat* and its derivate *satya* are also interconnected with one of a number of key concepts of Indian thought that defy translation: by way of approximation, we will call this the idea of "truth." *Sat/satya* is what is true, what is marked with the power of that which is truthful, what has for its vehicle the word of truth. *Satya* might be defined as a word of truth whose efficacy causes what is to be.[38] Indeed, it is because it proceeds from the eminent quality of being true (and also of being uttered truthfully, with a sincere heart) that true speech *creates* beings and situations.

In India, Speech is more than merely the goddess Vāc, that divine being and object of endless speculation and reverie.[39] It has the power of making things exist. In order to comprehend what follows, one must imagine that things with names are but the supports, in a sense the simulacra of the words used to designate them. They are born—one might even say genetically—out of the very process of being named. We find this typically Indian approach, which consists of granting absolute value to abstract qualities and relative value to concrete beings, in every sphere of Indian thought. More exactly, this process consists of having concrete beings emanate from abstract qualities that have themselves become entities. In a discussion of Buddhism, in which this phenomenon manifests itself to the greatest extreme, Eugène Burnouf noted in 1844 that

> [I]t is not easy for our European minds to conceive of qualities without substance and attributes without a subject, and still more difficult to understand how those qualities can form an ideal individual, who will later become a real individual. But nothing is less familiar to Indians than the realization and, in a sense, the personification of absolute entities, detached from the being that we are accustomed to seeing attached to such entities; and all their systems of creation are but more or less direct and rapid transitions from abstract quality to concrete subject.[40]

One must not think that these reflections on the powers of Speech are only of interest to indologists or historians of religion—not, at least, when we have seen *satya* shake an empire. The "grasping of truth," the famous *satyāgraha* of Mahatma Gandhi, a novel strategy of passive resistance first developed and tested in South Africa before being launched as a total weapon against British domination in India itself, succeeded in lending unprecedented cohesion and breadth to the nationalist movement of the 1920s.[41] As for *sat* itself, it becomes endowed with an autonomy of sorts: as quality, substance, energy, and power, it acquires the opacity of a "being"—of which flesh and blood satīs are mere emanations, as it were. Here we see that these notions, which are distinct for us—being, virtue, truth, and speech—become fused together and condensed in a single term which, prismlike, diffracts all their potential meanings.[42]

Satī, then, designates a woman who immolates herself and not the rite or custom of widow-burning. It was the British who, at the close of the eighteenth century, officialized the confusion—expressed by many travelers before them—between the immolated woman and the sacrifice of widows, adding to this fine mess such delightful orthographic innovations (for which they seem to have had the patent) as *suttee, sattee, sutee,* and other variants, to which may be appended the elegant French transcription of *sutty.*[43]

The Sanskrit language knows of no specific term or explicit denomination to designate this rite; rather, it resorts to periphrastic expressions: "going with" *(sahagamana)* or "dying with" *(sahamaraṇa)* if the woman burns herself with her husband; and "going after" *(anugamana)* or "dying after" *(anumaraṇa)* if she later burns herself on a different pyre. One also finds "ascension" (of the pyre: *anvārohaṇa*), a more literary euphemism, and at a late date, the "burning of the satī" *(satīdāha),* a neologism especially prevalent in Bengal. Are we to see in the allusive distance of language a resistance to a loathsome reality? All we can say with certainty is that the metaphor of accompaniment, of "following into death," constitutes an ideogram of sorts for the sacrifice of faithful wives, in India as well as Bali.

Speech as Instrument

The women of Bali wounded themselves with a kris as a means of marking their determination to die. In India, the wife proffers a series of words. She "breaks out," as it were, in the same way that a fever, a fire, or a passion breaks out. She cries "I am going to eat[44] fire," "I am going to follow my husband," "I am going to become a satī," "Praised be such and such a god, such and such a goddess!" (here, she invokes her personal deity, in whom she will take refuge). She shouts "*Hari bol*" (this *mantra* can have a funerary connotation)—but also, and most importantly, and in a single breath, "*Sat, sat, sat.*" This formula—so compact, enigmatic, and imperious—reveals her nature and her calling as a satī. People will then say that "the *sat* has risen" or that "the *bhāv*[45] has come on," impersonal expressions indicating the irruption of the supernatural force of the *sat* into the profane world. Then, in order to describe the frenzy that takes hold of the satī in that tragic instant in which her fate is sealed, another old Sanskrit term, *āveśa*—formed from the root *viś-,* "to penetrate"—is used, even down to the present day.[46] In the devotional literature, this term signifies the state of absorption into a divinity, the penetration of a *mantra* into oneself, or indeed possession by a god or demon *(bhutāveśa)*. The possessed individual becomes the vehicle of the god or spirit, which penetrates into him and spirits him away.

The irruption of the *sat* introduces an irreversible breach, if not a tear, in the fabric of reality itself. Radiating outward from the utterance of a word, the power of the *sat* spreads like wildfire. This hidden force is perceived as something concrete, almost tangible: it is a *presence,* the stuff of imagination, and of dreams. People speak of it as if it were a living thing. The "rising of the *sat,*" that indescribable state of agitation, transport, and fervor, culminates in the moment in which the vow to burn oneself is enacted in a rite.[47]

A court clerk from Nagaur District in Rajasthan, attempting to describe to me—and with what reticence!—the sensations he had experienced upon attending the sacrifice of Sohan Kanvar in Neemri Kothariya on February 29, 1980, told me "Everything went dark. I no longer saw anything. The funeral pyre blazed up, and the flames were enormous. My whole body began to shake, I couldn't stop. I was no longer myself." He had insisted on speaking in English in order to emphasize his status as a *clerk.* In Marwari, the expression "the shadow comes," which in common parlance means "to no longer see anything," is also used in a technical sense to designate the onslaught of the state of possession, the moment in which the possessed individual begins to shake convulsively. This takes the form of spastic seizures that seem strangely disconnected from the body, as though the body of the possessed individual were no more than a piece of cloth, a sheet covering another body that moves as if racked by sudden, massive contractions. We shall see how Hindus react to these scenes of cremation. But what emerges already from this fragment of an interview, despite the masking effect of the use of English, is that the native onlooker, when he sees a satī being burned alive, finds himself in a state comparable to that of a possessed individual. The rapture that so shocked foreign observers is to be taken literally, in the sense of being transported to a supernatural world.

There is another image popular tradition links with the *sat.* The *sat* is not merely a being called into existence by speech, a force, and a power. It is also a substance: fire itself. According to belief, the pyre is ignited solely through the inner flame of the *sat.* The visible, earthly flames drawn from the domestic hearth that is installed at the time of the nuptial rite (and which are to be used, theoretically, in the cremation rite), erect around the satīs a kind of hedge that conceals the "true" spectacle of their death: an instantaneous death, devoid of either burns to the body or physical suffering, by "self-combustion." Fire is not the agent of the satīs' death, but rather the essence of their being. This is a fundamental distinction whose full implications we will assess when we turn to the present-day state of the question, and the positions of the Hindu fundamentalists.

It is, therefore, an intimate bond that unites fire with the woman who declares her intention to burn herself. An account that may be qualified as hagiographic (even if its author, the journalist Nandkishor Parik, belongs to the "enlightened" intelligentsia of Jaipur) describes the first manifestations of the secret presence of the *sat* in Dayal Kanvar, the daughter of Ram Singh. *Ṭhākur* Ram Singh, who died in 1971, was a deputy police inspector in Jaipur who upon retirement in 1944 took up the path of a Sufi "holy man." His eldest daughter, Dayal Kanvar, ascended the pyre of her husband in Khud, a village in Sikar District, in 1948 (on the twelfth day of the bright half of the month of *Kārttika,* in year 2005 of the *Vikrama* era, for the pious Hindus who venerate her memory and who erected a temple to her). From her earliest childhood, Dayal Kanvar had shown an irresistible fascination for fire: at age eight, as Parik reports in his pamphlet (published in 1987), she would struggle frantically to draw close to fire. One day she succeeded in rushing headlong into a burning blaze and plunging her face into it. Her family's panic turned to amazement when they saw that, with the exception of a fleck the size of a mustard seed in the corner of one eye, the child bore no burn marks whatsoever.[48]

The inner fire of the *sat* is assimilated with the sun via an esoteric connection, as illustrated in popular religious imagery. Here we see the sun shooting its rays at the satī who, seated to the side of the blazing pyre, has her hands clasped in an attitude of solemn salutation to her master or husband, while the three great gods of the Hindu pantheon, Brahmā, Viṣṇu, and Śiva, shower her with multicolored flowers in an invitation to ascend to heaven. The sun is depicted either as a heavenly body or as a god. A small satī temple in Banaras contains a relatively ancient image of this type, in which the conjoined souls of the deceased are transported to the world of the gods in an airship borne upward by a *haṃsa.* The *haṃsa,* a kind of wild goose, has symbolized the *ātman* (the imperishable self) since the time of the Upaniṣads (fig. 5).

Sexual Colorings

In order to dispel the frenzy of the *sat* and divert a woman from her baneful resolution, one must sprinkle the satī with water that has been dyed with indigo. This impure substance has the property of "bringing down the *sat.*"[49] In India, there is a subtle and elaborate hierarchy of color symbolism. This will vary according to the social group to which one belongs by birth (*jāti,* caste), and to the order (*varṇa,* a term whose primary sense is, precisely, "color") with which that caste is ideally linked. Each *varṇa* has its own emblematic color: white for the Brahmans, red for the Kṣatriyas, yellow for the Vaiśyas, and finally blue indigo for the Śūdras.[50] The hierarchy of colors is not the same for the two genders and is subject to an infinite number of permutations across the broad expanse of India. In a general sense, however, it may be said that what is dyed is tainted with impurity, whereas that which is not dyed—i.e., what is white—connotes purity and detachment. This is the color of *sattva,* the first of the three composite elements of Nature and the brahmanic quality par excellence.[51] The dyer castes are more impure than those of fabric-printers, and among the former, those specializing in indigo dying are by far the most impure of the lot.[52] These people have traditionally lived in segregated quarters on the outskirts of villages or towns; they tend to be Muslims (former Hindus who in the past converted en masse to Islam, in order to escape their Untouchable status). This is especially the case with the Nilgars, the "blue indigo makers," as well as with certain Khatris, and the Chhipas who are also fabric-printers in Rajasthan and Gujarat.[53]

Light, vivid, or bright colors such as red, pink, and yellow are associated with happiness, prosperity, and passion; or, on the contrary, with "dispassion" *(vairāgya).* All depends on the perspective one takes and the "stage of

Fig. 5. Painting of a satī at small Banaras temple (private collection).

life" *(āśrama)* in which one finds oneself.[54] Here it would be more appropriate to say "the reds, the pinks, and the yellows," since these are differentiated from one another in clearly contrasted shadings. Thus whereas yellow ocher *(geruā)* symbolizes world renunciation, "turmeric" yellow *(haldiyā)* is associated with marriage and marital happiness. This latter color is reserved for "fortunate" wives *(saubhāgyavatī)* whose husbands are alive,[55] and the expression "to yellow one's hands" is commonly used for "to marry." A yellow veil or sari with circular tie-dyed patterns and a red border indicates that the happy wife is furthermore a mother.[56] Saffron yellow *(kesariyā)* evokes the sacrifice of a heroic warrior: when their citadels were besieged by the enemy, the Rajputs would go off into the final battle in attire that had been dyed in a decoction of saffron *(kesariyā bānā)*.[57] Virile energy reappears (but with an erotic—rather than a tragic—valence) in *khyāl*s, songs with double meanings:[58] in these, women allude to the sexual potency of their husbands by calling them "*kesariyā*."

On the other hand, dark colors—dark blue, dark green, brown (which is not distinguished from gray), the reddish-brown cashew color, the two principal shades of maroon (purplish red and the color of the areca nut), and finally black—are reserved for beings stigmatized by inferior status, by misfortune, infamy, and defilement. For Hindus, these adverse states are the results not of some biographical accident, but rather of moral necessity: one is born into this or that social category, or this or that sex; one meets with misfortune, disgrace, and other vicissitudes of fate along the path of one's earthly life in exact proportion to deeds *(karma)* perpetrated in former lives. For Hindus and Buddhists alike, it is the notion of *karmadoṣa* (the "flaw" or "fault of karma") that accounts for an individual's fate.[59] The doctrine of retribution for one's acts, when internalized by the individual in the form of a belief, provides a theory of universal causality "transported into the moral sphere":[60] "one is reborn as one has lived" might well be the adage.

Elsewhere, black may indicate a group's social affiliation: until relatively recently, the Minas of western India wore black woolen garb, as did the Rabari breeders.[61] In fact, the Minas are classified as a tribe, and not a caste. The association between brahmanic culture and light colors on the one hand, and aboriginal culture and dark colors on the other, continues to be perceived, at least dimly, as a number of practices make plain. In certain regions of Rajasthan, when a child catches cold, a compress dipped in indigo-tinted water is applied to his chest because, people say, the cold comes from the north and the sky, and consequently from the direction of the brahmans. Here then, indigo, the color of the vile and the impure, drives away an evil brought on by the brahmans. In order to protect a newborn child against the evil eye, a cotton thread dyed in indigo and strung with blue-colored earthen beads is attached to its wrists and ankles (the maternal uncle or a surrogate is expected to offer this ritual gift).[62] Alternatively, the child will be made to wear a black silk thread around his neck and waist. Following the celebration of the sixth day after birth, in which worship is made to Chaṭhī Mātā, the goddess of the Sixth Day (also known as Vidhāta Mātā, the goddess of Creation), kohl prepared from the smoke of the lamp that had been used in worship is applied to those parts of the infant's body most coveted by evil spirits—the palms and the soles of the feet.[63] We could give numerous other examples of the impurity attached to the color black and its derivatives in both language and practice—in Sanskrit, the term *śyāma* is applied to black as well as blue-black, dark green, brown, or gray. The impurity of indigo is so strong as to have left its stain on the lighter shades of the color. No Hindu woman, whether steeped in tradition or simply superstitious, would dare to wear a light blue sari if her husband were alive, because that color is associated with mourning. In addition, in those castes in which widows are allowed to wear bracelets on special occasions, it is blue or light blue plastic bracelets that will be chosen, since plastic is a material devoid of symbolic value.

If we are to believe the religious treatises, only members of the lowest social order, the śūdras—the category comprising the serving castes that form the fourth class of the *varṇa* system—were authorized to wear clothing dyed in indigo. The three highest classes of this idealized ordering (grouped under the rubric of the "twice-born," brahmanic initiation constituting a second birth) were to avoid all contact with that impure substance. Voluntary or accidental violation of this rule could result in loss of caste. A twice-born person who cuts himself on a branch of this plant while crossing an indigo field under cultivation, or who swallows food that has been wrapped in indigo-dyed cloth, becomes an outcaste who, in order to regain his original status, must perform a rite of expiation, which will vary according to circumstance. He must ingest the "five products of the cow" *(pañcagavya)*, a supreme source of purification consisting of milk, clarified butter, curds, urine, and excrement, or submit to "severe penances" *(kṛcchrāyaṇa vrata)* or to an expiation lasting for a lunar month:

> Cultivating, selling, or living by trading in indigo: thereby does the Brahman lose his status. He purifies himself by undergoing the three severe penances. Ritual ablutions, gifts of charity, recitation of sacred *mantras*, personal recitation of the Veda,[64] and water-libations to manes: these five sacrifices are without fruit for him who wears a garment dyed in indigo.[65]

Land that has been cultivated with indigo becomes impure and must lie fallow for a period of twelve years.[66] Well into the middle of the nineteenth century, the indigo planters of Bihar found it difficult to recruit laborers, as Jacques Pouchepadass has noted, since "only Untouchable or tribal coolies would accept . . . to enter waist-deep into the foaming, ill-smelling, colored liquid"[67] of the fermenting vats.

It bears noting here that women are constantly associated with śūdras in ancient India and in the tradition that perpetuates the ancient ideology. Like śūdras, women have no access to Vedic knowledge and therefore may not receive the initiation that integrates the "twice-born" into society—or rather, into the religious ordering upon which society is founded. Although one is born a Brahman, one only accedes to brahmanic status through apprenticeship in the Veda at the feet of a teacher, through the ascetic way of life one adopts during that period, and finally through the "perfecting" and "consecration" effected through initiation. Like *śūdras,* women, to whom the Veda is forbidden, nonetheless enjoy considerable privilege in this Iron Age that is the *kaliyuga:* for both, devotion throws open the gates to salvation. One is subject to the same punishment for the murder of a woman as for a *śūdra,* a light punishment as such things go in the hierarchy of penalties. A wealth of other examples may be marshalled to illustrate the equivalence of women and *śūdras* in the great chain of being. So it is that blue indigo, which is the emblematic color of *śūdras,* may also well be the secret color of women. The *Āpastambasmṛti* informs us that "there is no sin attached to women (wearing dark blue garments) in bed during love-making just for fun."[68] Is it purely coincidental that the next chapter in that volume treats of the impurity of menstrual blood? Might there not be secret affinities linking menstruation, lovemaking, and indigo? Whatever the case the *Nirṇayasindhu* (1612) of Kamalākarabhaṭṭa, citing Gārgya, makes the following statement:

> Fortune smiles on a woman who wears a white garment at the time of her first menses; she who wears a stoutly woven garment [in the same circumstances] becomes a woman faithful to her conjugal vow (*pativratā*); she who wears silk meets with success; happiness is promised to her who wears a new garment; she who wears a used garment is destined for sorrow; she who wears a garment stained with blood is hounded by disease; she who bears a blue indigo garment on the day of her first menstruation becomes a widow.[69]

Living Satīs

The story of the holy Bala demonstrates that even today the fire of the *sat* is neutralized by the impurity of indigo. Bala, whose real name was Rup Kanvar, was born in 1903 in a village near the small town of Pipar (in Jodhpur District) to a Rajput Shekhavat family. Widowed in 1919, and with no children of her own, she adopted her nephew Man Singh (an altogether common practice). In 1943, when that adopted son died as well, Bala announced her intention to follow him onto the pyre. The "madness of the *sat*"[70] also overcame Rasal Kanvar, one of Man Singh's daughters-in-law. The situation was finally resolved by forceful measures (Rasal Kanvar was forced to drink water polluted with indigo), as well as through trickery (a man from the Goldsmith caste, a Sunar, was asked to throw a blue veil—or according to another version, a blanket of the same color—over Bala). Polluted by this act, Bala continued to live—against her will. But from that day onward—February 15, 1943—she maintained a total fast that lasted until her death (of cancer, on November 15, 1986).[71] It is said that she survived without taking any food for twenty-three years. The reputation for saintliness of this woman, who was worshipped as a "living satī,"[72] was and remains considerable. This paradoxical designation is applied to women who were possessed by the *sat,* but who for one reason or another—family or police interference, a monsoon rain that unexpectedly extinguished the pyre (John Masters built a novel around this theme in 1952)—were unable to carry through on their solemn vow to sacrifice themselves.[73]

The case of the "living satī" of Jodhpur is not unique. In Devipura, a village near Shahpura (Jaipur District), the police forced another Shekhavat Rajput named Jasvant Kanvar to descend from the pyre on March 12, 1985. Since that time, she has become in the eyes of all a hybrid being, living at the junction of the earthly and the supernatural realms. People consider her to be a *joginī* (*yoginī:* an emanation of *śakti,* divine energy, in the tantric perspective). A temple built for her has become an important worship site.[74] I went to Devipura in April 1993: the intense and troubling hours I spent with Jasvant Kanvar will be discussed below. It was *Rāmnaumī*—the festival celebrating the birth of the god Rāma. A crowd of worshipers thronged to the great temple of the god whose birth was being celebrated all the more ostentatiously for the fact that the events at Ayodhya in December 1992 had galvanized popular fervor. The worship of the "Mother Satī" at her shrine did not, however, seem to suffer from the competition of the cult of Rāma. The offerings of coconut, flowers, sugar candy, and cakes consecrated by Jasvant Kanvar, the custodian of her own cult,[75] and then placed at her request upon the small altar to Śiva, Pārvatī, and Gaṇeśa, had formed an impressive pile by the time I took leave of her. The emotion that must have been visible on my face was perhaps the reason for the unexpected gift she then made to me. Showing for the first time genuine spontaneity, she handed me, as a form of *prasād* ("consecrated remains"), a color photograph: one sees emerging from a pile of coconuts—on the funeral pyre where the body of her husband, Ganpat Singh-ji, had been laid—a head covered with a red veil *(cūndṛī),*[76] a symbol of marriage, and a right hand raised in a gesture of benediction (fig. 6). The image *(mūrti)* that serves as the object of her worship in her temple is a stylized copy of the same Polaroid snapshot. On it one sees "The Illustrious, Holy, and Virtuous Satī Jasvant Kanvar Shekhavat of Devipura" with haloed head, veiled in red and adorned with her auspicious marriage finery, seated on a pyre depicted as an enormous heap of coconuts. In the background, one can make out the nearby temple of Brahmāṇī. The reality effect emanating from this image (an effect further enhanced by the presence before me of the altogether living satī, who could have stepped right out of the painting) was still not sufficiently powerful, however, to prevent my being struck by the distance separating the bare fact from its mythification (figs. 7 and 8).

Returning now to the blue veil thrown over Bala, it is more than coincidence that the person assigned that mission was a Sunar craftsman. The Sunars' profession as artisans traditionally links them to the *śūdra* class in the *varṇa* hierarchy.[77] To dispel the *sat,* no one is better equipped than a *śūdra,* since he is to the social order what a woman is to the sexual order: a being marked at birth with the seal of impurity. This episode underscores the natural identity that obtains between women and *śūdras,* as the canonical texts never tire of proclaiming. But it also brings to light the connection made between woman, the *śūdra,* and indigo, a link clearly supported by information gathered in the field. In Rajasthan, people traditionally have recourse to three techniques in order to destroy the *sat:* the satī is sprinkled with water stained with indigo *(guḷī);* an Untouchable (or, in his absence, a person of low caste) is called upon to pollute her by contact; or a menstruating woman *(rajasvalā)* is asked to do the same. For all this, it remains quite rare for any person, including Untouchables, to be willing to run the risk of being cursed by a satī. For this reason, people will resort to a variety of expedients: for example, one of the coconuts piled up on the pyre where the satī is to take place will have been secretly contaminated with indigo.[78]

Travelers' accounts confirm these data. They inform us that it was enough for a satī to be touched, even accidentally, by a man of "lowly caste," and *a fortiori* by a foreigner, for her to no longer be permitted to burn herself: profaned in this way, she became an object of rebuff. As for the culprit himself, he risked grave danger if he did not acquit himself through the payment of a considerable sum of money in compensation.[79] So it was that widows forced to burn themselves would occasionally throw

Fig. 6. Polaroid photograph of Jasvant Kanvar on the pyre, March 12, 1985 (private collection).

Fig. 7. Jasvant Kanvar at her Devipura (Rajasthan) temple, April 1, 1993 (private collection).

Fig. 8. Devipura (Rajasthan) temple image of Jasvant Kanvar (private collection).

themselves on such men, who had come to view the spectacle of their death. Bernier observed that such women were the prey of what he called the *Gadous* (scavengers, removers of human excrements) "who occasionally gather as a group when they know that it is some fair young woman who is to be burned."[80] Long before Jules Verne's *Around the World in Eighty Days,*[81] in which the beautiful Parsee Princess Aouda is saved *in extremis* from the pyre by Phileas Fogg (fig. 9) and eventually becomes his bride, travel literature was rife with examples, as real as they were romantic, of young widows being snatched from the flames by gallant foreigners. Or else, in error as to the day and time, the would-be rescuers arrived too late—the wall was still hot, the ashes still smoldering—and they returned, with an "inexpressible pang" in their hearts, as did Degrandpré, an officer

Fig. 9. Princess Aouda being brought to the pyre: Bennett's illustration from the 1873 Paris edition of Jules Verne's *Tour du monde en quatre-vingts jours.* Courtesy Bibliothèque Nationale, Paris.

in Bengal, in 1789.[82] According to legend, Job Charnock, an agent of the Bengal East India Company who in 1690 built several huts on the banks of the Hooghly—thus laying the foundations for the small trading post from which Calcutta would emerge—carried off a young Hindu woman, whom he made his mistress, under much the same circumstances. He is said to have given her a Christian burial, but also to have sprinkled the blood of sacrificial cocks over her grave.[83]

Blue as Blood

The casting of water stained with indigo appears in another context in Rajasthan. Here the focus is on ancestors who have met their death while battling livestock thieves. Their acts of bravery, violent and premature deaths, and selfless sacrifices grant them access to the "Path of Heroes." They have become territorial guardian deities, locally known as *bhomiyā* (from *bhūmi*, "earth"). One of the most popular of these is the celebrated Pābū-jī, whose saga, painted on a cloth scroll *(paṛ)*, is sung by castes of specialists (the Nayaks) in performances that are first and foremost rituals.[84] His shrine is found in Kolugarh (between Jodhpur and Pokaran), but the house of every Raika camel driver harbors a small domestic altar *(sthān)* devoted to him. As for the Nayak, who even today are rarely sedentary, the painted cloth of Pābū-jī serves as their *sthān* and mobile temple.

Many of these narratives contain an episode in which the hero, who has been decapitated by cattle rustlers, nonetheless continues to battle relentlessly. It is as though the headless body, perched on its mount and armed with a sabre in each hand, were inspired by a martial ardor that had been greatly increased by its very mutilation. A lotus flower sprouts from the severed trunk of the body and eyes are lodged in its chest. The hero emerges victorious, frees the cows, and leads them back to the village. But nothing can allay his fury. The village women throw indigo-blackened water over him and he falls to the ground at last, vanquished by death. Shrines are built over each of the places where his head, body, and horse fell. Thenceforth he is worshiped and celebrated in songs sung in ritual night vigils (*rātījagā*s). These headless heroes are designated by a special name: they are called *jhūjhār* (or *jhūñjhār*), from the Sanskrit *yuddhakārin*, "warrior." Many are the villages in Rajasthan that count a local *jhūjhār*. At Bapini (between Osian and Nagaur), one can worship at the grave—now become a cult site *(samādhi)*—of Mehā-jī Māñgaliyā, which is nothing other than a stone symbolizing the head of that decapitated hero.[85]

The motif of a lotus sprouting from a severed trunk evokes the famous *cakras* ("wheels" or "circles"), the energy centers of the subtle body located at various points along the spinal cord, according to Indian yoga theory. These have been viewed as so many lotuses which flower when they are awakened, if not "pierced" *(cakra-bheda),* by the rise of energy *(śakti),* which is depicted as a coiled serpent *(kuṇḍalinī).* The final lotus, possessed of a thousand petals *(sahasradala-padma),* is situated at the top of the head, above the cranial vault. When the practitioner succeeds in raising his energy, breath, and semen up to the cranial vault, the thousand-petaled lotus blossoms out and fills with the nectar that transforms the practitioner into an immortal being. Now during the medieval period Rajasthan was a veritable melting pot for sects practicing the techniques of yoga. So it is that the lotus replacing the decapitated head may well symbolize an immortality won through voluntary death. In this symbol system, moreover, heroic sacrifice, renunciation, and yoga are so many mirror images of one another.

The lotus flower has been associated with the head offered in oblation from very ancient times.[86] In Saurashtra as in Rajasthan, the expression used to designate the sacrifice of the head out of devotion to Śiva or the Devī is precisely *kamalapūjā,* "worship of the lotus." Often a husband and wife performed this particular *pūjā* together, as depicted on stele in the Porbandar region.[87] This motif is also to be found in myths belonging to (or associated with) the "great tradition." Retracing the cycle of the goddess Khoḍiyār in Saurashtra, Harald Tambs-Lyche cites two "classical" myths which her Gujarati hagiographers link with her miraculous birth. Viṣṇu solemnly vows to offer a thousand lotus flowers to Śiva. But Śiva conjures up a *līlā* (God's Play) with which to test his follower, such that no matter what he does, Viṣṇu always finds himself short one lotus flower. Whereupon he plucks out one of his eyes in order to replace the thousandth flower. The demon Rāvaṇa (who is the picture of the perfect devotee in this and many other myths) offers nine of his ten heads to Śiva. It is only when Rāvaṇa makes ready to chop off the tenth that the god is finally satisfied.[88] An episode from the famous *Naiṇsī Chronicle,* written between 1658 and 1666, relates the exemplary tale of Narbad Sujavat: this Rajput of the Rathor clan loses an eye in battle, but his valor wins him the favor of the Rana of Chittorgarh, the leader of the enemy army, who makes him a gift of land. Narbad serves his new master with a devotion that is reported as far away as Chittor. The Rana decides to put him to the test, sending a slave to demand of Narbad his only eye. Narbad obliges without hesitation.[89]

The story of Kallā-jī, a Rathor of the Mahecha branch thought to have lived toward the middle of the sixteenth century, clearly illustrates the interpenetration of all these themes. Upon the death of his father Meghraj, Kallā went to Chittorgarh, where he received from Maharana Udai Singh a parcel of land lying in the Salumbar region, to the southeast of Udaipur. Becoming a disciple of a famous *siddha* (a tantric master and expert in supernatural powers), he was initiated into yoga under his master's guidance. Kallā was to marry the daughter of Rao Krishna Dutt Chauhan of Shivgarh. On the day of the wedding, upon learning that emperor Akbar had laid siege to Chittorgarh, Kallā-jī forsook the marriage canopy for the threatened citadel. After several months of resistance, when all hope had been lost, the Rajputs carried out a mass immolation of women and children: this was the third *jauhar* of Chittorgarh (1568). Then, donning their saffron-hued renouncer's garb, they leapt into battle to gain entry into heaven (such a fight to the death, assimilated with sacrifice, is called *sākā* in Rajasthani). Kallā-jī was decapitated in the combat, but his body kept up the bitter fight. Receiving a premonition of his death, his betrothed, Krishna Kumari, had a pyre of the most precious woods prepared. And when she took her place on it, the decapitated head of Kallā-jī, which had now sprouted arms with a sword in each hand, came to rest in her lap: through the rite of *sahagamana* ("going with") a marriage of ashes was celebrated.[90] The Minas worship Kallā-jī, as do the high castes (the priest of the temple, located near Kesariyaji, is a Brahman). Kallā-jī is depicted as a warrior on horseback, brandishing his lance and sword, or in the form of a serpent. Other deified ancestors of the region, such as Gātod-jī, who gave their lives in the defense of cows, appear in the same form to their devotees, who worship them for their miraculous healing powers. Not so long ago it was customary to lead criminal suspects to the hole where Gātod-jī lay coiled. There they were made to introduce their hand, smeared with saffron, into the opening. If they were innocent, Gātod-jī accepted their offer of saffron and spared their lives.

Trial by Fire

Attempts at dissuasion, evoked when we embarked on this long excursus on indigo, are in fact quite rare. There is no lack of examples of the pressures brought to bear on women consumed by the madness of *sat* to listen to reason. In most cases, however, such exhortations are a pure formality, or mere trappings of the mythology of satīs intended to heighten the prestige of their heroic deeds, or means by which families may exonerate themselves when such sacrifices are halted by the long arm of the law. In communities in which the ritual has been extant, it is rather the case that all the elements are in place to encourage a widow to burn herself alive. Furthermore, once she has declared herself a satī she may no longer recant, even though she in fact has the right to do so: the religious lawbooks that sanction the practice (which was quite controversial, as will be seen) make provisions for a ritual of expiation (said to be "of Prajāpati," the great cosmogonic god of the second period of Vedic mythology) for a woman who regrets having taken the vow.[91]

Declaring one's "intention" (*saṃkalpa,* in Sanskrit) constitutes the necessary preliminary for any person preparing to perform a sacrificial act or religious observance. The sacrificer must begin by clearly stating his desire, his intention, to undertake the ritual task he has set for himself. He makes use of scriptural formulas, which he adapts to his specific situation: "I, so named, of such and such a lineage, on such and such a day of such and such a (light or dark) fortnight, during such and such a month of the lunar calendar, in such and such a place and on such and such an occasion do declare my intention of performing such and such a rite." Without that declaration of intention, the rite cannot take place; conversely, once it has been uttered it must be acted upon. This is borne out by an 1185 inscription from the Shikarpur District of Karnataka: a man who had pledged to immolate himself upon the death of the queen offered up his head when the time came "because a word uttered with full resolve cannot be broken."[92] So too, the widow's declaration is fatal for her: whether it escapes her lips or is extracted from her by force, she shall have to burn herself.

The original sense of the term *saṃkalpa* is "conception" or "resolution"; it simultaneously indicates desire, will, intention, and intended goal. But in the ritualists' vocabulary it took on the technical meaning of the "sacrificer's determination." Finally, it ended up specifically designating a widow's determination to accompany her husband onto the pyre. This semantic drift marks the historical turning point following which the faithful wife became obliged to undergo a trial by fire to prove her fidelity.

Trial by fire is not a simple metaphor here. It also evokes a matter of fact, a ritual sequence that is itself an enigma. Several travelers' accounts provide ample witness to this, yet no trace of it can be found in Indian sources prior to the end of the nineteenth century. What we are dealing with here is a kind of pre-sacrifice reminiscent of that of the Balinese *satia*s. At first blush, it appears to be linked to the foreign presence in India.

The burning of widows was held in equal horror by Christians and Muslims. In the event, it actually was not: of all the eyewitnesses whose accounts have come down to us, there is but one who nearly lost consciousness and would have fallen from his horse had his companions not come to his aid. He was a Berber, a native of Tangiers, and reputedly the greatest traveler in all of Islam. He journeyed across the northwest of India in the middle of the fifteenth century; while passing through the city of Amjhera near Dhar (in present-day Madhya Pradesh), he witnessed the self-immolation of three Hindu women whose husbands had been killed fighting the Sumra of Sind.[93] This was the celebrated Ibn Baṭṭūṭa. The horror shared by the Portuguese, Dutch, Danes, and French who set up trading companies in the East Indies during the sixteenth and seventeenth centuries seems to have been still more insurmountable among the Muslim faithful. There were, to be sure, notable exceptions: the poets Amir Khusrow (1253–1324) and Muhammed Riza Nau'i (d. 1610) made no secret of their admiration for satīs.[94] The Moghul rulers, from Akbar to Aurangzeb, sought by every possible means to reduce the number of these sacrifices even as they strove to adhere to a policy of noninterference in the religious affairs of their "idolatrous" subjects, after the prudent example of the Sultans of Delhi before them. Thus, they did not directly prohibit the custom of widow-burning. If we are to believe Abu'l Fazl, his biographer, Akbar saved the daughter of the Rajah of Jodhpur and the daughter of Udai Singh of Jaipur from the pyre. The local governors used their power to veto the ceremony, which could not take place without their authorization. But when their efforts remained without effect, they demanded that the woman qualify for the torture awaiting her by undergoing a preliminary trial by fire. Here, for example, is what Jean-Baptiste Tavernier recounts in his famous *Travels:*

I remember anouther strange occurrence which happened one day in my presence at Patna, a town of Bengal. I was with the Dutch at the house of the Governer of the town . . . when a young and very beautiful woman, scarcely more than twenty-two years of age, entered the reception room where we were seated. She, with a firm and resolute voice, required the Governer's permission to burn herself with the body of her deceased husband. The Governer, touched by the youth and beauty of the woman, sought to turn her from her resolution, but seeing that all that he could say was useless, and that she only became more obstinate, and asked him with a bold and courageous voice if he believed that she feared fire; he enquired if she knew any torment equal to fire, and if she had never happened to burn her hand. "No, no," this woman then replied to him with more courage than before; "I do not fear fire in any way, and to make you see that it is so, you have only to order a well-lighted torch to be brought here." The Governer, horrified at the language of the woman, did not wish to hear more, and dismissing her told her in a rage that she might go to the devil. Some young nobles who were by him asked him to allow them to test the woman and to order a torch to be brought, herself with it. At first he was unwilling to consent, but they continued to urge him the more; so that at length, by his order, a torch was brought, which, in India, is nothing more than a cloth twisted and steeped in oil, and fixed on the end of a stick like a chafing dish; this, which we call a lamp *(fallot),* serves us at need in the crossways of towns. As soon as the woman saw the torch, which was well lighted, she ran in front of it, held her hand firmly in the flame without the least grimace, and pushed in her arm up to the elbow, till it was immediately scorched; this caused horror to all who witnessed the deed, and the Governer commanded the woman to be removed from his presence.[95]

This scenario remained unchanged after the British conquest. The British Resident or District Collector replaced the Moghul governor in exhorting women transported by the madness of *sat* to give up their plan:

My good lady, pray consider over the act once more; act not against your reason; you must be sure that we are your friends and not your enemies, that we would save you from the horrid death by all means at a slight signal of your consent, and would make an honorable provision for you during your life.

It is in these terms that Lieutenant Earle addressed a fifteen-year-old Brahman woman who was preparing to burn herself in the village of Maholi (present-day Maharashtra).[96] The year was 1824, five years prior to the abolition of "this inhuman and impious rite" by Lord William Bentinck, the Governor-General of India, in the territories under his jurisdiction. Since 1813, the government had been sending directives to district authorities, police officers, and magistrates, exhorting them to implement strict controls to limit the custom of burning widows, and to allow it only under certain conditions. Far from achieving their objective, these half measures were to contribute considerably to the propagation of the practice.

The lieutenant used all the eloquence he possessed to dissuade the "young beauty." In his perfect Marathi, he told her that he considered her death to be not a voluntary act but rather a murder, premeditated and in cold blood, by the priests. The Brahman officiants in these ceremonies (for which they receive a ritual honorarium) combined fanaticism with cupidity in consigning widows to the tortures of the pyre and the flames of Hell—suicide being a mortal sin for Christians. They used the power they held over the women in contempt of the "pure law of the Hindus."

It is necessary that we open a parenthesis at this point: the science of *dharma* (a notion encompassing both religion and law) was still very poorly known at this time. Orientalism, born around the year 1770, had exhumed but a few of the monuments of the Sanskrit language. One of the young discipline's pioneers, William Jones, a judge in the Calcutta Supreme Court of Justice, had left behind a posthumous translation of the *Laws of Manu* (Mānavadharmaśāstra or *Manusmṛti*), published in 1794.[97] But this treatise, whose authority is unsurpassed in India, does not contain a single reference to the rite of widow-burning. It was at Jones's request that Jagannatha Tarkapancana, one of the greatest pundits of his time, composed a digest for practical use.[98] Nonetheless, the vast *dharma* literature—aphorisms (*dharmasūtras*), treatises (*dharmaśāstras*), digests, and commentaries that set out the rules of Hindu theology and jurisprudence—remained largely unexploited. Magistrates only had access to this literature through the intermediary of literate brahmans, pundits, or *śāstrī*s (*śāstra* masters). So it is that when the government consulted them on points of jurisprudence *(vyavahāra),* they formulated opinions that varied according to the textual traditions of the school with which they were affiliated *(Mitākṣara* or *Dāyabhāga),* if not by simple venality or partisanship.

From the end of the eighteenth century onward, the sacrifice of widows had lain at the center of a religious and legal debate that had unleashed impassioned reactions in Great Britain as well as in India. Since they had asserted their supremacy, the British had never ceased to voice their resolution to avoid intervening in the religious affairs of Indians, whatever their religious beliefs, adopting in these delicate matters of native values the same reserve as had been the golden rule of the Muslim conquerors. This fundamental principle of British policy would never be called into question, regardless of the horror certain Hindu customs might have prompted at home. The task was thus one of tracing as clear a line of demarcation as possible between religion and superstition, between rituals and dogmas sanctioned by Hindu law as expounded in the *Śāstra*s ("the *Shaster,*" as it was called) and those that lacked legal foundation but partook of custom. It was in order to clarify matters that English magistrates adopted the habit of consulting specialists of *dharma* and of the exegesis of sacred texts. So it was that in 1817, in response to a government request, there appeared a report, written in Sanskrit under the aegis of Mritunjoy

Vidyalankar, Chief Pundit of the Supreme Court of Calcutta, that emphasized the optional character of the rite of widow-burning: the *Śastra*s, these scholars of Hindu law argued, far from recommending the sacrifice of widows, prescribe a life of abstinence, chastity, and mortification for women who have lost their husbands, allowing them (with certain provisions) the possibility (should they so desire) of perishing with him on the funeral pyre. In the following year, Raja Rammohun Roy published his first broadside against the burning of widows. (One of Bengal's greatest intellectuals, and the founder, in 1828, of the *Brahmo Samāj,* a religious society of reformed Hinduism, Roy is today considered to be the "father of modern India.") In it, he demonstrated with brio that the Vedas, the Upanisads, and canonical texts of unquestioned authority were completely unaware of this custom, which entered into Hindu practice through obscurantism, ignorance of the original religion, and the greed of priests and families. Two other incendiary tracts (in 1820 and 1822) expanded on this thesis, supported by references from sacred texts and the *Śāstra*s. Lieutenant Earle's words were thus inspired by a current of thought that was prevalent at the time.[99]

The young Marathi woman had simply answered that it was written in the book of her destiny to be the wife of her husband, that this sacred duty had precedence over all others, and that consequently it incumbed upon her to accompany him to any destination whatsoever. At this point, as a final means of dissuasion, it occurred to Earle to propose a trial by fire; whereupon she ripped her kerchief, tied it around her finger, and with an imperious smile, burnt it in an oil lamp. The finger was consumed slowly, like a candle, without the slightest sigh or sob coming from the woman. She continued to converse amiably with the people around her as the acrid odor of burnt flesh permeated the room. But her flushed cheeks and the beads of perspiration on her forehead were ample proof of the torment she was enduring.

Sir Frederick Halliday, a magistrate from the Hooghly District, was a witness to the last occurrence of legal widow-burning in Bengal, shortly before the promulgation of the law prohibiting the practice in 1829. Two of his compatriots, a physician and a priest (the governor-general's chaplain), accompanied him, and they of course attempted, by every possible means, to dissuade the widow. She listened gravely and then, showing a certain impatience, asked to be authorized to proceed to the pyre. The magistrate was obliged to yield to her request, but the chaplain begged him to ask the woman one final question: was she truly aware of the suffering she was about to endure? The rest of the account seems modeled on those previously mentioned:

Then steadfastly looking at me with an air of grave defiance she rested her right elbow on the ground and put her finger into the flame of the lamp. The finger scorched, blistered, and blackened and finally twisted up in a way which I can only compare to what I have seen happen to a quill pen in the flame of a candle. This lasted for some time, during which she never moved her hand, uttered a sound, or altered the expression of her countenance. She then said: "Are you satisfied?" to which I answered hastily, "Quite satisfied," upon which with great deliberation she removed her finger from the flame, saying: "Now may I go?" To this I assented and she moved down the slope to the pile.[100]

C. B. Elliott, another magistrate based in Bengal, resorted to the same technique in an attempt to prevent such a "gratuitous sacrifice of life"—a most lucrative sacrifice, moreover, for the officiating brahmans, who were receiving three hundred rupees from this satī, a considerable sum at the time, for purchasing "an entrance into Paradise through the agonies of martyrdom and the intercession of her holy murderers." Like his predecessors, the magistrate demanded a trial by fire, and observing that the woman was somehow cheating, he roughly held her hand in the flame. The woman would no doubt have repented of her resolution had not the brahmans, seeing their prey escaping them, quickly led her to the river to cool her burns, immediately prior to escorting her to the funeral pyre.[101]

It may be wondered whether this preliminary ritual sequence, which is nowhere codified in Indian tradition, belonged to India originally, or whether, on the contrary, it does not constitute a peripheral development arising out of an accident of history: the conquest of India. In other words, the question is one of determining whether we are confronted here with a case of backlash, by the indigenous society, against a foreign presence. The historiography of the subject provides us with numerous examples of this phenomenon. It has been noted, for instance, that the first measures taken by the British government to limit widow-burning triggered a spectacular increase in such sacrifices between the years 1815 and 1828 in the region of Calcutta, the seat and symbol of colonial power.[102] This obvious explanation is obviated, however, by the fact that in most of these cases it was the woman herself who called for the ordeal. It was she who took the initiative, and who insisted that fire be brought. So it is that we find the motivations at play here to be interpenetrating in these accounts. On the one hand we find Westerners resorting to trial by fire in order to regulate a custom that horrifies them; on the other hand are Indian women wielding the same as a strategy for aiding Hindu belief to emerge victorious over Christian prejudice, and for insuring that their own capacity for heroic sacrifice be universally acknowledged. The ordeal was an occasion for actualizing a declaration of intention. The vow to immolate oneself was proven out through the qualifying ordeal in which a woman made the oblation of a portion of her body stand for the whole: a burned finger, hand, or arm, slowly consumed by the trial fire, heralded and foreshadowed her total sacrifice.

In the Indian perspective, the trial by fire was also an "act of truth." The woman proved her "satī-hood" *(satītva)* by showing no physical pain at the time of the ordeal. According to belief, the *sat* protects the satī like an unguent, coating, or armor. Death on the pyre is compared to a "fire-bath" *(agnisnān)*. It is said that such and such a woman "has taken a fire-bath." It is also said that flames refresh the satī like sandalwood paste, a morning bath, or the still waters of a lotus pond.[103]

"My pulse has long since ceased to beat," William Sleeman was told on November 28, 1829, by the widow of Ummed Singh Upadhya, a Brahman from one of the most respected families in the Jabalpur district (of the Nerbudda Territories) where Sleeman was the Superintendent (this is the same Sleeman who would later achieve fame in his fight against the criminal brotherhood of the Thug stranglers). "My spirit has departed, and I have nothing left but a little *earth,* that I wish to mingle with the ashes of my husband. I shall suffer nothing in burning; and, if you wish proof, order some fire, and you shall see this arm consumed without giving me any pain."[104]

For five days Sleeman had denied the woman permission to burn herself (a bold initiative anticipating by a few months the promulgation of the law banning the sacrifice of widows), and for five days she had remained seated on a rock in the bed of the Narbada River where her husband's ashes had been scattered following his cremation. Shielded by only a thin sheet, she was exposed to the sun's burning heat and the night's piercing cold. She fasted—out of penitence, out of protest, and because in losing her husband, she had lost her very life. As a mark of the irrevocable character of her resolution, she had donned a red turban, the *dhajā,*[105] and had broken with her bracelets the symbols of her marriage and the bonds attaching her to the world. In the eyes of Hindu law, she was no longer part of the world of the living; and if she were to go back on her vow, she would have been excluded from her caste and spurned by her family.

Yet another piece of evidence comes to us directly from an Indian source. The Bengali essayist Shib Chunder Bose, the author of a number of works on Hinduism, was, in his childhood, an eyewitness to a trial by fire. His mother informed him that his aunt was about to become a satī. When he failed to understand what this meant, she added, her eyes shining with tears, that his aunt was about "to eat fire." The child rushed into his aunt's bedroom. He saw her draped in a red silk sari, the part in her hair coated with a thick layer of vermilion paste, her feet dyed with red lacquer, chewing her betel as if she were a young bride on her wedding day. A lamp of clarified butter burned in front of her. She appeared to be "wrapt in an ecstasy of devotion," yet each of her gestures betrayed complete serenity. Then, as an old Brahman woman beseeched her to show her resolve, she held her finger in the flame of the lamp, imperturbable. "The perfect composure with which she underwent this fiery ordeal fully convinced all that she was a real Suttee, fit to abide with her husband in *Boykonto,* [Viṣṇu's] paradise," wrote Bose in 1881.[106]

We encounter yet another episode of this type in 1959, if we are to believe *The Exemplary Life of Sugan Kunvari,* a religious pamphlet published in Kishangarh in a series devoted to the new Mother Satīs of Rajasthan. Sugan Kanvar, who burned herself in that year in the village of Ujoli (near Rupnagar in Jodhpur District), declared her intention to follow in death her stepson Himmat Singh, whom she had adopted and whom she loved more than her own children (he was nineteen years of age and she twenty-eight). She was told that such sacrifices were forbidden by law and that dying for a stepson ran contrary to the *Śāstra*s. Then her two little children (of which the younger was not yet six months old) were brought to her. But she would not be stopped. Manifesting her "terrible" form, the satī threatened to curse all those who would stand in the way of her desire. Then someone among the onlookers asked her to prove that she was indeed possessed by the *sat.* She had burning coals brought in, which she placed in the palm of her hand. These were slowly reduced to ash, but no trace of a burn was visible.[107]

That which qualifies a satī for her heroic sacrifice is her insensitivity to pain, her immunity to fire. This prodigy makes plain, in broad daylight, the supernatural and secret power of the *sat.* This is a power that, transferred to the satī, becomes refracted into a panoply of powers—protective power, as well as healing and thaumaturgical powers. Ascetics who allow themselves to be buried alive in the rite known as *samādhi*[108] (a reference to the seated meditative posture of yoga of the same name), as well as yogis who have mastered the eight supernatural powers (*siddhi*s), also possess the gifts of divination and miracle-making.[109] Wonders and miracles are also demanded of satīs, who are required to prove their "satī-hood" through similar means. Burning oneself is not sufficient to become a Mother Satī: one must also "give *parco,*"[110] reveal one's true nature as a satī through those miraculous deeds that effect the recognition *(parco deṇo)* of one's "satī-hood." If, for example, a satī has been locked in a room to prevent her from burning herself, the door will open on its own; the red marriage veil *(cūndṛī)* will rise up as if by enchantment out of her clothing trunk and come to rest on her head; water will take on the color of henna; milk will rise in the breasts of sterile women; the police, once alerted, will not reach the premises in time because a storm of unprecedented fury or the sudden rise of the river to be crossed has barred their path; the satī will generate fire with her hands or, conversely, the fire will leave no trace of a burn on her body: all of these are so many signs of her possession by the *sat.*

Fire and the Fault of Karma

In a different perspective, immunity to fire stands as proof of a woman's unfailing marital fidelity in the heavenly judgment that constitutes the ordeal. The god of fire Agni is summoned to vouchsafe that the wife in question has indeed been chaste and faithful to her husband in this as well as previous lives: the faithful wife is married in each of her rebirths to the same husband, for whom she proves deserving and whom she wins through her virtue. It is her flawless conduct through cycles of past births as well as her ever pure and well-oriented "dispositions" that have, through the germination and accumulation of "psychic residues" (*pūrvasaṃskāra*s in Sanskrit[111]), produced that which forms both the nature and the power of the satī: her *sat.* The woman who sacrifices herself suffers only in proportion to the sins she has committed in her past lives, sins that are the immediate cause of her widowhood in this life. For, according to the *dharma* treatises, a faithful spouse ought to accompany her husband in his earthly existence and precede him in death. From this standpoint, the death of the husband is interpreted as the manifest sign of the sins of the wife. She is assumed to have failed in her "wifely duty" or seriously violated her "conjugal vow." The gravity of her fault is inversely proportional to her age: the younger the widow, the greater the guilt. An additional yardstick is provided by the intensity of her suffering at the time of her ordeal and, to be sure, her death.

In a general sense, the Hindu worldview associates pain and bodily ills with sin. In the traditional medical treatises of Āyurveda, the very word for "sin" *(pāpman)* designates fever or, in a broader sense, illness itself—so much so, as Francis Zimmermann writes, that "divine matters and the weight of deeds accomplished in past lives are placed on the same footing as changes in the humours."[112] A malady or physical disability is never ethically neutral; it betrays misdeeds committed in past lives. The illness is treated by attacking it at the root. Expiation and the redress of sin *(prāyaścitta)* become remedies (*bheṣajas*): Caraka, one of the great theoreticians of Āyurveda, uses the terms synonymously.[113] Here, fire emerges as the supreme form of purification and consequently of healing. In the middle of the nineteenth century, lepers were burned alive in order to afford them access to a higher rebirth (the British abolished this custom).[114] Leprosy was thought to be repulsive less for fear of contamination or for its symptoms than because of the hideousness of the crimes whose delayed manifestation it was taken to be. Even at the beginning of the twentieth century, incidents of purification by fire were still frequently found among local press reports. In 1906, in Vasad, a large village in the Kaira District of Gujarat, nine villagers (including five women), fanaticized by a *sādhu* passing himself off as a divine incarnation, burned themselves alive by leaping into a flaming pit. He had succeeded in convincing them that the ordeal would win them entrance into heaven.[115] That same year another wandering "holy man" burned a low-caste woman in a poor Calcutta neighborhood in an exorcism aimed at extirpating from her body the demon responsible for her insanity.[116] Such popular practices are to be compared with far more elaborate forms of purification by fire, including the tradition of the voluntary death of the sage or ascetic (attested to from the time of Alexander) or the self-immolation of Buddhist monks.[117] Even today, in certain regions of India (most especially in Tamilnadu), suicide by fire is by far the most common form of voluntary death. We may surmise that the idea of self-purification is not wholly unrelated to the choice of death by fire, reputed to be the cruelest death of all.[118]

Although both men and women resort to the "fire-bath," there nonetheless exists a more specific link between the feminine and the igneous. This is because purification impacts women in a particular spot, in the common congenital flaw of their sex, in a sin that has been committed ever anew throughout their history. What is at issue here is the impurity of women. By "impurity" is meant nonchastity, and by chastity the observance of the conjugal vow committing a wife to absolute fidelity. Fidelity in turn implies (in accordance with the consecrated formula) body, speech, and thought.[119] To these should be added unconscious thought, since a dream or impulse has the same status as an act in the hierarchy of faults. Mythology illustrates the matter quite well, as in the story of Reṇukā, decapitated by her son Paraśurāma on the order of his father Jamadagni ("Devouring Fire"). While bathing in a river, Reṇukā is witness to the love-play of the king of the Gandharvas (the celestial musicians) and his wives. The image of carnal pleasure momentarily distracts her mind. Jamadagni punishes her for her crime by transforming her into one of the decapitated goddesses that remain one of Hinduism's specialties and are worshipped as such by their devotees.[120]

The fidelity of virtuous wives ought not to be imagined as a homogeneous quality. There are at least four varieties (governed by a subtle hierarchy), as the great poet Tulsī Dās (ca. 1550–1623) teaches us in his Holy Lake of the Acts of Rāma *(Rāmcaritmānas),* a veritable Bible for the Hindus of north India:

> There are in the world four grades of faithful wife, as the Vedas, the Purāṇas, and all the saints declare. The best are perfectly convinced that there is no other man in the world at all. The next in order look on another's husband as their own brother, father or son. The woman who preserves her chastity merely because it is her duty and because she regards the honour of her family is said in the scriptures to be low; but account that wife lowest of all in the world whom fear alone restrains and want of opportunity.

And Tulsī adds:

> She who deceives her husband and enjoys an intrigue with another's is cast for a hundred aeons into the depths of the lowest hell. Who so vile as she who regards not the torments of innumerable lives for the sake of a moment's pleasure? . . . [S]he who is disloyal to her husband, wherever she be born, becomes a widow in her early youth.[121]

Here we can see that it is the law of the retribution of acts *(karma)* and its corollary—the transmigration of souls from birth to birth—that places infidelity at the source of widowhood. Tulsī Dās's *Rāmcaritmānas* also contains an episode that may throw some light, if only indirectly, on the riddle of trial by fire. This is because its heroine Sītā, the wife of Prince Rāma and the model of the faithful wife, undergoes a trial by fire following the victory of Rāma and his army of monkeys over the demon Rāvaṇa. This sequence, which also figures in the *Rāmāyaṇa* of Vālmīki as well as, fleetingly, the Sanskrit dramas of Bhāsa, Kālidāsa and Bhavabhūti,[122] functions less as a turning point in the plot than as a first crescendo in the misfortunes of Sītā. Exiled into the forest for fourteen years with Rāma and his brother Lakṣmaṇa; abducted and then imprisoned by the demon of Lanka, who attempts in vain to seduce her; repudiated by her husband, who doubts her chastity, Sītā voluntarily submits to a trial by fire *(agni-parīkṣā)* to prove her innocence before the entire universe.

In the *Rāmāyaṇa* of Vālmīki, Rāma greets his rescued spouse with cruel words of repudiation:

> There are doubts about your past behavior, and your presence before me is quite as afflicting as a lamp before a diseased eye.
>
> Therefore, go! You have been dismissed. Go wherever you wish, O daughter of Janaka. The world lies before you, fair woman. I no longer have anything to do with you.
>
> A woman who has sojourned in the house of another man—what noble, well-born man could be so ruled by his affections as to take her back?
>
> Rāvaṇa has sullied you with his breast and roved over you with his wicked eyes. How can I take you back, I who claim noble birth?[123]

Distressed, Sītā protests her innocence, and then asks her husband's younger brother Lakṣmaṇa to build a pyre for her, the sole possible remedy for her ills.[124] Lowering her head in shame, Sītā then circumambulates Rāmā three times, keeping him to her right (as a sign of devotion),[125] before entering into the flames as she calls out to the god Agni (here called Pāvaka, the "Purifier"):

> Since my heart has never released Rāghava [Rāma] from its embrace, may Pāvaka, who is eyewitness to [all that takes place in] the world, grant me his complete protection!
>
> Since my conduct is pure [even though] Rāghava thinks me to be defiled, may Pāvaka, who is eyewitness to [all that takes place in] the world, grant me his complete protection!

Agni restores Rāma's wife to him as he vouches for her purity; Rāma then accepts her, since her chastity has triumphed over her trial by fire.

Tulsī's narrative is embedded in another context. In the "Book of the Forest," Rāma confides to Sītā his secret plan: to produce a divine game for human consumption *(nara-līlā)*.[126] Here it must be understood that the fabulous plot of the epic, with its gods, their "descents" (*avatāras*), demons, humans, and deified animals such as the monkey Hanumān—in sum the totality of characters and events in this fantastic story—are but the "effects of *māyā*" produced out of the Play of Viṣṇu in his seventh earthly incarnation as Prince Rāma, the son of Daśaratha (*māyā* is cosmic illusion, the weapon and prerogative of the gods). The notion of God's Play, one of the keys to *bhakti* religion, is, quite naturally, not absent for Vālmīki's poem. However, the idiosyncratic use Tulsī Dās makes of it in this episode is foreign to the original *Rāmāyaṇa*.

Rāma therefore asks of Sītā that she hide herself in fire until his victorious return from the island of Lanka. Sītā enters into the blaze, leaving behind "the image of her shadow": a delusive double of herself, a false appearance. In the "Book of Laṅka," Rāma addresses Sītā with the cruel words that are to be the cause of her ordeal. She protests her innocence and casts her body into the flames, but none of this is true since Rāma is in a sense playing his own role in this illusory drama in which Sītā's double gives him his cue. "Her shadow and her apparent defilement were consumed in the blazing mass: no one noticed this stratagem of the Lord's."[127] Now the real Sītā emerges from her hiding place like the goddess Lakṣmī from the Ocean of Milk. When she goes to sit at Rāma's left side, she shines like a golden lotus bud whose brilliance eclipses the blue lotus flower.

The changes Tulsī Dās makes to the original plot of the Acts of Rāma allow us to gauge the popularity of devotional religion *(bhakti)* and the vigor of the Vaiṣṇava cult of Rāma in north India at the beginning of the seventeenth century. As the object of devotion of this Avadhi (a medieval form of Eastern Hindi) poet, Rāma cannot be subject to the human failings tainting his behavior in Vālmīki's narrative.[128] He is the supreme God whose name, once uttered, suffices to obtain liberation for the utterer. His reign is the symbol of the golden age *(Rāmarājya).* And Sītā, as the incarnation of the goddess Lakṣmī, so participates in the divine nature of her husband that the coalescence of their names, when continuously repeated *(japa)* in the mystical formula *Sītārāma,* throws open the gates of salvation to their devotees. The figure of Sītā is too idealized for her purity to be open to suspicion or subjected to Agni's judgment. The biographical accidents punctuating her story (which are necessary to the working out of Viṣṇu's purpose in his seventh descent into the world of men) are thus transposed upon a factitious Sītā. "The image of her shadow" suffers all the trials and tribulations while the true Sītā takes refuge in the fire. It will be noted however that in both cases, for the deified heroine as well as for her counterpart, fire constitutes the necessary transit and, as it were, the very sign of womanly destiny.[129]

Sītā's ordeal brings to light the link, in this symbol system, between feminine chastity and fire. It would nonetheless be imprudent to see in this episode a myth of the origin of widow-burning, as has occasionally been done. On the other hand, the extraordinary spread of the Rāma tradition in its many forms may have given rise to a pseudo-tradition of trial by fire, for the edification of faithful wives.[130] And it may have been this model that served as a personal guide or religious precedent during the period in which foreigners, wearing the mantle of power in the land of the Indians, took it upon themselves to dissuade widows from burning themselves.

Fig. 10. Indian widow: illustration taken from Pierre Sonnerat's *Voyage aux Indes orientales et à la Chine, fait par ordre du Roi dupuis 1774 jusqu'en 1781 . . .* (Paris, 1782). Courtesy Bibliothèque Nationale, Paris.

Widows who did not immolate themselves were nonetheless also marked by fire, as Father Vincenzo reports in 1678:

In the States governed by Mohametans, it is rare that the permission [to burn oneself] be accorded: nevertheless, some women, in order to conform to sacred law and show themselves more faithful to their spouses, still purchase for a certain price the authorization to do so from the Governors. When I was in Suratte [in Gujarat], one of them requested this and when it was denied her, the woman let it be known to the Divan that she would burn herself in her own house, since she could not bear to live with such a reputation for infidelity. Others, condemned to perpetual widowhood, wear fiery red clothing for the rest of their days, as a sign of the debt they have incurred.

In the States in which Gentile [Hindu] Princes reign, above all in the Canara country [in Karnataka], it is common practice to burn widows. If any of them, vanquished by fear, refuses to do so, she must request permission for such from the governing authority who, forgiving her natural weakness, receives her in the name of the King as the Prince's perpetual slave, stripping her of all rights to inheritance, with the obligation that she shall always go about with shaven head and in Turkey-red garments, two signs of her infamy and shame.[131]

In the same period, John Fryer also observed that widows who survived their husbands were "rifled of all their Jewels, and Shaved, always wearing a Red *lungy,* whereby to be known that they have not undergone the Conflagration; for which cause they are despised, and live more Uncomfortably than the meanest Servant" (fig. 10).[132]

Fire-red, the sign of infamy, is as opposed to auspicious red, the emblem of connubial happiness, as day is to night. Shades of reddish brown and purple are associated with widowhood in western India (Karnataka, Maharashtra, Gujarat, and Rajasthan).[133] Even today Mahajan widows of Bikaner wear wide reddish brown skirts of cloth printed with black-encircled white patterns.[134] Fryer was certainly not incorrect in interpreting this red of dishonor as the mark of the fire whose flames the widow did not suffer. There is in fact a popular expression that concretizes this viewpoint. To those widows and female enemies upon whom one would wish the supreme misfortune of widowhood, one hurls the insult "burnt parting of the hair!" *(māṅg jalī).* In the course of the wedding ceremony, the groom combs his bride's hair and coats the part thus formed with vermilion paste or with *kuṃkum.*[135] If the wife loses her husband then other widows will wash away this vermilion after having broken her marriage bracelets on the night of the twelfth day of mourning. Among higher castes, a woman will have her head shaven. "Burnt parting of the hair" thus evokes the ritual moment of entry into the state of widowhood, whose painful intensity is exacerbated by a mortifying ceremonial. This lapidary formula also plays, however, on another connotation since it also refers (antiphrastically) to the sacrifice the widow has refused to perform. Not satisfied with having pitched her husband into the jaws of death through her evil karma, with letting him set off on his own into the other world, she has, by stealing away, betrayed him a second time.

HANDPRINT, DAGGER, AND LEMON

Mutilation and Voluntary Death

Wounding oneself with the kris and trial by fire—these marks of the solemn resolve to burn oneself take on yet another form in India, a form etched in stone and human memory. Before departing for the cremation ground, the satī presses the palm of her right hand, which has been coated with either vermilion paste or *kuṃkum,* against the walls or doorways of her house, or on the monumental gates of the palace or city if she is among those accompanying a deceased member of royal lineage.[1] The traveler who passes through the sites of Jodhpur, Bikaner, or Jaisalmer cannot help but notice on these fortified archways row upon row of little hands pointing upward as a sign of their "determination" (figs. 11 to 13). The impressive gridwork formed by these handprints, row upon row of individual lives pieced together over the centuries through the deadly vow that has made them one, constitutes the visible seal of their sacrificial calling, even as it concentrates within itself the magical power of the *sat.* In Jodhpur, between the Mehrangarh Fort and four of the six gates of the old city, I counted 222 satī handprints. It is from such imprints *(thāpā)* that a basic worship structure gradually emerged: sculpted, coated with vermilion or a thin veneer of gold and silver leaf, occasionally written over with inscriptions, these imprints have received offerings from members of the satī's lineage at particular moments in their domestic life. Aniconic platforms, commemorative stones, (square, rectangular, or *liṅga*-shaped) funeral pillars, small shrines containing

Fig. 11. Satīs' handprints at Bikaner Fort, Rajasthan (private collection).

the image of the satī or of the married couple, and finally temples were erected, grounding the cult in a specific locality. It is these handprints that one finds, once again, on the stele of the satīs. These may be found side by side with "hero-stones" at the outer boundaries of villages; at other times, they form vast funeral grounds stretching haphazardly as far as the eye can see (figs. 14 to 17). The handprint motif is most often a depiction of the hand and forearm: a single word—*hasta* in Sanskrit, *hāth* in Hindi—designates this part of the body, which constitutes an anatomical unit. On numerous stele in Karnataka one finds references to women who, in such and such a year and in such and such a circumstance, "have given arm and hand,"[2] a euphemism for these satīs' deaths. On either side of the open palm the sun and the moon are figured as images of eternity. More mysterious, even enigmatic, is a lemon. Occasionally the swastika is added as a symbol of good fortune, as if to underscore the auspicious nature of the sacrifice. As for the marriage bracelets, which are omnipresent in such images, they indicate that the satī has burned herself as a wife: *sahagamana* ("going with") renders the deaths of the two spouses simultaneous in the rite, if not in reality, thereby annihilating the spectre of widowhood (fig. 18).[3]

The hand, and most especially the finger, that extremity of what is already a liminal region of the body, had "powers" attributed to them—on

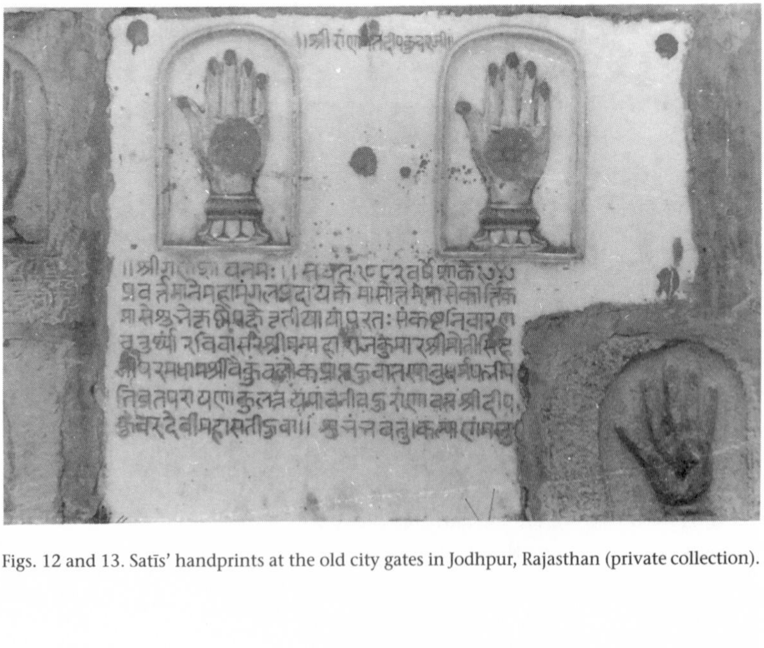

Figs. 12 and 13. Satīs' handprints at the old city gates in Jodhpur, Rajasthan (private collection).

Figs. 14 and 15. Hero stones and satī stones at the Wadhwan (Saurashtra, Gujarat) archaeological site (private collection). On figure 15, the presence of red minium and gold and silver foil overlays indicate that this satī stela is an object of worship.

Fig. 16. Hero stones, Wadhwan (private collection).

Fig. 17. "The Determination": stela from Vijayanagara Archaeological Museum. Copyright French Institute of Pondicherry and Ecole Française d'Extrême-Orient; reprinted by permission.

Fig. 18.
Marriage bracelets, lemon, swastika, sun, and moon: satī stela from Wadhwan. Copyright Archaeological Survey of India, New Delhi; reprinted by permission.

the fringes of Hindu orthodoxy, but nonetheless in intimate accordance with it—which nineteenth-century ethnographers and folklorists brought to light. The offering of a finger appears to constitute a surrogate sacrifice. An incident reported in the Calcutta press on March 25, 1925, is a good illustration. This case, of a combined human sacrifice and infanticide, was all the more scandalous for the fact that its perpetrator, an upper-caste Hindu named Mulchand Singh, was a government employee (he had the position of public scribe in the Mandla courthouse, in present-day Madhya Pradesh). He had sacrificed his daughter to the goddess Kālī in order to obtain a cure for one of his sons. The boy's illness, which erupted suddenly, had been diagnosed by a "holy man" as a case of demonic possession requiring a human sacrifice. The daughter-in-law had first cut the third joint of the little girl's pinkie. She allowed a bit of rice[4] to absorb the blood thus shed and left that offering at the site of the *sādhu*'s retreat. When this partial sacrifice failed to allay the fury of the Goddess (who is rarely satisfied with such half measures), the girl was offered to Kālī in a total sacrifice—by we know not what means—which ought to have succeeded. Yet the illness persisted. The parents then deprived the sick boy of food and exposed him naked, with his hands and feet bound in a sign of penitence, in the vicinity of the "territory" of the holy man, who was mediating between the family and the wrathful goddess. This treatment, which should have resulted in a cure, resulted in the death of young Lakshman Singh.[5]

The play of equivalence—between fragment, part, and whole in the sacrificial sphere—is to be noted in this case: the joint replaces the finger, and the finger the sacrificed body. Similarly, in the ordeal by fire, the satī's burnt finger, which prefigures her sacrifice, in a certain sense symbolizes its completion. The wounds or mutilations that constitute the necessary preliminary to certain types of ritual suicide, inasmuch as they epitomize the violence of sacrificial deaths, are also metaphors for them. Far from being an attenuated form of the ritual it anticipates, the pre-sacrifice may be viewed as its fullest expression.[6] A stela erected in Shikarpur District (Karnataka) in 1050 extols the memory of a man who, in order to protest against the donation of a small fort, had taken a permanent vow to tear out his fingernail. The day on which the fort was nonetheless given, he chopped off his finger and threw himself from atop a pillar onto a row of spikes.[7] Death by leaping onto sharp objects (especially spikes) was one of the preferred forms of devotional suicide in south India during the medieval period. Inscriptions also attest to the popularity of offering one's last finger joint to Śiva, Kāla Bhairava, or Mahālakṣmī. In the fourteenth century, the Kāla Bhairava temple at Siti was famous for such sacrifices. Konduri Sarojini Devi tells us that the Reddi and Marasu Vokkaliga farmers, who traditionally offered a finger joint to the god, and who then found themselves handicapped by that amputation for work in the fields, later had the idea of cutting off two fingers of each of their women.[8]

The Rhetoric of Protest Suicide

In western India, entire castes of genealogists and panegyrists raised the practice of self-mutilation to the level of corporate specialty. Bhats and Charans were considered to be holy: the inspiration that was the source of their art was taken to be a sign of divine possession, a fact corroborated by their readiness to take their own lives. Their origin myths (of which there are many variants) maintain that they were descended from Mahādeo (Śiva) and Pārvatī. As custodians of both Speech and History, they occupied the second rank in the hierarchical order, above their Rajput patrons. As the saying goes, *āge Brāhmaṇ pīche bhāṭ / tāke pīche aor jāt* ("first the Brahman, then the Bhat, and after them the other castes").[9] Without a bard to sing his praises or a genealogist to exalt his ancestors, it was impossible for a Rajput to assert his rank in the old society. Whenever questions arose concerning ancestral rights, privileges, inheritances, lands, or titles—or forming new alliances—he was dependent on their knowledge, which was transmitted through genealogies (*pīḍhiāvalī*s or "generational lines," and *vaṃśāvalī*s or "lines of descendants") and recorded in *bahī*s ("registers").[10] But he was also dependent on their savoir-faire: as certified mythographers, Bhats and Charans were capable of finding connections between a given clan or lineage and this or that prestigious dynasty, of adapting myth to history, and of weaving small and great traditions into a seamless narrative whole. Thus, they were simultaneously guardians of caste institutions (which were legally grounded in their antiquity) and craftsmen of social mobility.[11] The high favor they enjoyed with the Rajput chiefs (who received them as honored guests, sharing with them the lord's opium even as their service relationship also consigned them to the contemptible category of "those who beg") cannot be explained solely on the basis of these castes' authority in matters of social legitimation. Bhats and Charans made and unmade reputations, and had no qualms about subjecting their less than liberal employers to ridicule: speech turned to venom, and panegyric to satire while an effigy of the object of their resentment, tied together with a shoe (to add defilement to infamy) to the end of a long stick, was displayed wherever these essentially nomadic groups passed (this was the case at least for the Charans, who, originally pastoralists, later became cattle-drivers, livestock-traders, and haulers). Their very name likely derives from the Sanskrit verb *cārayati,* "to graze," the causative of *carati,* "to move, roam about."[12]

After the rainy season they would take to the road and travel from court to court in the service of their patrons, thereby covering considerable distances through mountainous and rugged terrain that was either heavily forested or swampy and desolate, both equally dangerous to travelers. Organized bands of thieves—from the Bhil, Koli, Kathi, and other "criminal tribes" (according to the colonial classification)[13]—also awaited the end of the rains to launch their campaigns of plunder. The Charans' inviolability, together with their nomadic way of life, singled them out as ideal caravan escorts and insurers of the safety of people and goods. When attacks came, they threatened to shed their own blood. They would generally begin by slashing their forearms with their daggers (*kaṭārī*s): one could judge a

Charan's prestige by the number of his scars. If the adversary did not yield, things would take a far more dramatic turn. Members of the clan would be put to death in a variety of ways, each more spectacular than the last, in a macabre crescendo whose purpose was to place unbearable pressure on the opposing party. In fact, nothing was more greatly dreaded than the vengeance of a suicide's ghost. Without fail, it would wipe out the guilty party and his entire lineage. Children and the elderly were sacrificed first, with priority given to girls and women: imbued with a particular type of sanctity within the caste, their violent death transformed them into terrible forms of the Devī.[14]

The Charans stood as sureties *(zāmin)* whenever a legal guarantee was required: pacts, engagements, transactions, transfers, recovery of debts, collection of land revenue, and even the signing of treaties. The security for such a guarantee was their body, their life. They collectively wounded, mutilated, and immolated themselves if the terms of the contract were not respected, if reparation was not made for a damage or offense and, quite naturally, whenever they were themselves victims of an injustice or affront. They served as sureties for the collection of land revenue from the sixteenth century down to 1816.[15] Even the British called upon the Charans to underwrite the Saurashtra peace agreements of the early nineteenth century.[16] The mark of the dagger, heavy with the threat of self-sacrifice, served as their signature. The Charans were, moreover, the traditional arbitrators of conflicts between the various Rajput clans or branches. In times of war, their villages became neutral zones and places of refuge.[17]

The body of practices involving mutilation and voluntary death as a sign of protest bore the name of *tyāg (trāgā* in Gujarati).[18] The word comes from the Sanskrit *tyāga* ("abandonment," "cession"). In Vedic ritual, it designated the formula used by the officiant when he cast an offering into the fire: "This for said god, not for me." J. C. Heesterman has emphasized the importance of that dedicatory formula in Vedic sacrifice, in which the essential act "is not primarily a gift or offering of food to the gods but an abandonment *pure and simple*"[19] of one's person. "The abandonment of the body" *(dehatyāga)* is a euphemism in classical Sanskrit for "sacrificing one's life." According to the *Laws of Manu* (10.62), "giving up the body instinctively for the sake of a priest or cow or in the defence of women and children is the way for even the excluded (castes) to achieve success."

Confirmed from Konkan to Kathiawar and Kutch, and from Saurashtra to Rajputana and Malwa, the custom of *tyāg* gave rise to a series of measures: struck down by law in 1795 and 1799, it was officially prohibited in 1827, but did not in fact disappear until the final decade of the nineteenth century.[20] Mutilations and voluntary death were at once techniques and rites. Whereas their ritualization conferred on them an impersonal and immutable character, the notoriously innovative bards were constantly developing variations on the deadly scenario. Gashes and wounds were comparable to poetic flourishes, with both being objects of emulation as well as competition between clans. There existed no fewer than thirty-two ways of committing *trāgā,* each region of the tormented body being a symbolic seat of power. The sacrifice itself was preceded by the solemn declaration of intention *(saṃkalpa)* that inaugurates any ritual sequence, a purifying bath *(snāna),* an admonitory fast, and an invocation addressed to Jogmāyā or another form of the *Śakti* of whom the Charans are great devotees.

The most basic form of *trāgā* consisted of piercing both cheeks with a lancet and, without displaying the slightest sign of pain, taunting one's adversary in a frenzied dance—an imitation of Śiva's dance that incinerates the worlds, as well as a sign of possession. But the *trāgā* could also be elevated to the level of an art and a science. On certain stele, one sees a Charan piercing his own jugular vein in an act of autosurgical prowess known as "striking the throat" *(gaḷe ghālṇo)* (fig. 19).[21] The expression "doing *cāndī*" (the words means "wound") designates that particular form of protest suicide in which one allowed one's blood to flow from a wound until death ensued. "To do *khāḷiyo*" (another local term for "wound") meant to sever one's head. Nothing, however, could rival the violence of *trāgā* by fire, a macabre scene in which the act of burning oneself combined death and vengeance, rite and spectacle, hierophany and profanation. Transformed into a living torch, the Charan would dance before his adversary until he collapsed, before his very eyes, into a heap of ashes.[22]

In 1586, eleven thousand Charans whose villages had been confiscated by Rao Udai Singh of Jodhpur gathered in Auwa (Pali District) with the intention of "performing *cāndī*" under the protection of Gopal Das, a Champavat and the local Rajput chieftain, who embraced their cause. They sat before the temple of Mahādev (Śiva), blocking its access to register their solemn protest and demand redress. The Rao sent his envoy in the person of Akkha-ji, his royal bard (Barot[23]). Having come to negotiate the withdrawal of the Charans and the relinquishment of their deadly intentions, Akkha instead declared his solidarity with his caste brethren. With the Rao threatening to send his army, the Charans passed the night calling upon the goddess Jogmāyā with their chants and then, before dawn, had the drummer climb atop the temple spire to give the signal for mass suicide at the first light of dawn.[24] Not wishing to provoke a hecatomb, the drummer slit his throat and threw himself down from the temple. Taking up their

Fig. 19. Stela showing a Charan piercing his jugular vein, Rajasthan (private collection).

daggers and knives, the Charans then entered into the sacred precincts of the temple. One slit his throat and sprinkled the divine image with his blood; another cut off his head; a third disemboweled himself. Akkha-ji followed their lead. All was awash in blood. Gopal Das sought asylum for himself and his family in Bikaner, in the house of Rajah Rai Singh, whose brother Prithviraj convinced Emperor Akbar to return the confiscated villages to the Charans.[25] In 1846, an armed group of Charans, driven back at Jaisalmer, marched on Jodhpur and threatened to resort to the same extreme measures. A year later Maharajah Takhat Singh promulgated a law punishing such sacrifices on the same grounds as voluntary deaths.[26]

Captain Macmurdo, who accompanied Alexander Walker, the Resident of Baroda, on two daring missions into Kathiawar (in 1807 and 1809–1810), reported several cases of *trāgā*. On November 23, 1809, during a halt at Alia, he learned that two brahmans had slit their wrists down to the bone to protest the destruction of their sugar-cane field by a band of horsemen.

In the same *Journal,* he describes a case of *trāgā* that occurred several years earlier:

A Charon had become security on the part of Dossajee, the Raja of Mallia, for a sum of money due to the Moorbea Raja. The time specified for the payment arrived, and Dossajee refused to pay the money. The Charon, after repeatedly entreating the Raja to comply with his Bond, returned home, and after passing several hours in prayer called his family and desired his wife to prepare his daughter, a beautiful girl of 7 or 8 years of age, for death—the innocent child taught to reflect upon the sacred character of her Father and the necessity with which he was bound to fulfill his Bonds, such as those which he had contracted, required no adviser to point out the path to preserve for the honour of her family. She came forth a voluntary victim. After bathing [and] dressing herself in her richest clothes, she laid her head upon her Father's knee, and holding aside her long and beautiful hair, which had been unbraided for the purpose of bathing, she permitted herself to be murdered without a groan or struggle. The human heart can scarcely picture to itself a Father so cruel or a daughter so magnanimous.

The Raja who had been the occasion of this traga, alarmed at the Blood of a Charon being upon his head, did everything in his power to appease the wrath of the Supreme being by instantly paying the money, conducting the funeral ceremonies of the unfortunate little girl, in the most public and magnificent style, and erecting a monument to her memory. The inhuman Father received a Gift of lands, in return for the loss of his Daughter.[27]

Dizzying Heights of Vengeance

Alexander Kinloch Forbes recounts a case of *trāgā* described in a short work composed in Gujarati in 1849 by Dalpat Ram Daya, a Shrimali Brahman poet from Wadhwan.[28] Around 1819, a conflict pitted a Charan against a Sayla (in Kathiawar) chief who had refused to pay him his due. Accompanied by about forty members of his clan, the Charan prepared to "sit unto death" at the Rajput's door. This well-known technique, called *dharnā* (from the Hindi verb meaning "to place, hold"), consists of sitting at the door (thereby blocking access) of one's offender, in a sign of protest. Implicit in this act is the threat of not lifting the siege until one has received satisfaction, even if this means dying in the process. An exclusively Brahman prerogative in ancient India and religiously sanctioned since that time, *dharnā* is a modern form of protest suicide. The murder of a brahman—or responsibility for his death, which amounts to the same thing—is in fact the most abominable of all crimes, an inexpiable crime (at least in the absolute sense) that pursues its perpetrator, from rebirth to rebirth, with its disastrous effects. Indeed, its sole equivalent is the slaughter of a cow; but this is precisely because the cow incarnates the very principle of brahman-ness. It is in this context that we can understand how a brahman's threat of laying "siege" would have been a tremendously effective means of coercion. The archetypal form of this category of suicide was that of the creditor who fasted to death at his debtor's door, thereby making the delinquent party a brahmanicide.[29] Outwardly peaceful, the fast unto death was, basically, an act of extreme violence directed primarily against the other: if the injured party lost his life in the process, his offender, now become his victim, lost not only his reputation but also all hope for earthly happiness for himself and his descendants. The dark deed, set in motion by his own misconduct, locked its saturnian rings into the cycle of his future lives.

Brahmans were not the sole group to resort to protest suicide. Epigraphy and literature from the first millennium of the common era attest to the fact that members of every social order *(varṇa),* including śūdras, made use of this form of coercion or redress. On occasion, entire villages would immolate themselves in protest against the levying of a tax or some other iniquitous measure. During India's struggle for independence, fasting to death and *dharnā* would achieve new notoriety, this time political. In addition to wielding it as an absolute weapon to thwart the colonial power, Gandhi also used fasting for its purifying virtues. The Mahatma was a native of an Indian region (Gujarat) and milieu in which Jain influence predominated. No Indian path to salvation accords as much place to fasting as does that of the Jains. A fundamental element of life in the world, fasting is also the supreme path (in the form of *sallekhana,* death by starvation) to liberation, for monks and laypersons alike.[30]

Political protest suicide has thrust itself into the public eye once again: in September and October 1990, a wave of voluntary student immolations in New Delhi and other cities of north India threatened the peace, and was partly responsible for bringing down the government of V. P. Singh. These (Brahman or high caste) students, in a show of anger at a proposal to set aside quotas for "backward castes" in the public sector and government bureaucracy, began their protest by practicing *dharnā.* When their demands were not met, they resorted to self-immolation. The projected law, drawn up in 1983 by the Mandal Commission (so named for the magistrate that headed it), was, on November 16, 1992, the subject of a Supreme Court ruling. Refusing to quail at the prospect of setting off a new round of "caste warfare," the Court ruled in favor of prioritizing the allocation to the lower castes of 27 percent of the positions to be filled in the central public administration.[31]

Returning now to Sayla, the Rajput chief, attempting to avoid the worst, shut his doors, whereupon the Charans "gave *dharnā*" at the threshold to his palace. For three days they undertook an admonitory fast, and on the fourth day they "committed *trāgā*": they slashed their arms with their daggers and, cutting off the heads of three old women, hung those sinister trophies as a "garland" on the doors. Women cut off their breasts; men slit the throats of four old men with pikes and then, seizing two little girls by the feet, smashed their brains out against the doors. The Charan who was the principal offended party brought matters to an end by draping himself in cotton-lined garments, which he soaked with oil before setting them ablaze. As he died, he hurled threats and curses down on his offender: metamorphosed by his violent death into a "headless spirit" *(khabīsa),* he would wreak his vengeance upon him, take his life, and destroy his family line. This type of *trāgā* by fire, known as *teliyo* (from *tel,* oil) constitutes the supreme form of voluntary death for the Charans.

Although suicidal practices motivated by a desire for redress and revenge are found widely among other groups and in other regions of India (notably in south India), the Bhat and Charan communities of western India elevated the individual practice of *dharnā* to the level of caste duty, in quasi-contractual terms. In response, the Charans at least would further raise the stakes, in the luxuriant forms of violence that constitute *trāgā.*[32]

The Trammels of Resentment

The gods themselves can become trapped in this web of resentment, in which the victim is not he who sacrifices himself, but rather he who bears the responsibility for that act and will sooner or later suffer the consequences. A short piece in the August 30, 1926, issue of the *Calcutta Daily Newspaper* recounts the suicide of a Maghaya Brahman from Purulia (present-day Bihar). Stricken with an illness, the man had gone to the temple of Śiva to be healed. In vain he waited for the god to manifest himself, in the form of a dream or a cure—until the night he slit his throat with a dagger over the Śiva *liṅga.* This bizarre incident brings together the three predominant themes of the tradition of "murder of the self": expiatory suicide (recall here that illness is caused by karmic flaw), devotional suicide, and protest or revenge suicide. The blood shed on the *liṅga,* that form of the god which expresses his mystery and a cult object of Śaivite worship, calls vengeance down upon him who has forsaken his devotee.[33]

There was yet another facet to *trāgā:* it consisted of using a dagger not only to wound the body but also—in the event of an attack on the caravan, the violation of a contract, an offense, or litigation—to cast the blood of those wounds on one's enemy, a sacrilegious act. Sons of Mahādev in their origin myth, the Charans are also "children of the Goddess" *(devīputra*s). As such, they are possessed of her energy *(śakti),* and the holy terror it inspires. Together with blood, the Charans hurled curses, which served to reinforce the blood's efficacy. The gesture gave literal expression to the words of the malediction "May my blood fall back on your head." Naturally, this "act of truth" never missed its mark. Macmurdo relates the case of a Kutch chieftain whose village had been attacked by plunderers. He tried to flee with his wife and child; unable to escape, he turned and faced them, drew his sword, decapitated his wife, and plunging his weapon into the blood, threw it at his assailants as he cursed them.[34] Here the symbolism of blood plays itself out on three registers: impurity, magical power, and revenge. Like semen or saliva, blood is an eminently impure substance (menstrual blood heads up this negative hierarchy).[35] But for the very same reasons that it has a dangerous and polluting valence, blood can become an inexhaustible source of "powers."[36]

The casting of blood also served as a means of blackmail. Bhats and Charans became experts in the art of extorting enormous sums of money from their Rajput patrons, in the form of ritual payments, whenever a wedding was celebrated.[37] When the groom's wedding procession arrived at the bride's house (where the ceremony took place), the Charans traditionally stood at the door so as to be the first—even before the Brahmans—to receive gifts *(neg)* from the bride-takers. This privilege stood in counterpoint to their function as "guardians of the gate" *(poḷpāt)* or "guardians of the fort" *(gaḍhvī):* stationed at the principal entries of besieged forts or on the front line of combat, they blockaded the enemy with the holy shield of their bodies, and thereby were the first to perish. The Charans demanded the groom's finery, his mount (horse or elephant) or cash equivalent, as well as two handfuls of rupees (the "fistfuls of heroism": *vīrmuṭṭhī).* In addition, the father of the groom was required to give the Bhats and Charans (whose services were required on such occasions) a payment *(tyāg)* comparable to the sacrificial fee *(dakṣiṇā)* paid the Brahman officiants.[38] But whereas Brahmans accepted such honoraria without asking for more, the *tyāg* was the object of fierce bargaining. Bhats and Charans had no qualms about demanding three quarters of annual landholding revenues. A Rajput's reputation hung on the words of the bards, who, according to their mood, could just as easily let loose a volley of praise as fire off a string of satiric barbs that were all the more injurious to his honor inasmuch as the wedding audience was a large one, composed of the social elite. Worst of all, they threatened to cast their blood on the guests if their demands were not met—"and these threats have been too often carried into execution to make them be deemed idle by the superstitious Rajpoots," reports Sir John Malcolm, in telling how Bhim Singh, the son of the Rajah of Bagli, complained bitterly one day that his marriage with a close relative of the Rawal of Banswara was about to be postponed on the grounds of the enormity of the sum demanded by the Charans. He could not satisfy them without being ruined, nor could he refuse their conditions without incurring their revenge and the discredit that would ensue. He had thus been reduced to choosing between poverty and disgrace.[39]

This practice, which had become the general rule throughout the whole of Rajputana, was a veritable plague on society, since it could lead directly to female infanticide: if members of certain Rajput clans systematically did away with their daughters at birth, it was not only because they could not marry them off without suffering loss of status (due to the rule of hypergamy), but also because such marriages would in any event bring about their ruin. Maharajah Jai Singh of Jaipur and Bakhat Singh of Jodhpur tried to put an end to such exactions by setting a ceiling on the sumptuary expenses occasioned by weddings as well as the fees paid to bards. Their edicts (of 1731 and 1752–53), however, remained unenforced. *Tyāg* would continue down to the end of the nineteenth century, when it finally yielded before the concerted actions of the princes of Rajputana and Rajput and Charan leaders who, together with C. K. M. Walter, the political agent of the Governor General, founded a society in 1888 whose purpose it was to reform the most shocking practices of these two groups (the *Walterkṛt Rājaputra Hitkāriṇī Sabhā*).[40]

A Rite of Exorcism

The incident related by Forbes is but the prelude to a rite of exorcism. The suicide's spirit had indeed entered into the body (more precisely, the head) of the Sayla chief, and the most illustrious *jogīs*, *jatis*, fakirs, brahmans, and other demonology specialists had been summoned—to no avail.[41] The spirit continued to wreak havoc, wounding, killing, and spreading terror through the palace. Finally a *jati* from outside the region but highly reputed for his powers succeeded, after forty-one days of charms, incantations, and magical manipulations, in driving out the malevolent spirit. He had a sacrificial fire-pit *(kuṇḍa)* dug into the floor of the Rajput's upper room, and a lime placed between the fire-pit and the man. Then, after pouring a ritual offering of clarified butter into the fire, he ordered the spirit of the possessed man to enter the lime. The operation was a long and laborious one, but finally, after a number of hours, with the lime leaping into the air before the eyes of those present, the *jati* ejected it from the palace with great pomp and ceremony. He had a guard escort him with swords drawn as he drove the lime to the outer limits of the city, where it was buried in a seven cubit-deep pit that had been sealed with lead and pierced at its four corners with long nails over which spells had been pronounced.

Because of its beneficial and purifying virtues, the lemon is commonly used in exorcism. It dispels evil, breaks spells, and protects the living from those "beings" *(bhūta*s) who have been deprived of their funeral rites through violent death or other circumstances and who, for the same reason, are unable to reach the "world of ancestors," the abode of the "Fathers *(pitaraḥ)*." In his *Bhut Nibandh,* Dalpat Ram Daya, who himself served as an exorcist, distinguishes between several kinds of spirits. The category of the *bhūta*s groups together all those who have died a "bad death": suicides and accident victims, persons struck by lightning, drowned, burned, fallen from high places, crushed, or bitten by snakes, but also all persons who died in bed or in an upstairs room, or who were polluted after death through contact with a śūdra, or in some other manner. A word of explanation is due here. A dying person should be laid on the ground because earth is pure. In order to purify it further, one should carefully apply a coating of cow dung (one of the best filters against pollution) to the soil, and strew it with *kuśa* grass (this being the procedure for all sacrifices). Dying in one's bed—every Westerner's dream—is the worst of natural deaths for the Hindu because that position, of being neither here nor there, will be reenacted by the dying individual in his next life: he will be born neither in heaven nor on earth, but rather as a spirit doomed to wander in the intermediate region *(antarikṣa)*. People still object quite frequently to having a sick family member moved to a hospital, because people die in bed there. As for pollution after death, this may be explained by the holiness of the corpse: even as there can be nothing more impure than a body whose life's breath has abandoned it, there is nonetheless nothing so pure (and thereby so vulnerable to pollution) as a corpse that has been duly "perfected" *(saṃskṛta)* through the closing sacraments of the life cycle in which the deceased, in a total sacrifice, offers himself up to the gods without the intermediary of a victim. A pun plays well upon this ambivalence: the corpse *(śava)* is "auspicious" *(śiva)*; it is Śiva.[42] If the funeral ceremonies are interrupted before the final rite, in which he is made to join his assembled ancestors on the twelfth day *(sapiṇḍīkaraṇa)*, the deceased becomes trapped in limbo as a spirit *(bhūta)* or ghost *(preta)*, depending on the day on which the rituals were suspended. Some of these unhappy dead are a hybrid of *bhūta* and *deva*, half-spirits and half-gods. Others, even if they have been appeased through the rites, do not come to know the "happy ending" *(sadgati)* of becoming an ancestor under house arrest in the other world, because they have failed to break some earthly bond. These various spirits torment the living in a thousand different ways. As a result, it is common practice to place lemons inside the turbans of little children. And all over India, people cut lemons in order to exorcise spirits.[43]

By virtue of its rounded shape, the lemon—like the gourd, the pumpkin, and above all the coconut, the universal symbol of sacrifice in popular Hinduism—also evokes the sacrificial offering. The offering *is* the body of the sacrificer: in worship rites and ritual vigils alike, the "hair" of the coconut is cut, save for a "lock" *(cuṭiyā)* similar to that grown out of the central whorl by brahmans and pious Hindus. Satīs mounting the pyre held in their hand a coconut whose fibers were wound into a tuft imitative of the chignon of tangled locks *(jaṭā)* worn by ascetics.[44] At Girnar, one of the great pilgrimage sites of Gujarat for both Hindus and Jains, devotees of Bhairava threw themselves into a chasm from atop a crag known as *Bhairav-jap*, first standing on a coconut:[45]

> Laying a cocoa-nut on the dizzy verge of the rock, the deluded victim attempts to poise himself upon it, and in another instant he is beyond humanity's reach, and his body a prey to the vultures that soar under the lofty cliff. Such suicide has been for long forbidden, but only ten or eleven years ago three Kuṅbis, keeping secret their intentions, ascended and made the fatal leap; some Rabâris [camel herders] had also determined to do the same, but were restrained.[46]

The Offering of the Self

The dagger and the lemon turn up yet again as ritual accessories for the sacrifice of widows in the south Indian Vijayanagar Empire, which was founded in the middle of the fourteenth century.[47] According to the accounts that have come down to us, it was in this bastion of Hinduism—where the exaltation of heroic values reinforced by an anti-Muslim backlash created a favorable climate for it—that the practice of widow-burning reached its apogee. In fact, the women of Vijayanagar burned themselves in a particular manner (attested to in other regions of India, but on a lesser scale): they did not ascend their husbands' pyre, but rather waited three days, three months, or longer before throwing themselves into the flaming pit in which the crematory fire used for his obsequies had been kept burning (figs. 20 and 21). This pit is called a *kuṇḍa,* "basin," but also a "hole for the sacrificial fire." Nonetheless, the privilege of "dying after" *(anumaraṇa)* was reserved solely for women of "noble descent" or those who belonged to the royal gynaeceum as concubines or servants. As for women who were poor or of lowly rank, we learn from Duarte Barbosa, who in 1508–1509 was probably the first Portuguese to visit "Bijanaguer," that these carried the body of their husband to the cremation ground outside the city and burned with him, according to the tradition of "dying with" *(sahamaraṇa).*[48]

The reprieve accorded the satī was an opportunity for her to savor in advance the fruits of her sacrifice. Celebrated as befits a true heroic character, she moved freely through the streets or traveled the countryside with her royal retinue. She thus took leave of the world of the living, and sanctified via her passage through it a region whose protective deity, whose "Mother Satī," she would become after her death. Riding a white horse, the symbol of a victorious king (or carried on a palanquin or a howdah); glorified by another royal emblem, the parasol that shaded her;[49] and escorted by a throng of dancers and musicians, she would hold a mirror in her left hand, and in her right a lemon or dagger. The mirror is used in certain female puberty rites. In the classic wedding ceremony, the groom gives the bride a porcupine quill, a thrice-braided rope, and a mirror which she holds in her left hand.[50] The mirror sometimes serves as an attribute of the Hindu Goddess.

She rode on Horse-back about the City with face uncovered, holding a Looking-glass in one hand and a Lemon in the other, I know not for what purpose; and beholding herself in the Glass, with a lamentable tone sufficiently pittiful to hear, went along I know not whither, speaking, or singing, certain words, which I understood not; but they told me they were a kind of Farewell to the World and herself; and indeed, being uttered with that passionateness which the Case requir'd and might produce they mov'd pity in all that heard them, even in us who understood not the Language. She was follow'd by many

Fig. 20. The burning pit: illustration taken from J. W. Massie, *Continental India: Travelling Sketches & Historical Recollections*... (London, 1840). Courtesy Bibliothèque Nationale, Paris.

Fig. 21. Burning pit with stairway: illustration taken from *Viaggio de M. Cesare de' Fedrici nell'Indie Orientale* (Venice, 1587). Courtesy Bibliothèque Nationale, Paris.

other Women and Men on foot, who, perhaps, were her Relations; they carry'd a great Umbrella over her, as all Persons of quality in *India* are wont to have, thereby to keep off the Sun. . . . Before her certain Drums were sounded, whose noise she never ceas'd to accompany with her sad Ditties, or Songs; yet with a calm and constant Countenance, without tears, evidencing more grief for her Husband's death than her own, and more desire to go to him in the other world than regret for her own departure out of this . . . They said she was to pass in this manner about the City I know not how many dayes, at the end of which she was to go out of the City and be burnt, with more company and solemnity.[51]

Pietro della Valle, a "Roman gentleman," describes this event in a letter sent from Ikkeri (in present-day Karnataka) on November 22, 1623. Della Valle is one of the rare travelers of his time to have held an extended private conversation with a satī.[52] This "colloquy" with the woman he calls "Giacamma," a woman of the lowly "Terlenga" (Telinga) caste, an interview of sorts conducted with the help of an interpreter, constitutes an exceptional document inasmuch as one finds in it an expression of the innermost feelings of a woman about to burn herself.

The young and lovely woman whom Gasparo Balbi saw burn herself in Negapatan (Nagapattinam, in present-day Tamil Nadu) at the end of the sixteenth century (his account appeared in 1590) played "all sorts of games" with her lemon on the road to the place of her death.[53] At the beginning of the nineteenth century, Jan Haafner notes yet again that the kṣatriya woman who leapt into a flaming pit in Vellore held in her hand "a sour lime stuck with cloves,"[54] which served, he said, as an incense burner for Hindu women. In other accounts—such as the invaluable relation left by the Venetian jeweler Cesare de' Fedrici, who visited "Bezeneger" (Vijayanagar) in 1567, two years after the sacking of the city—the satī holds a mirror in her left hand and a dagger in her right.[55] Drummond observed in 1808 that the satī carried a mirror, into which she gazed constantly, in her left hand; and a dagger whose tip had been driven into a lemon, in her right.[56]

As fleeting as all of these references may have been, they nonetheless are supported by the oral literature:

Mother Satī, O Queen, you bear at your waist a dagger with a curved blade *(kaṭārī)*. Mother Satī, you hold in your hand a Saurashtran sword *(saurathī)*. Mother Satī, O Queen, you ride a horse whose white coat has a bluish shine and whose bridle is studded with diamonds. Mother Satī, O Queen, a gleaming spear flashes in your hand and your shield is covered with rhinoceros hide.

Fig. 22. Mahiṣāsuramardinī, the Goddess as Slayer of the Buffalo Demon (Gujarat Museum Society, Ahmedabad).

These emblems of martial bent underscore the affinities between the heroic sacrifice of the faithful wife and the battlefield death of the hero: in both instances, the heroic mood *(vīra rasa)* dominates.[57] Songs dedicated to deified satīs form an integral part of their adoration and worship. Sung by women, they list, in a standardized form, the insignia, accessories, and magical properties that form the common stock of satī folklore in western India.

A replica of the ancient Indian sacrificial knife and an emblem of the warrior castes, the dagger is the instrument with which the hero or devotee wounds his body or cuts off his head in those forms of devotional, votive, or expiatory suicide that involve the "terrible" *(ugra)* image of the Goddess (or of Śiva-Bhairava). Moreover, the dagger and its variants (the straight-edged sword, short sword in the shape of a bill-hook, cleaver, or shears) partake of the classical regalia of the Durgās, Kālīs, and other terrifying "Mothers" of Hindu iconography (understood in its broadest sense). It is a sword that the goddess Durgā "Slayer of the Buffalo-Demon Mahiṣa" *(Mahiṣāsuramardinī)* brandishes in her upper left hand while her lower left hand holds by the hair the decapitated head of her victim, dripping with blood (fig. 22). It is a sword, scimitar, or shears one sees in the right hand of the "decapitated Goddess" Chinnamastā, while her left hand proffers her own severed head, as if it were an offering. The blood that squirts from her mutilated trunk splits into three streams. The widest of these feeds the severed head, while the two others are caught and mystically ingested by the two feminine figures placed on either side of the goddess: these are the *yoginīs* Ḍākinī and Varṇiṇī, who, while they emanate from her own body, also symbolize her devotees (figs. 23 and 24).[58]

With Chinnamastā we enter into the universe of Śāktism, that particular orientation within Tantra that highlights the cult of the *Śaktis*, the energies of the divine. This perspective, long regarded as foreign to Hinduism and exiled from its gates, is one in which the world teeters on the brink of nonworld[59] and the senses are rendered senseless in the dazzling light of the inexhaustible illusory reality of things. This is the land of *māyā,* a Feminine territory. Moving from image to image, from the severed head of the sacrificial buffalo that Durgā (in the form of Kālī or Caṇḍī) offers to the gods in the *Devīmāhātmya* ("The Glorification of the Goddess"), to the head of the decapitated Goddess drinking her own blood, a common symbolism is at play here, even as it carries us from orthodox devotional religion to one of the most radically heterodox sectarian trends in all of Hinduism. This symbolism is exemplified in a passage taken from a ritual text used in the worship of Durgā in the royal temples of Orissa and quoted by Madeleine Biardeau in her *Histoires de poteaux.* What follows is a list of victims with whose blood the Goddess is appeased:

> Śivā [the spouse of Śiva, one of the "thousand names" of the Devī] is satisfied for two hundred years with the blood of a ram; she is satiated for ten years if she is worshipped with the blood of a goat. Bhava's spouse experiences supreme satisfaction for a hundred years with [the blood] of a buffalo. But she is joyful for a thousand years if she is worshipped with the blood of a human victim. Śiva's beloved knows unrivalled satisfaction for a month with the [blood] of a cock, and she is contented for fourteen years with the blood of a boar. But she rejoices for an infinite number of years with the blood offered from her own body.[60]

Dagger and lemon have the same symbolic value. They are both images of sacrifice, or rather of that component which provides sacrifice with its meaning and substance—the victim. A consenting victim, to be sure, participating of its own free will in its own ritual killing—this being the cost of "liberation" *(mokṣa* or *mukti)*—and a victim from which one awaits a sign of assent, without which the sacrifice cannot take place. The officiant charged with the ritual killing was called the "appeaser" in ancient India,

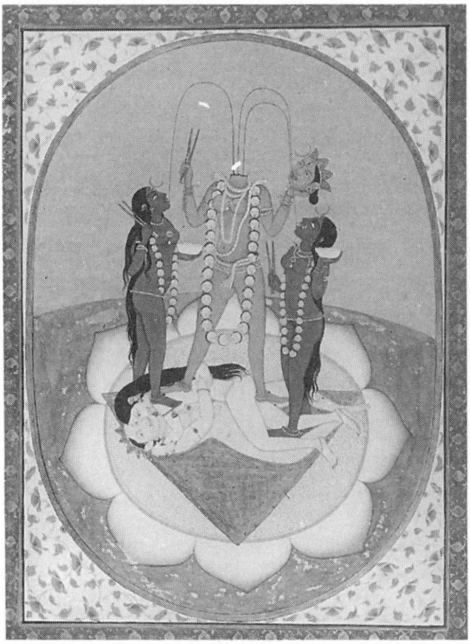

Figs. 23 and 24. Chinnamastā, the Decapitated Goddess (Gujarat Museum Society, Ahmedabad).

a euphemism that speaks volumes on the scotomization of the violence inherent in sacrifice, but also on the special status of the victim, who acquiesces expressly to the violence done to it. The very idea of violence is, in fact, entirely evaded here,[61] whence the aphorism in the *Laws of Manu* that "killing in a sacrifice is not killing."[62] This consent, which in a certain sense seals the religious contract between men and gods in sacrificial activities, stands out in its highest relief in those forms of sacrifice in which man, the sole true victim in the final analysis, willingly offers up his own life. In 1898, Sylvain Lévi epitomized this viewpoint with the lapidary formula that "the only true sacrifice would be suicide."[63] It is in this perspective that we may understand how ancient India and, in its wake, Hindu India could condemn desperation suicides and simultaneously exalt the ritual suicide of ascetics and devotees, even going so far as to glorify the heroic death of the warrior and the self-immolation of widows, instances which typify the total convergence of voluntary death and sacrificial ideology. While "murder of the self" is odious, the sacrificial killing of the self is the most direct path to liberation.

Coconut, dagger, and lime, which are so many images of self-sacrifice, appear together in full sequence (with a mirror) in an incident recounted by James Forsyth, whose book, published in 1872, deals with less somber matters, as indicated by its title: *The Highlands of Central India: Notes on Their Forests and Wild Tribes, Natural History and Sports.* It was by chance that Forsyth one day came upon a manuscript lying among a mass of other dusty papers in the Government record room of Nimar District (in present-day Madhya Pradesh). This was a report made by a certain Captain Douglas, the political assistant in Nimar, who on November 29, 1822, witnessed "the truly appalling scene" of the suicide of a devotee of "Bhyroo" (Kāla Bhairava, a "terrible" form of the god Śiva) at the Omkar-Mandhatta shrine in the region of Indore. This small rocky island in the Narbada, associated as it was with the cult of Śiva and Pārvatī, had long been renowned for its suicides by precipitation. At the time, the site was situated within the principality of Gwalior, thereby escaping British jurisdiction. Captain Douglas, who had been sent to Omkar-Mandhatta with a company of Sepoys in November 1820, received orders to prevent such sacrifices by every possible means short of force.[64] After having attempted in vain to convince the young potential suicide to renounce his intentions, Douglas decided to accompany him to the fatal site: a lofty pinnacle towering over the image of Bhairava with a sheer drop of ninety feet. Escorted by a small group of musicians, the man first went to the worship site of his chosen god Bheru-ji, represented as an aniconic stone—"a rough block of basalt smeared with red paint"—before which he prostrated himself. According to legend, it was this same Bhairava who required an annual sacrifice on the part of his devotees. "[H]e who boldly casts himself over, each step that he takes is equal in merit to the performance of a sacrifice. . . . A devotee who has broken his vows, a parricide, or one who has committed incest, shall by thus sacrificing himself, become sinless": these are the words one reads in the *Narmadā Khaṇḍa,* a devotional text attached to the *Skanda Purāṇa,* according to local tradition. In Douglas's words, the man "approached the amorphous idol with a light foot, while a wild pleasure marked his countenance." Then he began his ascent. Having arrived at the peak of the "fatal eminence," before precipitating himself "in a most manful leap" into the abyss, he whirled down into it, in order, a coconut, a mirror, a dagger, and a lime. According to the author, this suicide was the last of its type. Two years later, the State of Gwalior, coming under British rule, forbade by law these "bloody rites," which it judged to be "contrary to humanity."[65]

According to the testimony of colonial historiography, sacrifice by leaping from high places was especially practiced by low-caste peoples, by Untouchables or "tribals," the Camars, Kunbis, Dhers, and Bhils. Such often occurred in cases of sterility: the mother prayed to a particular "terrible" divinity to grant her offspring,[66] pledging to sacrifice her firstborn son to it when he reached adulthood. The child was then raised in anticipation of his eventual sacrifice. But it could also happen that couples would sacrifice themselves in this way without anyone ever knowing the reasons that drove them to it. Malcolm reports the case of a young Kunbi and his wife who in April 1819 flung themselves hand in hand into the abyss, despite the protests of the brother of the Rajah of Partapgarh. Malcolm also notes that, according to local custom, if a man miraculously survived his fall from the rock of Omkar-Mandhatta, he could lay claim to the kingdom. In order to prevent such a happenstance, the potential suicide was given a heavy dose of drugs, while armed guards blocked the path of retreat.[67]

The Fruits of One's Acts

The lemon, a fruit, symbolizes the auspicious and fruitful side of sacrifice. Here literality plays itself out on several levels. The idea of "fruit" is intimately connected to the notion of karma: acts ripen like fruit, and it is the fruit of their acts that people reap in their successive rebirths. In a less obvious manner, certain fruits symbolize the ancestors, as will be shown. Or rather, they symbolize the funerary rice-balls offered to them.

The lemon's color *(vasantī* or *nīmbuā raṅg)* bears a positive valence. It is produced, in practical terms, by immersing the cloth to be dyed in a bath of turmeric and whey, which rank among the most auspicious of substances: turmeric because it is associated with the marriage ritual, love, and its fruits (offspring); and whey because it is one of the "five products of the cow" *(pañcagavya),* which in combination are the source of complete purification and redress of sins. The lemon yellow color can also evoke the golden yellow hue of the sacrificial fire. Finally, its proximity in the spectrum to yellow ocher and orange-yellow, colors emblematic of world renunciation, completes this symbolic pallet in which may be found, in its principal shadings, the entire color range of the auspicious *(śubh, maṅgal).*[68]

Even today, lemons are impaled on the wheels of processional cars in the "Worship of the Weapons" that concludes the *Navarātri* (the Nine Nights of the Goddess) festival in south India. These lemons are substitutes for the young water buffalo or piglets that were formerly impaled in Andhra Pradesh and the Tamil country before those sacrifices were banned by law in 1947.[69] They still go on today in a private and semiclandestine way. The last legal buffalo sacrifice was performed in September 1974 by Savai Bhavani Singh, the Maharajah of Jaipur, in his Amber palace (I attended the ceremony, together with Madeleine Biardeau).[70] On that occasion, eleven young buffalo were sacrificed and their heads, garlanded with flowers and crowned with earthen oil lamps, were offered to Śilādevī. This goddess (who is a form of Kālī) of official functions is eclipsed in domestic ritual by Jamvāī Mātā, the tutelary goddess *(kul-devī)* of the Kacchvaha clan, to which the royal family of Jaipur belongs. It is in the secrecy of her small shrine, located to the northeast of Jaipur, that the ceremony of the first shaving of the head of the young Maharajah takes place.

When one cuts the lemon or coconut, one transfers the impure and inauspicious aspect of blood sacrifice onto a benign (and nonviolent, because vegetal) ritual expression of the same, which both bypasses it and stands as a powerful image of it. It would appear that this symbolic power is linked to the round shape of the fruit. It forcefully evokes for the Hindu imagination the sacrificial rice-balls offered to the dead in funerary rites and ancestor worship.[71] The offering of such balls, which are called *piṇḍa*s, constitutes a source of liberation for the living, since it is through this act that one pays off—at least in part—the congenital debt owed to one's ancestors.[72]

The Corporality of the Dead

At death, the deceased is conceived as a disembodied being, possessed of neither coherence nor stability, and stained with the defilement of death. The cooked rice-balls offered to him by his son or, failing this, his closest male relative (the agnatic relationship being expressed by the category of *sapiṇḍa:* "those who have the offering of funeral rice-balls in common"[73]) during the ten days following death, at a rate of one per day, have the explicit function of giving a body to the deceased, with each ball corresponding to a body part: the head on the first day; then, successively, the neck and shoulders; heart and chest; back; stomach; thighs and intestines; legs and skin; knees and hair; and finally the genital organs.[74] This highly enigmatic transitional body, which comes to fill out the "subtle body" cremation has left intact, and which takes the place of the "gross body" burnt by the crematory fire, is sometimes called the "nourishment body." It is by virtue of this body of sorts that the departed *(preta)* may become an ancestor *(pitṛ),* one who feeds on the rice-balls that constitute the basic ingredient of the post-cremation rituals in the cult of the dead (collectively known as *śrāddha,* derived from *śraddhā,* "faith").[75] It is only on the twelfth day of mourning, however, that the deceased will truly accede to the status of "Father," through the rite of *sapiṇḍīkaraṇa* ("making the deceased *sapiṇḍa*").[76] Once again, this involves the offering of rice-balls—one to the deceased, which the sacrificer divides into three equal parts, and one to each of his three forefathers (his father, grandfather, and great-grandfather)—followed by the careful blending of each third taken from the deceased's rice-ball with the three balls representing his ancestors. Through this ritual process, the officiant incorporates the deceased into the mass of the ancestors, with the consistency and stickiness of the rice-balls marking his cohesion with that group. The rice that remains stuck to the sacrificer's fingers forms that portion of the offering known as *lepa,* which is set aside for the ancestral host, beginning with the fourth generation. The Vedic formulas that punctuate the rite, formulas whose transparency masks their opacity as concerns the actual destination of the deceased,[77] underscore the homogeneity of the deceased and those who are sometimes called "Fathers having faces of tears," his three immediate ancestors—in contradistinction to the "Fathers having faces of joy," who are the undifferentiated horde of the dead, eaters of the *lepa,* a multitude packed into some corner of the cautiously oblivious memory of men.[78] When a wife follows her husband onto the funeral pyre, the rite of *sapiṇḍīkaraṇa* symbolically marks the symbiosis of the two spouses, given the fact that a single rice ball represents the deceased couple in this case:

> When there is ascension [of the funeral pyre: *anvārohaṇa],* the rite of *sapiṇḍīkaraṇa* is performed conjointly for both spouses. The *Śātātapa* ordains: "she who in dying follows her husband shall have her *sapiṇḍīkaraṇa* performed with her husband. She wins heaven until the end of a cosmic age."[79]

It is true that authors of works on *dharma* are divided into three schools on this point: while the first prescribes the offering of a single *piṇḍa,* the second recommends preparing two separate rice-balls that are to be blended during the rite of *sapiṇḍīkaraṇa* prior to incorporating their mixture into the ancestral balls. The third school holds that two separate unblended *piṇḍas* are to be offered. In practice, however, according to corroborating sources, a single ball (or two subsequently blended into one) is offered.[80] The *Garuḍa Purāṇa* introduces an important distinction in this regard:

> If the woman ascends the pyre of her husband on the same day, then no separate sāpiṇḍya *[sapiṇḍīkaraṇa]* is prescribed for her. If husband and wife are cremated together, there is one cooking *(pāka),* one ritual time *(kāla)* and one officiant *(kartṛ).* . . . If she ascends the pyre on a different date, she should be offered a separate piṇḍa on the separate date of death.[81]

The bodily and spiritual unity of the couple—the ideal of every Hindu marriage, which the satī's sacrifice alone is capable of fully achieving—is ritually signified by the unity of the offering: a single funeral ball, a single ancestral body, will afford the couple access to the Heaven of Heroes, or the Paradise of Indra, Viṣṇu, or Śiva. The *mantras* used on these occasions are declined in the dual (the number which, in Sanskrit, designates two persons or things). We will see that in the world of religious practice the postmortem destinies of the two spouses are more highly contrasted than in the scholarly treatises, for if it is the case that the satī enjoys eternal bliss in the company of her husband in his celestial abode, she nonetheless possesses, in her cult, a supernatural life that is hers alone.

Unlike women who have died an ordinary death, satīs are not honored with offerings of funerary rice-balls in *śrāddha* ceremonies. The former receive a *piṇḍa* on the one-month, three-month, six-month, and twelvemonth anniversaries of their death, as well as on that day which corresponds, within the "Fortnight of the Fathers" *(pitṛpakṣa),* to the day of their death. This custom is observed for as long as one's son and grandson are alive. Summoned by the food offering and the water libation that assuage the hunger and thirst of the dead, the deceased women are called upon by name in the ritual formulas,[82] thereby underscoring their well-defined personalities as female ancestors (*pitrāṇīs*). Nothing, however, is given to the most glorious of all deceased women, the satīs. This is something of a paradox. The texts tell us, at least implicitly, that because the satī has through her sacrifice abolished every principle of differentiation between her own being and that of her husband, and because that act has forever incorporated her with him, offerings are made to the husband alone in the *śrāddha* rites, in the same way that a single rice-ball concretizes a dual body that has been restored to its underlying unity through *sapiṇḍīkaraṇa*. This explanation, however, is contradicted by other ritual acts: when their bones are collected from the cremation ground (in a procedure known as *phūl bīnnā* "culling flowers"), care will be taken to sort out the bones of the satī (which are smaller) from those of her husband.[83] Moreover, a portion of the ashes will be preserved. Judging from their use in the satī's worship, one has the distinct impression that it is the husband's being that has been incorporated into the celestial body of the satī. If the ashes signify the abolition of all duality, they nonetheless only become miraculous (protective and curative) because they constitute the final remains of the woman's sacrifice. This reversal of perspective may be further observed on certain stele where the husband is depicted in a miniaturized form, with his heroic wife manifesting her preeminence in stone, territory, and worship.

Informants I have questioned on the subject explain that satīs have no need of food since, unlike ancestors, they have been stationed in a separate "abode" (a "world," *loka)* located midway between heaven and the world of ancestors *(pitṛloka)*. This abode of the satīs, with its fuzzy borders, also harbors fairies, celestial musicians (Gandharvas), and goddesses "born of a womb" *(yonijā)*—in sum, a fluid host of gods in the making. It is these goddesses who come to dance nightly in closed temples which, shut off from human gaze, serve as their arena *(akhāḍā)*. Theoretically, goddesses "not born of a womb" *(ayonijā)* never show themselves to the world of men, except in secret—that is, except in those splinters of eternity in which the devotee is suddenly transfixed by their splendor, in his trance states, dreams, or mystic visions.[84]

It seems to me that we must push our interpretation further if we are to understand why satīs are deprived of food offerings this way in the cult of the dead. This is all the more paradoxical considering that in their worship rites, commemorative religious fairs, and night vigils, as well as on every occasion in which boons or blessings are sought, devotees celebrate them with songs and offerings of coconut, as well as their favorite flowers, the odoriferous jasmine and frangipani. This peculiarity evokes the case of the world renouncer at the moment of his death who, because he is buried, is in fact an exception to the general rule of cremating corpses. And in a highly remarkable manner:

> A pit is dug, generally by the shore of a river; the corpse is placed in it and made to sit in the meditative posture known as *samādhi.* The pit is then filled in with salt, such that the corpse is packed in and held in that posture by the mass of salt that surrounds it up to the chin. Only the head is left exposed; the skull is broken by striking it with a coconut or a large shell: according to popular belief, the soul is more certain to reach the world of Brahman if it escapes through the opening made at the topmost extremity of the body. Above this pit, a tumulus, also called *samādhi,* is raised around the head. This tomb is a veritable place of worship, shrine, and pilgrimage site, since people who feel bound spiritually to this dead man (the question of kinship has no place in this context) regularly come to commemorate—through offerings, prayers, and ablutions—him whose remains have been deposited at the site.[85]

The contrast of such cases with the fate reserved for the great majority of the dead is most striking here. Whereas the remains of an ordinary man are burned and carried up to the gods on the crematory fire, and whereas nothing furthers the memory of the deceased—neither a stela nor inscription of any sort nor individualized ancestral worship (from the fourth generation onward)—the body of the renouncer occupies a terrestrial space both physically and spiritually, and the community of the living perpetuates the memory of his act (if not of his person)—his "escape into eternity," to use the powerful words of Charles Malamoud. Malamoud further explains the reasons for the special disposal of the corpse of the renouncer: he who has been burned and cooked by ascetic heat *(tapas)* during his earthly life; and who, by internalizing his sacrificial fires, has performed his own funeral while still alive in the course of the ceremony marking his entry onto the renunciant path—that person need not be consigned to the crematory fire or expedited to the gods. His quest for liberation has made him his own divinity.[86]

If it is the case that lineage members do not offer *piṇḍa*s to a woman who has burned herself alive, this is no doubt because the satī, burned while still alive and purified and liberated through the offering of her bodily envelope, has no need of receiving either the surrogate body symbolized by the funerary rice-ball or, consequently, food to appease that body and ensure for it consistency and stability during the ritual year. Pundit Girdhar Narayan Joshi, the domestic priest of Gaj Singh-ji, the Maharajah of Jodhpur, confirmed this hypothesis for me. Questioned on the subject in March 1993, he exclaimed: "Satīs are like renouncers. We don't offer *piṇḍa*s to either one of them." The affinities between renouncers and satīs are remarkable. In both cases, the same logic is brought into play. The radical break that occurs in the life of the "man-in-the world" when he enters onto the path of renunciation,[87] far from betokening a heightened degree of individuation, may be interpreted as a will to shed the excess weight of his individual personality. The renouncer's goal is to escape forever from both the phenomenal world and an illusory and outmoded notion of self. In fact, the satī's desire is of the same order: the sacrifice of the self in its perishable form is carried out in favor of an entity that is, for women, the symbolic equivalent of the absolute. That sacred entity is the couple whose miraculous preservation beyond death is enabled solely through the sacrifice of "true wives." From the orthodox Hindu standpoint, the sacrifice of women, far from constituting a perversion of it, is embedded within the very ideology of marriage.

A rite specific to the Rajputs expresses this idea on the dual register of literality and symbolic overdetermination. According to tradition, a critical moment in the wedding ceremony (called *hath-ḷevo* "taking the hand") consists of attaching the bride's right hand to the right hand of her future husband with a red cord. In the hollow of their joined palms the officiant places a ball of henna *(hāth-piṇḍa),* which leaves an indelible coloration on both in a symbol of the indissoluble union of their bodies.[88] Concerning this custom, Norman Ziegler cites an episode from the *Naiṇsī rī Khyāt* (Naiṇsī Chronicle): upon returning to his village with his wife Mohil, Sadul Bhati dies while fighting for his honor. Mohil cuts off her hand. The hand "accompanies" her husband onto the pyre, whilst the young woman journeys to her in-laws to offer them her respects before immolating herself on a separate pyre.[89]

The fact that satīs are excluded from the group of ancestors who are to be fed, even as Hindus fulfill this ritual obligation (which carries with it a hidden desire for self-preservation) with the meticulousness that characterizes them in such matters, may also be explained in another, more mysterious fashion. A woman who has immolated herself in such a manner has herself become a sacrificial offering. The word *piṇḍa,* whose mosaic of meanings brilliantly illustrates the notion of the corporeal nature of the deceased (his substance, his food, that which fleshes him out), has, through an extension of its primary meaning of "round, compact, undifferentiated mass" (which may also be composed of clay, flesh, dough, or paste), taken on the sense of "body." A *piṇḍa* is an unformed (headless) body, similar to an embryo. Elsewhere, as Lakshmi Kapani reminds us, the word designates "the ball of flesh formed in the womb from sperm and blood, at the very beginning of pregnancy, when the embryo is a male."[90] In Śaiva literature, the meaning of *piṇḍa* is extended to apply to Śiva's liṅga.[91] *Piṇḍa* also has the sense of a "ball used in a game." Playing with a ball is one of the images of cosmic sacrifice found in epic and devotional literature, in which the round earth becomes the oblatory substance. Gasparo Balbi's apparently innocuous remark about the satī of Nagapattinam playing with her lemon (we can imagine her throwing it in the air, catching it, and twirling and sliding it through her hands) may also be elucidated from another perspective. The satī's sport, in which she is as if playing with a ball, is immediately expressive of her lightness of heart: the fiery pit awaits her, with its wealth of promises of glorification and immortality. Arriving at the site, she sings and dances in a show of joy before taking off her clothing and finery (which she will distribute among her relatives and friends) and finally leaping, "belly to the fire," into the pit. On a deeper level, this simulated ballplay also bears a highly powerful sacrificial connotation: it is a sacrifice of herself, of her own body offered as an oblation, that the woman symbolizes through her movements.

It must be understood here that there is nothing artificial to this bringing together of the satī's body and the funerary rice-ball. According to the *dharma* treatises (those recommending the custom), the faithful wife who follows her husband onto the pyre purifies through her voluntary death three lineages—her father's, her mother's, and her husband's—for three or seven generations. In this way, no less than three groups of ancestors are seen to have a stake in the matter. The satī's sacrificed body may be viewed as an offering to the ancestors and a source of liberation for the living, just as are the funerary rice-balls.[92] The power unlocked in the act of self-sacrifice, however, confers special redemptive and magical virtues upon this offering. The energy released in this supreme form of heroic death, a death that has fire for its transit, becomes concretized via the same process we observed earlier with reference to the *sat:* an abstract quality is made into an entity, a "being." The satī becomes *Śakti,* a manifestation of divine energy and an incarnation of the Goddess.

DEATH IN THE TELLING

Nay, but on the other hand, again and again our foe, religion, has given birth to deeds sinful and unholy. Even as at Aulis the chosen chieftains of the Danai, the first of all the host, foully stained with the blood of Iphianassa the altar of the Virgin of the Cross-Roads. . . . For seized by men's hands, all trembling was she led to the altars, not that, when the ancient rite of sacrifice was fulfilled, she might be escorted by the clear cry of "Hymen," but in the very moment of marriage, a pure victim she might foully fall, sorrowing beneath a father's slaughtering stroke, that a happy and hallowed starting might be granted to the fleet. Such evil deeds could religion prompt.

—Lucretius, *On the Nature of Things*[1]

If it were desired to po[u]rtray a scene which should thrill with horror every heart, not entirely dead to the touch of human sympathy, it would suffice to describe a father, regardless of the affection of his tender child, in having already suffered one of the severest of the miseries which flesh is heir to, with tearless eye leading her forth a spectacle to the assembled multitude, who with barbarous cries demand the sacrifice, and relentlessly delivering up the unconscious and unresisting victim to an untimely death, accompanied by the most cruel tortures.

—Letter of July 31, 1817, from R. M. Bird, Magistrate of Ghazipur, to M. H. Turnbull, Register of the Court of Criminal Justice of Calcutta[2]

Rite and Belief

We have chosen to enter into the history of Indian widows at its geographical and religious periphery, and in a disconnected fashion, not unlike that of a jigsaw puzzle. To this point, we have only assembled a few of the outermost pieces, and have left the center in shadow as a means to "puzzling" the reader into an apprehension of the bare facts of the matter—knowing all the while that there is no such thing as a bare fact. And since this history remains mysterious, we will attempt to retrace it from the only perspective capable of affording us any degree of perceptual certainty—that of ritual, of the spectacle of death, the macabre scenography of which may be reconstituted through the narratives of eyewitnesses who have lent us their eyes. For satīs only live on through the lingering aftertaste of their death accounts. They only gain their identity, their fullness of being, and ultimately their immortality, through the transfiguration and apotheosis of their passage through fire. The story of the satīs, unveiled in the ceremonial of death itself, and laid bare in the obscure yet articulate language of the rite, will aid us most especially in restoring the problem of belief to its proper perspective.

In fact, the first question that arises with regard to widow sacrifice, a question that casts its long shadow across the entire field of its historiography, is that of knowing whether these immolations were voluntary acts or whether, on the contrary, women were forced to burn themselves; whether their immediate circle (family, priesthood, caste) and the dominant religious ideology they emerged from did not exert upon them—at the time of their declaration of intent and *a fortiori* in their hour of death—every sort of pressure and violence to force them onto the pyre. According to one's choice of viewpoint, one will interpret widow-burning as a form of suicide, sacrifice, or murder. And a murder made all the more odious by the fact that it is also a matricide: it is the closest male relative of the deceased—the son—who lights the pyre on which his mother will be burned alive. And a murder that also takes on the dimensions of a collective homicide, since thousands of men and women attend such events and because the responsibility of society as a whole is deeply implicated in it. Carrying this line of reasoning a bit further, one could consider the rite to be a form of torture inasmuch as the death of the husband is ascribed to sins committed by the wife in her past or present lives: by dying on the pyre, the widow theoretically expiates her crimes.[3]

The distinction between suicide and sacrifice is more subtle. By suicide one normally means voluntary death, freely consented to; whereas with the notion of sacrifice one introduces an element extraneous to the subject—a religious structure that inspires the individual act and bends it in the direction of social conditioning or fanaticization. The statement that widow-burning is a sacrifice may be understood in several ways. When in 1821 Joseph de Maistre used the term in his *Éclaircissement sur les sacrifices,* he was referring to the "sinister ancient practice of human sacrifice," which persisted in Hindustan "despite the influence of our arms and sciences"—in short, to those cruel customs, impelled by superstition, that drove widows to their husbands' funeral pyres, devotees of *juggernaut* (Jagannāth) beneath the wheels of their idol's processional car, and sectarian followers of "Calabhairava" into terrible chasms. He further comments: "These horrors take place in a country where it is a horrendous crime to kill a cow; where the superstitious bramine dares not kill the vermin devouring him."[4]

Although he substituted the term "altruistic suicide" for sacrifice and the rigor of sociological analysis for de Maistre's vituperations, Durkheim's overall interpretation in 1897 of ritual suicide in "lower societies," where "insufficient individuation" leads to such barbarous practices as the suicide of Indian widows, is not embedded in a radically different perspective. In such societies, according to Durkheim, "the ego is not its own property . . . it is blended with something not itself . . . the goal of conduct is exterior to itself, that is, in one of the groups in which it participates."[5] To be sure, the vocabulary has changed, the desire to understand has won out over condemnation, and the subtlety of the approach has come to serve as a rampart against the old demons of disparaging discourse on primitive societies. When Durkheim suggests, for example, that the forms of voluntary death he has grouped under the category of "obligatory altruistic suicide" are to be explained by the fact that between a widow and her husband, a client and his patron, and a servant and his prince the relationship of dependence is so close and the very idea of separation so unthinkable that the fate of the one must necessarily be bound to that of the other, he quite nearly shares the native point of view. But a short while later, when he makes mention of that variety of altruistic suicide which he qualifies as "optional"—because society, even if it encourages him to it through the philosophical and religious dogmas it professes, does not make it an imperative for the individual—he reintroduces (with regard to devotional suicide) the idea of fanatical suicide and makes India "the classic soil for this sort of suicide."[6]

On the other hand, when one of my informants, a Supreme Court judge and a man of the Jain faith, harps on the difference between sacrifice and suicide and maintains, with the full weight of his authority, that because these voluntary deaths are grounded in belief and because emotions are born out of that belief over which society has no hold, the satīs' deaths are sacrifices and not suicides (and *a fortiori* even less murders); and when he adds that his own tradition, which accords a prominent place to the ideal of nonviolence, has always exalted this Hindu practice, he is injecting the word "sacrifice" with a very different content. Offering up one's life as an oblation in answer to deeply held convictions of fervor and devotion is indeed quite a different matter than committing a fanatical act of violence directed against oneself, and thereby disclosing one's own social and religious alienation.[7]

Let us recall in this context that it is precisely the Jain tradition that most sharply draws the line between suicide, which it rejects because suicide implies passion and violence and arises out of ignorance, and the voluntary death of the sage or, better still, the "death of the sage among sages" *(paṇḍitapaṇḍitamaraṇa),* which requires partial or total freedom from all desire (including the desire to abandon one's life), mastery over all the senses, a rigorous apprenticeship with a spiritual master, and finally, keeping the rule of nonviolence to the point of self-mortification unto death.[8]

Nothing can better clarify this fundamental matter of the connection between ritual and belief than an examination of the hard facts. What is important here is to know just what happened, what acts were performed, what words were proffered or exchanged, what objects or substances were used and to what ends, what techniques or formulas were employed and in what circumstances, what actors were mobilized, and what emotions, attitudes, and forms of behavior marked each sequence in the ceremony. Working from this starting point, we may undertake to explore even more problematic or impenetrable bodies of data: in a word, anything that partakes of subjective or collective value judgments, or the viewpoints individuals, groups, or societies (as well as the cultures that arise out of them) project on practices of this order—viewpoints that are, moreover, neither permanent nor homogeneous.[9]

Having said this, the question remains: with what do we begin our reconstruction of this history? The data are as vast as they are varied. Vast in their profusion, as well as in their spatial and temporal scope; and varied because they draw on two types of sources that are only partially reconcilable. On the one hand there are the Indian sources, which prove elusive in the sense that they present us with a reality that is filtered through (normative, prescriptive, or embellished) discourse—in other words, a reality that has been adjusted to a cultural pattern. On the other hand there is the foreign documentation, impressive in its volume, precision, and attention to rigor, to be sure, but whose trustworthiness (at least on certain points) is subject to doubt. In the first instance, texts, stele, practices, and cults: an edifice of words and deeds in which bare facts are dissolved into ideology. In the latter, accounts, reports, investigations, and, belatedly, statistics: direct observation, in which the spectacle is recreated in all its luxuriant detail and infinite variations, but only as a means to portraying India as a land of *mirabilia* or of barbarism, according to one's outlook. The observer's troubled and sententious gaze is transfixed by his fascination and distorted by his preconceptions.

Even when it unfolds before our very eyes—as in the last case of widow-burning, which occurred at Deorala, in the state of Rajasthan, on September 4, 1987—the phenomenon eludes all perception as it is instantaneously transmuted into a cultural stereotype or a public scandal. And it is no less a paradox to see the national press, in its current denunciations of "the barbarity of a primitive practice that blemishes the face of Indian democracy," marching in lockstep with the colonial legislator who abolished the custom of widow-burning in 1829. Rup Kanvar's[10] immolation at Deorala, the last in a sequence of widow-burnings that have occurred in that same region of Shekhavati to the north of Jaipur since the 1940s, received exceptional press coverage, whereas the sacrifices of Tara Kanvar, Jugal Kanvar, Savitri, Sartaj Kanvar, Sarasvati, Sohan Kanvar, Om Kanvar, and other satīs whose deaths had preceded Rup's raised very little outcry. And yet one cannot help but noting that the young Rup, the central character in the tragedy, appears solely as a vehicle for impassioned polemics, a fetish of popular devotion, or the unhappy victim of religious fanaticism. Of her life prior to the drama, of the spectacle of her death which drew an estimated crowd of three to five thousand to her cremation site, what has remained in the collective consciousness? A marriage photo cleverly doctored into a funeral scene of the deified satī embracing her husband's corpse amidst the flames (fig. 25). An image in a series of satī images, themselves so many interchangeable parts in a popular religious iconography whose reds and pinks, symbols of marriage, vie in their garishness with saffron yellow, the color of world renunciation. Religious posters, devotional pamphlets, rumors that hardened into legends, fervent invocations to the "Mother Satī," a solemn commemoration of the twelfth day of mourning *(cūndṛī mahotsav)* that brought together some two hundred thousand devotees, acts of worship that transformed the site into a shrine before our eyes: so many walls built up around the calcinated body, so many trappings of death masking death's mystery, a public death viewed as the *tableau vivant* of a timeless sacrifice.

Before unraveling the thread of the ceremony, before unfolding in the process the symbol system that is its very fabric, we will first juxtapose two accounts of the death of satīs. The first is taken from travel literature, which devoted remarkable attention to the "burning of women in the Indies." From Strabo to Jules Verne, no other Indian rite was held in such great fascination by foreigners. This *topos* of the journey to the East, which

Fig. 25. Popular religious image of the "Venerable Great Satī Rup Kanvar": collage of Rup Kanvar's cremation at Deorala (Rajasthan), September 4, 1987 (private collection).

during the Enlightenment became a standard fixture in discussions of Asiatic despotism, and which the novelist's craft illustrated so brilliantly, continues to sell: perpetually readapted and reworked, it turns up in novels, essays, and films. One is tempted to say that it has the innate power to evoke, in its very immediacy and quintessence, an image of India forged in the West over two millennia, in which *realia* and *mirabilia* become so intertwined as to be lost in one another.[11]

That widow-burning was perceived as defining, in a single stroke, the culture of this vast country in which not only men and gods, but also the most extravagant beliefs and the cruelest customs proliferated, is demonstrated (to limit ourselves to a single example) by the iconography of one of the great classics of missionary literature on India: *La Porte ouverte pour parvenir à la connoissance du Paganisme caché, et la vraye représentation de la vie, des moeurs, de la Religion, & du service divin des Bramines, qui demeurent sur les Costes de Chormandel, & aux Pays circonvoisins* by Abraham Roger (Rogerius). This work was published in Leiden in 1651; the French translation appeared in Amsterdam in 1670. The title page of the original edition is illustrated with eight vignettes that faithfully reproduce a number of scenes described by the Dutch missionary, scenes he witnessed himself while stationed in Pulicat, in south India, between 1630 and 1640. Here one finds illustrations of bodily mortification by fire and iron (the iron hook of the *cakra-pūjā,* an expiatory and devotional practice which greatly impressed the imagination of observers; the chains in which yogis shackled themselves; and a heavy iron collar mounted with pickets that literally fenced in the face[12]); a widow-burning scene; the hunt of a sacrificial fox or he-goat; the ritual procession of a divine image's processional car; the suicide of fanatical devotees beneath the wheels of another divinity's processional car; and finally, placed directly above the title at the top and dominating the entire page, the worship of idols in their shrine, a focal image heading up, in a cause and effect relationship, the depiction of these scenes of bodily mortification, religious suicide, bloody sacrifice, and parades of idols, whose purpose it was to introduce us into the mysteries of Paganism. The French edition (which was embellished with the eloquent subtitle of *Le Théâtre de l'idolâtrie*) does not provide the reader with the same imagery; or rather, it treats it in a different way: seven engravings are inserted into the text. The eighth, which serves as the frontispiece, takes up a full page and has been entirely transformed: what one sees is a young half-naked widow dancing on a pyre amid a throng of musicians, priests, and onlookers; above, igniting the scene, an oversized demon emblazoned with his symbolic attributes blows into a trumpet whose ensign bears the

Fig. 26. Illustration from the title page of the first edition (1651) of Abraham Rogerius's *De Open-Deure tot het Verborgen Heydendom*. Courtesy Bibliothèque Nationale, Paris.

work's title: *le PAGANISME caché* (Hidden Paganism). The meaning is clear: when widows burn, it is Satan who leads the dance. This particular custom, we see, epitomized more than any other the paganism of the "Gentoos" of Hindustan and the horror it inspired among the Christians of Europe (figs. 26 and 27).[13]

Fig. 27. Frontispiece of the French translation (1670) of the same work, *La Porte ouverte pour parvenir à la connoissance du Paganisme caché*. Courtesy Bibliothèque Nationale, Paris.

We have had to choose from among these innumerable accounts, remarkable both in their diversity and their repetitiousness, because despite the wealth of variants, their basic story lines betray the same somber monotony. This monotony is compounded by yet another circumstance: these macabre scenes were observed by foreign witnesses not only with their own eyes but by way of reminiscence, through the accounts of all those who had gone before them, most particularly the classical authors. "So many Travelers will write that women burn themselves in the Indies that I think people will end up believing there is something to it; as for myself, I in turn shall proceed to write of it as others have, but will nonetheless begin by having you note that it is not at all what it is made out to be." It is with these words that Bernier, having placed himself in a long line of raconteurs of the rite, immediately distances himself from them. In so doing,

Fig. 28. "Le brûlement des femmes aux Indes": illustration taken from the 1724 edition of *Voyages de F. Bernier (Angevin), contenant la description des Estats du Grand Mogol, de l'Indoustan, du royaume du Kachemire* (first edition 1699). Courtesy Bibliothèque Nationale, Paris.

he is further imitating his predecessors, every one of whom, jealous of his knowledge, claimed it to be his alone. He then concludes his account, which he has foreshortened ("I will not stop to tell you the story of every woman I saw burn herself; it would be too long & too boring"), with the famous words of Lucretius: "*Tantum religio potuit suadere malorum* (Such evil deeds could religion prompt)."[14]

The pyres of India's widows burn bright with the fires of classical mythology (figs. 28 and 29). So it is that behind the girl of twelve (she who trembled and wept so vigorously that she had to be bound in order to finish the matter), burned in Lahore in the presence of Bernier, that "fair philosopher" and disciple of Gassendi, there stands another: the shade of Iphigenia sacrificed by her father to cruel Artemis surreptitiously flits onto the scene via the reference to Lucretius. This citation sprang quite naturally again to the mind of the Comte de Modave, following his first eyewitness experience of the cremation of an Indian woman, on December 31, 1774, in the city of Faizabad (in present-day Uttar Pradesh):

That horrible spectacle so preoccupied me that for two days I could think of nothing else. The image of that woman is so deeply etched in my memory that it will never be erased.

102 *Des Guſurates & Banianes.*

FIGVRE OV SE VOID COMMENT LES FEMMES des Bramenes ſe bruſlent auec leurs maris treſpaſſez.

CHAPITRE XXXVII.

Des Guſurates & Banianes de Cambaia.

Guſurates & Banianes à Goa & leur profeßion.

IL y a pluſieurs Guſurates & Banianes du pays de Cambaia qui ſe tiennent à Goa, Diu, Chaul, Cochin, & autres lieux des Indes, pour le fait de la marchandiſe, laquelle ils y exercent en froment, Riz, Coton, *Anilo* & autre denrees, mais ſur tout en perles & pierres precieuſes, en la cognoiſſance deſquelles ils ſont tenus fort experts. Ils ſurpaſſent auſſi en la ſcience d'Arithmetique non ſeulement les Indiens, mais auſſi les Portugais, & ſont naturel-

Fig. 29. "Figure ou se void comment les femmes des Bramenes se brûlent avec leurs maris trespassez": illustration taken from *Histoire de la navigation de Jean Hugues de Linscot* (Amsterdam, 1610). Courtesy Bibliothèque Nationale, Paris.

She displayed neither confusion nor agitation and complied with each of those ghastly ceremonies as though it were the most unimportant thing in the world. *Tantum religio potuit suadere malorum.*[15]

"Tantum religio potuit suadere malorum!" exclaimed Courtney Smith, second judge at the Criminal Court of Justice of Calcutta in 1821, during the trial of the Brahmans Sheolal and Bishuk Tivari, accused of having twice pushed their relative Humaliya, a young widow of fourteen, into the fire, and then of having had her finished off with a sword by a Muslim attending the ceremony when she attempted to escape for the third time, horribly burnt and pleading for help. The incident took place on November 20, 1820, in a village in Gorakhpur District, in present-day Uttar Pradesh. Yet Smith argued for the release of the accused, citing the power of custom and the stranglehold of antiquated ideas even as he denounced the pusillanimity of the half measures taken by the government and declared himself an advocate of the immediate abolition of the rite.[16]

In reading this interminable sequence of true-to-life accounts, one cannot help but feel that these facts, described in such surfeit and even *ad nauseam,* have become fiction. It may be that the foreigners present at these scenes were attempting in this way to soften the shock of coming face to face with a form of otherness that appeared to them to be a repudiation of humanity itself. Once again, we must quote Bernier here, since he expresses this sentiment with greatest force:

The woman I saw burn as I was leaving Sourate [in Gujarat] to come to Persia, in the presence of Monsieur Chardin of Paris & several Englishmen and Dutchmen, was approaching middle age and was not uncomely; to depict for you the animal intrepidness & savage mirth of her features, the aplomb with which she walked, allowed herself to be washed, spoke to this person and that, with what self-assurance & indifference she regarded us, looked upon the small Hut made of well-dried Millet stalks woven together with twigs, entered into the Hut, seated herself on the pyre as she took her husband's head in her lap, took a torch in her hand, & herself lit the fire from within, while I know not how many Brahmens armed with poles to stoke the fire kindled it from without on every side; to depict for you all of that, I say, is something impossible for me to do, in fact I can hardly believe it at present, even though it was, so to speak, only three days ago that I saw it.[17]

In the final analysis, these eyewitness accounts, which abound in priceless detail, ought to be read with the same circumspection as the indigenous documents, of which we will also provide an example—hardly a typical one, as it turns out, inasmuch as the text is quite exceptional. Its author, a Gujarati poet named Durlabh Ram, was in fact an eyewitness to the scene he records with great precision and unusual reserve. These qualities stand in contrast to the redundancy (and impoverishment in terms of factual data) of descriptions of similar scenes found in ancient Tamil Sangam poetry, classical theater, medieval chronicles, the poetry of "saints" and Sufis, bardic epic literature, and oral literature. They also contrast with the allusive distance and euphemistic style that characterize such learned works as the *dharma* treatises, law codes, digests, catalogues of observances, and guidebooks, all of which contrive to empty the rite of all its loathsome elements in favor of a pure ideality. It is true that certain normative texts, such as the *Śuddhitattva,* attributed to Raghunandana (who lived ca. 1520–1570), the *Nirṇayasindhu* of Kamalākarabhaṭṭa (1612), or the *Dharmasindhu* of Kāśīnātha (1790–1791), contain descriptive passages.[18] It is also the case that one can glean useful information from the rhetorical flourishes of the poets, chroniclers, and bards. But one rarely finds oneself in the presence of a continuous narrative in which dispassionate observation of the ritual facts wins out over the excesses of religious fervor or stylistic embellishment.

The eyewitness accounts of Durlabh Ram and Stavorinus are from more or less the same period: the manuscript of the Gujarati poet dates from 1741, and the Dutch traveler's relation may be placed around the year 1770, as the French title indicates. In both cases, the ceremony is presented to us in its most common form: that of a cremation (and not of a live burial of the widow together with the corpse of her husband). In both accounts, a single wife (and not a group of wives, concubines, and servants) burns herself alive. But what distinguishes these two testimonies (apart from the "machinery of death": a pyre in Bengal, a flaming hut in Gujarat) is that the first example depicts a "going with" or "dying with" *(sahagamana, sahamaraṇa),* and the second a "going after" or "dying after" *(anugamana, anumaraṇa)*—in other words, a joint cremation and a deferred cremation, which constitute the two facets of the rite. Here now are the two accounts, quoted in their entirety.

A Satī on the Shore of the Ganges (Stavorinus)

On the 25th of November, having received intimation that the solemnity would take place about noon, I went betimes, with some of my friends, to the place which had been pointed out to us; it was a few paces out of *Chinsurah,* upon the banks of the *Ganges.*

We here found the body of the deceased upon a *kadel,* or couch, covered with a piece of white cotton, and strewed with *siri,* or betel-leaves.

The woman, who was to be the victim, sat upon the couch, at the foot-end, with her legs crossed under her [in the lotus posture], and her face turned towards that of the deceased, which was uncovered. The husband seemed to me, to have been a person of almost fifty years of age, and his widow was full thirty. She had a yellow cotton cloth wrapped around her, and her arms and hands were adorned with rings of *chancos* [*śaṅkhas*: shells used as conches in rituals or for bracelets]. Her hair, which hung loose all around her head, was plentifully strewed with ground sandalwood. She had a little green branch in her right hand, with which she drove away the flies from the body.

Round her, upon the ground, sat ten or twelve women, who kept supplying her with fresh betel, a portion of which she had continually in her mouth; and when she had half masticated it, she gave it to one of her female friends, or to others of the bystanders, who begged it of her, wrapped it up in pieces of cloth, and preserved it as a relic.

She sat, for the greatest part of the time, like one buried in deepest meditation; yet with a countenance that betrayed not the least signs of fear. The other women, her relations and friends, spoke to her continually of the happiness she was about to enjoy, with her husband, in a future life. One of these women, who sat behind her, upon the couch, frequently embraced her and seemed to talk the most, and very earnestly with her.

Besides the women, several men, as well her relations, as brahmins, were present, who at intervals struck their cymbals and beat their drums, accompanied by the songs, or cries of the women, making a most deafening noise. At half past ten, they began to prepare the funeral pile, at the distance of a little more than eight feet from the spot, where the unfortunate woman was sitting, but which she beheld with the most stoic indifference, as if it in no way concerned her.

The pile was made by driving four green bamboo stakes into the earth, leaving about five feet above the ground, and being about six feet from each other, forming a square, in which was first laid a layer of large firewood, which was very dry, and easily combustible; upon this was put a quantity of dry straw, or reeds, which hung beyond the wood, and was plentifully besmeared with *ghee* [clarified butter] . . . This was done alternately, till the pile was almost five feet in height; and the whole was then strewed with fine powdered rosin. Finally, a white cotton sheet, which was first washed in the *Ganges,* was spread over the pile, thus completely prepared for consuming the devoted victim.

The widow was then admonished by a brahmin, that it was time to begin the rites. She was then taken up by two women, from the couch, carried a little further, and put down upon the ground, while the others made a circle round her, and continued to offer her fresh betel, accompanied by entreaties that, as she would, in so short a time, appear with her husband in the presence of *Ram,* or their highest god, she would supplicate for various favors for them; and above all, that she would salute their deceased friends whom she might meet in the celestial abodes, in their names.

In the meantime, the body was taken up from the couch by four men, and carried to the river, where it was washed clean, and rubbed with turmeric, but which was afterwards washed off again. Upon this, one of the brahmins took a little clay out of the river, and marked the forehead of the deceased with it, wrapping the body up in white linen; which, when this had been done, was carried to the pile, and laid upon it.

The woman, who had beheld all these preparations, was then led by two of her female relations to the *Ganges,* in order to wash in the river. When she came again upon the bank, her clothes were pulled off, and a piece of red silk and cotton gingham was wrapped round her body. One of her male relatives took out her gold nose-jewel [*nath:* one of the symbols of marriage], while she sat down, and gave it to her, but she returned it to him for a memorial of her. Thereupon she went again to the river, and taking up some water in her hands, muttered some prayers, and offered it to the sun. All her ornaments were taken from her, and her amulets were broken, and chaplets of white flowers were put upon her neck and hands. Her hair was tucked up with five combs, and her forehead was marked with clay in the same manner as that of her husband. Her head was covered with a piece of silk and a cloth was tied round her body, in which the brahmins put some parched rice.

She then took her last farewell of her friends, both men and women who had assisted her in the preparation, and she was conducted by two of her female relations to the pile. When she came to it, she scattered from that side, where the head of the deceased lay, flowers and parched rice upon the spectators. She then took some boiled rice, rolled in a ball, and put it into the mouth of the deceased, laying several other similar balls of rice under the pile. Two brahmins next led her three times round it, while she threw parched rice among the bystanders, who gathered it up with eagerness. The last time that she went round, she set a little earthen burning lamp at each of the four corners. The whole of this was done during an incessant clamor of cymbals and drums, and amidst the shouts of the brahmins, and of her relations. After having thus walked three times round the pile, she mounted courageously upon it, laid herself down upon the right side next to the body, which she embraced with both her arms; a piece of white cotton was spread over them both, they were bound together over the arms, and middle, with two easy bandages, and a quantity of firewood, straw, *ghee,* and rosin, was laid upon them. In the last place, her nearest relation, to whom she had given her nose-jewel, came with a burning torch, and set the straw on fire, and in a moment the whole was in flame. The noise of the drums was redoubled, and the shouts of the spectators were more loud and incessant than ever, so that the shrieks of the unfortunate woman, had she uttered any, could not possibly have been heard.

What most surprised me, at this horrid and barbarous rite, was the tranquillity of the woman, and the joy expressed by her relations, and the spectators. The wretched victim, who beheld these preparations making for her cruel death, seemed to be much less affected by it than we Europeans who were present. She underwent everything with the greatest intrepidity, and her countenance seemed, at times, to be animated with pleasure, even at the moment when she was ascending the fatal pile.

Her feet appeared from between the firewood, on the side where I stood; and I had an opportunity of observing them, because a little breeze, playing upon that side, cleared it of the flame and smoke; I paid particular attention to her, in order to discover whether any convulsive motions agitated her feet, but they remained immovable, in the midst of the conflagration.

The women who were present, and who all, sooner or later, would have to undergo the same fate, if they survived their husbands, appeared to rejoice at the sacrifice, and showed every token of exultation.[19]

A Satī in Surat (Durlabh Ram)

In September 1741 A. D. (V. S. 1797 Bhadra) Shivabai, a lady of the Nagar community, came to know about the death of her husband. Thereupon she began to live on milk having acquired "*Sat.*" The sensational rumour spread throughout the city and each one who heard the news went to see her. The relatives of the lady tried to dissuade her from the course. But the lady persisted and said that she would show the proofs of her *bona fide.* Shivabai took the letter conveying the news upon her lap and gave out that she would burn herself. She then threatened the people with curses if they refused to believe her. Thereupon Lālā Sadānand, one of her kins, locked the doors of her room. But the lock broke by itself and the frenzied lady threatened to set the building ablaze [by the power of her *sat*]. Lālā Sadānand came to see the *satī* (presumably to test her "*sat*") and asked her to tell what he secretly held in his hands. The *Sati* said, "Lālā Sadānand, take the name of Ambā, you have betel-nut in one hand and rupees two in the other. Look, I can also produce "Kumkum." Being convinced by these proofs positive, Lālā Sadānand rode to the darbār. There he consulted Thakore Karsandas, Mehta Manekchand, and Diwanji. Having deliberated on the matter, the four approached the Khan Sahib. The Khan Sahib having heard the case obtained permission from the Nabob. Lālā Sadānand returned with the permit. The lady kept up self-possessed surrounded by the servants and attendants begging for gifts [as relics]. She rubbed her palms and produced live coal.

Lālā Sadānand requested her if she would care to proceed riding a mare or a *Rath* [chariot]. Satimā asked to get ready a bullock *Rath.* She then proceeded with pomp and dignity. Her sister and maternal aunt sat by her side. The *Rath* passed through the principal streets of the city, followed by a huge crowd shouting "Jai Ambe, Jai Ambe" [Long Live the Goddess Ambā]. The *Sati* alighted at Lāl Darwaja (the city gate) and made hand impressions with "kumkum" on the doors. A torch was lighted on the way near Ashvani Kumar. The procession came to Gupteshwara (the burning ghāt) at dusk. The *Sati* refused to perform the ordeal after the sunset and requested her relatives to wait till the daybreak.

The relatives being afraid lest her spirit might droop advised her not to delay. The *Sati* confirmed her resolve to enter the fire early morning and expressed that the people might doubt whether the *Sati* did not escape in the dark of night. She felt confident to keep up her spirit for five days.

Lālā Sadānand sent for the Patel (headman) of the town and asked him to prepare "Madhuli" (canopy of faggots) for which he would be rewarded with gifts (shirpāv). The lady came to the river-bank (Tapti) all elated early in the morning. She took Tulshi (holy basil) from the priest and went for a bath. She dipped herself one hundred and eight times [this number, indicative of completeness, magnifies ritual acts and formulas] all alone. Lālā Sadānand stationed himself on the bank and asked the Brahmins to watch her lest she might give herself in the water [to save herself from the torment of fire]. The *Sati* came out of the water and worshipped a cow. She went round the priest and his wife and the cow. She gave her ornaments to the priest and his wife and fed grass to the cow. She performed Havan (Fire worship). The relatives of the lady presented seven cocoanuts to her and began to shed tears. But the *Sati* forbade them to weep [since such was a sign of evil portent reserved for ordinary mourning]. Satimātā had kept a platter of "Kumkum" at Havan. She took off her "chudo"[20] (the costly mark of a married woman whose husband is alive) and gave it as a gift to the wife of the priest [an act of benediction which has the sense of "may you forever remain a happy wife, with a living husband, so that you may wear these bracelets"]. However, she wore the nose-ring. She once more took her bath and performed "Tarpan" (*[tarpaṇa]* the act of propitiating the dead). Then she put on a white *sari* and came to the "Madhi." By that time the sun had risen hence she worshipped the Sun. She took the sun's permission to burn herself. She went five times round the "Madhi." She held a cocoanut in one of her hands and a torch in the other. She bowed to the sun and entered the "Madhi." She called her relative Lālā Venilal and blessed him with a gift of cocoanut. Lālā Sadānand stood with a drawn sabre near the "Madhi." The *Sati* asked to cease beating the drums as she would not scream or shriek. She then took "ghi" [clarified butter] and put it on the pyre. Finally, she entreated Lālā Sadānand to approve the act as auspicious. She took the letter [announcing the death of her husband] upon her lap and remembered her lord. The pyre was made of sandalwood, Tulshi, and Agaru. At first the *Sati* set fire to her hair [with the torch she held in her hand] and then ignited straw all around. The full blaze of the fire was revered by throwing betel-nuts, coins, and almonds by the crowd. The event became memorable in the annals of the people. Thus the *Sati* went to heaven by Viman [celestial vehicle].[21]

The Dream as Proof

While the solemn utterance of the "declaration of intent" *(saṃkalpa)* is in fact what irrevocably sets the rite in motion, this act of speech, this act of truth has a history of its own.[22] How do the fatal words burst from the satī's lips? At what moment and in what circumstances is her vow conceived? What impulses cause it to break out of the world of fantasies? . . . So many questions whose answers will never come to light. Whatever the case, they seem not to have posed a problem for our sources, since they already had implicit answers at hand. In the native perspective, the "rise of the *sat*" is an explanatory principle that suffices unto itself. If further explanation were necessary, it would come from notions relative to the virtue of faithful wives and to *satītva,* satī-hood, fleshed out with speculations on karma and fueled by images of the power of the Feminine. The *sat,* molded and increased through the assiduous practice of marital devotion in previous lives, is manifested in this life, upon the death of the husband, in that speech act which, while seemingly unpredictable, uncontrollable, sudden, and violent, has its origins in a history of the "longue durée": past lives, the slow germination and inexorable ripening of acts, the generation of immediate as well as deferred effects, and the production of such principles/substances/powers as the *sat.*

Furthermore, the violent yet anticipated irruption of the *sat* is foreshadowed by signs that betray a woman's vocation as a future satī: an irrepressible passion for fire (as we have seen in the case of Dayal Kanvar), miracles, or the disclosure of her destiny through a dream or vision—all of these being shared in common by the "saints" (*sants*) of popular hagiography.[23] Their earthly trajectory is as if punctuated with portents that, incomprehensible at the time of their occurrence, become altogether clear once their sacredness has revealed itself. Dream visions play a particularly important role here. A mere premonitory sign, such a vision can also be a direct source of information: a woman whose husband has gone off to war, taken a perilous voyage, or long since disappeared receives news of his death through a dream. Yama, the king of the dead, occasionally delivers the message himself. Thus in the epic of Pābū-jī, the ritual recitation of which still marks the rhythm of rural life in Rajasthan, the lovely Gailovat, wife of the elder half-brother of the deified hero, is visited in her sleep by Jamṛo (a local name for Yama):

> 'O son of Jamaṛī, go back hence;
> Pābūjī will come and kill you painfully with the point of his spear!'
> 'Queen Gailovat, do not be so very proud of Lord Pābūjī!
> Pābūjī has passed on to the court of the innocent (god) Rāma.'

The dream is tantamount to proof: upon awakening, the woman has the pyre prepared, and it is not uncommon for her to immolate herself without even awaiting a confirmation of death. This motif, which appears in satī myths, is also found in real-life accounts and verifiable testimony. Lieutenant George Francis White reports the case of a Brahman woman who, having had the death of her husband announced to her in a dream, burned herself near Baroda, in the princely State of Gwalior, in the presence of one Captain Grindlay. Deeply distressed, she had become entirely convinced that her dream was real when, some time later, it had taken the tangible form of a sinister omen: a crow had flown off with her wedding necklace, which she had left atop an earthenware jar. At that point, she let down her hair to mark her death to the world, and declared her intent. Once alerted, the British Resident, Sir James Rivett Carnac (who was later to become the Governor of Bombay), attempted to dissuade her, but when the woman showed herself to be intractable, he petitioned the prince to intervene. Daulat Rao Scindia did in fact make the journey, in the company of a large escort, whereupon the young widow took up a dagger and threatened to shed her blood if permission to burn herself was refused, adding that her Brahman blood would forever stain the forehead of the prince with the guilt of her death. The Rao chose to withdraw and the woman burned herself that very day. The news of her husband's death was confirmed in the course of the following three weeks and—quite disturbingly, the author tells us—the date of his death tallied with that of her dream.[25] Blood extortion (which reminds us of the Charans) appears to be an upper-caste woman's final recourse in such circumstances: a report from the Foreign Department (Political) dated September 20, 1843, informs us that six women—the rani, four concubines, and a maidservant—had declared their intention to burn themselves together with Man Singh, the Maharajah of Jodhpur, on the fifth day of September of the same year.[26] When the British political agent and close relatives attempted to dissuade them, they threatened to stab themselves in their apartments—and won their case. As for women of more modest origins, they often resorted to the same rhetoric—if not the same weapons—and, in countless cases, carried through on their vows.[27]

Sleeman reports a similar incident: one of his Jabalpur informants told of a fisherman who had left for Banaras (around 1810) and from whom no news had been received for six months. One night, his wife, dreaming that he had died on the road, uttered the fatal cry: "*sat, sat, sat.*" In the morning, a pyre was piled up, at her request, on the north bank of a large tank, adjoining the temple of the god Hanumān, that was reserved for ablutions. There she burned herself with a turban belonging to her husband. Then, ten days later, he returned.[28] There was also the 1823 case of an illegal widow-burning that was ruled on by the Court of Criminal Justice in Calcutta. Ganesha had burned herself according to the practice of *anumaraṇa* ("dying after"). Now it happens that she was a Brahman woman and that that form of the rite had been forbidden to Brahmans in British territories ever since the government—in consultation with the pundits, who were specialists in religious matters—had transformed that highly controversial issue into a rule of Hindu law. Not only had Ganesha violated the law by dying on a separate pyre, but in addition, no one knew for sure whether her husband, who had disappeared several years earlier, was dead. The fatal decision had been taken in the wake of a dream. In this instance, the British judges and Indian pundits entered into serious discussions regarding the legal status of a person's innermost convictions as founded on dreams which, according to the Hindu traditionalists, legitimized the sacrifice.[29] According to popular belief, what one sees in a dream is a mirror of reality. The question the dreamer asks himself is not whether the dream will come true, but rather *when*.[30]

The dream leitmotif continues to spin out tales of women being called upon to sacrifice themselves. The custodian of the Kothri temple (Sikar District, Rajasthan), where a woman of the Goldsmith caste burned herself on April 1, 1973, told me that Savitri was in her natal village when her husband, Makkhan Lal, a great devotee of Śiva, died of snakebite. No one had heard the news; and yet, that very night, it came to Savitri in a dream. The following morning, she asked her mother to bring her the red marriage veil that satīs of Rajasthan wear when they go off to burn themselves.[31]

Occasionally, dream visions will play a different role in satī myths: the woman who has burned herself appears in a dream to demand that a temple and worship cult be raised. Such was the case of the celebrated Nārāyaṇī Satī of Alwar, in Rajasthan, who, according to tradition, sacrificed herself on the ninth day of the bright fortnight of the month of *Vaiśākha* in the year 1016 of the *Vikrama* era—i.e., in 959 C.E. This humble Barber's wife had a passionate desire to become a satī. With the aid of a stranger, who prepared the funeral pyre, she immolated herself in the forest in which her husband had met his death. Then, in a dream, she ordered the king of Alwar to honor her with a shrine, and to build a temple to Śiva adjacent to it.

Territorial deities ("Mothers" and minor figures of the Hindu pantheon);[32] dissatisfied and irascible spirits (*bhūta*s) deprived by their sudden deaths of their share in this-worldly pleasures; and the dead, in sore want of deification make their demands on the living through the conduit of dreams, shamelessly clamoring for worship, offerings, and observances. As unpredictable as they are capricious, thin-skinned, and, on occasion, tyrannical, they show themselves to be beneficent when they are appeased through the fulfillment of their terms. The dream (like the trance or mystic vision) is the locus in which the impossible encounter—between human beings and divine entities, between living descendants and departed ancestors—takes place in ways that, while mysterious, are accessible through interpretation. If a woman in white appears in a dream, she is undoubtedly a ghost *(pitrāṇī):* so I was told by Anup Kanvar, a Chauhan Rajput from Jaipur, originally from the small town of Uniyara (in the Bundi region). Seeing a serpent in a dream may be a sign that a "father" *(pitar)* wishes to be honored through a worship cult, or requires of the dreamer that thenceforth he should wear around his neck an amulet in his effigy *(patrī).*[33] The spirit who prefers to remain anonymous and whose identity can only be established through divinatory techniques thus maps out his territory within the symbolic space of men and renews his bonds, from beyond the pale of death, with the community and family from which he was so violently torn. His premature death is compensated, in a sense, by this long-lasting inscription in the collective memory.

The will of the dead who speaks through a dream is thus the expression of an unfulfilled desire. Satīs, however "altruistic" their sacrifice may be, are not exempted from this rule. This, at least, is what may be inferred from the use they make of ritual prohibitions when they are about to ascend the funeral pyre. This forswearing *(ān)* obliges the women of the husband's family line to abstain indefinitely from wearing certain items of clothing, finery, colors, or objects associated with conjugal happiness or maternity. The satī will forbid those women fortunate enough to outlive her from wearing this or that veil or piece of cloth of a given color, pattern, or hem; gold and silver jewelry; ivory bracelets, or glass or lacquer bangles; or anklets or toe rings, other symbols of marriage. Elsewhere, she will prohibit them from bedding their children down in the traditional cradle, from rocking them in the little swing that always hangs in inner courtyards, or from tying around their waist the gold or silver belt or the black silken thread that ensures their protection against the evil eye. It may be thought that the satī avenges herself in this way on a family in which she had not been well received, and in which the women in particular—her mother- and sisters-in-law—had mistreated her (women leave their natal village to take up residence with their in-laws after marriage, or following the *gaunā* ceremony marking the effective beginning of spousal cohabitation). But we may also surmise that the satī is giving vent, albeit indirectly, to her resentment at the cruel fate that will forever deprive her of both her earthly happiness and her life.

In his essay *Bhut Nibandh,* Dalpat Ram Daya notes a particular variety of the dead whom, due to their excessive attachment for a son or a place, the funeral rites have failed to install in the "world of the ancestors": they go on living in their former house as its serpent guardian; or else coil themselves beneath a fig tree or a *khejṛā* (*Prosopis spicifera,* a type of thornbush). These are, in the words of the author, the ancestor-gods *(pūrvaj-dev),* spirits "of the best class."[34] The *khejṛā* tree, which is sacred to Bhairava, is one of the favorite haunts of the *bhūt-prets,* spirits of every sort—but especially of *bhūtnīs,* spirits of the feminine gender, malevolence being an art in which women excel, in the beyond as well as in this world. In Narsinghpuri, a village in Sikar District, I was shown a *khejṛā* tree, which my ignorance in matters of botany had at first rendered unidentifiable.[35] It is growing on the left side of the temple built upon the cremation site of Jugal Kanvar, the thirty-five-year-old Rajput mother of five who immolated herself in 1966. Her eldest son, who lit the pyre and who is today the officiant of his mother's cult, told me that "the hundred eight times very holy satī Jugal Kanvar" had granted a *vardān* (a divine boon) to the people of the village before ascending the pyre: any possessed person who performed a two-day ritual circumambulation of the *khejṛā* tree, following a purifying fast, would be released. Upon being forced to tell its name, the spirit would forever leave the body. When I then asked him if there were many candidates for such exorcism, his only response was to lead me to another tree from which a profusion of votive coconuts were hanging by red cotton threads. If Jugal Kanvar fulfills their wish, these devotees untie a coconut and split it open over her altar.

We may ask ourselves what function dreams play in the satīs' stories. For Hindus, to burn oneself on the basis of a dream is a matter of belief, while to appear before someone in a dream to exact a worship cult is part of the "psychology" of ancestors: dreams are a means for the unhappy dead to express their frustrations and unfulfilled desires. These cultural rationalizations are no doubt highly important to those who formulate them. But what exactly do we know about the wishes of the dead? and when we speak of belief are we doing anything other than throwing sand in the eyes of nonbelievers? Gananath Obeysekere has in a sense already answered these questions for us. In an essay published in 1981 on the subject of individuals possessed by the god Kataragama in Sri Lanka, he has shown through a series of case studies that a dream—like an ecstatic trance or mystic vision—can be interpreted as the symbolization of the guilt felt by the living in relation to the dead.[36] This interpretation throws light on a number of obscure phenomena. Tara Kanvar, a Chauhan Rajput born in the village of Balwari (Gurgaon District), burned herself in 1953 in Madho-Ka-Bas, a village in Sikar District.[37] Shortly after her cremation, she appeared before her mother Jarav Kanvar in a dream. The latter questioned her with an anxiety that can easily be imagined: how had she been able to endure the torment of the fire? Had she not suffered horribly? Tara Devi answered serenely that she had experienced no suffering in taking the "lustratory fire bath" *(agnisnān)*.[38] This dream is clearly disclosive of the guilt of the mother, who had transmitted the ideology of "satī-hood" to her daughter.[39] The dream happily freed her of her maternal anguish even as it negated any possibility of revenge on the part of the satī against the community of the living—primarily her family, but especially her mother (in the dream, Tara Devi was smiling and affectionate.)

But what happens when it is the satīs themselves who dream? I find myself very hard pressed to explain the "dream clairvoyance" of certain satīs. It does seem to me, however, that *to dream the husband's death* and then to pay for that dream with a burning and painful death can be understood as an abreaction to unbearable feelings of guilt. It must be recalled here that evil thoughts—even when they are unconscious—are as imbued with sin as evil acts;[40] and that dreams present people with images of a reality that has yet to occur. The horror and self-loathing awakened in the dream of death can only be abreacted through the wish to die. It is in fact the only way for the satī to eliminate from her consciousness an unbearable psychic conflict. The woman who becomes possessed by the "madness of the *sat*" is internalizing a behavioral pattern—from the outside world, from the collective culture—that enables her to objectify the traumatic content of her dream. By giving form and substance to the dream (the woman burns herself *as if* her husband were dead), the madness of the *sat* repairs and voids the fault of karma *(karmadoṣa)* revealed in her dream: to have conceived in the depths of sleep that darkest of all thoughts can only be explained through some hidden sin, whose effects have inexorably come to fruition. Recall here that the life of a man hangs on the "virtue" *(satītva)* of his wife: she protects him from the evil hand of fate and ensures his well-being and survival through her devotion, vows, and religious observances. How could her husband possibly die without it being her fault? How could she have seen him dead in a dream if he were still alive? And since her death wish cannot surface consciously, what is expressed in broad daylight when the woman emerges from sleep is her own desire to die.

Javitri burned herself on July 11, 1979, in Jari, a village in the Banda District of Uttar Pradesh. She was in her natal village when her husband, Ram Kant, an engineering student, was killed by hoodlums, along with his brother Shiv Kant. The tragedy of their deaths was nonetheless revealed to her in a dream. She immediately rushed to the home of her in-laws, who welcomed her with a volley of curses: it was *she* who was the guilty one, and she who had cast a spell on her husband's family line. Overcome, Javitri declared her intent to burn herself. She was not yet eighteen. A temple was erected to her (the income from which goes to her in-laws). There she is worshipped together with her husband and brother-in-law: Javitri, Ram Kant, and Shiv Kant are represented by worship images reminiscent of Sītā, Rāma, and Lakṣmaṇa, the trio of epic heroes in the *Rāmāyaṇa.*

The Transmission of the Deadly Vow

How can one be a satī? Foreigners who have expressed opinions on this particularly delicate subject have, on the whole, adopted a position quite different from (and occasionally antithetical to) that of Hindu traditionalists. Religious fanaticism, the power of custom, the weight of religious beliefs conjoined with the trauma of a husband's death; the terrible fate of widows; pressure exerted by the family, one's social group, and brahman priests; and the desire to immortalize oneself through this heroic act: these are the reasons most frequently invoked to explain a phenomenon whose mystery, in the final analysis, remains unplumbed. Gustave Le Bon, the author of the celebrated *La Psychologie des foules* (1895), which was a source of inspiration for Freud, developed a passion for India. One of the first travelers to undertake an exploratory expedition into the Kathmandu Valley in 1885, he summarizes this point of view rather well:

> The unmarried woman and, above all, the widow, are two types of beings that Hindu society rejects from its bosom. And by widow, we mean even the young girl who has lost her fiancé in the first years of her life. Such a misfortune is irreparable. The abandoned creature falls even beneath the level of pariahs themselves.
>
> The death of a Hindu, says M. Malabari,[41] is a crushing blow for his wife; she can not recover from it. The Hindu widow remains in mourning for the rest of her life. She is no longer treated as a human being. Her sight brings misfortune and she sullies all that she touches. She is scorned and neglected. Life is but a burden to her. Nothing remains to her than to give herself over to impure customs or drag herself through a miserable and

lonely life. I speak here of the young widow; one who has the consolation of having had children is less at the mercy of caste prejudices.

It will now be understood from what bitter fount the Hindu woman has drawn the marital devotion that we find so admirable and which, vindicated from century to century, has become an inner sense. The same reasons explain in part the perpetuation, if not the foundation, of this custom of *sutti* which required that widows burn themselves alive with the body of their husbands. Between the wondrous joys the heroic widow was to savor alongside her husband in another life and the abominable misery in which she would live out her days while remaining on earth, the choice was quickly made by these ardent and credulous creatures, whose enthusiasm was brought to a pitch by the tears, applause, prayers, and sacred chants that resounded all around them and that cheered their exalted death.[42]

Walter Ewer, the Acting Superintendent of Police in the Lower Provinces, pleaded as early as 1818 for immediate abolition of the rite, arguing that the authorities were sanctioning, under the cover of the religious prejudices of the Hindus, the murder of women by their families (a crime punishable by death in Great Britain). Ewer dismantled the mechanism of the satī's declaration of intent in a letter addressed to W. B. Bayley, the Secretary to Government in the Judicial Department.[43] He demonstrated that Hindu women were at no time in their lives the architects of their own destiny; that they had no freedom of decision or choice; that, being deprived of education regardless of their rank, they had no knowledge of the purport of the Law, and relied entirely upon men—relatives and priests whose opinions they accepted as gospel truth—for advice and interpretation. Trained from childhood to be totally submissive, steeped in an attitude of holy veneration toward Brahmans, the incarnation of the gods on earth, women did not have the strength to resist the pressures of family members and priests, all of whom had a stake in their perdition. In the state of extreme confusion in which they found themselves following the traumatic loss of their husband, they were counseled at length as to the merits of sacrifice and its advantages for future births; the bright prospect of the glory that awaited was held out to them, and the disgrace that would follow them were they to refuse to burn themselves was portrayed in the darkest terms. There was no one to guide or protect them in this baleful situation. A few hours would elapse in this way, and the widow would then be burned before she even had time to ponder the fate that awaited her:

Should utter indifference for her husband and superior sense enable her to preserve her judgment, and to resist the arguments of those about her, it will avail her little,—the people will not, on any account, be disappointed of their show; and the entire population of a village will turn out to assist in dragging her to the bank of the river, and in keeping her down on the pile [with bamboo poles].[44]

The satī's words, her resolution, and her attitude are thus simple matters of convention. At no point in the drama that seals her fate can she legitimately be called a free agent. "Whether she shows a joyful face or desperation, appears to be glad or sorry, stupid, composed or distracted, is no manner of proof of her real feelings."[45] Consequently, to establish the legality of the rite on the grounds of a woman's free will as legal subject (while she is, to all appearances, a victim) is to close one's eyes to the truth or to fall into a trap. In any event, to do so is tantamount to becoming an accomplice in a particularly odious crime. And Ewer notes, in a marginal paragraph: "How should we act if human sacrifices to the goddess Kalee were frequent? They are declared by the Kalika Poorana to be highly meritorious."[46]

Charles Grant had already put forward these same arguments in a report written in 1792; his report would not, however, be submitted to the Court of Directors of the East India Company until the first phase of the conquest had been completed, in 1797:

Are we bound for ever to preserve all the enormities in the Hindoo system? Have we become the guardians of every monstrous principle and practice which it contains? Are we pledged to support for all generations, by the authority of our government and the power of our arms, the miseries which ignorance and knavery have so long entailed upon a large portion of the human race?—Is *this* the part which a free, a humane, and an enlightened people, a nation itself professing principles diametrically opposite to those in question, has engaged to act toward its own subjects? It would be too absurd and extravagant to maintain that any engagement of this kind exists, that Great Britain is under any obligation, direct or implied, to uphold errors and usages, gross and fundamentally subversive of the first principles of *reason, morality,* and religion.

If we had conquered such a kingdom as Mexico, where a number of human victims were regularly offered every year upon the altar of the sun, should we have calmly acquiesced in this horrid mode of butchery? Yet for nearly thirty years we have, with perfect unconcern, seen rites in reality *more* cruel and atrocious practised in our Indian territories.[47]

To the powers of persuasion of relatives and priests may be added those of the bards, in circles in which widow sacrifice is a badge of honor for the deceased and their families and even, it has been said, a criterion of "Sanskritization," of upward social mobility. In his 1821 *Report on Malwa,* Sir John Malcolm (Governor of Bombay from 1827 to 1830) provides us with a proof *a contrario* of the bards' influence. Recalling that there had not been more than three or four satīs annually over the previous twenty years in a region ruled first by the Muslims, and then by the Mahrattas, who were wise enough to ignore the practice rather than ban it, Malcolm remarks, not without humor:

> When the Rajah Bhanswarrah died last year, not one of his wives desired to burn, though the bards of the family sung to them the fame of the former heroines who had acquired immortality by perishing in the flames which had consumed the body of their lords.[48]

Oral traditions undoubtedly had a direct impact on the number of women who answered the call to become satīs. It suffices to find oneself in the throng of devotees when the cult of a satī is being celebrated, or among a group of women gathered together for a night vigil—or even to view a performance that includes the episode of a faithful wife's "fire bath," as found in the epics of Pābū-jī or Devnārāyaṇ—to gauge the intensity of the emotion generated by the overwhelming power of the *sat.* In 1978, Komal Kothari told me that he had been obliged to rewrite the scenario of a film based on a popular tale from Rajasthan, cutting the final sequence of the immolation of a satī, because neither the director nor the producer had wanted to run the risk of setting off an outbreak of mass hysteria during the screening of the film. (To be sure, he did not use the word "hysteria," but rather the Hindi *jos̈,* "excitation, uncontrollable transport, fervor." I do not believe, however, that I am misrepresenting his thoughts by phrasing it that way here.) Later, I will give an account of the *pañcamī* worship ceremony offered to Om Kanvar (who was burned on August 30, 1980), which I attended on April 11, 1993. It was a secret ceremony (since 1988, all glorification of satīs has been prohibited by law) that was nonetheless held in a domestic shrine open to the throng of her devotees in a residential neighborhood of Jaipur. The atmosphere of religious transport (heightened by the secrecy of the proceedings) quite nearly carried me away, so much did its infectious warmth—redoubled by the sacrificial fire that burned before the altar, and borne on the chants, invocations, and ardent prayers I heard—break down all my resistance for the period of several hours.

Even in present-day Rajasthan, rites of passage considered to be auspicious must necessarily include in their initial phase a song cycle dedicated to five categories of deities: ancestors (*pūrvaj*s), young ghosts (*bāḷā pitar*s), female ancestors (*pitrāṇīs*), satīs, and finally the god Bheru-jī. When a newborn child is given a name, when he takes his first solid food, when his baby hair is cut or ears pierced, or when a son is offered his deceased father's turban twelve days after his death, these songs are sung to these deities who, irascible and dangerous when ignored, become protective and generous in the granting of boons when their favor has been won through acts of devotion.

Women gather together for night-long song sessions whenever a night vigil *(rātījagā)* is required—upon the birth of a first son; on the eve of the child's first *Durgāṣṭamī;*[49] when the marriage engagement has been sealed by an exchange of coconuts between the two families; on the eve of the worship of the god Gaṇeśa, which occurs at an auspicious moment a few days prior to the marriage ceremony; and on the day on which that union is consummated. Sixteen divinities (including satīs) are hailed in succession. The first song is sung to the ritual lamp, which will burn until sunrise, and the last to the cotton mat upon which the divinities are invited to take their places. Of course, satī songs are also sung during satī worship, and whenever a boon is asked of one's chosen satī *(iṣṭ satī).* Associated with happy events (or at least events considered to be so[50]), with ceremonies in which religious fervor and the violence of the emotions are raised to a fever pitch, these songs suffuse the mind from infancy, instilling it with an affective charge of extraordinary intensity that can be reactivated at any moment.

The transmission of the call to satī-hood within a lineage aptly illustrates the role of these traditions: the heroic ideal is adopted all the more spontaneously when it is embedded in family history; the woman receives it not only from the outside world, in the form of a behavioral pattern, but also as a hereditary trait, a kind of birthmark ensuring the continuity of generations through her deadly vow. The "founding" satī protects the family line, grants sons, and wards off diseases and calamities—but it is as if she requires in exchange that she be appeased, even nourished, with the repeated spectacle of her death. The fact that one finds ten or twelve satīs in a single family line need not necessarily be explained by the violence inflicted on women: this motivation may simply be due to her chance connection with a line of satīs. The woman thus chosen, so to speak, will be naturally inclined to declare herself a satī when she loses her husband. One finds, for example, the following description of a case noted in the margin of the official list of widow sacrifices for the year 1824. The matter is that of the cremation of Mahasundari Devi, a thirty-three-year-old Brahman woman who immolated herself on November 24 in a district within Murshidabad Division:

> Every exertion was made to dissuade the widow from becoming a suttee, but without effect; she had been waiting for the death of her husband who had been transported to the bank of the river. . . . She was a native of Kishunagore, and the second wife of the deceased, and had one son about 8 years of age; her mother, she alleged, had also burnt as a suttee, and that the rite had invariably been performed by the females of her family.[51]

Sleeman's report, mentioned with reference to trial by fire,[52] offers one of the rare eyewitness accounts of the germination of the deadly vow. The old Brahman woman to whom he refuses permission to burn herself is sitting on a rock in the bed of the Narbada River as a sign of protest *(dharnā):*

> I asked the old lady when she had first resolved upon becoming a suttee, and she told me that about thirteen years before, while bathing in the river Nerbudda, near the spot where she then sat, with many other females of the family, the resolution had fixed itself in her mind as she looked at the splendid temples on the bank of the river erected by the different branches of the family over the ashes of her female relations who had at different times become suttees. Two, I think, were over her aunts, and one over the mother of her husband. They were very beautiful buildings, and had been erected at great cost and kept in good repair. She told me that she had never mentioned this her resolution to any one from that time on, nor breathed a syllable on the subject till she called out 'Sat, sat, sat,' when her husband breathed his last with his head in her lap on the bank of the Nerbudda, to which he had been taken when no hopes remained of his surviving the fever of which he died.

While fixing her gaze on the sun (the fiery heavenly body which, according to belief, lights the satī's pyre), she added, with an expression that left Sleeman deeply moved: "I see them together under the marriage canopy!" [an allusion to the wedding ceremony, whose counterpart is the joint funeral of the husband and his widow], "and I am satisified," Sleeman noted, "that at that moment she really believed that she saw her own spirit and that of her husband under the bridal canopy in paradise."[53]

The role played by satī temples in the genesis of the sacrificial calling may be seen in the field down to the present day. The construction, between the years 1956 and 1960, of the monumental temple complex dedicated to the celebrated Rāṇī Satī in Jhunjhunu explains at least in part the sudden resurgence of widow-burnings in that region of Rajasthan. Fieldwork studies conducted by Indian sociologists have arrived at conclusions that leave very little doubt on the subject.[54] It is no longer the case today, however, that the esthetic and religious emotions triggered by the vision of the temple are alone in awakening the call to become a satī. An elaborate propaganda apparatus disseminated through satī temples (hagiographical pamphlets, religious poster art, worship, religious fairs, commemorations and celebrations of every sort, "satī defense" committees, fundraising, campaigns for the glorification of satīs, and the sale of religious articles and "relics") insinuates itself between spontaneous individual reaction—even if such is induced in part by the milieu—and the mass production of the same.

Visual perception appears to have been another determining factor in the call, in the past as in the present. Thus the Comte de Modave notes in 1775 that "two or three girls, aged between three and four," are paraded around the pyre "in the arms of servants and are quite plausibly fated to offer the same spectacle some day."[55] The detailed report of the number of widow-burnings in Bareilly Division for the year 1823 relates the case of Rukmini, a twenty-year-old Brahman woman who burned herself in a village in Shahjahanpur District five years after the death of her husband, even though "dying after" had been prohibited to Brahmans under Hindu law and British legislation. She was survived by a small child, an aggravating circumstance that rendered her cremation illegal on two counts. Yet Shahjahanpur District was one of those that stood out for the infrequency of the practice: in the course of the previous year only three satīs had immolated themselves there (in comparison, 309 widows had burned themselves in Calcutta Division in 1823, as opposed to 12 in Bareilly Division). The sacrifice of Rukmini, moreover, constituted the sole case of widow-burning occurring in Shahjahanpur District that year. Now the entry describing the episode points out the fact that the woman had chosen for the site of her death the very place where a satī had burned herself five months earlier. We may surmise that Rukmini had been among the crowd that saw Kundin, a thirty-year-old Rajput woman, immolate herself on November 23, 1822. This episode must have been all the more sensational in that Kundin, exhibiting a generosity worthy of a rani, let fly fifty rupees before ascending the pyre.[56] The same phenomenon may be observed in recent cases: the villages in which satīs burn themselves are situated only a few miles from each other in the Shekhavati region, to the north of Jaipur.[57] Banda District, in Uttar Pradesh, famed for three self-immolations between

1979 and 1983, contains a number of satī stones and small, rather primitive shrines from a relatively early period. We will return to this matter below, in a discussion of the revitalization of the rite in Shekhavati.

If widow-burnings have always attracted considerable crowds, it is because the vision *(darśan)* per se of a satī—at the moment in which she performs the sacrifice that makes her what she is and enshrines her forever in human memory—unleashes a veritably unrivalled redemptive power. *Darśan,* the sanctifying vision of an object of worship in which the devotee becomes so absorbed as to lose himself in it, is a rudimentary form of devotional practice. The transference, from the religious to the subjective—of merit and ideals of conduct, as well as of love, one of its essential elements—is effected through this mute yet all-pervasive exchange of glances.[58] After the satī's death, all the trappings of her worship play the same role: *darśan* of the burning place *(satī sthal)* will be performed—most particularly, of the miraculous ashes in the sacred enclosure that houses them—and subsequently of the satī shrine *(devḷī)* or temple *(mandir)* containing the divine image *(mūrti)* or one of its symbolic representations, such as the trident, a symbol of *śakti.* But people also take *darśan* of profane sites, such as the house of the satī's husband, transformed into a religious museum of sorts, and in any case an obligatory pilgrimage stop. Finally, religious posters are used in domestic worship.

Over the past few years, another type of imagery has taken over: skillfully doctored photographs of the satī, alone or in the company of her husband, are placed nowadays in domestic shrines. Garlands of flowers frame these photographs, and incense is burned before them; they are, in a word, used as worship images. There are at least two sites in which one finds photographs used as divine images in a temple. The shrine dedicated to Sugan Kanvar, wife of the *ṭhākur* Jaba Singh, who died in 1954, contains a photograph of each of the spouses placed on either side of the (somewhat rudimentary) altar, which is topped by a polychrome depicting a satī seated serenely on the pyre, her right hand raised in a sign of blessing and her husband's body in her lap, according to the conventions of the genre. This worship site, situated in an outlying but populous neighborhood of Jodhpur, seems to be relatively deserted.[59] That of Hathideh, on the other hand, attracts large numbers of devotees. It shelters a large black and white photograph, taken on January 12, 1978, by a professional photographer from the neighboring city of Ajitgarh in Sikar District, just as the flames were about to engulf Sarasvati, a thirty-five-year-old woman of the Agarval caste (fig. 30). One sees Sarasvati dressed in her wedding sari, her hands joined in a sign of worship, seated on a coconut-covered pyre. Her husband lies in her lap. This is the photo (retinted as a polychrome) that was used for the mass production of images of Sarasvati, in which the lividity of the corpse contrasts with the brilliant colors (reds, golds, and yellows) of the sari and halo surrounding the holy woman. The realism clashes with the mythological treatment of the image: in the upper right corner, the sun casts its rays on the pyre, which ignites; on the left, a miniaturized Śiva and Pārvatī emerge from clouds to bless the faithful wife; and two swastikas add a final touch of sacredness to the scene (fig. 31). The temple in which this photograph was enshrined remains half-built as a result of caste conflict as well as of the ban on the glorification of satīs. It rather resembles a ritual shed. Nevertheless, the photo of Sarasvati receives twice daily that form of worship known as *ārtī,* which consists of whirling a tray containing an earthen lamp with either five or seven (in any case, an auspicious number) burning wicks, together with the other elements of worship, in a clockwise direction before the divine image. These acts, performed by the custodian of the temple (a Brahman who witnessed the burning of Sarasvati) are accompanied by the muttered recitation of *mantras.*[60] In addition, a religious fair *(melā)* formerly brought her devotees together each year on January 12. That celebration has not taken place since 1988, at which time it too was struck down by law.

Since there is no stopping progress, there was even a cameraman bold enough to cover a cremation from beginning to end. Charan Pal Gupta captured on film the high points of the ceremony. One can see Dasiya exchanging words with police officers (who were present in force among the crowd of onlookers, which also included two highly placed district magistrates) before ascending the pyre. Dasiya, wife of the *ṭhākur* Benketesh, burned herself in the village of Kusuma (in the Banda District of Uttar Pradesh) in 1981. She is said to have declared her intent to become a satī eleven years prior to the death of her husband.[61]

Even in life, satīs seem to take part in the play of their metamorphosis into images, either by imitating the conventional attitudes of satīs in their gestures, or by inventing a new style, nevertheless derived from the ambient sacrificial culture. Om Kanvar, a sixteen-year-old Shekhavat Rajput woman who burned herself on August 30, 1980, in Jharli (a village only three miles from Hathideh), made no solemn declaration of her intention to burn herself. When the body of her husband, who had died in a Jaipur hospital, was brought to the village, she even joined the group of mourners. From the moment a woman decides to become a satī, lamentations are

卐 श्री श्री १००८ सती सरस्वती माता हाथीदह वाली 卐
जिला सिकर (राजस्थान) (बांसल गोत्र अग्रवाल समाज)
मी० पोष शुक्ला ४ सं० २०३४ ता० १२-१-१९७८ ई०

Fig. 30. Photograph of Sarasvati used as worship image at her temple in Hathideh, Rajasthan (private collection).

Fig. 31. Monochrome of Sarasvati Satī. The legend reads "The One Thousand and Eight Times Venerable Mother Satī Sarasvati, of Hathideh, Sikar District (Rajasthan) (of the Bansval lineage of the Agarval community), January 12, 1978."

to cease: given the fact that one is leaving behind the world of grief, impurity, and danger that ordinarily characterizes the period of mourning, to enter into that of sacrifice, such would be of evil portent. But when she was asked to perform his funerary rites, she took a coconut and silently lifted it toward the sky in the gesture of offering to the divinity.

The coconut is intimately associated with funerary ritual.[62] Prior to the removal of the body, it is customary for daughters-in-law to place a coconut on the bier, at the feet of the deceased; family members offer an auspicious number (1, 5, 51, 101, 251, 501, . . .) of coconuts, which are piled onto the pyre. It is with a coconut that a son or the closest male relative will proceed with the "breaking of the skull" of the deceased in order to liberate the *ātman.*[63] The symbolic function of the fruit, which at once stands for the sacrifice and the person of the sacrificer (the meat of the coconut is called "skull"—*khopṛā*[64]), is even more highly marked when the funeral ceremony is accompanied by the burning of a satī. Traditionally, satīs made their way to the burning grounds with coconuts in hand, the which they either distributed to relatives and friends as "consecrated remains" *(prasād)* or offered to the deceased.[65]

Om Kanvar's gesture—unexpected, enigmatic, but charged with funerary connotations—appears to have created a certain sensation among those present. Om Kanvar then circled the corpse four times, keeping it to her right. Now, before mounting the pyre, satīs will circle it three or seven times in the auspicious direction *(pradakṣiṇā).* When a wife does not accompany her husband in death, the chief mourner will circle the pyre in the opposite direction *(prasavya).*[66] The satī's circumambulations *(pherā)* seem to replicate the "seven steps" *(saptapadī)* the bride and groom take around the sacrificial fire in the wedding ceremony. Although they number seven in classical tradition, they are often reduced to four in practice, since it is on her fourth time around that the girl becomes the wife of the man leading her. During the first circumambulation, she will have been the wife of the god Agni; during the second, of the god Soma; and during the third, of the Gandharva, who gives her to her earthly husband during the fourth. By setting herself apart through this idiosyncratic behavior, Om Kanvar did in fact, and quite unbeknownst to her, come very close to the true spirit of the custom. She then cried out *"Hari Om."* This *mantra* is used on different occasions. It is silently recited when one is engaged in meditation, intoned in devotional hymns (*kīrtans*), and chanted while accompanying the deceased to the cremation ground. Unlike "the name of Rām is truth," the ritual formula most often used in this context, *Hari Om* does not have an inauspicious connotation.[67] Om Kanvar followed the procession dressed in her wedding finery, as is the custom when a wife burns herself. She carried a stick of incense in her hand. This was the stick she herself would have used to light the pyre, to her right (the pure side). This version of events is vouched for by witnesses who claim that despite Om Kanvar's pressing requests, no one was willing to light the pyre on which she was to die. There was a police investigation in Jharli that led to the arrest of a number of Rajput leaders as well as the head of the local caste council; these were released and the case was never adjudicated "for want of witnesses." According to another version, more in keeping with popular beliefs concerning the death of satīs, the sun, after Om Kanvar had worshiped it, miraculously engulfed the pyre in flames. Yet another version has it that a young nephew of the husband, assuming the role of a son, carried out that religious duty. The detail of the incense stick takes on its fullness of meaning when one recalls that with her last words, Om Kanvar exacted that *pañcamī* worship (observed the fifth day of each lunar fortnight) be made to "Satī Om Kanvar" and that she be offered "white *pūjāpā*." This is a word that designates the entire range of ingredients used in *pūjā*—the adoration of divine images in a temple or domestic shrine. White *pūjāpā* is so named because all of the constituent elements offered ought in principle to be white, the color symbolizing purity and detachment from earthly goods: milk-based *(barfī)* or confected sugar *(patāśā)* sweets, white flowers, coconut meat, and sugar candy. In her hour of death, Om Kanvar thus saw herself (and above all displayed herself) as a divine image and object of worship. And in fact, a rather impressive temple was erected to enshrine her marble effigy (fig. 32). Savai Bhavani Singh, the Maharajah of Jaipur, attended the ceremony in which the image of Om Kanvar was consecrated in Jharli, on April 17, 1983.

Love in the Extreme

Although the Indian and foreign sources have highly contrasting outlooks with regard to the satī's sacrificial calling, they appear to agree, if nowhere else, in their recognition of the crucial role of love in the matter. Whatever horror the deed inspired in them, the notion of a woman dying out of an excess of conjugal love appeared admirable to a great number of fervent Christians. The Jesuit Roberto de Nobili, founder of the Madurai mission, who was present in 1606 at the burning of four hundred women during the funeral of the Nayak Muttu Krishnappa,[68] rued the fact that they were not his coreligionists, since such would have further heightened the glories

Fig. 32. Worship image of Om Kanvar at her temple in Jharli, Rajasthan (private collection).

of Christian martyrology.[69] In the middle of the sixteenth century, the Lusitanian poet Garcia de Resende evoked the satī's pyre with a lyricism that Kabīr and Jāyasī, the mystical poets of Hindustan, would not have disavowed. Underscoring the "authentic, total, free will" of the Indian women who "cruelly kill themselves out of love and fidelity," Resende exclaims:

> Women of such perfection
> who out of honor and love of their spouse
> suffer such a death
> deserve honor
> and are worthy of praise.[70]

The works of Kabīr (mid-fifteenth century[71]), one of the great "saints" (*sants*) of medieval India, teem with references to the death of the satī. It becomes for him a metaphor symbolizing the supreme form of devotional love *(prem)* and the ultimate goal of mystical experience: the blissful and ineffable union of the wife-soul with her divine Husband. Kabīr links—to the point of fusing the two—the glorious death of the hero *(sūr)* out of loyalty to his master and the sacrifice of the satī for the love of her lord and husband. *Sūr* and satī are emblematic of the pact with death required of anyone who would betake himself upon the steep path to salvation (through union) in God. By way of example, we quote the following couplets, which are part of the corpus of Kabir's *sākhīs* ("witnesses"):

Now has come the time
  when she has obtained her heart's desire:
How could [a Satī] fear death,
  when she has taken the sindhūr-box in her hand?[72]

That death which the world dreads
  is joy for me:
When shall I die? When shall I behold the One
  who is Plenitude and Joy supreme?

Climbing the pyre, the Satī calls and cries:
  'Listen, O my Friend Masān![73]
All the people, as passers-by, have gone away,
  only you and I remain at the end!'

Kabīr, towards that House of Love,
  the path is rough, impassable:
Cut off your head, put it under your feet,
  if you wish to taste Love's flavour!

The Satī has gone out to the pyre,
  remembering her Lord's love,
[And so] hearing the Śabda,[74] the soul has gone out,
  forgetting the body.

Kabīr, that house of Love
  it is not your aunt's house!
With your own hands, cut off your head—
  then you may enter that House!

Love is not grown in the garden,
  love is not sold in the market:
King or commoner, whoever craves for it,
  can have it for the price of his life.

Kabīr, in that liquor shop of Love,
  many have come to sit:
He who pawns his head can drink,
  otherwise, there's nothing doing!

I ask you, O my friend,
  why don't you burn when you are still alive?
After death the Satya will be performed,
  why don't you do it while alive?[75]

This mystic love lies at the heart of the *Padumāvatī* (or *Padmāvat*), an allegorical novel in verse composed in the middle of the sixteenth century by Mālik Muḥammed Jāyasī, a Sufi from the Chishti order who had been influenced by Kabīr. In north India, the Sayings of Kabīr and Jāyasī's *Padmāvat* are second in popularity and "holiness" only to Tulsī Dās's *Rāmcaritmānas.* Now the whole *Padmāvat* may be considered as an illustration of the idea—quite prevalent in Sufi traditions—that love *('iśq),* suffering, and death are inseparable and can only be adequately expressed through the language of fire.[76] The novel's final scene, in which the queens Padmāvatī and Nāgmatī ascend Ratansen's pyre (and the historical backdrop for which would have been the celebrated episode of the mass immolation *[jauhar]* of the Rajput women together with Queen Padminī during Alā ud-din Khiljī's 1303 invasion of Chittorgarh),[77] constitutes a veritable apotheosis, rather than a denouement, of this imagery of mystic love, which can only find its consummation in the incandescence of fire (fig. 33).

This, at least, is the interpretation implicitly advocated by the lawmakers who quite recently decided to expunge from Jāyasī's text this and a number of other passages that were equally suspect of contributing to the glorification of widow sacrifice, which glorification has been condemned by law since 1988. This, however, leaves the way open for supporters of Hindu revival—especially those who in this new version of Quarrel between Ancients and Moderns have declared themselves champions of satīs—to reply that one would, on the same grounds, have to ban those very literary and religious monuments upon which the civilization of "eternal India" was built, and censor Vyāsa, Vālmīki, Kālīdāsa and, closer to our

जौहरकी ज्वाला
जाग उठी चित्तौर-दुर्गमें जौहरकी भीषण ज्वाला ।
हँसती हुई धर्म-रक्षा हित कूद पड़ीं क्षत्रिय-बाला ॥

Fig. 33. The *jauhar* of Padminī and the Rajput women of Chittorgarh, Rajasthan: illustration taken from the "Special Issue on Women" of the Hindi-language *Kalyāṇ* series (Gorakhpur: Gita Press). The legend reads: "The fearsome blaze of the Chittorgarh Fort *jauhar* rose into the sky. The young Kṣatriya women threw themselves into it, laughing, in the defense of *dharma*."

time, Vivekānanda and even Tagore, a defender of women's emancipation and a supporter of Hindu reform who nonetheless paid homage to the satīs of a bygone age.[78] To be sure, one would also have to pillory Ananda Kentish Coomaraswamy, that brilliant art historian so admired by Romain Rolland, who put his polemical talents to use by playing the devil's advocate in favor of the cause of satīs, Indian conceptions of love and marriage, and the "Oriental Woman." She alone, Coomaraswamy argued, was capable of fully asserting her freedom and femininity, through that very quality which her detractors took to be the mark of her alienation and servitude: her boundless devotion to her husband. This, he explained, was because in Asia, love and marriage are not founded, as they are in the West, on passion (the "accidents of sensibility"), but on "the fulfillment of a traditional design." Rather than using the bond of marriage to artificially perpetuate a passing fancy, the two partners are expected to conform to cultural models. So it is that in India at least, "the way of ego-assertion cannot be a royal road to realization of the Self," since "Hinduism justifies no cult of ego-expression, but aims consistently at spiritual freedom." An Indian woman can only obtain this liberation by adhering to the role the group, society, and tradition have assigned to her from time immemorial: that of a "true woman," a perfect wife—in short, of a satī. What this means is that in order to realize her femininity, she need only *be:* moreover, as he reminds us, "the root meaning of the word *[satī]* is essential being." The Western Woman, on the contrary, at least since the advent of the industrial age, has lost her femininity and her power since, in her struggle to stand up for her rights and lay claim to her autonomy, she has adopted the values, language, and even the behavior of men. Thus, without being intrinsically superior, the Eastern Woman "is perhaps an older, purer and more specialised type, but certainly a universal type,"[79] while the woman of industrialized society, because she has strayed from that feminine ideal, represents a perversion of the same. (In 1912 Coomaraswamy presented the London Sociological Society with a provocative paper on this theme.[80])

It is interesting to note that in the 1987 *Kalyāṇ* series special issue on women *(Nārī Aṅk),* the illustration of this duality between the traditional woman and the modern woman no longer portrays the latter as a foreigner, but rather as a westernized Indian (figs. 34 and 35). Under the title "The Old Style Woman," a plate comprising twelve illustrations with legends depicts the "meritorious life" of the housewife: dressed simply, humble and smiling, she sweeps, pounds rice, grinds spices, churns butter, does the cooking by herself, works the spinning-wheel, sews, dresses her child, recites ritual religious texts, fans her husband as he takes his meal alone, keeps the household accounts, and listens with hands joined in prayer as a brahman reads devotional texts to her. On another page, "The Modern Woman," elegantly and meticulously dressed, self-assured if not arrogant, reads her newspaper, smokes a cigar in her club, puts on make-up, plays tennis, goes to the movies with men other than her husband *(par-puruṣ),* turns the complete care of her children over to a nurse, asks her husband to bring her a glass of water as she works at her desk, eats out alone, speaks out at meetings in which she addresses her male audience in a loud voice (the traditional woman, in the upper castes at least, is expected to speak, out of modesty, in a nearly inaudible voice, and to avoid as much as possible all contact with men other than her husband), takes walks with her male friends, takes tea in the company of other men, and does her own shopping.[81] *Kalyāṇ* is not simply a Hindi monthly with a wide readership; its special editions, such as the present issue on Woman, with its 800 pages of serried text supplemented with numerous illustrations, takes the role of a *vade mecum* and catechism for the present Iron Age (the *kaliyuga*) in which Tradition, threatened by Modernity, is compelled to have recourse to the media in order to ensure its own survival.[82]

Whereas Coomaraswamy saw in the sacrifice of faithful wives the most striking proof of perfect spousal unity within the Indian conception of marriage as well as the mark of India's spiritual calling in opposition to the materialism of the West, Hindus who have recently mobilized themselves in a crusade against acculturation and the loss of their national identity—and who, in order to preserve their cultural heritage, have rallied around the banner of "Hindu-ness" *(hindutva:* the word, ironically, is a neologism—worse yet, a hybrid formed from the Persian *hindū)*—have buttressed the theme of conjugal love with a veritable defense and glorification of the voluntary death of satīs, an argument whose extremism would no doubt have deeply troubled our refined historian, who passed away in September 1947, a month after India gained its independence.

Omkar Singh, a former high official in the Rajasthan state government and activist within the Committee for the Defense of Satī *Dharma*[83] (founded in September 1987), later wrote and signed a petition against the Commission of Satī (Prevention) Bill, which was made law in 1988. In that petition, he makes the following argument: Love is the foundation for the ideology of *bhakti,* the great devotionalist movement that has constituted the dominant form of Hinduism since the beginning of the common era. Furthermore, since earthly love has forever been recognized as the primal impulse of the human being, it has become the symbolic expression of sublimated Love for the Godhead, even as it has integrated this religious

प्राचीन नारी
स्वच्छ रखती है घर-द्वारको बुहार सदा , धान कूट लेती औ चाकी भी चलाती है ।
सूत कातती है और माखन बिलोती घर , भोजन विशुद्ध निज हाथसे बनाती, है ॥
करती सिलाई है, लड़ाती लाड़ लाड़लेको , पाठ करती है, निज पतिको जिमाती है ।
आय और व्ययका हिसाब लिखती है , हरि-गाथा सुनती है पुण्यजीवन बिताती है ॥

Figs. 34 and 35. "The Old Style Woman" and "The Modern Woman": illustrations taken from the same "Special Issue on Women" from the *Kalyāṇ* series (Gorakhpur: Gita Press).

आधुनिक नारी

पढ़े अखबार, है सिगारका उड़ाती धुआँ , करती सिंगार भी पामेड पाउडरसे ।
क्लब और सिनेमा जाती पर-पुरुषोंके साथ , दाईपर बच्चोंका उतार भार सरसे ॥
पतिसे मँगाती जल, खाती खुद होटलमें , वक्ता सुनाती पुरुषोंको तार स्वरसे ।
मित्रों संग घूमती है, जाती चायपार्टियोंमें , आती है बाजारमें निकलकर घरसे ॥

dimension of sublimation into the very social institution that ratifies it—marriage. This constant transference, from the religious to the subjective, together with the inscription of said transference into that sacrament upon which the entire social edifice as well as the perpetuation of the "race" is founded, explain the valorization of concepts like *satītva* to define a woman's boundless fidelity, chastity, virtue, and devotion. In the final analysis, it is in women that family stability is grounded, a family stability that is the foundation for social order as well as the purity of the "race"—a word that returns like a leitmotif throughout this thick document. Moreover, the spiritualization of marital love leads to the principle of absolute interdependence, from rebirth to rebirth, which in turn leads quite naturally to the desire (on the part of the woman, it goes without saying) to give up her life upon the death of her spouse. The notion of any possible symmetry between men and women is unthinkable to the Hindu traditionalist.[84]

It is on these premises that Omkar Singh rejects any idea of violence brought to bear against women: their immolation was and remains a voluntary act, a proof of a supreme love, modeled on Devotion, the same Devotion to which the majority of Hindus adhere. It follows that to ban these sacrifices is to violate the most sacred values of "Hindu-ness" and consequently to pave the way for the disintegration of India. There may perhaps have been a few scattered cases in history of women who were forced to burn themselves, but these unfortunate episodes, showcased by missionaries in the colonial period, and by anyone whose interests lie in projecting a negative image of Hinduism, are but the exceptions that make the rule. And in Rajasthan at least, the state of the Indian Union most directly targeted by the 1988 Act, no woman was ever burned against her will.[85]

Another petition, dating from 1989, goes even further in this direction.[86] Its author, Jeevan Kulkarni, a freelance journalist from Bombay and a militant in the RSS, intersperses his argument with quotations drawn from the corpus of foreign and Indian eyewitness accounts. These quotations are for the most part truncated, distorted, or couched in a tendentious discourse that undermines their intended meaning. So, for example, one discovers that Bernier was a staunch supporter of the rite. Without giving an extended account of the author's rhetoric (a feverish defense of an "eternal India" threatened by a secret plot between the West and Islam) at this juncture, we simply make mention of a passing remark he makes in a discussion of the strictly voluntary nature of these immolations:

Let me elucidate Satis presumed screaming 'in agony' when actually fire flares up. There are many cases of Satis meeting their end without uttering a shriek or betraying any sign of agony. (It is also wrong to presume that they were stupefied or intoxicated.) And even if they screamed . . . it is not unnatural. Is it not a fact that sometimes one shrieks in the state of ecstasy?[87]

While the deliberate perversion of an orthodox value—love, the sacred duty of women—and the highly idiosyncratic view of amorous ecstasy these polemical texts use to the sole end of justifying widow sacrifice quite legitimately shock us, they nonetheless should not blind us to the fact that Indian tradition acknowledges the potentially lethal side of love. Whereas normative Hindu ideology makes a place for it, recognizing in love one of the four essential goals of human activity (*puruṣārtha*s), the medical literature as well as scholarly treatments of erotica (Vātsyāyana's *Kāmasūtra*[88]) classify it among the *doṣa*s, a term that denotes, as we have seen, a flaw or fault as well as a humoral disorder. Once again, we see that sin and pathology are intimately intertwined, and that the body is the mirror of the passions.[89] These texts describe the ten stages through which the pains of love lead inexorably to death, unless one applies the necessary means for halting their progression. For Caraka, this takes the form of purification and expiation; for Vātsyāyana it is the immediate satisfaction of amorous desires, since in such circumstances unrequited love is a life-threatening situation, to be counted as a case of *āpaddharma*—the licit transgression of *dharma* in times of distress. In south India there exists a tradition of love as a fatal illness; this seems not to have been a mere convention of ancient poetics, since one finds stele in the Tamil country erected in memory of betrothed girls, hopelessly in love, who died of despair.[90] In north India, and most particularly in Rajasthan, bardic literature abounds with similar stories, and there is no lack of memorial stones to women who became satīs "before their time." Given the extent to which Indian funerary culture, as has been noted, is characterized by its minimal individuation of the dead, the erection of those stele is all the more remarkable. It is as if these women who died for love had attained the same individuality, the same freedom, as the renouncer, the heroic warrior, or certain ancestors who had died a "bad death." In the midst of transient earthly existence, the funerary inscriptions stand as a foretaste of eternity.

This tacit accord between Eros and Thanatos, which plays itself out so differently in India than in the West, opens the way to every sort of excess: brides-to-be throw themselves on the pyre of a fiancé whom they have never seen; female lovers flaunt their husband by immolating themselves together with the body of their paramour; adulteresses and even murderesses expiate their crimes, with brio, by becoming satīs;[91] women follow their young brother-in-law (the *devar,* a possible substitute for the husband in the obsolete tradition of levirate, which lives on in feminine fantasies) into death;[92] proud Rajput women have a pyre raised if their husband appears before them alive, but defeated in battle; ranis, anticipating a glorious death, burn themselves without further ado, as if to force the hand of fate; co-wives argue bitterly over the privilege of being burned or leaping first into the burning pit; sisters ascend their brother's pyre,[93] and mothers their son's.[94] Women even become satīs for a stepson or grandson. The height of paradox is attained when the husband is one whom the satī has fled and loathed: such was the case with Guman Kanvar, the eldest daughter of the famous Shardul Singh (1681–1742), a prince of Shekhavati who wrested Jhunjhunu and Fatehpur from the hands of the Nawabs of Hissar. Married in 1739 to the Rao Chater Singh Hada of Indegarh, she refused to live with her husband, who on their wedding day had insulted her brother Zoravar Singh. Yet she burned herself on a separate pyre when she learned that her husband had died suddenly.[95] In the Deshnok temple of Karṇī-jī (the deified Charan woman who is the tutelary goddess of the Rajahs of Bikaner), there is a cenotaph containing the image of two women: these are Mankumari, Karṇī's granddaughter, and her friend Sakhi, a woman of the Carpenter (Khati) caste who burned herself along with Mankumari when the latter, upon receiving news of her husband's death, declared herself a satī.[96] Finally, one may also immolate oneself for the love of an animal: in the village of Miti in Gujarat, one can see the stele of twelve young Charan girls who followed a nilgai—a type of antelope with a bluish hide—in death.[97]

Matters may at times take a fantastic and even a "camp horror" turn, as in the case cited in a questionnaire addressed, on May 8, 1817, to pundits in the employ of the Court of Appeal of the British East India Company. According to the questionnaire, a Jogi widow had had her husband exhumed in order that she might burn herself with his corpse. The Jogis of Bengal belong to those communities that bury their dead instead of burning them.[98] Faced with this particularly cruel variant of the rite, in which the wife is buried alive in her husband's tomb, the British decided to prohibit it, arguing that it was not sanctioned by the *Śāstras*. The macabre scenario contrived by Bastari as a response to the new legislation at once illustrates the extremes of an Indian woman's love and the ironies of history, as will be shown below. By insisting that the rite be performed in conformity with the tenets of Hindu law, the British ended up creating unprecedented ritual situations.[99] An 1823 ruling by the Court of Criminal Justice in Calcutta sentenced a Brahman from Gorakhpur District (in Benares Division) to seven years in prison: Digambar Pandey had lit the pyre upon which his daughter Achar-ji had been burned; he had gathered the wood and raised up the pile with his own hands. Achar-ji "accompanied" her brother Jagmohan, who had died in his father's house. Jagmohan's wife, who was visiting her natal village at the time of his death, burned herself there with her husband's turban, which had been sent to her for that purpose. In the eyes of the law, two prohibitions had been disregarded in this case: in the first instance, "dying with" is restricted to wives (to *pativratās*, "wives faithful to their conjugal vow" according to the strict wording of the *Śāstras*); in the other, "dying after" *(anumaraṇa)* is forbidden to Brahman women. According to the reading adopted by the new rulers of India, the sister-in-law had thereby violated indigenous law. While Digambar Pandey's life was spared, it was only because he had been granted extenuating circumstances: as he claimed in his defense, he had "consented to be instrumental to [his daughter's] destruction on her imprecating the wrath of heaven on his head"—and nothing can be more dreadful than a satī's curse. According to W. Dorin, the fourth judge of the Court, the legal opinion of the pundits consulted on the case was "a good specimen of their absolutely nonsensical ideas on the subject of criminal law." What did the pundits say in their learned legal finding, composed in Sanskrit? Among other things, the following:

> Although it is not allowable, and indeed is contrary to law and usage, for a sister to sacrifice her life by burning her body on the funeral pile of her brother, yet it must be presumed that she, in some former stage of existence, did some act, the effect of which was to impress her with an irresistible belief that burning with her deceased brother was the only means of salvation in the next world, or that the excessive love for her brother caused her to form a violent resolution to burn herself on her brother's pile, and to curse those who attempted to dissuade her from her purpose.[100]

The pundits pointed out that it falls to the father to light his son's pyre in such a circumstance—when the son dies before his father. Although the father's act was the *material* cause of his daughter's death, one could not hold him responsible for a death that she had freely chosen. One can well imagine the ways in which a sensationalist author might milk such a story in which, when all is said and done, one has a father lighting the pyre of his daughter, who is unlawfully sacrificing herself out of love for her brother, while her sister-in-law, infringing the same laws, burns alone a few miles away.

The *Parliamentary Papers,* a veritable "ocean of stories" of modern India, are rife with cases of mothers yielding to the fatal power of love for the sake of a son. Tradition considers these to be the most exalted of satīs (within the group's internal hierarchy), as evinced in their designation as *mahāsatīs* (or *māstis*)—"great satīs."[101] So it is that the list of women burned in 1820 includes the case of a forty-year-old Rajput woman who immolated herself in Kanpur (in the Patna Division), on September 8. "The wife of Chutta Sing was with child when he died, and about 16 years after his death, she burnt herself with the corpse of her son, in contradiction to the tenets of the Hindoo law."[102] On November 13, 1822, a seventy-year-old Brahman woman, who had also been a widow for sixteen years, immolated herself with the body of her son in a village in Ghazipur District (in Benares Division).[103] One might suppose (and this was the official interpretation at the time) that these women died out of despair, rather than as genuine satīs: already afflicted with the calamity of widowhood, they would lose all reason for living if their son died as well. It seems to me that we need to go further in our reflections, and recall that in Indian tradition the son is the replica of his father. This is an important point: he does not replace him at his mother's side; he *is* his own father, "re-born" as an embryo in the maternal womb.[104] It is difficult to say whether these highly archaic notions, which were likely unknown to many Hindus at the beginning of the nineteenth century, played the role of unconscious stimuli. In any event, they continue to subsist in the symbolic realm, in Rajasthan if nowhere else. In certain castes and on certain occasions, a widow who has a son may wear the sari or veil called *pīliyā,* which is emblematic of both conjugal happiness *(suhāg)* and motherhood.[105] She will no longer be permitted to wear a nose ring *(nath),* an ornament of marriage, but she may keep the discreet nose stud *(loṅg),* which has the same value, albeit with a lower level of prestige. It is as if the presence of a son maintained the fiction of conjugal happiness, above and beyond the reality of her widowhood, inasmuch as he is the physical and spiritual incarnation of his father. As the saying goes, "the mother of a son is only half a widow."[106] Whatever the case, we are clearly brought back here, I believe, to the theme of guilt. I have already indicated that a wife who has not burned herself upon the death of her husband may find herself haunted by the feeling that she has wronged him on two counts. Guilty of his death according to popular belief, the guilt of the "husband eater" *(khasam khānī)* is compounded by the weakness that allows her to outlive him. Year after year, she will know in her heart of hearts that she has failed him in her wifely duty. The trauma of losing a son reawakens her painful guilt feelings. At this point, the woman may give in to her despair and throw herself on her son's pyre. Her sacrifice redeems and annuls her fault even as it transports her to the firmament of faithful wives, to that same Heaven in which the "great satīs" shine with the brilliance of a thousand Arundhatīs (the incarnation of the ideal wife, Arundhatī, wife of the sage Vasiṣṭha, is also the personification of Alcor, a star in the Great Bear). And if she is pregnant when her husband dies, as in the case of the Rajput woman from Kanpur, her guilt feeling at surviving him is shifted away from her husband and onto her unborn child.

UNDER THE SPELL OF SACRIFICE

In the preceding pages, we have sought to better understand the formation of the deadly vow, and to uncover the complex motivations whose interplay induces that subjective state that collective representations portray as a phenomenon of possession: the *bhāv* "comes on" and the *sat* "rises." These two expressions give a fair account of the transition from impulse to objectification. When people say that the *bhāv* comes on *(bhāv ānā),* they are referring to a subjective experience, even if this indirect grammatical turn of phrase already betrays a process of objectification. Indeed, in its most common usage, the Sanskrit word *bhāva* designates the dominant emotion coloring a given moment in one's affective life, an emotion rooted in one's intrinsic nature, one's *svabhāva*—an Indian variant on the notion of idiosyncrasy.[1] On the other hand, when people speak of the rise of the *sat,* they are alluding to a power that is external to the subject, a power they also consider to be the most free and spontaneous manifestation of the ego (and this is part of what makes it problematic). In fact, the *sat* rises because the woman is already possessed of this exceptional virtue: "satī-hood" is its outward manifestation, as revealed by the *sat.* Like a fire brooding beneath the embers, it remains in a latent state until the day it discloses itself in the *bhāv.*

The symbiosis between this power and the woman who has conceived or received it within the innermost recesses of her ego is such that many Hindus imagine the cremation of satīs to be a magical phenomenon of self-combustion: through her miraculous powers, the woman produces within her own body the fire that will consume her. This belief, moreover, is in perfect keeping with the myth of the goddess Satī, who was the wife of the god Śiva in a previous life (she is later reborn as Pārvatī): in order to avenge an outrage against Śiva, she withdraws to the sacrificial ground and burns herself with the fire of her yoga *(yogāgni)*. Some have seen in this primal Satī the eponymous goddess of human satīs, and in the "Episode of the Destruction of Dakṣa's Sacrifice" *(Dakṣa-yajña-vidhvaṃsa)* the origin myth of widow-burning, a matter to which we will return.

What should we retain from the story-, dream-, and interview-fragments we have brought together in this jigsaw puzzle of a book? While the real-life experience of the *bhāv* remains impenetrable to us, we can perhaps better grasp the psychological processes that are brought into play when "satī-hood" irrupts. The disparate parts of the whole that we have used to piece together the case histories of these satīs seem to bring an essential element to light: during the short span of time (usually a few hours) separating her declaration of intent from her death on the pyre, the satī becomes transformed—for her family circle, for her throng of devotees, but also, it seems, for herself—into a supernatural being. Om Kanvar speaks of herself in the third person when she demands that "white *pūjāpā*" be offered to the satī Om Kanvar.[2] This way of objectifying oneself, of adopting a persona, and of taking an active part in the construction of one's own myth and cult is, in my view, what allows women who have declared themselves satīs to carry through on their deadly vow.

Earlier, I mentioned my encounter with one of the extremely rare "living satīs" of Rajasthan, a woman who had survived her own sacrifice through timely police intervention.[3] The events transpired on March 12, 1985, in the Shekhavati village of Devipura. Jasvant Kanvar had seen her vow through to its very end. She had taken her place on the pyre. Her body had been buried in coconuts, with only her veiled head (since the satī, in the moment of her death, pronounces words that are meant to be heard) and right hand (because a final gesture of blessing is expected) remaining uncovered. When I questioned her, however, she was unable to tell me how the *bhāv* had come on to her. A feeling of trust, if not complicity, had, after all, been created between us. Had she not given me, as *prasād* ("consecrated remains"), a Polaroid snapshot of herself on the pyre on which she had nearly died, as well as a tiny piece of folded newspaper containing the miraculous ashes *(vibhūti)* from the unfinished cremation? She looked at me with a gaze so intense that I shall never forget it and said "It is He. It is by His grace. It wasn't me." She deferentially pointed to Śiva with the gesture a devotee makes when receiving a divine boon *(vardān)*. And she spoke the truth, in the sense that eight years after the fact, she truly saw things that way. Perhaps that is how she also experienced them. Śiva, whom her deceased husband had chosen from among all the other gods as his object of worship, had possessed her in the *bhāv:* it was He; it was not she. There could be no more powerful expression of objectification, of that process through which the subject voids from consciousness a given traumatic content, by dissociating it from his experience in order to project it onto an object belonging to what Georges Devereux has called the "cold storage" of culture.[4] When Jugal Kanvar's eldest son spoke to me of his mother, saying "the One Hundred-eight Times Holy Satī Jugal Kanvar," he who, when still a child, had lit the pyre on which she went up in flames, I felt myself to be in the presence of the same psychological process. Transforming a mother whom one had seen burn with one's own eyes—and by one's own hand—into an abstract figure absorbed, through the magic of an impersonal designation charged with symbolic efficacy (the number 108 is one that actualizes ritual acts and formulas[5]), into a faceless crowd of blissful deities may be interpreted as an unconscious strategy for ridding oneself of guilt feelings by couching them in acceptable and soothing terms from within one's cultural idiom.[6]

The interpenetration and ongoing interaction between subjective experience and cultural idioms may be observed with great clarity through recent (i.e., post-1940) case histories collected in the field. The death of Hem Kanvar, as recounted to me by her female in-laws, is exemplary in this respect. This Rajput woman from the Chauhan clan, married to a Rathor of the Jodha branch, burned herself in 1943 in Devpuri, a hamlet in Ajmer District not far from the town of Kishangarh (renowned for its school of miniature painting). She was the first satī of her lineage and, so far as I can gather, the first of the new satīs in that region. When her husband Narain Singh was taken to the hospital, Hem Kanvar received from the god Tejā-jī the order to leave her *sasurāl*—the in-laws' family home, in which Hindu women traditionally live.

In Rajasthan, Tejā is a highly popular deified hero whose specialty lies in curing his devotees of snakebite. Other deities—Gogā-jī, Kallā-jī, Kesariyā Kuñvar, and Bhabhūtā Siddh, to name but the best known—also possess this skill, so useful to villagers in this desert region. The Saga of Tejā combines the theme of heroic death in the protection of cows with that of the immolation of the faithful wife.[7] There are several markedly different variants of the story, all of which are nonetheless consistent in holding up Tejā as the model of heroic sacrifice. Tejā learns that his parents have married him off in his childhood but have hidden that bond from him. Mounted on a horse with a bluish-white coat, he sets out to seek his wife in her village. On

Fig. 36. Popular religious image of Tejā-jī. The legend reads "The Venerable True to his Word Hero, Tejā-jī Mahārāj" (private collection).

the way, he saves a cobra from death by fire. The snake, however, far from showing him any gratitude, threatens to bite him: wearied of his reptilian existence, he has been seeking death. Tejā asks him for a few days of grace: if only for one time, he would like to see the woman who is his wife, but promises the serpent that he will then return and offer him his life. Upon arriving at the village, he discovers that Minas have stolen its cows.[8] He makes a solemn vow to free them and courageously carries out this sacred duty. Horribly wounded in combat, he appears once again before the cobra. "Where can I bite you," the latter asks him. "You are covered with wounds; no part of your skin can take my bite." Tejā sticks his tongue out at him (fig. 36). His wife Pemal De (or Bodal De) later becomes a satī.

Jat farmers are great devotees of Tejā-jī.[9] Many Jats wear a silver amulet around their neck depicting the god astride his mount, brandishing a sword as the snake bites his tongue. Songs to Tejā are sung before plowing-time to insure a good harvest. Commemorative religious fairs (*melās*), which take place in several towns of Rajasthan from the fifth to the fifteenth day of the bright fortnight of the month of *Bhādrapada* (August-September), are occasions for colorful livestock fairs. The Kishangarh region is an important center for Tejā's cult. The god is supposed to have been married at the holy site of Pushkar, to which his parents would have gone on pilgrimage; or else in the village of Paner, where his in-laws lived. It is said that he saved the snake in Rupnagar, and that the snake bit him fatally in Sursura; all of these sites are located within a twenty-five-mile radius of Kishangarh. There is not a single town in the region that has not dedicated a shrine to the god, and the hamlet of Devpuri (situated a few miles from Kishangarh) is no exception.

Narain Singh died and his body was sent to the family, who raised their voices in lamentation, as dictated by custom. At this point Hem Kanvar exclaimed "Rām, Rām, do not cry," and her words were immediately interpreted as a declaration of her desire to become a satī.[10] Suddenly, as I was told by a young aunt of the husband who had been present at the scene (she is now in her 80s), Hem, who had previously been dark complected, became white and radiant. The hair on her head and over her entire body stood on end. She purified herself with milk and Ganges River water that had been brought back from a pilgrimage. The *pīliyā* veil she wore prior to taking her ritual bath remains enshrined in the house to this day.[11] It is possessed of miraculous powers: in order to stave off labor pains, pregnant women sprinkle the veil with lustral water, which they drink as "foot nectar" (*carṇāmṛt:* the consecrated water with which a disciple or devotee has washed a divine image or the feet of a guru or a holy man, which the disciple then drinks). Hem Kanvar herself cleansed the corpse and saw to all the ritual details. Then she climbed onto the pyre, a coconut in her hand, and her youngest brother-in-law lit the fire. By way of thanking him, Hem Kanvar tossed him her wedding bracelets, promising him offspring; her sister-in-law conceived shortly thereafter. (Her daughter, whom I met, presently lives in Hem Kanvar's former house.) The cremation took place at five o'clock in the afternoon, and drew an enormous crowd. The old woman who told me the story, still elated by the memory of the event, assured me that the satī remained smiling until the very end—that her head, her veil, and her bearing remained unaffected as the flames consumed her body.

Since the event, her in-laws have resided in the house where Hem Kanvar became a satī. It is both a place of residence (like any other) and a religious site, with certain areas set apart: the place where the satī performed her ablutions before burning herself has become a *sanctum.* Narain Singh's aunt, who officiates in her cult, performs the morning and evening worship of the "Mother Satī," who is depicted in the abstract form of the Goddess as *Śakti* (here the goddess Durgā Jagadambā, "Durgā, Mother of the World"), in the form of a trident set between a sun and moon, the whole painted in vermilion. Hem Kanvar appears in her human form in the memorial built to her eight years after her death. Seated serenely in the midst of the flames, she holds her husband on her lap, with a silver-bordered red veil haloing the sacred image. A lengthy inscription is found beneath the tableau, while to the right, a crude stela portrays the satī in a standing position, with her hands joined in reverence to Narain Singh who, while turbaned after the fashion of every self-respecting Rajput, is barefoot. As for Hem Kanvar's former house, it contains another image of Durgā Jagadambā—that of a vermilion trident housed inside a stylized niche surmounted by a sun and moon. Her dimension as *śakti* is highlighted by the great sword *(talvār),* the emblem of the terrible aspect of the demon-slaying Goddess, that rests diagonally across the niche. Here, however, the satī receives no worship (figs. 37 to 39).

We must resign ourselves to the fact that we shall never know anything about the real-life woman whose name was Hem Kanvar. The short religious booklet (a *khyāl* in the Marwari tongue) a poet from the city of Byavar dedicated to her in 1953 enables us only to gauge the fullness, the opacity, of her mythification.[12] Moreover, all the "life stories" of the new satīs *(satī-caritr)* resemble one another to the point of confusion. These publications serve as bases for ritual worship *(jot);* the biographical elements in them are inserted into the devotional songs, invocations, and prayers addressed to a given "Mother Satī" in her cult. The same vignettes, and occasionally the same cover illustration, reinforce the sense of *déjà vu* that permeates the corpus.

What can we hope to learn from the reconstructed persona that informants and the hagiography present to us? The story of Hem Kanvar's call to satī-hood is related in an indirect fashion: her vision of the god Tejā-jī and her change of domicile are so many signs of her transition from profane experience to the sacredness of "satī-hood." Tejā, who embodies all the virtues of supreme sacrifice (faithfulness, abnegation, heroism) shows Hem Kanvar the way by manifesting himself in her presence: he announces the death of her husband in a veiled manner, and invites her to leave the "world of acts" *(karma-bhūmi).* The vision plays the same role as do dreams in other accounts.[13] The order to leave her husband's house is even more explicit, even if at first blush it appears obscure. According to one of the

Fig. 37. Shrine of Hem Kanvar at Devpuri (Rajasthan). The satī is represented in the abstract form of the goddess Durgā-Jagadambā (private collection).

legends in the Tejā cycle, the god, unhappy in Kishangarh, appeared in a dream to the headman of Parbatsar (in present-day Nagaur District) to command that he establish his image and cult there.[14] In this light, Hem Kanvar could have projected an episode from the god's story into her own experience.

If this account is about objectification, it is also connected to another order of signification, which partakes of a most ancient stratum of religious ideology. Here, the husband's house would symbolize the world of acts, and the new domicile both the celestial abode and the hut in which the preliminary phase of sacrifice, called *dīkṣā*, is performed. In *dīkṣā*, the "consecrated one" *(dīkṣita)* withdraws into a hut, an image of the womb, within which he returns to an embryonic state, relinquishing his profane body as a means to generating a sacrificial body through extenuating and purifying

Fig. 38. Image of the goddess Durgā-Jagadambā in the marital household of Hem Kanvar at Devpuri, Rajasthan (private collection).

ascetic practices.[15] The use made of Hem Kanvar's veil commends this hypothesis. For while the number of satī-related miracles is beyond count, to my knowledge there is no other example of a veil being used prophylactically against the pangs of childbirth.[16] In fact, the initiand is made to wear a sheet representing the fetal caul *(ulba),* and over it a black antelope skin representing the placenta *(jarāyu).*[17] To be sure, the women of Devpuri have no notion whatsoever of the symbolism of *dīkṣā,* which makes it all the more remarkable that they could unknowingly have rediscovered so archaic a theme. Tradition reinvents itself by drawing on the bric-a-brac of cultural artifacts at hand.[18]

The metamorphosis of Hem Kanvar at the time of her possession affords us additional proof of this dynamic. Although dark-skinned, she became white and radiant in the eyes of the women around her.[19] This brings to mind an episode drawn from the mythology of the goddess Pārvatī. Although the Purāṇas contain several variants on the story,[20] the plot can be summarized in a few words: wounded in her pride by Śiva, who has insulted her by calling her "Black," Pārvatī, through a series of harsh austerities, obtains a complexion of incomparable brilliance, which earns her the name of Gaurī, the "Fair." In Rajasthan, people celebrate the divine couple of Śiva and Gaurī, which constitutes the model of Hindu marriage, during

Fig. 39. Memorial to Hem Kanvar at Devpuri, Rajasthan (private collection).

the *Gaṅgaur* festival, which is especially observed by women—girls of marriageable age and "happily married wives" *(saubhāgyavatī)* alike.[21]

Hem Kanvar not only changes her skin: all the hair on her head and body also stands on end. "To have one's hair stand up" is a popular Hindi expression designating a state of heightened terror. Unbound hair, knotted into a tangled mass or, on the contrary, standing on end like a mane or halo of flames, is the mark of the "terrible" form of the Goddess, especially in tantric iconography, where she is known as Kālī or Cāmuṇḍā. We cannot enter here into the jungle of Hindu expressions regarding hair and the wearing of hair, a territory into which anthropologists, historians of religion, and a few psychoanalysts have ventured.[22] Let it suffice to recall that hair that is unbound—i.e., uncombed, unbraided, or unknotted—denotes the impurity that befalls a woman during menstruation, childbirth, and mourning, as well as during intercourse. This is an impurity charged with ambivalence since the social and sexual avoidance occasioned by pollution in the first three cases is commensurate with the erotic power of (usually luxuriant) feminine hair, which is allowed to hang freely in a woman's lovemaking. In addition, long hair (that has never been cut) has a sacred value for women, since it is required for marriage, in the same way as virginity.[23] It is associated with *suhāg,* the auspicious state of wifehood. When a high-caste woman becomes a widow, it is a canon of orthopraxy that she shave her head like the Buddhist or Jain nun. Comparable to being branded with a hot iron, this act stands as a badge of infamy, of punishment for those sins and omissions of wifely duty that are the cause of her widowhood. So it is that the mere sight of scissors can occasion anxiety or panic. Shanta, whom a doctor had advised to trim her hair slightly as a protection against lice, exclaimed in horror: "But I have both a son and a grandson!" (widows who have children are spared having their heads shaved). Those *dharma* commentators who recommend that widows offer their hair *(keś caṛhānā)* explain that a widow's braids, like a noose, would strangle her husband in his celestial abode.

According to popular belief, the hair (of both sexes) is the favorite haunt of sin, which lodges and proliferates in the profusion of its natural vegetation. Hair would be to the human body what the forest is to socialized space: an image of disorganization, nondifferentiation, instinct, and taboo, but also of spiritual liberation. Even today, all persons who profess to be ascetics symbolize their antisocial stand through two distinct bodily characteristics: nudity and the rejection of conventional hairstyles. This group is divided into those who are "hairy" *(keśī),* with their impressive piled-up matted hair *(jaṭā),* and those who are "shaven" *(avkeś).* So it is that the Jogatis of Karnataka, servants of the goddess Yellammā and "sacred prostitutes" (*devadāsīs*), have as their principal attribute a head of hair that is as unkempt as possible: never cut, never combed, and never washed.[24] Conversely, a woman's hairdressing is one of the insignia of her status as a married woman. During the first part of the wedding ceremony, the young bride leaves her freshly washed hair undone. But following the rite of the "seven steps" around the sacrificial fire, the husband parts her hair and smears the part so formed with vermilion.[25] Thereafter, with the exception of the circumstances mentioned above, the woman must always have her hair dressed. Her hair must be tamed—braided, knotted into a chignon, or held in place with combs.[26] In this way, the exuberance, attraction, and danger of that part of her body which seems to escape her can be neutralized.

Gananath Obeysekere has shown how the sudden growth of matted locks on the heads of women possessed by the god Kataragama—whose shrine, located in the southeastern extremity of Sri Lanka, has drawn an ever-increasing throng of Hindu and Buddhist devotees—may be interpreted as a symbol of the god's *śakti.* The unconscious motivations underlying the outbreak of this symptom in the different cases he has studied mirror a symbol system that derives for the most part from Tantra and yoga. Intrapsychic conflicts and private tragedies find their resolution in an ecstatic trance that radically modifies their content and inscribes itself on the body in the extraordinary manifestation of matted locks that seem to belong to another order of nature.[27]

It seems to me that this interpretation casts the unusual metamorphosis of Hem Kanvar in a new light. The satī is viewed as *śakti,* and the sudden pallor of her skin and her horripilating hair as somatic expressions of the duality of the Goddess (Gaurī/Kālī). This last feature partakes of the miracles commonly attributed to satīs: in their moment of death, their hair stands straight up toward heaven, in defiance of the flames. If objectification is what makes it possible for satīs to carry through on their resolve to burn themselves (when no violence has been used, it goes without saying), their transformation into *śakti*s is what makes the spectacle of their death bearable to onlookers. This, at least, is my personal feeling. Hindus who believe in the supernatural powers of satīs do not see human women burning, but rather the divine energy revealing itself in broad daylight. This is not a primitive belief to be contrasted with higher forms of a religion that has been purged of all impurity. The satīs' followers are found in every milieu and walk of life, although it is true that satī cults undeniably have a folk dimension to them. To be sure, there are many Hindus who do not share in this belief: the "Deorala affair" (the September 1987 cremation of

Rup Kanvar) has shown to what extent Indian public opinion is divided on the issue. Finally, we must also take into account those persons who, without subscribing to it, exploit popular belief for political or economic ends.

In the long list of miracles attributed to Bala (whose real name was Rup Kanvar,[28] Bala being her husband's village), the woman who was, between 1943 and 1986, the most famous "living satī" of Rajasthan, we find the same phenomenon of the inherent duality of *śakti* being given somatic expression: according to her devotees, her skin was fair *(gaur-varṇ)* at times and dark *(śyām-varṇ)* at others. Questioned about this change in her appearance, the Mother Satī would answer, laughing: "It's just a question of outlook. I am the way God made me."[29] Bala, whose story I evoked with reference to the blue veil that an artisan of the Goldsmith caste threw on her to dispel the *sat,*[30] wished to "accompany" a nephew whom she had loved as a son (Man Singh, the son of her husband's elder brother) onto the pyre. There is no shortage of examples of women dying for the love of a son, a stepson, or an adopted son.[31] The case of Bala is nonetheless exceptional, given the fact that this satī, who gained a reputation for holiness through her ability to live on for twenty-three years while observing a total fast, was the *cause* of her husband's death.

Rup Kanvar was married at the age of sixteen to Jhumjhar Singh, a Jodha Rajput from the village of Bala (in Jodhpur District). Actually, it was her elder sister whom Jhumjhar Singh was supposed to marry, but Sayar Kanvar had died in the cholera epidemic that decimated the region in 1918 (the two girls' father was also a victim). Young Rup, possessed of a religious bent from childhood, had no desire to marry. Nonetheless, she yielded to the wishes of her grandmother, who had become the head of the household. May 10, 1919, was set as her wedding day. Due to ill omens, the brahman astrologer advised a postponement. His advice went unheeded, and the ceremony began. Then came the ritual moment in which the groom takes the hand of she who would thenceforth be his wife *(hath-ḷevo).*[32] It was as if Jhumjhar Singh had been thunderstruck by her touch. This shock, comparable to an electric charge, was taken by him to be the satī's *tej.* This untranslatable word (from the Sanskrit *tejas,* "shining energy") designates the imperishable being that transmigrates from rebirth to rebirth, and which is characterized by its luminosity. It is the soul viewed as an aura or fiery essence. According to the context in which it is found, *tej* is translated as "brilliance," "glory," "genius," or even "supernatural power" when it is employed to refer to possession by the *sat* (in which usage it has the same sense as *jośः* "frenzy," "divine furor"). Beneath the wedding canopy, the energy generated by the bride's hand caused the fever that seized Jhumjhar

Singh. The shock of revelation had made him lose consciousness. Doctors of every stripe (Unani, Ayurvedic, allopathic) as well as exorcists and healers were called upon—to no avail. Jhumjhar Singh lay drained of all energy (*aśakt:* "bereft of *śakti*"). A few days later, the young woman was asked to bring a glass of water to her husband. She obeyed, albeit reluctantly; however, as soon as he saw her, her husband, terrified, implored her to leave. He died fifteen days later. Then, while the entire household was sunken into a state of stupor and despair, Bala, by her own admission, felt overwhelming relief: the path to saintliness had been opened to her.

The fate of a young high-caste (Bala was a Shekhavat Rajput) widow in the India of the 1920s—and even moreso one from the unbeaten tracks of rural Rajasthan—was not, however, one to be envied. She was barred from remarriage, even though such had theoretically been legalized on the subcontinent in 1856.[33] Those Rajput castes that allow secondary marriage with a widow (*nāto* in Rajasthani)[34] are consigned, because of this practice, to a lower ranking within the group's internal hierarchy. Conversely, the prohibition of widow remarriage is a criterion for upward social mobility, in much the same way as the adoption of a vegetarian diet. The paradoxical designations of "co-wife" *(saut)* and "kept woman" *(rakhel),* which today are used as terms of insult addressed to women enmired in widowhood, bear eloquent witness to the fear of widow remarriage.

An object of universal repugnance, the widow must lead a life of asceticism and self-mortification. Her head is shaved, and she is deprived of every finery, every pleasure, and every comfort. In Rajasthan, her long-sleeved bodice marks her for public abuse. She must emaciate her body through the most austere of diets, sleep on the ground, and pass a full year in penance, living in a corner of the tiny room to which she is confined (*kunevālī*—"she of the corner"—is an insult).[35] Because she is a bearer of misfortune, she must avoid appearing in public for the rest of her days; her impurity, rather than being intermittent as in the case of other women, is permanent. An upper caste Hindu will purify himself with an ablution if the first person to cross his path (or upon whom his eyes inadvertently fall) is a widow. And married women whose husbands are alive are to avoid like the plague all contact with these women, who are considered to be earthly incarnations of Alakṣmī, the goddess identified with Evil Luck, Misfortune, and Ruin.

The widow is excluded from domestic festivities, even from the weddings of her own children; in very orthodox families, all contact with the children is prohibited.[36] Her existence is but a monotonous succession of fasts, religious observances, self-mortifications, and devotional practices. It can, however, become a veritable trial, given the fact that the hatred and resentment of her in-laws, legitimized by the belief that the widow has "eaten" her husband, knows no limits. She is subject to humiliation, insult, and abuse. She is beaten and made to subsist on leftovers (grudgingly given her);[37] she is called a "whore" *(rāṇḍ),* a "burned parting of the hair" *(māṅg jalī),* and a "witch" *(dāyan).* The catalogue of insults on the theme of female widowhood comprises (in Rajasthani alone) some fifty expressions: epithets, adages, aphorisms, couplets, and proverbs, some of which are derived from the *Laws of Manu* or Tulsī Dās's *Rāmcaritmānas.*[38] A Marwari saying evokes the case of a woman widowed at the very beginning of her marriage (like Bala): "The wedding bed just made, and she's already a whore" *(sej caṛhte hī rāṇḍ),* which means, by extension "to be a failure from the start," or "to nip in the bud."

The young widow is especially execrated, since in order to deserve such an unhappy fate, she must have committed abominable sins in a past life—adultery or the murder (literal, in this case) of her husband. The torments of but a single lifetime cannot redeem a karmic fault of such magnitude. No fewer than seven successive rebirths in that impure sex, and seven successive experiences of the torments of widowhood, will be required to expiate the sin that is at the root of her dire condition. Before dying, a satī will sometimes utter or make a hand gesture to indicate two numbers, whose sum is always seven. The meaning here is that she has already burned herself *x* number of times with this same husband, and that she has still to burn herself *y* number of times before attaining liberation.[39] Child marriage, which was commonplace until the end of the nineteenth century, often led to early widowhood. A father was expected to marry off his daughters before menarche, since every menstrual cycle lost (from the standpoint of fertility) was tantamount, according to orthodoxy, to "foeticide" *(bhrūṇa-hatyā).* The father (or the relative serving as guardian) who failed to carry out this religious duty would upon dying be thrown into *Raurav* hell, the most horrific of all the infernal regions. This is why girls (especially among the higher castes) were married while still in their infancy (a custom that has not entirely disappeared).

A widow's youth also carries an element of risk, since pregnancy would cast an indelible stain on the reputation of her husband's lineage. The crowded living conditions of the joint-family encourage sexual abuse, and a young widow is easy prey since she has no one to protect her. If she becomes pregnant, she is thrown out into the street, and since her own family usually refuses to take her back, all that remains for her is to make good on her reputation as a "whore."

In the India of the 1920s, it also happened that families would resort to another strategy to save their honor. As Margaret Sinclair Stevenson reported in a book that has become a classic on the social and religious practices of the Brahmans of Kathiawar in Gujarat, "kerosene is not expensive." Either the widow's clothes were set afire or she was poisoned. Such crimes (which are precursors of the dowry murder of daughters-in-law, known by the name of "bride-burning") remained unpunished, disguised as they were as suicides or household accidents.[40] While this dark picture of the condition of widows in traditional India at the beginning of the century does not always correspond to reality, which was at times kinder to them, it nonetheless conveys a quite realistic idea, still widely embraced today, of the horrors widowhood held for women.[41]

Bala went through her trial unperturbed: she lived only for Kṛṣṇa, her chosen deity, and Man Singh, her sole earthly attachment. But when the latter suddenly succumbed to typhoid on February 15, 1943, the *sat* that had briefly revealed itself twenty-four years earlier suddenly erupted. And it took hold of two women: both Bala and Rasal Kanvar, the wife of Man Singh's eldest son (I know of no other case of a daughter-in-law wishing to die for a father-in-law). They began to shake in symptomatic fashion, and to speak in the gravelly voice that is the sign of possession. Already they had begun to prepare for the funeral ceremony. At this point Man Singh's mother (who was also a widow) forced her daughter-in-law to drink water tainted with indigo. As for Bala, we have already described the subterfuge through which her *sat* was dispelled. From that day on, she undertook a fast that endured until her death. Her miraculous survival made her a "realized" saint.

This story, the only one of its type, is nonetheless exemplary inasmuch as it contains a hidden truth underlying the satīs' mystery. For what does it tell us if not that any woman can be fatal to the man who unites with her? This truth has an extremely long history, belonging as it does to normative discourse rather than to the language of misogyny. In the course of the fourth-day marriage ritual, which precedes their first sexual union, the husband offers oblations to various divinities and sprinkles holy water on his wife's head while uttering the following *mantra:* "I change the evil residing in thee, bringing death to thy husband, thy children, thy cattle, destroying home and reputation, into that which brings death to thy lover. Live with me then, until the end of our days, thou thus named."[42]

A myth whose major themes go back to the *Atharva Veda* links women to original sin, or to what passes for it in Vedic mythology: Indra, the king of the gods, kills the three-headed Viśvarūpa, thereby committing brahmanicide. In order to rid himself of the stain of his crime, he calls upon the Earth, Trees, and Women, asking each of them to take upon themselves one third of his sin, in return for a compensation. Women win the blessing of taking pleasure in intercourse up to the time of childbirth. However, the menstrual cycle would thenceforth inscribe upon their bodies the indelible mark of Indra's sin.[43] This compact has all the appearances of a fool's bargain: the periodic impurity of women has resulted in their demotion within the chain of being. It implies a permanent status of social asymmetry that has altered their destiny.

Women's menses appear in the myth as the counterpart to their capacity for sexual enjoyment. This unbridled sexual desire, which only abates in childbirth, carries within itself the seeds of disorder that are a woman's prerogative. A fantasy that appears and reappears across the entire span of historiography, from Strabo (who refutes it) down to Chevers (who holds it to be true, in 1854),[44] embroiders on this theme with an etiological account of the rite of widow-burning in India. Foreigners claim to have heard it from native sources.[45] Indian women, inclined to lust, had practiced the custom of poisoning their husbands in order to take a new mate. It was in order to punish them and spare men such unfortunate incidents that a legislator (a king, a god, or the god Brahmā in person) instituted the custom that obliges widows to follow their husband in death:

> The [first] cause [and occasion] why the women are burnt with their husbandes was (as the Indians themselves do say), that in time past, the women (as they are very leacherous and inconstant both by nature, and complexion) did poyson many of their husbands, when they thought good (as they are likewise very expert, therein:) thereby to have the better means to fulfill their lusts.[46]

This account is part and parcel of the Western fantasy of India. The inventive cruelty of the Indians, their immoderate appetite for sensual pleasure (most highly pronounced among women), and their reputation as unrepentant poisoners are so many stereotypes that enjoyed exceptional longevity in Europe.[47] But the fantasies spun out by the Indian traditions themselves on the theme of the feminine do not lack in parallels to this fictional narrative, woven around the dual theme of the deadly power and innate guilt of women.

The analyses of Sudhir Kakar have familiarized us with the splitting of the maternal *imago* in India, a cleavage that finds expression in myth, custom, and clinical practice.[48] Indological and anthropological studies have brought the same duality to the fore. Although such views have occasionally been criticized, we can nonetheless affirm that the split image of the Goddess-Mother-Woman triad in south Asia has become a part of the researcher's conceptual apparatus.[49]

What strikes me as remarkable in the case of Bala is that the fantasy of the "murderous woman" should play such a conspicuous role in the life story of a female saint, let alone that of a satī. Let us review the salient points of her earthly adventure. The supernatural power emanating from the hand of a girl who has manifested since childhood a predisposition for holiness drains away the life-force of a man at the very moment when the marriage rites unite their destinies. The groom immediately recognizes the satī's *tej:* the luminous emanation of the inner flame of her *sat,* which strikes him down. One may well wonder what it was that so terrified Jhumjhar Singh. After all, many Hindu men have dreamt of having a satī for their spouse. Historiography abounds in examples of husbands who have exacted this pledge of fidelity from their wives. According to Nicolo di Conti, two thousand women—among those chosen to be wives of the sovereign of Vijayanagar—had to consent to being burned with him. Their wedding would only be performed on that condition:

> The inhabitants of this region marry as many wives as they please, who are burnt with their dead husbands. Their king is more powerful than all the other kings of India. He takes to himself 12,000 wives, of whom 4000 follow him on foot wherever he may go, and are employed solely in the service of the kitchen. A like number, more handsomely equipped, ride on horseback. The remainder are carried by men in litters, of whom 2000 or 3000 are selected as his wives on condition that at his death they should voluntarily burn themselves with him, which is considered to be a great honor for them. . . .[50]

Rogerius noted an analogous custom among the Brahmans of Pulicat, where he lived between 1630 and 1640.[51] In the eighteenth and nineteenth centuries, the gift of a symbolic object had replaced the taking of ritual vows, with the husband giving his wife an object that symbolized his person. This could be an item of clothing, such as a turban, loincloth, sandals,[52] or a piece of cloth with which he mopped his brow; an emblem of his caste and craft—a tool, instrument, or weapon; a rosary or holy book to bear witness to his spiritual inclinations; or else some trifling object connected with pleasure or amusement: a betelnut case, hookah, purse, or ring. This gift implied a counter-gift on the part of the woman, which took the form of sacrifice. On January 15, 1825, the Assistant Magistrate of Kumbakonam (in present-day Tamilnadu) informed the Magistrate of Tanjore of a case of widow sacrifice he was unable to prohibit since the woman had been bound by a promise her husband had extorted from her.[53]

Jhumjhar Singh was gripped by a deadly fear: he fainted, lay unconscious in his bed, his vital breaths "dried up," and he died. At the source of all these phenomena was a fire, an aura, a power, an energy. It was as if male and female energies communicated like sand through an hourglass, with male virility and vigor being drained in order to feed a reservoir of female *śakti* until the husband's remaining life force was entirely spent. However, Bala, the involuntary cause of his untimely death and a potential satī, had not "declared" her resolve to burn with him. Far from following the well-trodden path of dying on the pyre, she chose the sole path of freedom open to women—to answer her spiritual calling (it will be recalled that her marriage had not been consummated).

Twenty-four years later, the *sat* reawakened. This time, Bala wished to die—for the love of another man. The *sat* having been broken through human trickery, it was only now that the cry of eternal sorrow, which the death of her husband had not torn from her, rose to her lips as she sighed: "the airship is leaving empty" *(vimān khālī jā rahā hai).* The soul of the deceased is conveyed to the abode of Viṣṇu or Śiva in an aircraft, which is depicted in Hindu religious imagery.[54] What she meant, then, was that the deceased was departing alone for the other world.

In spite of the anomalies of her career track, Bala is worshipped by her devotees as a full-fledged satī. She has even risen to the rank of "Mother Satī," which is usually the culmination of a satī's trajectory. Bala claimed, moreover, that she had been a satī in past lives. Before ascending the pyre for the first time, she had, in her fury, cursed her in-laws' family, thereby destroying the entire lineage. In order to expiate that sin, she had been reborn only to "re-die" on the pyre. Bala used to add that the man who broke the *sat* was subject to grave danger. According to the two extant versions of her story, the artisan who had thrown the blue veil (or blanket) over her died suddenly, a few months later.

This dark and tangled tale becomes clearer once one understands that the true story of the life of Bala the Mother Satī is actually a myth of *śakti,* with the title "Mother" concealing a dual identity. While Bala is undeniably a Mother Satī *(Satī Mā),* she is also a *Mātā-jī,* a "Mother" *tout court*—i.e., a local territorial deity, considered to be an incarnation of the Goddess in her "terrible" aspect. As such, she demands worship, offerings, and human victims. This helps explain Jhumjhar Singh's terrified reaction, the fury of the satī in her first life that caused the ruin of her in-laws' lineage, and the dead bodies left in the wake of this female saint. The simple fact that this woman adopted a toponym for her holy name is significant in this regard. In fact, in Rajasthan, as in other regions of western India (especially in Gujarat), "Mothers" whose origins are regional as opposed to classical are known most often by the name of a village, city, street, or caste. Their original name is forgotten.[55]

Ḍhāṇḍhaṇ is the most prestigious satī of the Fatehpur region (Sikar District). Every year thousands of her devotees—from Jaipur, Kanpur, Calcutta, Bombay, and Gauhati, in Assam—gather together for her worship. Now, Dhandhan is a place-name. Although it does not figure on maps of Rajasthan—which are sparsely detailed for security reasons, since that state borders on Pakistan and is the location of a number of important military bases—it can nonetheless be reached by following a sandy track for about twelve miles beyond the limits of the city of Fatehpur (itself a regular tourist destination over the past few years by virtue of the wall decorations of its stately residences, called *havelīs*, which make it one of the "jewels" of Shekhavati).[56] A sign that looks like it came straight out of a western reads "The Ideal Village of Dhandhan." The temple-*dharamśālā* (a rest house for devotees and pilgrims) complex surges up out of a lunar landscape. The temple is located inside the "house of *dharma*." Upon entering the sacred compound, one comes upon a shrine, on the right, containing a "hero stone" in traditional style: a husband astride his mount brandishes a sword, while his wife stands at his side, with hands joined. Another stela depicts the spouses side by side. Above the monumental temple door, which was renovated some forty years ago, one finds an inscription reading: "*Śakti* Temple" (fig. 40).

The worship image is a Durgā mounted on a lion, her classical vehicle. This is a replacement for the original image, which was a vermilion-colored trident whose rounded form suggested a face. The enormous eyes and the outline of a nose wearing the ring symbolizing marriage *(nath)* accentuated its anthropomorphic character. This earlier depiction is retained in the form of a motif found over the silver doorframe to as well as on either side of the altar, with the trident-shaped face set atop a *ghāghro,* the wide pleated skirt worn by women in Rajasthan. If this appears to be the anthropomorphization of an abstraction, such is but an illusion, since the image thereby produced evokes the mystical representation of the union of Śiva and Śakti in tantric iconography (fig. 41).

It was explained to me that Ḍhāṇḍhaṇ took on the name and appearance of Durgā-jī following the 1988 Act banning the glorification of satīs.

Fig. 40. "Temple of Śakti": temple lintel at Dhandhan, Rajasthan. The satī is represented, on either side of the god Gaṇeśa, in the form of a trident outlining her face, which extends into a traditional skirt (private collection).

In other worship sites of Shekhavati, I was able to observe the same use of this ingenious strategy for circumventing the law: devotion to the satīs goes on; only the externals of worship have changed. Struck in their Achilles heel—immortality—by the long arm of the law, India's satīs have proceeded to swell the ranks of the Durgā-jīs, Jagadambā-jīs, Bhavānī-jīs, and the other "establishment" *śakti*s. One should not conclude, however, that this set of circumstances has created an unprecedented religious situation: on the contrary, it has confirmed that situation. The bond between satīs and *śakti* is probably as old as the practice of widow sacrifice itself.

At Jhunjhunu, Rāṇī Satī has always been represented by a trident, an attribute of both Śiva and the Goddess, which concretizes the symbolic efficacy of the divine *śakti.* "Why do we worship the Trident and not another form [of Rāṇī Satī]?" one reads in the religious leaflet in Hindi distributed at the temple entrance.

> There are several reasons, but the principal reason is that in the Hindu religion only the Trident has been consecrated as the symbolic representation of Lord Mahāśiva, of the primal *Śakti [ādiśakti]* Mahāgaurī and Mahākālī, of Durgā the Mother of the World, and other Great Energies. At the time of the *Navarātri* [the "Nine Nights of the Goddess"]

Fig. 41. Worship image of Dholi Satī of Fatehpur, Rajasthan (private collection).

festival, millions of Hindus, united in their faith, celebrate the adoration and worship of the Nine Durgās, who are represented in the form of a Trident. In the same way, the divine Rāṇī Satī is worshipped as a manifestation of the *Śakti* in the form of the Trident.[57]

Whenever one worships one's lineage satī, one begins by applying vermilion to trace a trident on the wall near the altar. Following this, one uses one's ring finger (the sacred finger) to add nine or thirteen dots (*ṭīkīs*), using first a mixture of turmeric powder and quicklime *(rolī),* then henna, and finally kohl. These dots are nine in number because there are nine Durgā goddesses, worshipped over the Nine Nights; and thirteen, because it takes thirteen days for a satī to become a *svarginī,* to reach the heavenly abode in which she rejoins her husband. One offers nine or thirteen pieces of copra, and nine or thirteen ritual cakes prepared with flour, brown sugar, and various dried fruits. A lamp is lit, following which one may at last begin the worship.

The brahman temple priest at Dhandhan does not know the true identity of the divine image whose service occupies the greater part of his time. Morning and evening, he is engrossed in a worship ceremony that lasts for no less than two hours; twice a year, in the spring and fall, and in the company of other brahmans, he performs the elaborate ritual practices required for the Nine Nights of the Goddess; and once annually the All Satīs' Festival takes place, falling a month prior to the Hindu homologue of the Day of the Dead *(sarvapitṛ amāvasyā),* which is traditionally observed on the new moon day of the dark fortnight of the seventh month of the lunar calendar *(āśvin kṛṣṇā amāvasyā).*[58] In addition to these, not a day goes by that he is not called upon by devotees for a votive rite, in which a family will come to offer Ḍhāṇḍhaṇ the baby hair of a child born through her grace. At the gate to the Jhunjhunu temple, the displays of the sellers of worship paraphernalia are heaped with piles of scissors, to be used for the "sacrifice of the first hair" offered to Rāṇī Satī, the bestower of sons. Ḍhāṇḍhaṇ is the "Number Two Satī" (after Rāṇī Satī) when it comes to the fulfillment of wishes, her ritual servant told me with pride. So it is that red threads signifying the "fulfillment of wishes" *(manautiyān)* are tied to the branches of the votive banyan tree her devotees circumambulate in clockwise fashion, and offerings to thank the satī for the boons she has granted *(savāmaṇī)* are heaped up before her altar. There are also ceremonies reserved for members of her lineage: Ḍhāṇḍhaṇ was an Agarval from the Sharaf branch, whose ancestral homeland is Hissar District, in the present-day state of Haryana. Behind the temple, there is a row of eleven empty niches, broken by a central niche that is higher than the others. Bearing the inscription *"Śrī Pitar-jī"* (venerated Ancestor), each of these has a few flowers placed in front of it. These are memorial stones for the lineage ancestors, who have no image or identity of their own.[59] Their emptiness fills the space, just as the evanescent village of Dhandhan lends consistency and reality to its local satī. The temple priest has one final ritual task—to lead the devotees of "Kālī Satī" to her small shrine adjacent to the temple. She cures the skin diseases of those who offer her worship on seven consecutive Saturdays.

From Ḍhāṇḍhaṇ I learned that behind one satī there may stand another, and that the indivisible divine entity bearing this name is a dual one. They were in fact two sisters, who died together in the fifteenth century for the love of a brother.

The Goddess's Body

In India, divine society is as mobile as that of men—and so densely populated that its census ought to be taken. Whereas at the base of the pyramid, worship cults may fall away and die, hurling obsolete deities into oblivion, obscure gods may be skyrocketed to fame on unpredictable trajectories: Santoṣī Mā, for example, was brought into the limelight through a box office hit.[60] And, to be sure, new deities constantly bring new blood into the local pantheon. These issue from several different sources. There are those that are borrowed and adapted from the great tradition; those stolen from one's neighbors (cults form the baggage of migration and conquest); those emanating from some primordial divine figure; and finally, those drawn from the human pool.

It is not easy to find one's bearings in the tangled genealogy of the gods. While the distinction between divinities "born of a womb" *(yonija)* and divinities "not born of a womb" *(ayonija)* appears at first blush to be an altogether basic one, drawing a theoretically impassable dividing line across the universe, the life stories of the gods in fact show it to be highly permeable. A continual back-and-forth movement connects the earthly to the heavenly sphere. While it is the case that the great gods of devotional Hinduism *(bhakti)* periodically "descend" into the world of men to restore cosmic order, settle scores with enemies who have become rivals for universal hegemony (the famous *asura*s), found dynasties, and renew their ties with devotees, it is also true that a certain number of humans ascend to the Heaven of Indra, Viṣṇu, or Śiva after death or even while still alive. While there are many paths to immortality, the Heroic Path, and self-sacrifice in general, is one of the most commonly traveled in the present Iron Age. It is a path that, of necessity, passes through violence. Moreover, as has been noted on several occasions, brutal—violent and premature—death can in itself be a springboard to deification, independent of any heroic act. Such violence is special inasmuch as it requires a precondition—the inscription of the deadly vow onto the body in the form of wounds and mutilations, a harrowing of the flesh that expresses in its literality the desire to "die with," "die for," or even to "die against." In such matters, love and bitter resentment, fidelity and vengeance are not as far apart as one might believe. These contrasting emotions often go hand in hand, as the history of the various sacrificial callings makes plain.

Like the great gods of Hindu *bhakti* of whom she is the emanation, the Devī takes earthly incarnations. Her births from a human womb splinter off from one another like rays of sunlight diffracted through a prism. Thus, for example, the goddess Hiṅglāj, who appeared in eastern Baluchistan and who is considered to be a partial incarnation of the primal Śakti, "descends" into Āvaṛ, who is incarnated now in Khoḍīyār and now in Karṇī, while a multitude of minor descents mark the earthly peregrinations of the divine energy. All the incarnations of the Devī whose names have just been cited have the western portion of the subcontinent for their territory: Hiṅglāj's "seat" *(pīṭha)* is on the Makran coast (the Las Bela District of present-day Pakistan), while her incarnations spread, in different periods, into the Sind, Kutch, and Saurashtra to the south and the Thar Desert to the north. This space is bounded by a sacred quadrilateral whose female guardians are Hiṅglāj at Makran, Āvaṛ in Jaisalmer, Āśāpurā at Matanomadh, and Khoḍīyār at Bhavnagar.[61] The divine identities of these figures are not clearly defined, but rather telescope into one other. Their mythologies overlap and even borrow piecemeal from their neighbors, with this or that royal foundation myth bringing Hiṅglāj, Khoḍīyār, Vārudī, or some other "partial descent" into play. What remains constant throughout is the affiliation of this divine genealogy with a single social group: these are the Charans who, as we have seen, raised mutilation and self-sacrifice to the level of caste duty. No fewer than nine hundred thousand *śakti*s incarnate are counted among the "Nine Hundred Thousand of the Black Veil" *(nau lākh lovṛīyāl)*, so named because Charan women (like Jat and Rabari women)wear a black woolen veil *(lovṛī)* that has become a sign of caste brotherhood.[62] Charan men consider themselves to be "Brothers of the Black Veil" *(lovṛībhāī)*, which is tantamount to calling themselves the "Sons of the Goddess" *(devīputra)*.

James Tod emotionally describes a halt he made at Murlah on February 8, 1820, at a time when this small Mewar town was populated by Charans of the Kachela clan who were "Banjaris [haulers] by profession, but poets by birth":

> I was highly gratified with the reception I received from the community, which collectively advanced to me at some distance from the town. The procession was headed by the village-band, and all the fair Charunis, who, as they approached, gracefully waved their scarfs over me, until I was fairly made captive by *the muses* of Murlah! It was a novel and interesting scene: the manly persons of the Charuns, clad in the flowing white robe, with the high loose folded turban inclined on one side, from which the *mala,* or chaplet, was gracefully suspended; the *naiques* [*nāyaks*], or leaders, with their massive necklaces of gold, with the image of the *pitriswur* [*pitreśvaras*, the ancestors] depending therefrom, gave the whole an air of opulence and dignity. The females were uniformly attired in a skirt of dark brown camlet, having a bodice of light-coloured stuff, with gold ornaments worked into their fine black hair; and all had the favourite *chooris, or rings* of *háti-dânt* (elephant's tooth), covering the arm, from the wrist to the elbow, and even above it.[63]

Out of the host of the Nine Hundred Thousand a group of eighty-four "Great Śaktis" emerges. These figures are, however, substantially lower than the fact of the matter, since by virtue of her very birth into the caste every Charan girl is a potential *śakti.* And like the ideal of "satī-hood," the powers of the *śakti* are transmitted from mother to daughter, according to Kishor Singh Varhaspaty, historiographer of Ganga Singh, the Maharajah of Patiala:

> From earliest childhood onward, girls born into this caste are schooled in their divine nature by their mothers. The mother repeats to her daughter such sayings as: "You are the Devī in person; Bhagavatī [another name for the Goddess] created you out of a part of herself."[64] By virtue of this continuous schooling, the little Charan girl considers herself at a very early age to be the *"suāsaṇī"* of Mātā-jī, in other words the "sister of the Devī."[65] This tendency, which becomes an acquired mental disposition *(saṃskāra)* inherited from childhood, attains its fullness at the time of adolescence, when the Charan girl's love for the Great *Śakti* quite naturally reaches its climax. This is why Bhagavatī-Mahāśakti or Śrī Jagdīśvar [Śiva] considered the Charan to be the most suitable caste in which to take incarnation in the form of a woman. Thus one periodically finds *avatāras* of the Goddess in this caste.[66]

Deified Charan women are frequently depicted in groups of seven, with the principal *śakti* being one of the "Seven Mothers" (*saptamātṛkās*), another basic theme of the Goddess's mythology stemming from her early history. Among the premonitory signs of the divine nature of these human heroines is the sudden desire to drink the blood of the water buffalo in place of milk, through which the radical break from the world of brahmanical values in favor of the call of wild energy manifests itself.[67] In fact, ever since the gods created the Devī by pooling parts of their own bodies, or their sweat or rage, as a means of slaying the Buffalo-Demon Mahiṣa, the Goddess has had a taste for the blood of the buffalo or of human victims, and even, in certain sectarian traditions, for her own blood. The *Kālikā Purāṇa* contains a "Chapter on Blood" *(rudhirādhyāya)* that provides an anatomy of this passion. Through its translation by Blaquière at the end of the eighteenth century in the collection entitled *Asiatick Researches,* nascent Orientalism gained a glimpse of this text, the discovery of which fired many imaginations and contributed to the forging of a loathsome image of Tantra.[68] The "Chapter on Blood" opens with the following bizarre enumeration:

Birds, tortoises, alligators, fish, nine species of wild animals, buffaloes, iguanas, bulls, he-goats, *ruru* (a species of antelope), wild boars, rhinoceros, black antelopes . . . *śarabha* (an eight-footed mythical animal), lion[s], tiger[s], and men, [as well as] blood drawn from the adept's own body are considered as the proper sacrifice *(bali)* to the goddess Caṇḍikā, [the god] Bhairava, and others. It is through offering sacrifices that [the] devotee obtains liberation (from the bondage of the world) [and] heaven, and [that] a prince [gains] victory by conquering his enemies.[69]

Following this, we find a detailed description of the choice of victims, of the rules and prohibitions that are to be respected if the sacrifice is to bear fruit, and of the ritual to be performed, as well as of haruspicy.[70]

Colonial historiography has assembled an impressive collection of cases of human sacrifices to "terrible" forms of the Goddess (Kālī, Cāmuṇḍā, or Caṇḍikā), "a dark, fierce, sanguinary divinity, who is represented in the most awful forms, garlanded with a string of human skulls, besmeared with human blood, and holding a skull in one hand and an uplifted sabre in the other."[71] But the Indian sources make no mystery of these matters, and so it is that the heroine of the Sanskrit drama *Mālatī-Mādhava,* written by Bhavabhūti (who lived in the seventh-century court of king Yashovarman of Kanauj), is captured by Kāpālikas who prepare to sacrifice her to the goddess Cāmuṇḍā in order to obtain the supernatural powers known as *siddhis*.[72] The Kāpālikas were a tantric Śaiva sect notorious for its transgression of the purity regulations and tenets of nonviolence adhered to by Hindu renouncers. Initiation required the murder of a Brahman, whose skull thereafter served the initiate as a begging bowl—which thus explains their name, *"kapāla"* meaning "skull" in Sanskrit.[73] Edward Gait (who painted a lurid tableau of human sacrifice in India for the *Encyclopaedia of Religion and Ethics*) relates in his *History of Assam* that in 1565, in the course of the consecration ceremony of the temple of the goddess Kāmākhyā, Nar Narayan, the king of Cooch Bihar, sacrificed one hundred forty devotees, whose heads were offered to the Devī on copper trays.[74] The sacred site par excellence of Śākta devotionalism—for which Assam is, together with Bengal and Orissa, an important stronghold—this temple is thought to have been destroyed, along with the celebrated Jagannāth Temple of Puri, by Rajivlocan Roy, a brahman convert to Islam. Standing atop the Nilacala (the "Blue Mountain") a few miles outside the city of Gauhati in Kamrup District, the Kāmākhyā Temple is one of the principal "seats" (*pīṭhas*) of tantric sacred geography. Here we should note that geophysical India, the land mass of the subcontinent, has been identified with the body of the

Goddess since a very early date.[75] This identification, whose strata have been layered one upon the other over the course of history, is a central Hindu belief. Even today, "Eternal India," which Hindu nationalism claims to be defending against Islam and the West, is depicted in popular imagery as a goddess. Temples have even been erected to Bhārat-Mātā ("Mother India") in the holy cities of Banaras and Hardwar.[76]

What is special about the temple of Kāmākhyā is that it contains no image of the Goddess: wedged into a cleft in the rock out of which a natural spring arises is a stone slab into which the rough image of a *yoni* has been carved. This is a symbolic depiction of the female sexual organ, more exactly of the vulva, which is usually inset with the *liṅga* of the god Śiva. It is this naked *yoni* (without a *liṅga*), permanently moistened by the water oozing from the rock face, that is the object of her devotees' adoration.[77] The religious dimension of this symbol, in abstraction as well as in the infinite number of reworkings for which it serves as the base in texts and in rituals, ought not to make us lose sight of the fact that what is plainly visible in the dark cave of the shrine *is* a part of the Goddess's body—her sex—just as the Nilacala Mountain *is* the body of the god Śiva. This womb in fact belongs to a character in Puranic mythology, whose story we must evoke at this juncture. This divine biography will cast the enigma that is the subject of this book in a new, albeit indirect light.

Satī Divine, Earthly Satīs

Every rite in India is accompanied by its shadow, which is at times so thick and ramified, shooting out in all directions like the aerial roots of a banyan tree, that the rite itself nearly disappears from view. This shadow is the rite's origin myth. Oddly enough, widow sacrifice has no such narrative support. There does, however, exist a Hindu goddess who bears the name of Satī and who, precisely, burns herself. Her mythology, moreover, seems to be fully encapsulated within the act of self-immolation—by fire, or better still by the inner fire of her yoga *(yogāgni)* and the desire to abandon her body in accordance with the ascetic model of autocremation. For James Tod, the origin of the rite was to be traced "to the recesses of mythology, where we shall discover the precedent in the example of Sati, who to avenge an insult to Iswara [Śiva], in her own father's omission to ask her lord to an entertainment, consumed herself in the presence of the assembled gods." And Tod concludes boldly: "[F]emale immolation, therefore, originated with the sun-worshipping *Saivas,* and was common to all those nations who adored this most splendid object of the visible creation."[78]

In this myth, however, the goddess Satī dies out of vengeance, in the pure tradition of protest suicides surveyed earlier in the present volume. Still more curious is the fact that Satī sacrifices herself while her husband is yet alive. For Śiva is alive, so alive in fact that the myth (in its sectarian versions) culminates in a sequence Heinrich Zimmer entitled "Shiva Mad."[79] In despair over the loss of his wife and tormented by the five arrows that have flown from Kāma's (the Hindu God of Love's) bow, Śiva dances as he carries the corpse of Satī on his head. It is a dance that shakes the worlds and threatens the gods. Alarmed, Viṣṇu hurls his discus, cutting Satī's body into several pieces. But Śiva continues his frenzied dance, scattering in the process the dismembered body parts of the goddess.[80] The earth gathers them in at locations (whose number varies from four to one hundred and eight) that have become sites venerated by her devotees and major pilgrimage centers. These are the *śākta pīṭha*s, the "Seats of the *Śakti*"—here her feet, there her ankles, in still other places her umbilicus, sex, breasts, shoulders, and head—with the anatomy becoming ever more ingenious as the "seats" increase in number. The relative importance of these sacred sites varies according to tradition, but four (or occasionally five) of them are especially sacred. In western India, people generally include in this group the "seats" of Hiṅglāj in Baluchistan and Kāmākhyā in Assam, the two being separated by the vast expanse of some two thousand miles.[81] Hiṅglāj is the place at which the Goddess's "cleft of brahman" (*brahmarandhra,* the fontanelle) fell to earth. The Kāmākhyā *pīṭha* was established at the very venue of Satī's passion: it was there that the divine couple secretly gave themselves up to the pleasures of love, and there that Satī's sexual organ fell, turning the mountain blue. It remains there, in the form of that visible cleft in the rock. The name Kāmākhyā (and its variants: Kāmākṣī, Kāmeśvarī) derives from the word *kāma,* which means "love" or "desire."

What possible relationship can there be between the Satī of mythology and the faithful wives who burn themselves on earth because the marital bond that unites them physically and spiritually with their husbands, in this life as in lives past and those still to come, constitutes the sole justification for their existence, its ultimate end and very raison d'être? Rather than entering at this juncture into the narrative jungle of the Goddess's mythology, let it suffice us here to follow some of the paths leading through it. To begin, the main story line, which appears in both the Epic and the

Purāṇas under the name of the "Destruction of Dakṣa's Sacrifice":[82] Dakṣa (the Dextrous), one of the "lords of creatures" (*prajāpatis*), has made preparations to perform a sacrifice on an unprecedented scale—no small matter, in this context. For the nonce, he has invited all the gods of the Hindu pantheon, the *ṛṣis* (those sages who had a vision of the Veda), and a host of supporting players from the heavenly pageant. All the gods except one—Śiva—who is, after all, married to Satī, his own daughter. This is because Śiva has given himself over to impure acts, and because he frequents the cremation grounds and has transgressed every taboo. Are his followers not heretics and social outlaws, addicted to various sorts of intoxicants, wearing that awful matted hair, those ashes, and those necklaces of human bones? Satī comes to Dakṣa's sacrifice alone—or accompanied by Śiva in certain variants of the myth. Seeing that no portion of the sacrifice has been assigned to her husband, she becomes indignant and pronounces a sermon to her father on the mysteries of Śaiva devotion. But Dakṣa remains obstinate. Whereupon Satī withdraws to the north of the sacrificial ground, enters into *samādhi* (total yogic integration), and cursing her father, the gods, and the sages, perishes in the fire of the yoga generated from within her own body.

In order to understand this myth, we must go back in time, or rather—since this is the sole meaning it has for the world of Indian mythology—back to the (perpetually recurring) beginning of time. When Brahmā emitted creatures, he created his ten "mind-born sons" (*mānasaputras*), while from the depths of his inner vision a girl of wondrous beauty named Saṃdhyā was born. He had hardly laid eyes upon her before he found himself in the grip of a strange emotion. Out of this emotion was born Kāma, the god of Love, to whom Brahmā assigned his divine function, smitten as he already was by his arrows. Kāma decided to test his power on the spot, and found no one to try it upon except the Creator, his sons, and his daughter. All were immediately overcome with desire. One of his mind-born sons, Dharma, managed to regain his self-control, and, calling upon Śiva, asked him to intervene. Śiva mocked Brahmā, whose feelings of shame had caused him to perspire, his copious sweat giving rise to the Manes, from whom the human race would descend. The mind-born sons of Brahmā were also filled with shame, with similar results. Out of the sweat of the eldest (named Dakṣa) a girl possessed of boundless powers of seduction was born: this was Rati, Sexual Pleasure. Two other categories of ancestors, "those who die when the time comes" and "those who eat offerings," completed the cycle of this primordial creation, which would flow into another and yet another cycle, mirroring India's oceanic mythic imagination.

Furious over his humiliation, Brahmā uttered a curse, condemning the god of Love to perish, thunderstruck by Śiva. Kāma, however, protested his innocence, saying that he had done nothing other than to follow to the letter Brahmā's own injunctions. Brahmā could not take back his words, so he lightened the punishment: Kāma would be reborn from his ashes on the day that Śiva took a wife. As for Dakṣā, he had given his daughter Rati to Kāma as his bride: Love and Sexual Pleasure are indissociable. But what of Saṃdhyā, the primordial Woman, who had caused this fine mess through the desire she had awakened, quite nearly at birth, and who was responsible for the appearance on the planet of the ravaging god of Love? Saṃdhyā wished to expiate her crime, for it was her lasciviousness that had awakened the desire of her father and her brothers. She decided to sacrifice herself in fire, at which point Brahmā sent one of his mental sons, the sage Vasiṣṭha, to her to school her in matters of penance. Following an expiation that lasted for four cosmic ages, Śiva agreed to fulfill Saṃdhyā's wishes: no being would ever again be touched by desire at birth, which is why desire only arises at puberty; Saṃdhyā would be renowned for her chastity in the three worlds during her next rebirth; and any man looking upon her with lust would lose his virility. Saṃdhyā went to the sage Medhātithi's sacrifice (which had been in progress for the past twelve years) and entered into the sacrificial fire, where her body became a sacrificial cake *(puroḍāśa)*. Agni, the god of Fire, divided this into two halves: the upper part became the Dawn and the lower part Dusk—the common Sanskrit noun *saṃdhyā* designating these two twilight times. Saṃdhyā was immediately reborn out of the sacrificial fire as Arundhatī, the daughter of Medhātithi and future wife of Vasiṣṭha. Arundhatī, identified with the star Alcor, is called upon by chaste and faithful wives in India, and in particular by satīs when they utter their solemn declaration of intent to burn themselves. Brahmā still wished to avenge himself for Śiva's mockery of him when he had lusted after his own daughter. But how could one break the concentration of the great ascetic absorbed in his austerities? All of Brahmā's efforts failed until the day he obtained a promise from the goddess Durgā that she would incarnate herself in the form of Satī, the daughter of Dakṣa who would become Śiva's wife.[83]

Out of these mythic fragments, we shall retain the idea that women are fundamentally desirable, desiring, and guilty of the desire they inspire and experience. Their sensuality, which defines them completely and has its seat in their sex, is the cause of a man's ruin, rendering him incapable of taking part in those religious activities that distinguish the human race from lower creatures. Such, at least, is the risk men would run had social and religious laws not set matters aright by clearly demarcating the subordinate position into which women had been placed by nature, legitimating in the process the reigning asymmetry in gender status. In order to expiate their sin of being doomed to love, as it were, and to prove their chastity (which is never innate), women must either cast their bodies into the fire or lose the principal attributes of their femininity. The myth of the origin of menstruation lays bare the link between original sin and the insatiable sexual appetite of women. The epic account of Sītā's ordeal in the *Rāmāyaṇa* illustrates yet another undemonstrable truth—namely, that fire is an obligatory stage in a woman's life, even if she be a paragon of virtue of the same order as the wife of the god Rāma. This is because fire purifies women of those sins that caused them to be born within that impure sex. Unlimited devotion to one's husband will allow a woman to attain salvation,[84] but only purification by fire can redeem her of her "fault of karma" *(karmadoṣa).*

Yet another lesson may be drawn from the myth of Satī. For in the end, the goddess's voluntary death, motivated by hatred and resentment, is a proof of her high degree of autonomy: anger prevails over love, and a desire for vengeance wins out over faithfulness to the marriage vow. A wife must follow her husband's lead at every turn, and always stand by him. Yet the goddess Satī abandons Śiva. This behavior runs so strongly against the grain of the "duty of women" *(strīdharma)* that a number of present-day commentators have used all manner of ingenious argumentation to reinterpret it. Thus Puspa Bhati, evoking this mythic precedent in the paragraph she devotes to the satīs of Rajasthan, explains to us that the goddess Satī had a sudden awareness of her guilt: her father's insult to her husband could have no other cause than a sin she had committed in a past life. Satī therefore threw herself on the fire to expiate her crime.[85]

Psychological tinkering of this sort is eloquent testimony to the depth of the guilt and self-hatred that women have imbibed—from the outside, to be sure—but have so internalized since childhood that every trial of married life appears to be just punishment for the sins they carry secretly within, like some shameful disease. Munshi Premchand (1880–1936), the "Gorky of Hindi literature" who championed the cause of women long before the blossoming of Indian feminism, expanded on this theme in one of his short stories, entitled *Kusum* after the name of its heroine.[86] The only child of a wealthy lawyer, Kusum has been ignored since marriage by her husband, whose behavior seems all the more inexplicable inasmuch as Kusum is a young woman of many accomplishments and great beauty. In order to set matters straight, she takes it upon herself to write to him. The poignant letters in which she begs for his affection remain unanswered:

> You are not to blame; the one at fault is I. I must have committed some odious sin in another life to merit such unhappiness in this one. I wish I could show you the same indifference, ignore you, stifle the feelings in my heart, but I don't have the strength, God knows why. Can a creeping plant exist without the tree that supports it, a plant that was created to wrap itself around it? Tear it from the tree and it will wilt. I cannot even imagine my existence apart from you. You are present in every one of my deeds, thoughts, and desires.[87]

Eventually, the reader discovers that the husband has adopted this attitude because his father-in-law has not provided him the means with which to pursue his studies abroad, as he had been led to hope in preliminary marriage negotiations. Here Premchand is denouncing one of the "blemishes" *(kalaṅk)* of modern Hindu society: the perversion of marriage, which has become a business. The ruthless pursuit of dowry money and the consumer goods acquired through marriage has recently taken the radical form of "bride-burning." Such is the term applied to the murder of a young woman whose dowry is judged insufficient by her in-laws. The young woman is subjected to threats, harassment, and even cruelty, all of these being so many ways of pressuring her family into ponying up the money or assets her in-laws desire. If this blackmail remains ineffective, the husband, with the backing of his family, does away with his wife. These murders are invariably disguised as accidents, the most frequently employed strategy consisting of setting the wife's sari aflame with kerosene. The husband is then free to take another wife (something he may not do while his wife is still living, polygyny having been banned in 1955).[88] First appearing in the early 1970s in north India, and especially widespread within the wealthy Marwari community, this practice is thought to claim five hundred fifty victims per year in Delhi alone.

Field accounts have brought to light the role of guilt feelings in the formation of a woman's sacrificial calling. The death of a husband reactivates a vague yet universally latent sentiment. It is as if guilt were an endemic affliction from which women could only free themselves by uttering the fatal words *"sat, sat, sat."* As soon as one turns to mythology, however, the affective landscape and spectrum of emotions are entirely transformed. Satī immolates herself in order to satisfy the demands of her own ego. The desire to abandon her body springs from a narcissistic injury: Satī comes to know that she has not been invited to a ceremony to which her father has convened "[e]very living thing in all the reaches of space . . . gods and seers, men, birds, trees, and grasses."

Satī was struck, as by a bolt of lightning. Anger began to burn in her, and her eyes hardened. She had understood immediately, and fury increased in her beyond bounds. "Because my husband bears a skull in his hand for a begging bowl," she said, "we have not been invited." She thought for a moment, in order to decide whether to blast Daksha to ashes with a curse, but then she suddenly remembered the words she had uttered to him, the time she had mercifully granted the great boon of becoming flesh in the earthly status of his daughter: "If, for even a single instant, you should lack for me proper reverence, I will quit my body immediately, whether happy in it or no." And with that, her own eternal form became visible to her spiritual eye, complete and incomparably terrible, the form out of which the universe is made. . . . [S]he meditated: "The world period of the universal dissolution has not yet arrived; that is true; Shiva has not yet a son. The great wish that agitated all the gods became fulfilled for them: Shiva, caught in my spell, found his joy in woman. But what good did it do them? There is no other woman in all the worlds who could arouse and satisfy Shiva's passion; he will never marry another. That, however, is not going to stop me. I will quit this body, just as I declared I would. Some later day, I can reappear for the redemption of the world, here on Himālaya, where I have dwelt so long in happiness with Shiva. I have come to know dear Menakā, the pure and kindly wife of King Himālaya. . . . She shall be my next mother. . . . I will marry Shiva again, dwell with him again, and complete the work that all the divinities have in mind."[89]

Satī burns herself because Dakṣa has offended her. His insult to Śiva provides her with an excuse for carrying through on her threat. It is she who has been outraged. Her behavior is so self-centered that the very process of her death seems a virtuoso demonstration of her self-sufficiency: no accessory, auxiliary, or external element enters into its production. Death is a product manufactured by the body through the mere workings of will and mind, and obtained through a mastery of the techniques of yoga. There is no inner fire here, as in the other variants. The *Śakti*'s powers require no mediation:

Thus she meditated. Then her wrath overcame her. She closed the nine portals of her senses in yoga, stopped her respiration, and braced all of her powers. The life breath ripped through the coronal suture of her skull, out the tenth portal (the so-called Brahmā-fissure), and shot upward from her head. The body slumped inanimate to the ground.[90]

An unknown facet of the voluntary death of women reveals itself through this divine episode. The husband is neither the direct cause nor, *a fortiori,* the beneficiary of the sacrifice. Wounded in his love and deprived of his wife, he slips into the background, a mere device for the furthering of the plot; in brief, his role in this mythological fragment is simply an instrumental one. In the "true" story of the saintly Bala as well, we witnessed the same reversal of perspective—of the sacrifice as detached from the person of the husband, with no connection to him whatsoever; of the sacrifice viewed as a manifestation of the powers of femininity and no longer as an act of supreme abnegation; of altruism cast by the wayside, and *śakti* triumphant. A Rajasthani saying offers a fine illustration of this "egotistical" perspective on the sacrifice of satīs: *"khasam maryān ko dhokho konī, supno sānco hoṇo caije,"* which means literally: "What matter that the husband dies if his wife's dream comes true?"[91]

A few years ago, a Charan woman named Joma sacrificed herself while her husband was yet alive, in a village situated on the border between Rajasthan and Pakistan.[92] She was also survived by two young children. A series of calamities had rocked the village. Joma had offered up her life in order to appease the anger of the gods, following the traditional model of the heroic sacrifice of the Charan women, known in Rajasthani as *sagat*—i.e., *śakti.* The Charans whom I inteviewed lay great importance on the fact that *sagat* and the sacrifice of satīs were two distinct practices, which were by no means to be confused. Their repeated denials, which recalled the distinction made by other informants between suicide and the death of satīs, were a clear indication that widow-burning did not carry an odor of sanctity among these followers of *Śakti,* who were extremely proud to belong to the inner circle of the "Sons of the Goddess." There was always room for doubt concerning the voluntary character of the immolation of satīs. Contrariwise, heroic sacrifice as practiced by Charan women, precisely because it did not answer to any social imperative sanctioned by custom, could only be interpreted as the signal expression of the sacredness of the group, and specifically of its women.

In spite of this, Joma is venerated on both sides of the border as a Mother Satī, in secular life as well as in her religious cult. At the beginning of the century, all Charan women in Gujarat and Rajasthan were still addressed with the honorific and deferential title of "Mother Satī" or "Grand-Mother" (*Āī* in Gujarati), a name given to the incarnations of the primal *Śakti (Ādiśakti).* The last of these in this region of India was Ai Sonbai, another Charan woman, who died in 1973.[93]

With this, we have reached ground zero of our enigma. For the mystery of the origins of the rite and the interminable debate—over the freedom of women to burn themselves versus the violence done to them—conceal, in my opinion, another fundamental question: how are we to understand "satī-hood"? What exactly are we talking about? When I used concrete examples to retrace the history of the various forms of the sacrificial calling, I was attempting to bring to light the profound motivations that play a part in the production of the deadly vow. My intention has not been to psychologize the debate, but rather to lift it out of the rut in which conventional discourse on satīs ("for" or "against") has trapped us. What we realize, in fact, is that the very definition of "satī-hood"—the reality to which the term corresponds—eludes the narrow meaning that people continue to apply to it, and that it can be entirely dissociated from the idea of marital fidelity. From this alternative standpoint, the state of "satī-hood" is the mark of a woman's sacredness, rather than of her subordination. Hindus who honor Mother Satīs are nevertheless unconscious of this duality. The two facets of the satī's sacrifice form a seamless whole in their experience. And while they do in fact distinguish among numerous categories of satīs, the governing criterion is one of magical efficacy. It is the satī whose supernatural aura produces the most miracles, who grants the most sons, protects the locale, and drives away disease that will enjoy the greatest religious devotion, regardless of the conditions under which she sacrificed herself. Among the constellation of satīs in Rajasthan, there are a few that shine most brightly: Rāṇī Satī at Jhunjhunu, Nārāyaṇī Satī in Alwar, Sādh Satī at Ras-Bafra, Dholan Satī in Raipur, and Rāṇī Bhaṭiyāṇī in Jasol. Their cult transcends lineage, caste, region, and even the boundaries of Hinduism, given the fact that members of other religious communities also take part in festivals that bring together thousands of devotees annually. At Kathriyasar (Bikaner District), there is a tomb that commemorates the satī Kāḷal De: betrothed to the guru Jasnāth (fifteenth century), she chose to follow him in death when he took "living *samādhi*," a type of suicide through self-interment that appears to have been in vogue among sectarian renouncers of the period. Accompanying her beloved sister Kāḷal De to the grave was Pyāre De. While it is thought that the Jasnathis are a lost branch of Ismaili Muslims who have reconverted to Hinduism,[94] there nonetheless exists a temple in honor of this heterodox satī, who is considered extremely powerful in the region (fig. 42). A second shrine is dedicated to her in the village of Panchla, near Khimsar, in Nagaur District. Today none but the Jasnathis worship her; in the past, however, many local sovereigns and chieftains

Fig. 42. Popular religious image of Kāḷal De Satī at Kathriyasar, Rajasthan (private collection).

venerated her as highly as they did the holy men of their sect, who were renowned for their supernatural powers.

Cult and Apotheosis

On this April day in 1993, an even larger crowd than usual is pushing its way into a house that is at first blush indistinguishable from the other residences of this elegant Jaipur neighborhood. This is the home of a Rathor Rajput family whose son was miraculously healed a few years ago through the grace of Om Kanvar, the satī of Jharli, who died on August 30, 1980. The boy's mother, a Shekhavat Rajput, had gone to Jharli to obtain the intercession of her favorite satī. This town of eleven thousand inhabitants is located forty-five miles from the capital of Rajasthan in Sikar District, where cases of widow sacrifice have proliferated since the late 1940s. The family had solemnly vowed to install an image of Om Kanvar within the very walls of their house in order to worship her every day. Funds were raised among her devotees, the end result being a transformation of this residence into a branch of the temple at Jharli. But the celebrations that take place here are entirely unofficial. They are private, and even clandestine, following the implementation of the legal ban against every form of satī worship.

Mama-ji, another Shekhavat Rajput woman, who has brought me into this private house of worship—which is nonetheless open to all her devotees (from every caste, she maintains)—explains to me that it remains a well-guarded secret: none but those seeking the grace of the Mother Satī come there, and knowledge of the place is only spread by word of mouth, within the community of believers. Mama-ji is the wife of a well-known public figure: Bhishan Singh Shekhavat (affiliated with the Congress-I Party) was for years a journalist with *Rājasthān Patrikā,* the most widely read Hindi-language daily in the region.[95] His brother, Bhairon Singh Shekhavat, who was the leader of the BJP opposition in the Rajasthan State Assembly in 1987, has thrice been the state's Prime Minister (re-elected in November 1993, after he had been forced to resign, together with all of his peers, following the events that transpired at Ayodhya in December 1992).

"Satīs are exceptional beings," Mama-ji tells me, her eyes shining. "They are one in thousands, and even then!" And when I ask her why one would becomes a satī, she answers immediately: "Out of love. Without a husband, a woman is nothing. In Rajasthan, the power of the *sat* is special, like the power of Love." (She uses the word *prem,* a term with vivid mystical connotations.) "In other places, it can happen that women are burned against their will. In Rajasthan it is the women who force those around them to accept their sacrifice." Everyone I interviewed employed the same argument, with equal conviction.

This Sunday is not a day like any other. This particular April 11 corresponds to a fifth day *(pañcamī)* in the Hindu liturgical calendar.[96] Now it happens that Om Kanvar, who burned herself on a Saturday, which fell on the fifth day of the month of *Bhādrapada,* demanded before her death that she receive *pañcamī* worship.[97] The worship begins at noon, the hour in which the sun is at its zenith.[98] Throughout the rest of the year Om is, like any other deity, worshiped twice daily, in the morning and evening. The shrine remains open at all times, though, in order to welcome devotees who come with votive offerings or gifts of thanksgiving for her blessings. One enters the shrine through an antechamber where one's attention is attracted to a curious object—an automatic bell-ringing device that sounds whenever the officiant waves an earthen lamp or incense sticks before the divine image *(ārtī)*. Offerings of this sort are made with a continuous circular motion of the hand in the auspicious direction *(pradakṣiṇā)*. Theoretically these movements trace in the air the grapheme of the *mantra* used in the cult (or simply the sacred syllable *Oṃ*). The walls are covered with holy images, with Rāṇī Satī of Jhunjhunu placed alongside Karṇī Mātā, the tutelary goddess of the Rathor clan. Enshrined in the inner sanctum is a depiction of Om Kanvar in the classical style: the satī is seated on a flaming pyre with her husband on her lap, with her right hand raised in a sign of blessing. Her veil, skirt, and reddish orange apparel contrast with the white color of the offerings: Om Kanvar had demanded a white *pūjāpā*.[99] To the left of the altar there hangs, in a red velvet scabbard, a large sword with curved edge, the emblem of the Goddess. Above the sanctum is the name of Om, the quintessence of Hinduism.

Some fifty women in Rajasthani garb pile into the spacious room, making it feel quite small. The men remain standing respectfully in the doorway and the antechamber: with the exception of the young man who was miraculously healed, they are not allowed access to the inner sanctum. Throughout the entire ceremony, which lasts for more than three hours, devotees continue to stream in with their coconuts, garlands of marigold and jasmine, sweetmeats, and offerings of rupees. The mistress of the house, who acts as officiant on this occasion just as she does in the daily worship service, intones a traditional chant addressed to the Mother Satīs—which the group of women repeats in unison at the top of their lungs—and punctuates each couplet with an offering of red and white roses laid upon the altar. Then comes the cry, repeated again and again: "Long live Mother Satī!" It is proffered as an invitation: may Om descend from the world of the Satīs to tarry among her devotees; may She find embodiment in Her image. A woman from the assembled group, a native of Jharli, now takes up another chant dedicated to Om, which all the women then sing in chorus. Their shrill and fervent voices drown out the deafening roll of the drums. The officiant performs *ārtī,* cuts the coconuts, offers them, and then places them to one side.[100] Her son, the ritual cook, chops them up with a cleaver. He will later prepare small packets wrapped in newspaper containing pieces of coconut meat together with other elements of worship, which will then be distributed to the participants as "consecrated remains" *(prasād).* Another woman intones a third chant. The officiant then places a vessel of holy water over the image, following which she sprays the crowd with this "foot nectar" *(carṇāmṛt).*[101]

Their shouts of "Hail! Hail! Mother Satī!" rise in a single voice. Suddenly, the officiant begins addressing Om Kanvar. Like a distant storm that finally breaks, words burst forth out of the *bhāv,* out of the tumult of emotions unleashed by the vision of Om through her image: "Satī, come down and offer us your blessing," she says to her. "O Thou who hast saved the soul of thy husband, Thou who destroys the evil, Great Satī of Jharli, wife of Ram Singh, protect us, drive away all ills and calamities, O Thou who are the light of the *kaliyuga!*" This prayer is addressed to a well-defined divine entity, a woman whom some members of the audience had known and seen burn before their eyes: Om Kanvar, the little sixteen-year-old Shekhavat Rajput girl who had been married for six months to Ram Singh, a Bombay truck driver. Yet her epithets are the very ones used in the worship of the Goddess in her twofold nature—in her radiant (Gaurī) form and as the slayer of demons (Durgā). Throughout the entire ceremony, the vivats honoring "Mother Satī" alternate with acclamations of Bhavānī Mātā (a form of Durgā)[102] and Karṇī Mātā (a partial incarnation of the Devī, but a full-fledged *śakti*).

The sacrificial fire—or rather flame (*jot,* from the Sanskrit *jyotis,* "light," "brilliance")—is now installed. The ceremony itself is called *jot* ("adoration": this is not a *pūjā* in the ordinary sense of the term).[103] The officiant pours clarified butter over the live embers of a fire-pot, which is nested in a metal tripod. With each offering, she pronounces a *mantra* invoking *"Satī-Dev."* An enormous tongue of flame shoots upward. The officiant invites the assembled faithful to repeat each of her formulas in chorus. The crowd (consisting by now of more than a hundred women and children) obliges her with a religious enthusiasm bordering on frenzy. All the women are now standing. Beside themselves, they sing the glories of the satī as the bells clang, the incense sticks swirl, the offerings pile higher, the flowers are thrown, and the coconuts are chopped. The officiant's entire body is convulsing. Once again, she addresses the satī directly: "Thou art not a spirit *(bhūt),* Thou art not a demon *(piśāc),* Thou art not a female ancestor *(pitrāṇī)*—Thou art *Dev.*" In popular Hinduism, this masculine word is treated as a neuter: it designates one's chosen divinity, the supreme form of the divine that the devotee has enshrined in his heart. A religious poster depicts the monkey-god Hanumān, the model devotee, who opens up his heart to reveal the divine couple of Rāma and Sītā, the object of his devotion, inside.

The women are sitting once again. They run through every satī song in their repertoire as the officiant sprinkles holy water over the image of Om, presents each offering to her one at a time, and joins her son in preparing the little packets intended for the devotees. When these make their way up to her, before taking leave of the site, she marks their foreheads with a *tilak* of sandalwood paste, as a symbol of their sectarian affiliation and a sign of divine blessing. Cymbals have replaced the drums; their high-pitched beat rings out above the hubbub. The smoke, the heat, and the ardor of the devotees fill the air, which has become stifling.

Later, Mama-ji gives me a pamphlet published in Hindi by the "Mahāsatī Oṃ Kanvar Trust" in Jharli: my presence at the secret ceremony has made me a *de facto* initiate. In it I find the words that the mystic rapture of the *bhāv* had seemingly wrung out of the officiant.[104] Once again I realize that the spontaneity of personal experience expresses itself through a network of pre-established, external, and conventional words and images, and that it is impossible to encounter a religious sentiment, an emotion that has not been dictated by some cultural norm. What emerges most clearly, however, from a reading of this modest piece of propaganda aimed at devotees is the reinvention of both the person of the satī and the "objective" circumstances of her death. The space separating the world of men from that of the gods has been abolished. As the satī prepares herself for the sacrifice, the heavenly realms are in a state of exaltation. The multitude of gods throng the gates of Heaven to view the spectacle. Indra sends Agni, the god of fire, to the scene. The sun enters into the fray: it sends forth the spark that sets the pyre ablaze, as a malevolent onlooker threatens the sacrifice. The gods applaud the satī by showering her with a rain of flowers, in an ovation worthy of an opera diva. The satī ascends to heaven in Indra's chariot, escorted by Agni and the nymphs of Paradise. There Indra will throw a magnificent heavenly reception in her honor. There the "shining energy" *(tej)* of the human heroine will rival that of the gods. Om Kanvar is *Maheśvarī,* the supreme form of the divine, an incarnation of the *Śakti* come down to earth to restore *dharma.* Her cathartic sacrifice brings salvation, happiness, prosperity, and universal peace, by effecting a "revolution of the moral order." Moreover, the Great Satī goes on preaching to the very end, impassive amidst the flames.[105]

Whereas the story of Om Kanvar (retold by a religious committee that derives its existence and profits from her death) appears to be a new version of an *avatāra* myth, with the supreme deity descending to earth for the "good of the worlds," the text that serves as an introduction to this edifying tale focuses more specifically on the dangers threatening India and *dharma.* It is entitled "The Great Satīs and Our Civilization." Its author, Raghubir Singh Rathor, a lawyer from Bharatpur, begins by drawing up a list of the miracles accomplished by Om, as if to locate his heroine on the "scale of satīs." He then evokes her idealized death, in imitation of the goddess Satī's abandonment of her body *(deha-tyāga):* revealing her sacred nature, Om sheds her flesh-and-blood envelope through the sheer power of her yoga, as a means to obtaining liberation. The author reminds us that the history of India is spangled with the glorious sacrifices of its heroes, and the mass immolations of women (*jauhar*s) in the time of the Muslim conquest. These examples are naturally appropriated as symbols of "eternal India's" resistance to foreign presence. From this standpoint, heroic sacrifice becomes an emblem of Hindu nationalism.

This manifesto in support of satīs is worthy of a translation *in extenso,* for here, as in the writings of Coomaraswamy, or in the pamphlets cited above, apologetics go hand in hand with a denunciation of the demonized West. Here are a few excerpts:

> To be sure, it is human nature to wish to put a stop to the sacrifice of satīs. Yet sometimes we find ourselves faced with *Śakti*s who, when they reveal their extraordinary nature, make us forget the fine dictates of Reason. . . . The duty of anyone who loves *dharma* and freedom is to honor the satīs, those inexhaustible founts of inspiration who voluntarily became pillars of *dharma.* What is more, this Indian land has always been the homeland of the devout, of Savitrīs [models of marital fidelity], and of satīs. Were we to suppress these cultural traits, then the new page of Indian civilization would be written with the pen of Western materialism. It would become difficult to distinguish man from the machinery in which he is a cog in the realm of the spirit, and man from beast in the moral realm. Our ideals of conduct, of self-control, serenity, charity, devotion, non-violence, the elimination of untouchability, respect for elders, tolerance, patriotism and, lastly, the sense of sacrifice—all of these noble sentiments would be ineluctably erased from the map of India. . . . The real danger threatening our humanity arises not from our *dharma,* our ways and customs, but from our desire to compete with the West with weapons we have borrowed from it. At a time when countries like Russia and America are determined to annihilate the edifice of human civilization, we must not, through a lack of faith in this or that religious issue, allow the law of the fittest to reign over the pure and holy land of India. . . . What we need today, on the contrary, is to raise the spiritual energy of the population of this land of asceticism *(tapobhūmi),* and moved by our unshakable faith, to build a strong India that is an image of heaven on earth.[106]

SHEKHAVATI, AN ENDANGERED REGION

If the daughter-in-law burns, if her ashes fly,
then and only then does the honor of the lineage endure! —Shekhavati proverb[1]

The semi-arid region of Shekhavati, hemmed in by the kingdoms of Jodhpur, Bikaner, Loharu, Patiala, and Alwar, formerly constituted the northern portion of Jaipur State. Its territory, which spilled over into the neighboring regions of Churu and Nagaur, accounted for almost a third of the area and approximately one fifth of the population of that state. Since the creation of the State of Rajasthan in 1949, through the merging of the twenty-one Princely States of the former Rajputana, the name Shekhavati no longer corresponds to an administrative unit. The term nevertheless remains operative, designating the zone comprising the present-day districts of Jhunjhunu and Sikar, which have been the scene of the greatest number of widow sacrifices recorded since the 1940s. From this standpoint, Shekhavati may be considered an endangered region. And the question quite naturally arises of how one is to understand this phenomenon.

The region owes its name to Rao Shekha-ji (1433–1488), the grandson of Bala-ji, who ascended the throne of Amber in 1389. His descendants, the Shekhavat Rajputs, belong to a junior branch of the Kacchvaha clan, which reigned over Amber—and over Jaipur as well, following Savai Jai Singh's founding of that new royal city in 1727. At several points in their history, the *ṭhākurs*[2] of Shekhavati showed their rebellious spirit, in their refusal to recognize the suzerainty of their Maharajah. In spite of the 1818 treaty (between the East India Company and Savai Jagat Singh) that put an end to their independence, yet another Shekhavat prince rebelled, as late as 1938.[3] The abolition of the law of succession by order of primogeniture (laid down in 1650 by Todar Mal of Udaipurvati) accentuated still further the uniqueness of the Shekhavats within Rajput society: the equal division of property among all male heirs had a considerable impact on their future since it issued, on the one hand, in a series of internal feuds and, on the other, in a widespread division of their lands into smaller and smaller parcels that inevitably led to their decline and impoverishment. By 1731, when the victories of Shardul Singh over the Qaimkhani nawabs (who had been the masters of Fatehpur, Jhunjhunu, and Singhana since 1384) ensured Shekhavat dominance over the region, it had already been broken up into a patchwork of chiefdoms, fiefs, and estates. It should therefore not surprise us that the history of Shekhavati consists of an inextricable tangle of wars and raids, clan conflicts and fratricidal struggles, alliances and betrayals, all punctuated by the heroic and chivalrous exploits immortalized by James Tod in his *Annals and Antiquities of Rajasthan,* which afforded them the cachet of romance and glamour that the tourist industry has been using to its benefit of late.[4]

Although the Shekhavati, in its social and political organization, has provided historians of the colonial era with a model of Indian-style feudalism,[5] the region has also been associated with a social group whose traditional occupations have been diametrically opposed to those of the Rajput warlords: Shekhavati was in effect the cradle of the Marwari community, a designation applied to a hodgepodge of trading castes originating from western India, and most especially from Marwar. Eastward migrations, which began as early as the sixteenth century, gained full momentum after 1860, with the Marwaris fanning out into the cities of the Indo-Gangetic plain, from Farrukhabad to Calcutta, as well as into Assam, Bombay, Hyderabad, and finally, beyond the frontiers of India, into Burma, Singapore, and Hong Kong. Many struck it rich in the fields of business, banking, and industry: the Birlas, Bajajs, Dalmias, Goenkas, Poddars, Singhanias, Khaitans, and Jhunjhunuwalas were all originally from Shekhavati.[6] This diaspora has never severed its ties with its native land. Even if their actitivites opened them to the outside world and made them a modern community generally sympathetic to social reforms and democratic ideals, the Marwaris were and remain a socially and religiously conservative group. This conservatism is especially conspicuous in their attitude toward women. In Calcutta, a metropolis pulsating with culture, the nearly 100 percent illiteracy rate for Marwari women broke all records in 1921. The *purdah* (literally "curtain" in Persian) system, which forces women to live in the seclusion of the zenana, to veil their face in the presence of any man other than their husband and also, out of respect, before their mother-in-law and older sisters-in-law, was scrupulously observed. Marriage was another matter in which their strictness clearly manifested itself. The Birlas, who are of the Maheshvari caste, were outcasted in 1922 when Rameshvar Das Birla remarried a Kolvar woman. Even before the First World War, a schism had taken place between orthodox Hindus (*sanātanīs*), Jains (many Marwaris follow the Jain faith), and adherents of the reformed Hinduism of the *Ārya Samāj*.[7] The diaspora alone may suffice to explain this inward turn towards orthopraxy. The need to maintain an unaltered group identity probably played an important role in a community that, exposed more than most to alien forms of culture, found tradition to be a safe investment.

Neither their liberal ideology nor their contacts with the outside world, then, have prevented the Marwaris from vying with the Rajputs in the defense of *dharma*—most especially with regard to the "duty of women," a vulnerable point, and thereby a criterion of the social and religious norm. Since Independence and the abolition, in 1952, of the *jāgīrdārī* system, which delivered a fatal blow to Rajput dominance in the region, the cult of the satīs has become an element in the crystallization of religious feelings—which each side claims for itself alone.[8] What we are witnessing today is a bizarre backward race, for stakes of an apparently symbolic order, between two social groups that also compete fiercely for goods of a more mundane sort. While no one in Shekhavati would ever dream of denying the Rajputs their claim to exclusivity in matters of widow-burning, it is also true that medieval satīs born into the Jalan and Sharaf branches of the Agarval caste have, by virtue of the religious zeal and networks of the Marwaris, recently gained a prestige capable of overshadowing that of their Rajput sisters. One hundred eleven temples dedicated to Nārāyaṇī Devī—all branches of her main temple at Jhunjhunu (fig. 43)—blanket the subcontinent.[9] The business district of Burrabazar, where the throbbing pulse of Calcutta reaches its crescendo, is also the center for the propagation of the cult of Rāṇī Satī, the name under which Nārāyaṇī had asked to be worshiped after her death (figs. 44 to 46).[10] The neighborhood counts no fewer than fifty temples, to which may be added the head offices of the trusts, associations, and support committees implanted in the heart of the city by the Organization, the *Rāṇī Satī Sevā Saṅgh*. Prior to the promulgation of the anti-satī act, the two sisters of Dhandhan (whose temple is lost amongst the desert tracks of Fatehpur) received an annual tribute from their Bombay-based devotees worthy of a Maharani: shortly after *Holī*,

Fig. 43. Temple at Jhunjhunu, Rajasthan (private collection).

during the religious fair commemorating the day of their sacrifice, there took place a procession of 108 ritual pots—symbols of the Goddess—which were carried atop the heads of as many women.[11] This "procession of ritual pots" *(kalāś yātrā)* reached its climax in 1985 when the local committee for the propagation of Ḍhāṇḍhaṇ Satī had the idea of calling on Pushpak Airlines to send a helicopter streaking through the sky for three hours, to rain flowers down on the site. Donations from devotees, collected by the committee (which was founded in 1979 and is one of the sixty branches of the *Ḍhāṇḍhaṇ Satī Pracār Samiti*), covered the costs of the ceremonies (60,000 rupees, without counting that final caprice, which alone cost 20,000 rupees).[12] Spiritual and commercial goals, far from being incompatible, form a pair, and can be mutually reinforcing at times. If the cult of the satīs benefits from the Marwari money invested in temple construction and the setting up of trusts and support committees, the cult in turn brings huge profits to the Marwaris, who also use it as a convenient way of laundering money.[13]

Belief and Mystification

It has been argued that the appropriation by Marwaris of this emblem of Rajput nationalism has been part of a strategy. The argument runs as

Fig. 44. "The Most Venerable Rāṇī Satī-jī": popular religious image from Jhunjhunu (private collection).

Fig. 45. The satī as Śakti: Rāṇī Satī is invoked here with a tantric formula addressed to Cāmuṇḍā, a form of Durgā, and represented by the Trident (private collection).

Fig. 46. Worship image of Rāṇī Satī in the form of the Trident, at the Jhunjhunu temple, Rajasthan (private collection).

follows: the *baniyās* ("merchants": the term has taken on a pejorative connotation) borrowed this essential element of the local elite's *ethos* in order to elevate their status within the hierarchy and thereby overtake the Rajputs in a reconstructed history in which the latter would not have held a monopoly over the sacrifice of women. The region would have been relatively untouched by the rite: the handful of widows burned in the royal house of Amber and within the princely families of Shekhavati would not be evidence of a true tradition, especially if one compares these with the kingdoms of Jodhpur, Udaipur, or Bundi, in which the immolation of women belonging to the princely zenana was practiced on such a large scale that this ceremonial came to be considered an article of state religion.[14] Therefore, the sudden outbreak of widow sacrifices recorded in the region since the 1950s ought not to be viewed as the revival of an ancient custom, but rather as the deliberate adoption of a nontraditional ritual, by Rajputs and Marwaris, to further their caste interests in a variety of ways. As for the Brahmans, they have been only too happy to take part in such a venture, in which their expertise in manipulating blind faith has found fertile ground.

Such is the analysis Sudesh Vaid and Kumkum Sangari have put forward in a series of publications, and most especially in a long article titled "Institutions, Beliefs, Ideologies: Widow Immolation in Contemporay Rajasthan."[15] It is grounded in a powerful current of thought coming out of those intellectual circles that support secularism (i.e., state neutrality in matters of religion) and women's causes, and oppose all forms of cultural imperialism (a certain view of history and a certain Orientalist brand of knowledge, considered to be so many residues or avatars of colonial discourse, are also objects of their condemnation). Implicit in this school of thought is the postulate that religious experience is nothing more than an epiphenomenon and that religious beliefs are nothing other than social constructs. It is my feeling that research undertaken on the basis of such presuppositions cannot help but be skewed from the outset. If one is to hope to understand a body of data from within the religious sphere, then one must, regardless of one's personal feelings on the subject, give belief systems full credit, so to speak, even if one ends up with conclusions of a very different order.[16] Such is the stance adopted in this book—an uncomfortable stance, since it implies a form of self-discipline that consists of introducing a series of highly contrasting viewpoints without indicating one's preferences, or at least without giving them precedence over one's observations and the thoughts that flow from them. To be sure, this circumspect approach nonetheless presupposes an observing subject who bases his analysis on the facts he observes: writing a book is a subjective endeavor.

While it appears undeniable that the matter at hand is clearly subject to every sort of religious manipulation, this does not automatically imply that one may simply reduce the phenomenon to an act of mystification concocted by obscurantist forces from within a patriarchal society. Nor does it mean that there was no tradition of widow sacrifice, either in the Shekhavati or among indigenous or nonindigenous *baniyās*. Nor can one assert that the Rajputs used the rite in a purely instrumental fashion, to regain in symbolic capital the ground they had lost in real power, or to fuse anew a sense of caste identity sorely tried by economic setbacks and the erosion of traditional values, which had left the group, and especially its youth, frustrated and in disarray. All of this is true to some extent, but this element of truth conceals more than it clarifies an essential part of the question: it does not explain the move from "fanaticization" to the actual performance of the rite. It is no small matter to burn oneself alive. It is hard to imagine how women could conceive of such a plan, let alone carry it out, by simply yielding to the desires of external social actors, no matter how diabolical the machinations—of politicians, nationalist party ideologues, and elites who have lost or who are in search of legitimation—are made to appear to us. The scenario of a "widow-burning plot" is made all the less comprehensible when one starts from the hypothesis that there was no preexisting tradition. The problem disappears, of course, as soon as one identifies these sacrifices—*a priori*—as murders. This is, in fact, a basic tenet of the credo of "political correctness" inside—as well as outside of—India. The very possibility that another version of the facts might exist is held to be intolerable, if not sacrilegious. In the wake of the outcry raised against the immolation of Rup Kanvar in Deorala in September 1987, one can appreciate the power of this censorship against any interpretation not in keeping with the dogma of the "widow-burning plot."[17]

What precisely is at issue here? Between 1943 and 1987, some thirty women in Rajasthan (twenty-eight, according to official statistics) immolated themselves on their husband's pyre. This figure probably falls short of the actual number. Some sacrifices escaped the attention of the local authorities. While the deaths of satīs drew large crowds of Hindus in search of blessings prior to the late 1970s, it had not yet received the publicity it would later attract. Short news items would appear in the press depicting these as so many local oddities. But neither the authorities, nor public opinion, nor feminist organizations were interested in such incidents.[18] I discovered some of the aforementioned cases—which are not found in any official list—while rummaging through the dusty back room of a bookstore in Kishangarh. Lost in the clutter of its various and sundry items for sale were a number of hagiographic pamphlets devoted to the new Mother Satīs of the region. It was these religious propaganda tracts, written for the edification of devotees, that led me to the sites of these immolations, where I was able to undertake my investigations. Unfortunately, the bookseller had just sent a large portion of his stock of the Exemplary Lives of the Satīs to the pulp mill, in order to avoid any unpleasantness with the authorities concerning violations of the Act of 1988. The complete set would have afforded a more accurate idea of the scope of the phenomenon, of its historical depth for the recent period, and of the segments of the population it affected. For one cannot always trust informants who evoke this or that burning they may have witnessed in their childhood, but of which all trace has been lost: not all satīs are deified. Little more remains of these scenes than a residual impression, the distant rumor of a memory, with the name of the heroine, the exact date of her death, and the actual venue of her sacrifice being so many casualties of the ravelling of memory or the will to forget. It is, however, difficult to ignore their accounts, which occasionally overlap in ways that are troubling. There are also the unfinished sacrifices, cut short by police or family intervention—and one wonders whether or not these should be counted. And under what heading should one place Desu, who was struck down, on October 26, 1977, by a "blow to the heart" upon the death of her husband, in a village near Osian (in Jodhpur District)? The villagers burned her mortal remains by adding wood to her husband's still-smoking pyre, since her sudden death, following so closely on that of her spouse, could only be interpreted as proof of that wife's "satī-hood" *(satītva).* A shrine was built, and she continues to receive worship there.[19] Uttar Pradesh, Madhya Pradesh, and Bihar, other regions of India that have been touched to a lesser extent by the phenomenon, present the same problems to investigators. As a result of this, it is difficult to propose a definitive figure. We can, however, at least suggest a general order of magnitude: we would probably not be far from the truth if we were to set forty as the total number of immolations that have occurred in the entire country since the decade in which India gained its independence.

But is not such a temporal division arbitrary in itself? The authors I have mentioned maintain that the movement began in the 1950s: Tara Devi, burned in 1953 in Madho-Ka-Bas, would have been the first of the new satīs of Rajasthan. However, no less than three women had immolated themselves before her—Hem Kanvar in Devpuri (Ajmer District) in 1943, Dayal Kanvar in Khud (Sikar District) in 1948, and Jaet Kanvar in Khandela (Sikar District) in 1951. In addition, Rup Kanvar and Rasal Kanvar had attempted to become satīs in Bala (Jodhpur District) in 1943. It is true that the 1950s saw an increase in such sacrifices (six as opposed to two in the 1940s). Sudesh Vaid and Kumkum Sangari pinpoint the emergence of the phenomenon in about the year 1950 because they wish to establish a cause-and-effect relationship between such apparently isolated incidents and the social context in which they were embedded. In a nutshell, the situation would have been the following: there was, on the one hand, the religious agitation of the Marwaris, as evidenced in the transformation of the Rāṇī Satī temple in Jhunjhunu into a monumental complex and pro-satī propaganda base; and on the other, Rajput political agitation, which impacted the (otherwise greatly fragmented) entire caste, from the oligarchy of princes and holders of large fiefs (that of the Rao Rajah of Sikar covered two thirds of the lands not directly administered by the Crown)[20] down to the simple Bhumiyas, who enjoyed inalienable property rights over their holdings, but who had been reduced to farming a few meager acres, and whose fate was hardly more enviable than that of the Jat farmers—who constituted a majority in the region (they accounted for a third of the local population).[21] Although it is based on an analysis that is in many respects quite accurate, the reconstruction of the facts offered by these two authors nonetheless contains a number of insoluble problems. It is difficult to understand, for example, why the 1960s "produced" but a single cremation of a satī (Jugal Kanvar, burned in Narsinghpuri, Sikar District, in 1966), when the propaganda campaigns launched by the Marwaris and Rajputs were stronger than ever and the parties championing Hindu nationalism were gaining ground every day, most especially in Sikar District, where a coalition of the Jan Sangh, Swatantra, and Janata parties carried the 1967 elections.[22]

Seven women burned themselves in the 1970s, and another woman was prevented from sacrificing herself. The decade that followed was marked by a series of immolations: Sohan Kanvar in Neemri Kothariya (Nagaur District) and Om Kanvar in Jharli (Sikar District) in 1980; the near-sacrifice of Jasvant Kanvar in Devipura (Jaipur District) in 1985; and finally, the burning of Rup Kanvar in Deorala (Sikar District), on September 4, 1987. For what reasons, we may ask, was the outrage so slow in coming; and why did the sacrifice of this particular woman so suddenly appear as an act of intolerable barbarity to the same people who had been satī-blind for decades? In what ways was it different from those that preceded it? Through what process did this last in a long series of incidents become a national tragedy, a "pagan sacrifice" which "sullied the face of Indian democracy," as the English-language press wrote in its headlines? For it is clear that public opinion and the political class could not have been unaware of the fact that at the gates of the capital of Rajasthan, women were still succumbing to the power of a custom that colonial legislation had abolished, in 1829 and 1830, from the territories under its jurisdiction. A custom that the princes of Rajputana, led by the State of Jaipur, had finally banished from their states under the pressure of the British Residents, between 1846 and 1861.[23] And finally, a custom that the Indian Penal Code (1860) also condemns, since it makes every suicide a crime punishable by law.

The Indian psychologist Ashis Nandy, whose talents as an exorcist of social theories have made him famous, has provided us with a number of answers to these questions. If Rup's death had the repercussions we know it had, giving rise as it did to a national trauma of sorts, this happened, he tells us, because the actors who generated the critical discourse on the "Deorala affair" were from social sectors (namely, the *haute bourgeoisie* and an urban middle class in full economic expansion) that felt themselves to be directly threatened by it. Anglophone and Westernized, and thereby cut off from its roots, committed to modern values (the productivity principle and market morality), this new establishment, which has been producing a new kind of culture (through the media, which it directly or indirectly controls), practices what Nandy has termed a "new form of internal colonialism."[24] Its aims are embedded in a dual strategy that is both conscious and unconscious. These sectors are seeking to preserve their hegemony in the field of political economy, while the "semi-urban" classes are striving to rise to it by claiming the cultural high ground, a tactic whose effectiveness is no longer open to question. At a deeper level, all of these groups are seeking to protect themselves from the backlash of acculturation both by stigmatizing Hinduism and by conflating tradition with superstition, rural life with social backwardness, and belief with retrograde obscurantism. The sacrifice of a young woman whose level of education and social background linked her to these emerging elites could not help but trigger a defensive reaction, and a repudiation in the strongest of terms, since it demonstrated that the borderline between civilization and barbarism, upon which the entire edifice of "internal colonialism" had been built, had proven very easy to cross.[25]

There is much one could say about the aforementioned interpretive stances. I will nonetheless desist from entering into a debate from which I am not sure the reader would stand to benefit. I would only like to indicate in passing the common ground shared by these conflicting viewpoints. It seems that each camp is seeking to mark out and even define its position in contrast to a social, cultural, or historical *exteriority,* into which to repress this hard core of barbarism (which must, after all, be assigned a place). Many times in the course of my work on satīs I have encountered the same scenario, which could be encapsulated in the formula: "The barbarous is the Elsewhere" (instead of "The barbarian is the Other"). But when, in the present discussion, these camps refer to colonialism and use that construct to their own ends, each is putting a particular face—or rather mask—on that Elsewhere. It is as if the mere utterance of this magical word, endowed with imprecatory power and cast into the enemy camp, were sufficient, in and of itself, to remove all the difficulties that prevent us from understanding the facts. Ashis Nandy's critical distance from all the passions which the affair aroused may also be interpreted as a projection onto an Elsewhere, which finds its expression, in his case, in the paradoxical form of internal colonialism.[26]

True and False Traditions

I would prefer to approach matters from a different perspective and revisit the postulate according to which no genuine tradition of widow sacrifice ever existed in Shekhavati. This question is crucial. We may begin by asking what scale is appropriate for measuring a tradition. How many women must be burned before one can speak of a "true" tradition as opposed to a tradition cobbled together by social actors? To deduce from the relatively small number of satīs in royal families that the practice had a low rate of incidence in the region, as Vaid and Sangari have done, seems to me a bold move. Would the sacrifice of widows have been the exclusive prerogative of princes? Would one be not seeing the forest for the trees? The Rajputs represent less than 7 percent of the population of Shekhavati, and the royal families a minute fraction of the Rajput community.[27] To then assert that the significant number of women burned since independence is the result of the mystifying propaganda of a coalition of reactionary forces is somewhat of a paradox, since a total of thirty immolations of widows, in relation to the entire female population of the state of Rajasthan,[28] is without statistical value (it constitutes an infinitesimal percentage). One cannot make figures say both one thing and its opposite.

Anyone who travels through this geographical zone—which is more varied than it might first appear (wide open desert in the northwest, mountainous landscapes to the north and northeast, with a quite fertile and well-populated plain in the center)—will, at the outer limits of towns and villages or out in the countryside, come across a number of aniconic platforms, commemorative stones, and small shrines and temples that serve as so many boundary markers, and also bear witness to the passing, in the Shekhavati, of satīs of a bygone age. Some of these monuments are thought to be very old (five hundred years and more, according to informants), but there is no detailed benchmark survey to aid in determining their historical period. While many among them reveal, through their dilapidated state, the disaffection of former devotees, others have apparently never ceased their ritual activity: apart from daily morning and evening worship, an annual or biennial religious fair will bring their devotees together, most often on the last day of the dark fortnight of the sixth month of the lunar calendar *(bhādon badī amāvasyā)* or on the anniversary of the satī's death. Sikar District alone counts twenty-four cult sites where satīs are still worshipped, with ten of these located within the city of Fatehpur (nearly 35,000 inhabitants in 1971, a little more than 51,000 in 1981) alone. New satīs are instantaneously incorporated into the mass of their anonymous predecessors: their historicity becomes cloaked in the mantle of mythification, with their death-dates being entered directly into the liturgical calendar. Here as elsewhere in western India, most of the old satīs are known only by their place- or caste-name, or by some circumstance related to their sacrifice. In Thoi, a small town of five thousand inhabitants in the *tehsīl* of Sri Madhopur, a platform commemorates a certain "Blue Indigo Sati" *(Nīl Satī),* born into the Jat caste some three hundred years ago: it is alleged that indigo was thrown on her, but the power of the *sat* prevailed.[29]

These data are most useful since they allow us to form an idea of the geographical and social distribution of the practice on a district-wide scale. First of all, one finds that it covers the entire Sikar region, with the highest concentration in the eastern Neem-Ka-Thana subdivision, and that it furthermore encompasses nearly the entire spectrum of the social hierarchy: upper-caste satīs (Brahmans, Rajputs, Mahajans) jostle with satīs from intermediate castes (Jats, Mathurs, Baniyas), lowly artisan castes (Sunar goldsmiths, Lohar blacksmiths, Khati carpenters), and castes that are impure (Nai barbers) or of tribal origin (Minas). So the Rajputs of that earlier time never held the monopoly on the sacrifice of women in the region that presently corresponds to Sikar District. If we now take as our base the entire state of Rajasthan for the period between 1943 and 1987, we find an equal diversity in social origins: there is even a case of a street-singer Rani woman committing satī. This time, however, the Rajputs account for more than half of the immolations (19 out of 30).[30]

When we go back beyond the 1940s, we are reduced to gleaning the sparse information that Hindus born at the beginning of the century are willing to impart to us. In the course of my repeated stays in Shekhavati, I had many long interviews with women who were extremely advanced in age, octogenarians or nonagenarians—many villagers do not know their exact date of birth; and not so many years ago, the registration of births and deaths was regarded as a British eccentricity.[31] I consulted them on all sorts of questions—for example, color symbolism, menstrual pollution, women's rituals—since they are repositories of a knowledge that their daughters, granddaughters, and *a fortiori* their later descendants have generally lost. And naturally I asked them and their menfolk from the same generation about the place satīs had occupied in their own lives. Once their reticence had subsided, my interlocutors showed themselves to be inexhaustible on the subject. Satīs were everywhere in their life stories. There were the lineage satīs who had to be honored if one wished to have sons or shield oneself from the hand of fate; the chosen satīs (*iṣṭ-satīs*) one worshipped in one's heart of hearts; Mother Satīs whose intercession, blessing, and grace were solicited on important occasions and whom one visited on pilgrimages; the All-Satīs *(sarv-satiyān)* to whom one sang songs during night vigils; mysterious satīs who revealed themselves in the chiaroscuro of dreams; malevolent satīs who pronounced curses, provoked earthquakes, and brought sickness, sterility, and adversity; miraculous satīs who left a trail of wonders in their wake as a sign of their powers; adoptive satīs, introduced into the household by daughters-in-law; found satīs, whose worship site had been discovered, quite by chance, while on the road; satīs one had heard about but whose sanctifying vision *(darśan)* one had never obtained; and finally, for some, there were also those satīs whom they had known in their profane, human form, before their transfiguration by sacrifice. These satīs had descended to earth in order to restore order to the world. They refuted the proverb: "Neither satī nor *yati* [ascetic] in this Iron Age."

These interviews, conducted between 1978 and 1993 with Hindus from a wide variety of castes and conditions, have convinced me that this set of motifs—embedded in a mental and affective universe, transmitted through multifarious channels, and marking the rhythm of an important aspect of people's religious lives—taken together, formed a picture that very much resembled what is generally called a tradition; that that tradition, deep-rooted as it was, had persisted in spite of a ban intended to eradicate it; and that as a result, what was taking place before our eyes—the shocking reactivation of an antiquated ritual—could be explained in part by a remarkable persistence of religious attitudes toward the supernatural beings that satīs remain for so many believers.[32] In saying this, I am expressing neither approval nor admiration of any sort. Nor am I adopting the stance of the Orientalist voyeur delighting in "a notion of Bharat and her tradition-led masses which can profitably maintain India as a backward enclave and a cultural spectacle favoured by neo-colonialism."[33] Sudesh Vaid and Kumkum Sangari are right when they vigorously denounce the way Hindu nationalist ideologues and reactionaries have invoked popular belief to legitimate the immolation of women or, even worse, made such the symbol of a purified, essentialized Hinduism upon which the entire edifice of *dharma* would stand. Nonetheless, by countering this position, in the name of a different ideology, Vaid and Sangari are paradoxically led to take the same standpoint, that of the outsider, that characterized the widely disparaged colonialist vision.

Just as Shekhavati never formed a pocket of resistance to the rite's spread, so too women belonging to the merchant *(vaṇij)* class did not wait for the middle of the twentieth century to begin burning themselves. Epigraphy provides us with examples dating back to the middle of the first millennium C.E. From the end of the fifteenth century onward, travelogues are full of eyewitness accounts of the cremation of "banianes." Their zeal in ascending the pyre and burning themselves alive in specially built huts lacks none of the panache of satīs from the warrior castes. We can understand how the pomp of the funerary ceremonies of a deceased king or warlord, and the sometimes considerable number of wives, concubines, and servants immolated on such occasions, might have eclipsed more humble sacrifices. But it should be recalled here that the hypothesis that the custom was a kṣatriya prerogative that the lower classes adopted in order to imitate the royal model and raise themselves in the social hierarchy remains unsupported by any conclusive evidence. All that can be said at present is that originally the worship of satīs was probably linked to the glorification of the warrior's heroic death, which had come to be seen as a supreme form of world-renunciation.[34] More than this we cannot say. And yet the historical reconstruction outlined above has been elevated to the level of an article of faith. Its credit has been further enhanced by the backing bards and genealogists have lent to it through their rhetorical use of the deaths of satīs to legitimate their Rajput patrons. British historiography fell into lockstep with the native mythographers and found in James Tod its most gifted bard. The local culture adopted Tod's romantic vision for its own. Hindu nationalists—with the Rajputs in the vanguard—refer to the *Annals and Antiquities of Rajasthan* as a sacred source.[35] Returning to the Marwaris, while it is true that the *seṭh*s of Shekhavati—wealthy merchants, moneylenders, and treasurers attached to the princely courts—adopted a grandiose lifestyle, building sumptuous *havelīs* and sometimes even wearing the prestigious *tāzīm* (the anklet and honorific insignia bestowed by the Maharajah of Jaipur upon elite Rajput chieftains), there is no reason to believe that a similar process of imitation played a part in the immolation of women, given the fact that the historical legacy of the custom within the merchant castes renders it a tradition per se, regardless of whether it was originally borrowed from the warrior castes.

Cross-Examination of a District

The district of Sikar, where twelve women have burned themselves since 1948, was carved out of the former fief *(ṭhikānā)* of the Rao Rajah of Sikar on October 15, 1949.[36] Its population was 676,320 in 1951; 1,042,650 in 1971; and 1,377,245 in 1981. The sex ratio shows a significant imbalance in favor of males, which is characteristic of the region as a whole.[37] Essentially rural, the district includes 813 inhabited villages and nine cities, including Sikar, its capital, where the district's urban population is most concentrated (102,970 in 1981, 148,270 in 1991). Rural population density is the highest in the Sri Madhopur *tehsīl,* which comprises 170 villages and which has provided a significant contingent of new satīs.[38] The literacy rate was 15.7 percent in 1961 for the district as a whole, 13.2 percent for the rural population, and only 2.9 percent for women in the rural zone. It remains quite low today, though some progress has been recorded.[39] Hindus constitute an overwhelming majority (90.1 percent in 1971), with Muslims the strongest minority (9.3 percent), and Jains, Sikhs, and Christians together accounting for only 0.6 percent of the population.[40] As for the population distribution by caste, the latest census to give such data dates from 1931. Due to the war, the 1941 census could not be completed, and since India's independence, official documents no longer record caste affiliation.[41] While the central government's concern has been to obliterate caste differences as a means of battling discrimination, "the age-old social structure of the Hindu society based on *Varnashram* [*varṇāśrama-dharma,* the duties of class and stage of life] is still visible in the district," according to the 1971 census report's euphemistic formulation.[42]

It is impossible here to decant the details of a micro-regional analysis into a sociological profile of the Toravati, the territorial area grouping together those hamlets, villages, and small towns (situated within a twenty-mile radius of the small city of Neem-Ka-Thana[43]) that have been the scene for a succession of immolations since 1953 (which peaked between 1973 and 1987). Instead, we shall limit ourselves to an impressionistic overview that will permit us to restore the data to their own context, rather than to that of polemics.

At the close of the nineteenth century, Toravati constituted a division *(nizāmat)* whose administrative center was Neem-Ka-Thana, an artificial division that nonetheless corresponded to a perception, by the region's own inhabitants, of a cultural and territorial unity—what some geographers have termed a "folk region."[44] It owes its name to the Tanvar (or Tuar, Tomar, Tomvar) Rajputs, one of the thirty-six most prestigious Rajput clans, whose origin myth has them descended from the famous Pāṇḍavas, the heroes of the *Mahābhārata.* It is claimed that they founded Delhi on the site of the former Indraprastha, the capital of the epic's king Yudhiṣṭhira. The region is contiguous to that of Udaipurvati, the principal Shekhavat stronghold, making it a locus whose Rajput imagery is overdetermined. Most of the villages in which women have burned themselves in recent history were founded by Tanvars or Shekhavats. Jharli (where Om Kanvar immolated herself in 1980), located southeast of the small town of Thoi, is thought to have been founded three hundred years ago by the Tanvars, and later conquered by the Shekhavats under Gordhan Singh, who also founded Hardas-Ka-Bas (seven miles from Jharli), where Sarasvati burned herself in 1978.[45]

Jharli's foundation myth is a sort of reproduction in miniature of the myth of the birth of Shekha-ji, the eponymous ancestor of the Shekhavats. We find in it the theme of the Rajput chief whose wives are sterile and who obtains offspring through the miraculous intercession of a Sheikh, a Muslim holy man. The latter exacts a promise that the newborn's first bath be taken in the blood of a cow. As a good Hindu, the father cannot bring himself to commit such a sacrilege, and so substitutes goat blood for the taboo substance. The Sheikh is not fooled, however, and condemns him and his lineage to be but a he-goat among the lions (the Rajputs of royal houses).[46] This myth, which justifies status asymmetry through a respect for the sacred precepts of Hinduism and which, in a way, symbolically atones for this asymmetry, is paired with an account of the village's name: one day, Gordhan Singh spotted a female wolf and her cub in a brushwood thicket out of which there sprang a tiger, who wanted to eat the cub. An uneven struggle ensued, from which the she-wolf emerged victorious. Moved by the scene, Gordhan Singh decided to call the spot *Jhāṛlī,* "brushwood country." This story is reminiscent of one told at Thoi: about three hundred years ago a Jat saw a lion that was about to devour a cow, and died attempting to save it. His wife became the "blue indigo Satī" *(Nīl Satī Mātā)* whose aniconic platform south of the village commemorates the sacrifice.[47]

These narratives, collected locally, speak to us of hierarchy: hierarchy of status, of the "goals of man" (the *puruṣārtha*s), and of gender. These are stories about social stratification between Rajput clans or branches, but also about the opposition between power and *dharma,* whose symbols are the Lion and the Cow. By refusing to shed the blood of a cow, the Rajput chief placed *dharma* before *artha* (goal-oriented activity), but in so doing had to renounce kingship; in giving his life to save a cow, the Jat reached the "Path of Heroes" and attained liberation *(mokṣa),* thereby effecting a reversal of his status: farmers subjected to unpaid labor, arbitrary evictions, and exactions that would lead to the peasant revolts of the 1930s in the former *ṭhikānā* of Sikar, the Jats constitute (in other regions of India) a caste of fief-holding warriors, some of whom rose to princely rank.[48] Note here that when men are forced to give up their power or their lives, female figures show themselves to be all-powerful: the she-wolf triumphs over the tiger, and the Blue Indigo Satī takes the lion's share in her cult (it is she and not her husband who is worshipped). It is as if the supernatural powers of the Feminine compensate for the innate powerlessness of men. What filters through these stories, which are so simple in appearance, is that when the group is in a situation of declining status, it falls to its womenfolk to perform miraculous deeds, as signs of their *śakti,* to return things to an even footing and soothe wounded egos. The story line of the "widow-burning plot," far from being a 1950s *fabrication,* seems to have been woven into the *fabric* of the foundation myths of the villages within the specific area where the phenomenon would revive most widely.

We have therefore to choose here between two lines of argumentation. In the first, we must be prepared to allow that belief ultimately eludes social determinations; that in any case the archaic of belief has much to do with fantasmatic constructions; and, finally that while one or another coincidence of circumstances can at any time reactivate it, this still would not reduce belief to a mere product of circumstances. In the second op-tion, we are prepared to make an *a priori* identification between belief and mystification, a stance that is, in the final analysis, as legitimate as any other, provided that we carry through on it. If we were to follow this line of reasoning to its logical ends, we would find that it is the agents of mystification who are the first to be mystified; that they mystify in good faith; and that men and women are caught *together* in an interplay of mystifying forces of which they control neither the "production" nor the direct or indirect effects on their own lives. We also realize that just as denial and belief can go hand in hand, so too can mystification and belief coexist. This, I think, is where one of the keys to the puzzle lies. It is also the fundamental predicament currently facing Indian lawmakers. In saying this, I am in no way subscribing to the formulation of Kalyan Singh Kalvi, who was the head of the Janata Party in Rajasthan at the time of the immolation of Rup Kanvar, and who declared in this regard that "Sati was never a system. It is not one now, and will not be one in the future. It is a case of an individual decision. . . . People's beliefs and sentiments cannot be repressed." Kalvi was one of a number of persons who built their careers on the "Defense of Satī *Dharma*."[49] This argument, advanced by all supporters of the rite in my field interviews with them, seems to me a perfect illustration of the symbiosis between good faith and false consciousness. But it is also true that no legal action will ever abolish the archaic.

Each of the places where a woman has burned herself in recent history constitutes a world unto itself. Lost in the sands (even if it is relatively close to the small cities of Kanvat and Thoi), Madho-Ka-Bas is home to two hundred inhabitants (all of them Hindu), while Jharli and Deorala (Divrala in Rajasthani) are much larger, more accessible, and more highly developed population centers (11,025 and 10,500 inhabitants, respectively). Hathideh is a large village, but with a poor infrastructure (particularly in water); it has known both drought and famine, and half of its active population have migrated to other Indian states in search of jobs. Despite their contrasts, these villages have a number of common features: although they are all multicaste, the Shekhavat Rajputs are nearly always the dominant caste, both numerically and politically,[50] with most of the village councils in which local policy is drafted under their control.[51] In those places where this is not the case, intercaste tensions are greatly exacerbated, with the Rajputs remaining "masters" *(mālik*s) to be feared in the minds of most villagers. At the time of Om Kanvar's sacrifice, the head of the Jharli village council was a Mahajan. His anti-satī stance led to his replacement by a Rajput in the 1989 elections. In Divrala, where elections to the council were traditionally conducted on a consensus basis, the opposite occurred. In 1987, at the time of the "Deorala affair," it was a Mahajan belonging to the Congress-I Party who was the head of the village council. While it was not a Rajput who succeeded him, this was because Rup Kanvar's death and the aggressive attitude of the Rajputs on that occasion (an attitude provoked by the Rajasthan government's threats to ban the twelfth-day ceremony of the offering of the veil,[52] as well as by a series of anti-Rajput reactions on the national level) had alienated them from the other castes.

The second characteristic of these villages is that one finds in them vestiges of satīs from another time. Divrala (said to have been founded by Anant Singh in the early fifteenth century) thus houses, in its eastern quarter (the direction of the gods), a "satī site" *(satī-sthal)* at which two aniconic platforms commemorate the sacrifices of Kuman Kanvar and Mithu Kanvar, both of whom were married into Rup's husband's family line. Following Rup's immolation, a third platform came to complement this funerary group, which is held in great veneration by Rajputs, but visited by members of every caste. The worship rites of the eleventh *(ekādaśī)* and the last *(amāvasyā)* day of the dark lunar fortnight were victims of the ban on the glorification of satīs promulgated by the government of Rajasthan on October 1, 1987. Since that time, the Mother Satīs of Divrala have had to content themselves with a reduced worship service (limited to *ārtī*),[53] in which only women and children participate. At Jharli, a stela honors the memory of an unmarried girl from the Gujar caste who died for a lover from the Ahir caste; Kariri, another hamlet in the region, houses a shrine to a betrothed woman who became a satī. For the new satīs, the call to sacrifice is in a sense preinscribed, reflected back at them by these vestiges of the sacrifice which, even when forsaken and worn down by the workings of time and oblivion, retain their power of suggestion intact.[54]

The third point of similarity between these villages, one that flows from the strong Rajput presence in this microregion, is that one does not find any significant improvement in the condition of women. It is true that insofar as marriage is concerned, matters have changed somewhat, especially over the past two generations. Child marriages have decreased almost to the point of vanishing: infrequent in the rural areas, they have disappeared entirely from the cities, although traces of the practice were still present in the 1961 census. Premature widowhood (which, it will be recalled, is especially stigmatized) is in marked decline as a result of the increasing age at which marriage occurs.[55] Polygyny, in vogue among the Rajputs and Jats, was prohibited by law in 1955; moreover, a 1956 law gave daughters legal rights to inheritance, and widows access to their husband's property, under certain conditions.[56] Contrariwise, attitudes have not evolved concerning widow remarriage: the ban continues to be strictly observed among the higher castes (Brahmans, Rajputs, and Mahajans), whereas all other castes favor secondary marriages—often little more than sanctioned preferential relationship—usually with the husband's younger brother. The *nātā,* it will be recalled, is not considered to be a sacrament.[57] Intercaste marriages are extremely rare; divorce is not yet socially accepted, and although certain ritual minutiae no longer have any currency, marriages are still arranged and performed in the traditional manner: rules and degrees of endogamy, in particular, are strictly observed. Following the marriage ceremony, women leave the village where they were born to live with their in-laws, and all descendants in the paternal line continue to live under the same roof.[58] In rural areas, the extended or joint-family does not yet show the signs of disintegration that have been observed elsewhere in India as well as in cities within the district.

Nor does one see any significant changes in practices relating to the purdah system: in the higher castes, women rarely go out of the house. To be sure, they are no longer expected to cover themselves with the piece of white cloth *(cāndṇī)* that, like a mobile tent, formerly accompanied them wherever they went (which was, in any case, not very far). But they continue to hide their faces behind a veil *(ghūnghaṭ)* in the presence of their parents-in-law, elder sisters-in-law, and (it goes without saying) anyone from outside the family. When they wish to communicate with people around them, they still must go through third parties who act as intermediaries, or use sign language. Speech is not forbidden to them, of course, but it has to be tempered by an attitude of respect to their elders, which takes the form of a demeanor of diffident modesty and bashfulness *(śaram):* words rise inaudibly to their lips, while their eyes remain resolutely lowered. These interdictions and constraints disappear when the ravages of time neutralize the power of custom.

Just as every village or town in which a woman has burned herself constitutes a microcosm, so too each case history is unique and incomparable. What keeps us from perceiving this uniqueness is the process of mythification that begins as soon as the woman declares herself a satī, even prior to the enactment of her sacrifice. Acting in the fashion of a desiccating balm, it mummifies a life and a destiny, until nothing remains but the abstract contours. Locked away thereafter inside a preexisting category containing similarly impersonal and supernatural beings, the life story of each satī, which is irreducible to any other satī's story, nonetheless becomes interchangeable, and fades from view until it disappears into the distant recesses of her cult. Her rise to the heavenly spheres and attainment of immortality abolish all trace of the flesh-and-blood satī from the memories of her survivors. In most cases, her name is forgotten, and replaced with that of her caste or of the scene of her sacrifice. And when villages become deserted, the "nameless satī" is left standing by the roadside, lost in a space no longer marked by the ritual activities of men, a stone among stones.

THE RITE, THE LAW, AND THE CUSTOM

The time has now come for us to put together the pieces of the puzzle, a task whose intense difficulty was underscored by Georges Perec in a passage from *Life, A User's Manual,* under whose sign it has been my wish to place this book. Because in this case the interlocking elements are beliefs and symbol systems, and because the landscape to be reconstructed is a universe that is remarkable for its otherness, our task is made all the more arduous. The crucial pieces—whose interconnection with more marginal pieces has allowed a pattern to emerge that, even as it sheds light on the principal enigma, has become diffracted into a series of secondary enigmas—have appeared in these pages as so many contrasting elements. These apparent oppositions—between death and immortality (or rather, from the Hindu perspective, transmigration and liberation), between dying before and dying after, dying for and dying against, self-sacrifice and supernatural survival, commemoration and oblivion, violence and the denial of violence, sexual asymmetry and its inversion (i.e., male dominance versus feminine power), and finally between love, the passion of women that the stigma of menstrual blood inscribes in their bodies, and the lethal power of that passion: these oppositions are but a single facet of the greater bond that joins them together. In fact, these patterns show themselves to be tightly interconnected in an unexpected turn of events in the history of satīs.

Ritual and How to Use It

The case in point is a technical discussion of the ritual itself, which involved the judges and agents of the East India Company on the one hand, and on the other, pundits and *śāstrīs*, brahman repositories of knowledge and experts in the exegesis of sacred texts and matters of *dharma.*[1] As of 1777, a number of learned brahmans and specialists of Islamic law (*maulvīs*) were attached to the Supreme Court of Justice of Calcutta (established in 1773), the Court of Criminal Justice of Murshidabad,[2] and the four Courts of Circuit based in Calcutta, Murshidabad, Dacca, and Patna. It was their role to expound upon or clarify the theological and legal canons of India's two major "native" communities. It was through the cooperation of these pundits and *śāstrīs*, for example, that measures were first promulgated aimed at abolishing the ritual sacrifice of children on the island of Sagar at the mouth of the Hooghly River (where they were exposed or thrown to the alligators), the suicide of bards, and the infanticide of girls.

The British justified these breaches of their policy of noninterference in the religious affairs of India—whatever the confession—by claiming that such practices, in the opinion of the pundits consulted, were not based in scripture, but were merely matters of custom. They were without legal ground, it was argued, and had been introduced solely through human fancy, on account of the degeneration of the pure religion. Such abominations decked out in the finery of Rites were an assault on the Holy Scriptures of the Hindus, and it was the duty of an enlightened government to protect its subjects from themselves as a means to better defending the spirit of the indigenous law. Yet for all this, the rite that roused the greatest horror and indignation, and the one that had spread most spectacularly through the newly annexed territories (especially in the Bengal Presidency and, ironically, in the Calcutta Division, the seat of the British administration), was the same one that offered the most insurmountable resistance to the reformist zeal of India's new rulers, given the fact that, according to orthodoxy, the sacrifice of satīs constituted a veritable touchstone of Hinduism.[3]

If nothing else, the expert opinion of the pundits and *śāstrīs* established an essential point of doctrine: that there was no question that neither the Veda (in the broad sense of the term) nor the *Laws of Manu*—in other words, neither Revelation nor this universally acknowledged Tradition—made any reference to these sacrifices. Custom, then, did not stem from Law. In this case, Law had become the reflection of custom. It also became known that this rite had given rise, in the past, to all manner of theological dispute; that it belonged to the category of votive *(kāmya)* rites—no *dharma* commentator had made it an absolute necessity, and even those who recommended or exalted it left the woman with a theoretical freedom of choice[4]—and finally, that there existed a number of restrictions of a religious nature that placed limits on its execution. Disqualified from performing the sacrifice are: girls below the age of puberty, women suffering from amenorrhea or who, on the contrary, are having their period; pregnant women or mothers with infants; disobedient or adulterous wives; women who have not been good spouses (in the Sanskrit sense of the term *pativratā,* "she who respects her marriage vow");[5] who have not freely and solemnly declared their intention to burn themselves; who may have been drugged, tied down on the pyre, or pushed into the fire with bamboo poles; who at the last moment regret their decision; who are not of a pure caste and, conversely, Brahman women who would become "murderers of the self" (*ātma-ghātinīs*) by committing such an act. Certain *dharma* authors, however, grant Brahman women the right of self-immolation on the condition that it be on the same pyre as the husband, and not on a separate one. Other more liberal commentators confer on them the right of "dying after" *(anumaraṇa),* on the condition that they burn together with the bones or ashes of their husband, and not with a symbolic object or an effigy of *kuśa* grass as a surrogate for his person.[6] Naturally, each of these stipulations is a source of endless debate and fuel for a dizzying spate of casuistry. An example of this is "dying after," a thorny question that greatly preoccupied *dharma* specialists. Some were of the opinion that if a wife whose husband is away learns of his death and does not burn herself at once, she should by no means be authorized to do so subsequently, since her hesitation would be sufficient proof that she is not a truly ideal spouse.[7] At the close of the seventeenth century, Robert Challe, a writer in the service of the French king, had occasion to make the following observation, on the subject of the solemn declaration of intention by a wife who has become a widow:

> As soon as her husband dies she must declare that she wishes to burn herself with him, & inform some old bramène that appears suitable to her that he is the one she has chosen to perform the ceremony. Were she to allow a quarter of an hour's interval between the death of her husband & her declaration, she would no longer be received; because that declaration would be regarded as a result of her reflections & not as an effect of a tender and disinterested love whose sole object is that which it loves.[8]

Herewith another example of the pundits' finesse in matters of ritual: the "rules prescribed by the Veda" allegedly established different modes of performance for the sacrifice of satīs depending on whether the husband, during his life, had been a householder authorized to perform the solemn *(śrauta)* rites and possessed of the requisite three sacrificial fires (which the Sanskrit renders by the word *āhitāgni*),[9] or a twice-born householder possessing but a single fire for his domestic *(gṛhya)* rites:

The widows of ahitagnees, or such as preserve the sacrificial fires, are enjoined to proceed to the burning place in close conjunction with the corpse and the three fires. The widows of anahitagnees are merely enjoined to remain on the road in close company with the corpses of their husbands. In the place where the corpse is deposited, the formula attendant on the ceremony must be expressed in the dual number; and the widow must be made to sit down at the same time. All the ceremonies that occur on the road are to be observed in the same manner. Having arrived at the place of burning, the widow must be laid on the funeral pile at the side of her deceased husband. If she be then destitute of the wish to perform the act of suhagumun ["going with"], she must be lifted off. The widow being desirous of burning with the corpse of her deceased husband (provided he was an ahitagnee) is to be laid on the pile with its face upwards, and the sacrificial vessels having been applied to his members, the widow is to be laid upon him with her face downwards. At the time of applying the fire, the pile is to be lighted for both at once; and the formula on this occasion is to be recited in the dual number. The texts, propitiatory of Yama, are also to be recited in the same manner by him who officiates at the sacrifice, standing near the funeral pile. In the case of a widow of an anahitagnee, the sacrificial vessels termed *smarta* being applied, the widow is to be laid beside the corpse. The remaining ceremonies are similar in both cases.[10]

The British pondered: What was meant by "girl below the age of puberty"? How could one know for sure that a woman about to sacrifice herself had never had her period? Child marriages still being prevalent at the time, a significant number of young girls were being burned. In addition, early menarche was not unusual in those climes (Hindus generally set the age of puberty at ten). Was puberty to be identified with maturity (in the sense of legal responsibility, which began at age sixteen according to British law)? In short, what was the legal age for burning oneself alive? On which day of her menstrual cycle did a woman regain the purity necessary for performing the rite? What was meant by "a child in its infancy" (the Sanskrit makes a distinction between *kumāra, śiśu,* and *bāla*)?[11] Was weaning to be considered the criterion in this case? (It occurs rather late in India—children of six still suck at the breast.) What was meant by pure caste? Must the satī necessarily have been born in the same *varṇa* as her husband?[12] And how was one to know whether she was consenting, whether she had declared her intention to burn in accordance with the ritual formula *(saṃkalpa),* or whether she had not been "deranged" with betel, a decoction of opium, saffron, or datura? Was the pyre to be lit before or after the satī had ascended it? There were pundits who argued that if she were to ascend a pyre not already in flames, then her son would be guilty of matricide.[13] Others maintained that if she did not light the fire herself (with a torch or pot of oil to set her hair aflame, or with a wick placed between her big and second toes), the rite would not bear fruit, because there would be no way of knowing whether the sacrifice was voluntary. Was the live burial of a widow in her husband's grave, customary among castes and sects that inter their dead rather than cremating them (in particular the Jogi weavers of Bengal),[14] sanctioned by the *Śāstra*s? Ought the cremation of a woman who had never lived under the same roof as her husband be permitted? Such were legion in Bengal, where Kulin Brahmans took a multitude of lower-ranking Shrotiya Brahman wives. While this system of unbridled polygyny brought increased prestige to the Shrotiyas,[15] it afforded the Kulins benefits of a less symbolic nature, since they demanded payment in exchange. When a Kulin male died, it was not uncommon for his crop of secondary wives to be gleaned from the villages they had never left to be burned in a great fire. So it was that in 1799 the pyre of Anantaram, a Kulin from the Nadiya region, burned continuously for three days, while relays of women (thirty-seven in all) were sacrificed, in shifts, over its embers.[16]

These were not, then, abstract questions, or scholarly minutiae: the magistrates in charge of dispensing justice in their districts were faced with intractable matters of conscience in which their sense of duty, their own religious convictions, and their indomitable prejudice against the barbarity of the rite clashed with contradictory directives handed down from above. In fact, neither the Court of Directors of the Company nor the British Parliament were able to reach agreement on this matter (up to the year 1858, India was administered by a dyarchy, in which the Crown increasingly affirmed its hegemony over the Company). A great number of reasons may be elicited to explain their problems in promulgating a coherent policy, the most compelling of these being opportunistic considerations. For example, Britain was locked in a war with the Gurkhas and the Marathas until 1818. The Indian Army counted a large contingent of native soldiers (the famous Sepoys), many of whom were high-caste Hindus. The extreme prudence shown by the authorities may be explained in part by their fear of the reactions that might have been prompted by a drastic measure of prohibition.[17] And yet the abolition of widow-burning in 1829–1830 did not in fact give rise to any disorder in the ranks. On the other hand, there was trouble when a new rifle was introduced whose operation required that soldiers use their teeth to remove cartridges from their casings (which may have been soaked in cow or pig fat, to the horror of Hindus and Muslims alike), an incident that provoked the Sepoy Mutiny of 1857.

Circulars sent out to the authorities in the 267 districts under British rule opened the way to divergent interpretations. Collectors strove to follow to the letter the orders they were sent. Some attempted bold initiatives of their own, which were sometimes answered with reprimands or sanctions. Others, heeding only the powerful voice of human nature, took matters much further. Outraged by the horrific circumstances surrounding the September 27, 1823, cremation of a Brahman woman from within his jurisdiction, Captain H. D. Robertson, the Collector of Poona, devised an unprecedented pyre that corresponded to the descriptions contained in certain ritual compendia. His introduction of that *ad hoc* pyre onto the local widow-sacrifice market constitutes the central episode in a venture in which it may be observed that the British, in their vigilant attempts to ensure that the abominable rite was administered according to the rules of the art ("agreeably to the Shaster"), paradoxically became the masters of ceremonies for a practice they abhorred.[18]

A Satī in Poona

Bala-ji Pant died in Apte, in Konkan, of snakebite. His two brothers burned his body. A week later, they went to Poona to bring Radha-bai, the wife of the deceased, news of his death along with his bones, which they had saved. Radha-bai immediately declared herself a satī. The greater the pressure placed on her, the more obstinate she became. Finally, despite his revulsion and his doubts as to the legal basis for "dying after," Robertson granted her authorization to burn together with the bones of her husband on a separate pyre. Through an unfortunate coincidence, the police officers (the *jamādār* and his men), who ordinarily attended such ceremonies in order to assure their conformity to law, were busy leading a criminal to the gallows. While a number of Englishmen (both military and civilian) were present among the onlookers, none had been vested with any authority for the occasion.

Radha-bai ascended the pyre with great composure. In this part of the country, the traditional pyre was in the form of a hut *(koṭhī)*. A roof of palm fronds and logs was held up by posts and ropes that the officiant would cut once the fire had caught, causing the superstructure to come crashing

Fig. 47. The roofed pyre: illustration taken from James Peggs's pamphlet, *India's Cries to British Humanity, Relative to Suttee, Infanticide, British Connexion with Idolatry, Ghaut murders and Slavery in India . . .* (London, 1830). Courtesy Bibliothèque Nationale, Paris.

down and burn the satī (fig. 47). Radha-bai lit the hut herself with a burning wick. But the brahman was slow-handed, and failed to trip the fatal device quickly enough. Unable to bear her fiery torment, Radha-bai escaped. Two Englishmen came to her aid, taking her down to the river to treat her burns. In a burst of courage, she asked to try again, complaining that the pyre had been poorly built, and was burning her too slowly. When she found herself on the threshold of the hut, however, she recoiled, terrified. In order to finish her off, her relatives then took her by the feet, pushed her into the fire, and threw huge logs over her to make escape impossible. When the violent heat of the flames pushed them back, Radha-bai miraculously succeeded in fleeing the burning hut and dragging herself to the river, where her relatives would have drowned her had one of the English officers not saved her *in extremis.* Twenty hours later, death delivered her from her agony, which was atrocious, according to eyewitnesses. On September 29, 1823, "A decided Enemy to Suttees," who wished to remain anonymous, sent the following letter to the editor of the *Bombay Courier:*

I cannot describe to you the horror I felt on seeing the mangled condition she was in; almost every inch of skin on her body had been burnt off; her legs and thighs, her arms and back, were completely raw; her breasts were dreadfully torn, and the skin hanging from them in threads; the skin and nails of her fingers had peeled wholly off, and were hanging to the back of her hands. In fact, Sir, I never saw or ever read of so entire a picture of misery as this poor woman displayed. She seemed to dread being again taken to the fire; and called out to the "Ocha Sahib," as she feelingly denominated them, to save her. Her friends seemed no longer inclined to force her; and one of her relations at our instigation sat down beside her, and gave her some clothes, and told her they would not. We had her sent to the hospital, where every medical assistance was immediately given her, but without hope of her recovery. She lingered in the most excruciating pain for about twenty hours and then died.[19]

In no time, two hundred brahmans had gathered together in the Tulsi Bagh temple to challenge the right of the British to interfere in the course of a ceremony permitted by their own government (the presence of the magistrate or the *dārogā,* his Indian deputy, at the cremation site had reinforced orthodox Hindus' belief in the legitimacy of the rite). On the following day, the Collector invited the most famous pundits and *śāstrī*s of Poona to a "conference." He flattered himself in the hope that in their heart of hearts, enlightened brahmans desired an end to such cruel sacrifices. For hours, Robertson addressed, in Marathi, an audience of Hindu literati without using an interpreter, a fact that impressed them. He even succeeded in disquieting them through the force of his arguments. They remained speechless as the Collector, showing himself to be as skilled in casuistry as a brahman, made the point that no otherworldly benefits could accrue to a husband from a sacrifice that his wife had not had the courage to carry out to the bitter end. In spite of this, the meeting ended inconclusively.

Considering his to be a sacred mission, Roberston decided to act without first consulting his superiors (in particular W. Chaplin, the Commissioner of the Deccan, to whom he did not send his report until October 9). It was a chance he could not pass up. But what was he to do? Upon reflection, undertaking legal proceedings did not appear to be the best policy. At that point he had no other recourse than that of "enter[ing] on a strict examination of the origin and forms of suttee as laid down in the Shaster, to endeavour to find some plausible or substantial ground on which an order of government might rest," under the cover of which he might take urgent measures within his district. Such an action could not be challenged since it would be legally grounded in the authority of the *Śāstra*s. Robertson quite providentially came across a set of prescriptions concerning the construction of the pyre, in a number of legal compendia. Some time later, a famous *śāstrī* from Surat would confirm his findings in an answer to a query sent to him:

> Question 14th. In what manner is the pile to be prepared for a woman about to burn with her husband's body?
>
> The pile must be covered over with grass, laid upon branches or sticks. Shankhayum [Śāṅkhāyana] Rushee [Ṛṣi] writes in that Shakha, a branch of the Roogvedu *[Ṛg Veda]* bearing his name . . . ["]Build a room around the pile itself of seven cubits breadth, all around it (the pile) made of grass, with sticks, and let a door be on the south [the direction of Yama, god of the dead]; over it tie a roof of sticks, and cover it in.["][20]

In this case, the building material is of paramount importance: only a hut of sacred grass is approved in the *Śāstra*s. Apart from the fact that *kuśa* grass, from a ritual point of view, constitutes an *ad hoc* filter against pollution, it also guarantees total freedom to the woman, who is neither bound nor crushed, and who can at any moment escape from the hut through its southern door, thereby saving her life. The advantage of this material is also that it burns much more slowly than wood. This would undoubtedly prolong the woman's agony—which would, precisely, increase the dissuasive impact of the new measures.

The facts appear to prove the Collector of Poona right: not a single candidate for sacrifice would carry through on her vow once the fate awaiting her in the greenery hut was described to her in plain language. Five Brahman women and a woman from the Tailor caste would renounce their intentions. The most obstinate of the Brahman women (her husband was a carcoon in the district's Treasury Office) who, as Robertson noted on March 1, 1824, with a bit of regret, "would have shown a practical specimen of the effect of the new pile," appeared less terrified by the prospect of a still crueler death than by that of a loss of caste.[21] For it is true that when he decreed that cremations on the new pyre alone would be permitted, Robertson was careful to add that satīs who "defaulted" would no longer form a part of caste society. They would fall to the level of the Caṇḍālas, the prototypical Untouchables and dregs of the Hindu human race.[22] He knew, nonetheless, that the *Śāstra*s had made a provision for a rite of atonement that allowed a woman to recover her caste purity in such circumstances. He had evoked that point of doctrine in his discussion with the pundits. However, since the ends justified the means, he later used this expedient to place additional pressure on potential satīs. In any event, the provisions made in the *Śāstras* with regard to the retraction of satīs—i.e., taking recourse to the *prājāpatya* rite (concerning which, moreover, there is no consensus)—were never implemented.[23]

A Brahman woman was, however, to burn herself on the new pyre on February 5, 1825. What had inspired horror in others was to her eyes sublime, since the greenery hut would provide her the means of displaying a supernatural heroism.[24] The *śāstrīs* employed a veritable barrage of arguments to stop her from burning herself—not out of Hindu charity, but rather for reasons having to do with the magic of the ritual: since Radhabai's escape from the pyre, the region had not received any rain. Another failure to follow through would inevitably provoke a new calamity.

In reading the collector's report to the commissioner regarding the sacrifice of this woman of fifty or sixty years, one cannot help but note that the lofty sentiments that had inspired Robertson to act—pity, indignation, even horror—had by now given way to an all-consuming passion that he shared, all things considered, with his former adversaries, the specialists of Hindu law: the passion of ritual, i.e. of a ceremony performed properly and meticulously:[25]

The pile was constructed under my own superintendence. Four strong posts, ten feet distant from each other, and ten feet high above the ground, supported four cross beams fitted into deep hollows to prevent them from slipping. The space within the posts too was filled up with dry billets of wood to the height of four feet and a half, leaving a distance of five feet and a half to the top of the posts. The woman was less than five feet high. The upper part of the pile, from the wood to the top, was enclosed, excepting a door of two feet and a half wide at one corner with cusby and grass, and the roof was covered with rafters supporting first, grass, and then billets of wood. There was a fresh breeze from the south-west, and her position was on the north-east side of the pile. No combustibles were allowed to be used, excepting grass and the cusby straw; I estimated the intensity of their heat and the fury of their blaze by far too lightly; and I ought to have been more scrupulous in regulating their thickness just opposite to the woman's head: at the upper part of the pile there was only one bundle of straw in thickness, but bundles were piled downwards (like tiles resting on each other) at half their length, so that the thickness opposite the suttee's head was equal to three bundles. Perhaps the shastrees, who had before been so eager to prevent the suttee, and who must have known the fury of the conflagration that would ensue better than myself, did not care to point out this mistake to me, in the hopes that it might possibly effect the destruction of the suttee, for they looked with horror on the probability of her escape.[26]

Robertson did not conceal his admiration for that grey-haired woman whose bravery and composure would not soon be equaled. Nor did he make any mystery of his enthusiasm for the canonical procedure of widow-burning that he had brought back into fashion. "I shall take care on the next occasion," he noted, "to attend to the supply of these articles [grass and straw], with reference to the position of the suttee, and the direction of the wind. Officiating Brahmins will be able to be authorized, if it be deemed on high that such a concession is needed, to place below the wind a bit of the grass that ought not to be in the wind."[27]

Shared Passions

The voluminous corpus of the *Parliamentary Papers* on widow-burning in India,[28] published in London between 1821 and 1830 (but covering the period from 1797 to 1830) by the House of Commons, offers more than one example of this historical irony: through the force of circumstances, the Company servants had constituted themselves as the guardians of and sureties for a practice universally condemned by the nation. Having become the scribes and historiographers of the ritual, they drew up, at government request, a catalogue of satīs for each civil year. The lists of sacrificed women run into hundreds of foolscap pages. They consist of tables with multiple entries, in which are registered, division by division and district by district, the satī's name, age, and caste; her husband's name, caste, and profession (which does not always correspond to the caste's traditional occupation); the number of children; the date of the burning; and the Police Jurisdiction *(thānā)* of the locality in which the sacrifice took place. A final column contains the remarks of the magistrate present at the ceremony: he notes its particulars (*sahamaraṇa* or *anumaraṇa,* whether it was by burning or burial, whether it involved one or several women) and, when necessary, its irregularities, which would be brought to the cognizance of the judges of the *Nizāmat Adālat,* the Supreme Court of Criminal Justice in Calcutta. Each list is followed by an "ABSTRACT STATEMENT of the Number of Hindoo Widows who were burnt or buried alive, in the several Zillah and City Courts, during the year . . . ." These "Abstract Statements" are themselves followed by "REMARKS and Orders of the Court on the Suttee Reports and Statements for the Year . . . ." Corresponding to each remark is a short summary table, such as, for example, the following:

TOTAL NUMBER OF SUTTEES	
In 1821	654
In 1822	583
Decrease	67[29]

The stuff of human experience is made to vanish into the new world of statistics. Numerical analysis drains off all emotion, starting with that of unspeakable horror. Once again, entries in the logbooks of memory are placed in the service of oblivion. Satīs burned alive before people's eyes are transformed into paper satīs.[30]

The passion for the ritual, its ability to produce a factitious reality in which affects are censored, is highly conspicuous in the learned discussions among brahmans on points of jurisprudence concerning the burning of widows, as well as in the controversy that pitted orthodox Hindu supporters of the rite against their reformist Hindu adversaries. Nothing can better illustrate the paradox of Reason enthralled by the Rite than the arguments of Rammohun Roy in his two *Conferences between an Advocate for and an Opponent of the Practice of Burning Widows Alive* (1818 and 1820). Of course, the strategy of this defender of the cause of women was to attack the orthodoxy on its own terms, by showing that both the *dharma* authors who tolerated or encouraged widow sacrifice in the past and the pundits and *śāstrīs* who clung to those opinions in the modern era didn't know their Sanskrit, falsely interpreting the letter, but more importantly the spirit, of the sacred texts.[31] Roy's decisive argument in these imaginary dialogues between two protagonists to whom the author alternately lent his voice[32] treats of the rite per se, in its function and its essence. To promise the bliss of the Heavens of Indra, Viṣṇu, and Śiva in the company of her husband throughout the reign of fourteen Indras or for as many years as the human body has hairs; the expiation of her sins and of those of her husband, however unredeemable they may have been; the sanctification of her father's line, her mother's line, and that of her husband for three or seven generations—to promise these to a grief-stricken wife in mourning is to bedazzle her with the fruits of sacrifice. But only fools who are ignorant of the mysteries of the Veda (here, Roy draws most heavily on the Upaniṣads) and who have forgotten the teachings of Kṛṣṇa in the *Bhāgavad-Gītā,* the gospel of Hinduism, would act for the sake of enjoying the fruits of their acts in this or a future life. For "as in this world the fruits obtained from cultivation and labour perish, so in the next world fruits derived from rites are perishable."[33]

The devaluation of acts—and particularly of ritual acts—motivated by a desire to obtain visible or invisible, immediate or deferred benefits, and the valorization of the desireless act *(niṣkāma karman)* without expectation of either earthly or heavenly rewards, provided Roy with the theological and philosophical leverage with which to denounce the vanity, and even the madness, of "dying with." Led into temptation by brahmans, who are themselves deluded, the satī in fact sacrifices all promise of salvation and absorption into the Absolute for her desire for sensual pleasures—in the afterlife, it goes without saying. Conversely, only the widow who survives her husband by leading an ascetic life, in obdience to the injunctions of Manu, is assured of realizing the highest bliss.[34]

In his summary of the Hindoo law on the subject of widowhood, compiled for the judges of the Bombay Presidency, Arthur Steele noted in 1827 that

> [T]he most virtuous mode of becoming a suttee is to die of grief and affliction on the husband's death.[35] The usual practice is self-immolation on the husband's funeral pile. The pile should be constructed of light grass and leaves surrounding, as is the present custom at Poona [since Robertson's action]. A widow is excused from becoming a suttee: 1st, if pregnant; 2d, if under puberty; 3d, if she have a suckling infant; 4th, if she have a desire to attain moksh (absorption into the divine spirit); for a woman sacrifices herself on the pile in view to another happy birth with her deceased husband, and the Sanskrit term "suhugumun," applied to suttees, signifies "to accompany;" 5th, if the sacrifice is made merely with the view of escaping distress, from harsh treatment of relations, or want of maintenance; it must be purely voluntary.[36]

As extraordinary as these arabesques of thought turning around the rite (and especially their conclusion, that the widow burns herself, in the final analysis, out of a thirst for sensual enjoyment) may appear to us, they nonetheless alert us to a thorny doctrinal problem. For we may well wonder what constitutes the religious end of the rite for the woman performing it (the point of view of the man, his family, and the officiating brahmans seems clear enough). What is the satī seeking on the pyre or, less commonly, in the grave: release from transmigration and the suffering attached to all earthly existence, liberation from rebirth in a female body (a hope fostered by certain *dharma* treatises), or, on the contrary, a succession of rebirths as the wife of the same husband (which other, or sometimes the same sources promise her as a means to firing her enthusiasm)? The pundits whom the British consulted contented themselves with citing authoritative commentators and compilers, with the dilemma of these contradictory statements never acknowledged in their responses. What counted for them was having an array of religious injunctions to draw upon and adapt to any possible situation. But how did the future satīs themselves view these matters? It will be recalled that the death accounts often contain an odd element in which the satī, before the flames consumed her entire body, pronounced two numbers, whose sum was always seven. They meant: "I have burned myself so many times with this same husband; I have so many times left to burn before attaining liberation." It is my hypothesis that this ought to be seen as the pendant to the seven circumambulations of the sacrificial fire that seals the union of bride and groom in the marriage ceremony.[37] That bond is so powerful, and so difficult to loose, as to require no fewer than seven passages through fire before the slightest prospect of salvation can appear on a woman's horizon. The *śāstrī* of Surat consulted by Robertson cited the following passage from the *Nirṇayasindhu* of Kamalākarabhaṭṭa, a renowned legal scholar from the Deccan who lived in Benares in the early years of the seventeenth century:

> A woman should burn, because she thereby obtains absolution for the sins of both [her husband and herself], and enables him and herself to escape hell; moreover, she obtains for both the rewards of all the heavens, and finally she is absorbed in Brahma along with him, remaining his wife in the intermediate transmigrations in this world, in which they shall be blessed with issue, riches, and other good things.[38]

Menstruation and the Final Oblation

If speculation on the ritual can induce a derealizing effect, sometimes of extreme proportions, it verges on the fantastic when it comes to the question of when (and under what conditions) a woman who has been disqualified by menstrual pollution may burn herself, according to *dharma*. Generally speaking, that right is granted her after the fourth or, to be on the safe side, the fifth day. So it is written that:

> [On] the first day [of menstruation] she is a Caṇḍālī [Caṇḍālas theoretically descend from the union of a brahman woman with a śūdra man, which tradition views as an abomination]; on the second day she is a brahmanicide [it will be recalled here that women agreed to take on a third of Indra's sin, which manifested itself in the form of menstruation];[39] on the third day, she is a *rajakī*, a woman of the Washermen caste [washermen are impure because they wash linen stained with menstrual blood]; on the fourth day, she regains her purity [through a series of practices, including *snāna*, a ritual bath of purification].[40]

What is to be done then with the husband's corpse? The deceased must be cremated as quickly as possible, as soon as the requisite conditions for the "final oblation" *(antyeṣṭi),* the ultimate sacrifice that is cremation, have been met. This imperative entails all manner of practical complications: for example, if death occurs on an ill-omened day, at an inauspicious time of day, or in the course of an intercalary month during which, in theory, no rites may be performed. Yet there is great reticence about burning a woman on a separate pyre, even when she is not a Brahman. This is because the fundamental unity of the couple must be preserved through this sacrament, which stands as the model for every other rite of passage (*saṃskāra:* literally "perfectioning"), both because in it a Hindu finally offers his own person to the gods, without the intermediary of a victim, and because, according to ancient Indian ideology, he repays in full the short-term loan that was his life on earth to Yama, the god of the dead.[41] Thus, the *śāstrīs* introduced a new series of articles in their casuistry. If a wife is in the third day of her period when her husband dies, the cremation is postponed until the next day: once she has been purified by the fourth-day ritual bath, she may accompany her husband on the pyre. But if he should take it upon himself to die while his wife is only in the first or second day of her period, then he must be burned without delay. His wife will follow him on the fourth or fifth day. But what does one do in an emergency or cases of overriding necessity? Between 1817 and 1818, a cholera epidemic decimated Bengal. It would later ravage a number of regions in the Deccan, before reappearing in Bengal (with Bakerganj the hardest-hit district) in 1825, and claiming a total of at least twenty thousand victims, according to the statistics of the day.[42] The dead were burned in haste, preferably in the company of their wives. The *śāstrīs* devised an expiatory rite to provide a solution to this ritual impasse:

The penance is thus explained in the Devyadriyik Nibundh *[Devayājñika Nibandha]:* 'When a man dies at the time his wife is labouring under her courses, and the widow wishes to sacrifice herself before they are finished [from the religious point of view, menstruation lasts three days, even if biologically it is longer or shorter], she may thus render herself clean: let her pound with a pestle sixty-four seers of rice in the husk, and the impurities will by exercise flow from her body: let her then persuade herself that no impurities remain, and examine her body: let her five times clean her *whole body with five kinds of earth,* one to be taken from a horse's hoof, the second from under an elephant's foot, the third from a white ant's nest or any little mound in a jungle, the fourth from under a cow's foot, the fifth from under the foot of a rhinoceros (vurah); and let her on the first day give away thirty cows to the Brumhamuns [Brahmans], and the second twenty, on the third ten, on the fourth five, and on the fifth one cow: let her then be declared pure by the mouth of a Brahmun (vipr), and she may then burn.[43]

A woman who has died under normal circumstances may not be burned if she is in "flower" *(puṣpa),* in "season" *(ṛtu),* in her time of the "month" *(mahīnā),* in her "*dharma* of the month" *(māsik dharm),* "in her [menstrual] garments" *(kapṛe),* or "over-dressed" *(zyādā kapṛe)* at the time of her death—these being some of the current expressions for menstruation. One waits three nights before giving her the ritual bath that will cleanse her of her defilement. The rite of cremation will be performed without the use of *mantras*. An expiatory rite consisting of five *cāndrāyaṇa*s will be required.[44] It is nonetheless possible to burn the dead body without respecting this mandatory delay, on the condition that one perform three *cāndrāyaṇa*s and a series of purifications whose details I shall spare the reader. If the woman dies during the first three days of her period, the person performing the rites must undertake the prescribed expiation for three years; if she dies during the three days that follow, the expiation need last only two years; if she dies between the sixth and the ninth days, the expiation is limited to one year; finally, if she dies on the tenth day, the expiatory rite will be one *kṛcchrāyāṇa vrata* ("extremely severe penance").[45]

We can understand how the impurity of menstruation or childbirth might disqualify a woman, at least temporarily, from the sacrifice that would transform her into a satī. But why is it that a woman suffering from amenorrhea may not be burnt? The victim offered to the gods in sacrifice must be not only consenting but also in perfect condition. Amenorrhea constitutes the height of imperfection for a wife whose fertility is crucial to the biological and ritual survival of her husband's family line: the father is reborn through his son, and when he dies it is his son who liberates his *ātman* and relieves him of his debt to Yama; it is his son who ensures his transformation into a Father *(pitṛ)* and his survival as an ancestor, through the perfomance of the funerary and post-funerary rites.[46] The wife's fertility will thus be measured according to the standard of her procreation of sons; the womb of a woman who gives birth only to daughters is like a counterfeit money factory.[47] A woman who does not know the periodicity of the "seasons" and who eludes the laws of nature subjects her family and locality to grave risks, for she is nothing other than an incarnation of Alakṣmī, the goddess of Misfortune. Crossing her path brings bad luck, and she is barred from attending auspicious life cycle ceremonies, marriages in particular. In a word, such a "female eunuch"[48] is quite nearly as inauspicious as a widow.

In a book devoted to the rites of the *devadāsīs* of Puri, Frédérique Apffel Marglin showed that impurity does not necessarily correspond to inauspiciousness in India.[49] The *devadāsīs* of Puri are the very symbol of the conjunction between the impure and the auspicious: the sexual promiscuity that constitutes one aspect of their "service" *(sevā)* of the god Jagannāth, whose servants in the temple worship (as well as whose wives) they are, renders them eminently impure. At the same time, they are considered to be incarnations of the deity's consort, Lakṣmī, the goddess of Fortune. And menstrual blood, a source of pollution, is auspicious, since it is instrumental in reproduction. In Orissa, this author reminds us, the "season" of the goddess Pruthibī, the Earth, is celebrated for four days each year, in the month of *Jyeṣṭha* (May-June). Men neither plow nor approach their wives, because all married women are assumed to be in their period during the festival time. Moreover, women too respect the prohibitions observed in such circumstances. Following the Earth's "flowers," the rains will come to bear their fruit.[50]

The Goddess's menses are celebrated elsewhere in India, both in the secrecy of her shrines and in broad daylight.[51] The temple of the goddess Kāmākhyā—located near Gauhati in Assam, the "seat" *(pīṭha)* where the goddess Satī's sexual organ fell to earth—is the venue for a massive gathering of this *Śakti*'s devotees, who come there from every corner of Assam, Bengal, and Orissa for the festival of Ambuvaci (or Ameti), which falls in the first fortnight of the month of *Āṣāḍha* (June-July). The water that oozes from the vulva *(yoni)* cut into the rock as a representation of the goddess takes on a red ocher color in this season, and is identified as Kāmākhyā's menstrual flow. For three days, the doors of the temple remain shut to pilgrims, who are only allowed access to the inner sanctum on the fourth day. During these three days, one may neither plow the soil—not even with a needle—nor sow. Red flowers and vermilion—items of worship that are so many symbols of her menses—are offered to the goddess. And the *prasād* ("consecrated remains") her faithful devotees receive is a piece of red cloth, stained with the blood of Kāmākhyā.[52]

The Seasonal Fault

It remains the case that menstruation is a woman's *doṣa.* As we have seen, this Sanskrit word simultaneously means a flaw, a fault, a humoral disorder, and the passions that produce it. The cause of the "seasonal fault" *(ṛtu-doṣa)* is in fact passion. For by agreeing to take on one third (or one fourth) of

Indra's sin of brahmanicide, women received as their reward the capacity (not found in any other living creature) to enjoy sexual intercourse in every season, with childbirth being the sole natural obstacle to the unbridled desire characterizing the female sex: the intensity of a woman's desire is four times that of a man. There are no fewer than six types of menstrual flow, whose density and quality vary in exact proportion to a woman's sins. These have been used to draw up a typology of women—the passion for classification being an Indian fancy.[53]

Such sophisticated classifications extend to the realm of practice. When used with the proper precautions and within the context of a number of specific rituals by initiates of certain tantric clans (*kula*s), or by alchemists from the Siddha (or Nath) traditions, menstrual blood becomes a veritable precipitate of magical powers, a sacrificial substance *(dravya)* which, when combined with semen, becomes a source of liberation and an elixir of immortality *(kulāmṛta).*[54]

Werner Menski has recently brought to our attention another example of the ambivalence of feminine blood—in this case, virginal blood. According to two (obscure and much debated) passages from the *Ṛg Veda,* the husband who wishes to preserve himself after his marriage has been consummated gives the cloth stained with the hymenal blood to a brahman who is an "expert in the magic of Sūrya." Taking upon himself the highly dangerous power of the blood of virginity in his role of ritual scapegoat, this brahman must not enter into contact with the bride nor participate in the marriage ceremony (which did not involve a brahman officiant in its most ancient phase). In the *Atharva Veda,* his is a far more important role inasmuch as it is he who will perform a second marriage ceremony, held in the house of the groom, in order to counter the magical effects of the nuptial rites that had taken place in the bride's house. He will prepare the spouses for their first sexual union and receive the stained cloth. The later *sūtra* literature makes no reference to these practices. The blood of defloration, qualified in the Vedic sources as *nīlalohitam* (blackish red), would be changed into *raktakṛṣṇa* (reddish black). Menski sees in this change in terminology evidence of a successful attempt to obscure earlier expressions linked to the lethal power of virginal blood.[55]

A FOREWORD IN RETROSPECT

The reader who is about to close this book may perhaps wonder where I have wished to lead him by drawing him into this labyrinthine account. Was it really necessary to enter into all these digressions on the symbolism of the ritual, blue indigo, funerary rice-balls, decapitated heroes, the revenge suicide of bards, or menstrual blood, rather than broaching the subject *in concreto,* armed with facts and figures?

The form this narrative has taken was not premeditated: it came into being on its own, imposing its own logic, page by page. Upon reflection, however, it seems to me that this way of proceeding, through the diffraction and cross-checking of the data, was the sole possible means for giving a faithful image of such a multifaceted cultural enigma. By breaking the laws of the genre, this text will have respected other narrative rules, specific to Indian tradition, in which tales are nested one inside another in inextricable profusion. It may be that India still appears to me as it did on that first day of discovery when it was nothing more than a collection of words penned in an unknown script—a maze whose final goal was of little matter, since the way there represented a *saṃskāra* in itself, a perfectioning, a passage to another universe and another image of man.

What will we have learned about the history of satīs in this intellectual journey that has taken us from path to forking path, as well as down sidetracks that have often led us straight into the heart of Indian orthodoxy? The image that has emerged may well modify a number of preconceptions. The excursus into the offering of funerary rice-balls suggests that the sacrifice of women would not constitute a perversion of Hinduism but rather a fundamental article of faith, embedded in the very ideology of marriage. And what should surprise us is not that women—in past and recent history—could have burned alive on their husband's pyre, but that these occurrences were, all things considered, so rare (in a relative sense).[1] "Without a husband, a woman is nothing," were the words of Mama-ji, without whom I would not have discovered the secret shrine of Om Kanvar in Jaipur.[2] Those few simple words are an encapsulation, as it were, of one of the most widely shared beliefs among the defenders of the eternal *dharma (sanātana dharma).*

In order for that belief to become actualized in the rite of *sahagamana* ("going with"), it remains necessary that the ritual scenography bring into play that upon which the belief is founded. The fire will not burn a living woman and a dead man. Such an act would likely be as impossible for a Hindu to contemplate as its mere suggestion is for us. What burns in the cremation fire is a single body, comprising two indivisible halves, transformed into a sacrificial oblation and rice-ball—a *piṇḍa.* The more elevated one's ranking in the hierarchy, the more the "illusion of reality" must prevail.[3] The wife of an *āhitāgni* will burn herself in accordance with a set of special prescriptions because her husband possessed the three sacrificial fires necessary for performing the solemn rites: she must lie down on the pyre over her husband's corpse with her face turned toward his.[4] This face-to-face, body-to-body positioning materializes the symbiosis of the spouses, even as it offers an image of the *piṇḍa,* which *is* a body.[5] The hierarchy that obtained between the *bela*s and *satia*s of Bali ultimately reflects the same fiction: a woman mingling her ashes with those of her husband or master brings us close to the archaic notion according to which the sacrificing couple in a sacrifice not only acts in concert, but actually forms a whole whose parts cannot be separated. Conversely, a Brahman woman who burns herself after her husband on a separate pyre offends the conscience of ritualists, since the "belief effect" is not operative in this case.

Jonathan Parry's writings on death in Banaras have shown that the "final oblation" *(antyeṣṭi)*—the cremation rite of every Hindu—was a sacrifice in the fullest sense of the term: the offering of a living victim. The deceased remains animated by his vital breaths up to the moment when his son (or failing him, a close male relative) cracks open his skull, thereby affording him the *coup de grâce* that liberates his immortal self *(ātman).*[6] Elsewhere, Charles Malamoud has reminded us that in Vedic sacrifice, the sacrificed and dismembered animal was immediately restored to life through a number of ritual procedures—by sprinkling it with water and *mantra*s, in particular.[7] Its reunified body became food for the gods, since the victim "must go to heaven alive. A dead animal does not go to heaven."[8] When a satī accompanies her husband onto the pyre, the two halves of the offering forming but a single body would thereby be endowed with life. It is in this way that we may gauge both the power of the ideology of sacrifice in India—whose persistence seems so remarkable—and the chasm that separates the Hindu perception of *sahagamana* from what must be termed reality, which the *trompe-l'oeil* of the ritual spectacle hides from view.

This interplay of altered perspectives is reproduced on other levels. The satī dies as a happy wife whose husband is still alive *(suhāgin)* and not as a widow—or better still, as a young bride: she decks herself out, as she did on her wedding day, in the apparel of marital bliss. Death by fire becomes the mirror image of the marriage ceremony, with the pyre becoming the bed on which the couple was united for the first time. Here, however, these transports of the flesh will be prolonged for an infinite number of years in the world of the gods. From such a perspective, a woman who survives her husband can only be viewed as the impure remains of an uncompleted sacrifice. A "burned parting of the hair," she will bear the mark of the fire that failed to devour her until the end of her days. It is she, in the final analysis, who burns. For the satī, like the Sītā of Tulsī Dās's *Rāmcaritmānas* whose place in the flames was taken by a substitute shadow, suffers no harm. The fire of the *sat,* the essence of her being, brings about the phenomenon of a miraculous self-combustion, without burns or suffering, that transforms her into a divine entity before the eyes of the thousands of Hindus who gather to view the event. Can fire burn fire?

"Satis are exceptional beings," as Mama-ji insisted. Everyone I questioned most emphatically invoked this trait. We find the reason for this in the devotional literature: if satīs are so rare, it is because the present human race is living in the *kali* age, in which *dharma* stands on but one of its four feet. As the saying goes, there are no true women *(satī)* and no true hermits *(yati)* in this *kaliyuga.*[9] What appears to our eyes to be the height of barbarism, defying the laws of reason and nature, is viewed as a criterion of the golden age for Hindus "who love [eternal] *dharma.*"[10]

Women who have succeeded in preserving that exceptional quality despite the extreme deliquescence of those values upon which the edifice of Hinduism rests, and who prove the same by becoming "realized" satis, are perceived as earthly incarnations of the primal Śakti *(Ādiśakti)* or at least as partial emanations of the "descents" of that primordial figure into a human womb. With this, we find ourselves moving from an axiom according to which a wife is nothing without her husband to a proposition which posits that the "true woman," the satī, is all or a part of the divine energy.

Ought we to imagine that gender asymmetry—which manifests itself in the subordination of women in Hindu society, and which would have given rise, among other things, to widow-burning—might have been inverted (through circumstances about which we could speculate endlessly) in collective representations? Ought we not to consider, on the contrary, that a structural connection has from the outset linked satīs together with *śakti*s, and that the propagation of the rite within the subcontinent and into outer India went hand in hand with the spread of Śākta Tantra?

The mystery of the identity of divine *Śakti* with earthly satīs—as impenetrable for the nonbeliever as the dogma of the Incarnation or the Trinity—allows us in any event to better grasp not how things took place or followed on one another chronologically, but rather how they can actually form a part of human experience. Is this not the crux of the matter? The view from above, adopted by proponents of the various theories that have been constructed to account for this practice, throws no light on the act per se, which continues to be repressed into the recesses of the unthinkable. If we replace the question "how can one be a satī?" (which runs through the historiography of the subject down to its most recent developments) with a problematic of what the word really means and what range of experience it covers, then "becoming a satī" may convey a meaning—or even make sense. Such, at least, will have been the hypothesis of this book.

The singular fate of satīs, their sacredness, their birth into a human society that makes them the most sensitive of all intercessors to the prayers of their devotees once they have reached the world of the gods, the miracles they perform in transforming ashes—the very symbol of the precariousness of human existence—into a substance of immortality, the indelible imprint of their sacrifice as perpetuated through cults, myths, dreams, and fantasies—all of this is projected, instantaneously, beyond the reaches of consciousness. Mythification and commemoration, the supreme form of forgetting, erase all traces of the flesh-and-blood satī. The new deity shines like a constellation, chiselled diamondlike into a heaven that is even more undefinable than the world of the ancestors. Could it not be that the violence of death by fire eludes all attempts at denegation?

When one restores the rite of *sahagamana* to its place within the context of Indian traditions of self-sacrifice and the bodily mutilations that often constitute their preliminary—and, I would maintain, essential—phase, one sees that men and women wound and sacrifice themselves, individually or together, in isolation or en masse, in accordance with rules of conduct that are constantly being reinvented. In other words, one gauges a phenomenon that, when viewed in its totality, transcends issues of gender and social hierarchy. And so we are led to see that the constant in all of this, which plays the role of catalyst for both individual motivations and social constraints, is the idea that violence consented to and used knowingly—after the model of the primordial act and basis for all acts, sacrifice—that this violence alone releases a charge of energy such that he or she who accepts its *fatum* and knows how to benefit from it may, by shattering the circuits of the phenomenal world, of that ineluctable series of rebirths and redeaths, at last cross over the ford that leads to immortality.

NOTES

Funereal Prelude

1. Pierre Dubois, Letter no. 8: "Funérailles," in *Légère Idée de Balie, 1830 (Lettres adressées à Monsieur H. Y., demeurant à Z.)* (The Hague: Algemeen Rijksarchief). Collection no. 3087 contains the eight autograph letters by Dubois in French (30 unpaginated folios), coming from the Ministry of Colonies. Italics are in the original. Concerning Dubois, see Alfons van der Kraan, "Human Sacrifice in Bali: Sources, Notes and Commentary," *Indonesia* 40 (October 1985): 95–97. The passage quoted here is taken from van der Kraan's translation; other passages are translated directly from the original French.

2. Testimony of the British missionary W. H. Medhurst, "Short Account of the Island Bali," *Singapore Chronicle,* June 1830. See van der Kraan, "Human Sacrifice," 96 n. 17.

3. R. T. Friederich, *The Civilisation and Culture of Bali* (Calcutta: Sushil Gupta, 1959), 84. For the Dutch original, see below, note 7 to the present chapter.

4. Concerning the burning of widows in India, William Hodges notes: "Reason and nature so revolt at the idea, that, were it not a well known and well authenticated circumstance, it would hardly obtain credit." William Hodges, *Travels in India during the Years 1780, 1781, 1782, and 1783* (London: J. Edwards, 1793), 84.

5. J. F. C. Gericke and T. Roorda, *Javaansch-Nederlandsch Handwoordenboek,* ed. A. C. Vreede (Amsterdam-Leyden: Johannes Müller, 1901), 2:712–13. On *amok,* see H. B. M. Murphy, "History of the Evolution of Syndromes: The Striking Case of *Latah* and *Amok,*" in *Psychopathology: Contributions from the Social, Behavioral and Biological Sciences,* ed. N. Hammer, K. Salzinger, and S. Sutton (New York: John Wiley & Sons, 1973), 33–55. Nicolo di Conti (1395–1469) makes reference to the practice in Java. See *Viaggio di Nicolo di*

Conti Veneziano, scritto per messer Poggio Fiorentino, in G. B. Ramusio, *Navigazioni e Viaggi,* 6 vols. (Turin: Einaudi, 1978–1988), 2:801.

6. Françoise Mallison, *L'Epouse idéale. La Satī-Gītā de Muktānand* (Paris: École Française d'Extrême-Orient, 1973), 27; idem, "A Note on the Holiness Allowed to Women: *Pativratā* and *Satī,*" in *Ludwick Sternbach Felicitation Volume* (Lucknow: Akhil Bharatiy Sanskrit Parisad, 1979); and Catherine Weinberger-Thomas, "Cendres d'immortalité. La crémation des veuves en Inde," *Archives de sciences sociales des religions* 67, no. 1 (1989): 18.

7. For divergent interpretations of this terminology, see J. Crawfurd, *History of the Indian Archipelago,* 2 vols. (Edinburgh, 1820), 2:241; and R. T. Friederich, *Voorloopig Verslag van het Eiland Bali,* in *Verhandelingen van het Bataviaasch Genootschap, voor Kunsten en Wetenschappen* 23 (1850): 10–11. See also James A. Boon, *Affinities and Extremes: Crisscrossing the Bittersweet Ethnology of East Indies Studies, Hindu-Balinese Culture, and Indo-European Allure* (Chicago: University of Chicago Press, 1990), 40–44.

8. This is the title given to the Vesias (*vaiśya,* in Sanskrit), who constitute the third order of Balinese society.

9. Heinrich Zollinger, "Het Eiland Lombok," *Tijdschrift voor Nederlandsch Indie* 9, no. 2 (1847): 345–49.

10. H. van Kol, *Driemaal Dwars door Sumatra en Zwerftochten door Bali* (Rotterdam: Brusse, 1914), 323–24. On this matter, see van der Kraan, "Human Sacrifice," 89.

11. Emile Durkheim, *Suicide, A Study in Sociology,* trans. John A. Spaulding and George Simpson (Glencoe, N.Y.: Free Press, 1951), 217–40. On the category of altruistic suicide, see R. S. Gandhi, "*Sati* as Altruistic Suicide: Beyond Durkheim's Interpretation," *Contributions to Asian Studies* 10 (1977): 141–57.

12. For a critique of this point of view, concerning Scythian funeral practices, see Bruce Lincoln, *Death, War, and Sacrifice* (Chicago: University of Chicago Press, 1991), 188–97.

13. S. Settar and M. M. Kalaburgi, "The Hero Cult. A Study of Kannada Literature from 9th to 13th Century," in *Memorial Stones: A Study of their Origin, Significance, and Variety,* ed. S. Settar and Günther Sontheimer (Dharwad: Institute of Indian Art History, 1982), 31–35.

14. Marco Polo, *La Description du monde,* ed. L. Hambis (Paris: Klincksieck, 1955), 254. Marco Polo dictated an account of his travels to the writer Rustician of Pisa, his prisonmate in Genoa. The original manuscript of *The Book of Ser Marco Polo* has been lost. The translation here is based on the French edition, which provides greater detail than the standard English translation by Yule and Cordier.

15. Ibid., 255–56.

16. B. Lewis Rice, *Mysore and Coorg from the Inscriptions* (London: A. Constable & Co., 1909; reprint New Delhi: Asian Publishing Services, 1986), 104, 187–88; U. N. Thakur, *The History of Suicide in India* (Delhi: Munshiram Manoharlal, 1963), 61–62; Günther Sontheimer, "Between Ghost and God: A Folk Deity of the Deccan," in

Criminal Gods and Demon Devotees. Essays on the Guardians of Popular Hinduism, ed. Alf Hiltebeitel (Albany, N.Y.: SUNY Press, 1989), 334–35 and n. 21.

17. Among numerous contributions on this subject, see U. N. Thakur, *History of Suicide,* and David R. Kinsley, "'The Death that Conquers Death': Dying to the World in Medieval Hinduism," in *Religious Encounters with Death: Insights from the History and Anthropology of Religions,* ed. Frank E. Reynolds and Earle H. Waugh (University Park: Pennsylvania State University Press, 1977), 97–108.

18. See in particular Rice, *Mysore and Coorg;* M. L. K. Murthy, "Memorial Stones in Andhra Pradesh," and Günther Sontheimer, "Hero and Sati-Stones of Maharashtra," in *Memorial Stones,* ed. Settar and Sontheimer, 209–18, 261–81.

19. *Kṛtyakalpataru of Bhaṭṭa Lakṣmīdhara, Tīrthavivecanakāṇḍa,* ed. K. V. Rangaswami Aiyangar (Baroda: Oriental Institute, 1942), 258–64.

20. David N. Lorenzen, *The Kāpālikas and Kālāmukhas. Two Lost Śaivite Sects* (New Delhi: Thomson Press, 1972), 76.

21. On this text, see K. R. van Kooij, *Worship of the Goddess According to the Kālikāpurāṇa,* Part 1 (Leiden: Brill, 1972). R. C. Hazra places its composition between the tenth and eleventh centuries in his *Studies in the Upapurāṇas,* vol. 2 (Calcutta: University of Calcutta, 1963).

22. *Kālikāpurāṇa,* 67.20b–22b, in *Kālikāpurāṇa (Text, Introduction & Translation in English),* 3 vols., ed. B. N. Sastri (Delhi: Nag Publishers, 1992), 3:1004.

23. Jean-Philippe Vogel, "The Head-Offering to the Goddess in Pallava Sculpture," *Bulletin of the School of Oriental Studies* 6 (1930–1932): 539–43; S. Gurumurthy, "Self-Immolation in South India," *Bulletin of the Institute of Traditional Cultures Madras* 1 (1969): 44–49; A. Swaminathan, "Self-Immolation and Human Sacrifice in the History of South India," *Journal of Tamil Studies* 16 (December 1979): 10–18.

24. Or *gaṇḍagattera,* according to the transcription one adopts. See M. L. K. Murthy, "Memorial Stones," 215, and Konduri Sarojini Devi, *Religion in Vijayanagara Empire* (New Delhi: Sterling Publishers, 1990), 261, 263.

25. This is the modern-day Quilon in Kerala. See Geneviève Bouchon, "L'image de l'Inde dans l'Europe de la Renaissance," in *L'Inde et l'Imaginaire (Puruṣārtha 11),* ed. Catherine Weinberger-Thomas (Paris: Editions de l'EHESS, 1988), 72.

26. Nicolo di Conti in Ramusio, *Navigazioni e Viaggi,* 2:814.

27. *Manimekhalai* 6.50–53, in *Manimekhalaï (The Dancer with the Magic Bowl) by Merchant-Prince Shattan,* trans. Alain Daniélou with the collaboration of T. V. Gopala Iyer (Delhi: Penguin Books India, 1993). On the dating of this poem, see L. S. Leshnik, "Nomads and Burials in South India," in *Pastoralists and Nomads in South Asia,* ed. L. S. Leshnik and Günther Sontheimer (Wiesbaden: Harrassowitz, 1975), 62.

28. Jean Filliozat, "L'abandon de la vie par le sage et les suicides du criminel et du héros dans la tradition indienne," *Arts asiatiques* 15 (1968): 74–88. On Sangam literature, see George L. Hart, *The Poems of the Ancient Tamils. Their Milieu and their Sanskrit Counterparts* (Berkeley: University of California Press, 1975), 32; and François Gros, "La Littérature Sangam et son public," in *Inde et Littératures (Puruṣārtha 7),* ed. Marie-Claude Porcher (Paris: Editions de l'EHESS, 1983), 77–107.

29. S. Settar, "Memorial Stones in South India," in *Memorial Stones,* ed. Settar and Sontheimer, 189; M. L. K. Murthy, "Memorial Stones," 215–16; K. S. Devi, *Religion,* 260–63, 268–70; Dennis Hudson, "Violent and Fanatical Devotion among the Nāyanārs: A Study in the *Periya Purāṇam* of Cekkilār," in *Criminal Gods,* ed. A. Hiltebeitel, 373–404. On the Vīramuṣṭi, see David M. Knipe, "Night of the Growing Dead: A Cult of Vīrabhadra in Coastal Andhra," in *Criminal Gods,* ed. A. Hiltebeitel, 153.

30. This definition applies as well to a word belonging to the language of the bards of Rajasthan (Dingal, an ancient form of Marwari): *avsāṇsiddh* literally means "he who accomplishes [his duty by seizing] the favorable occasion." This honorific term designated the Rajput warrior who died in combat while fulfilling his caste duty.

31. Reference in S. Doshi, "Pāliyas of Saurashtra," in *Memorial Stones,* ed. Settar and Sontheimer, 168 and fig. 12. Doshi sees a human depiction in this motif.

32. Hart, *Poems,* 32. Concerning the hourglass-shaped drum, see also Mireille Helffer and Marc Gaborieau, "A propos d'un tambour du Kumaon et de l'ouest du Népal: remarques sur l'utilisation des tambours-sabliers dans le monde indien, le Népal, et le Tibet," in *Studia instrumentorum musicae popularis. Festschrift to E. Emsheimer on the occasion of his 70th birthday* (Stockholm: Musikhistorika Museet, 1974), 75–80.

33. On hero- and satī-stones see, in addition to *Memorial Stones,* ed. Settar and Sontheimer, also Romila Thapar, "Death and the Hero," in *Mortality and Immortality. The Archeology and Anthropology of Death,* ed. S. C. Humphries and H. King (London: Academic Press, 1982), 293–315, and idem, "Elegy in Stone. In Memory of the Sati and the Hero," *The India Magazine* (April 1982): 12–15. See also W. A. Noble and A. R. Sankhyan, "Signs of the Divine: *Satī* Memorials and *Satī* Worship in Rajasthan," in *The Idea of Rajasthan. Explorations in Regional Identity,* 2 vols., ed. Karine Schomer et al. (New Delhi: Manohar, 1994), 1:343–89; and Paul B. Courtright, "The Iconographies of Sati," in *Sati, the Blessing and the Curse. The Burning of Wives in India,* ed. John Stratton Hawley (New York: Oxford University Press, 1994), 27–53.

34. Hart, *Poems,* 38–39.

35. David Gordon White, *The Alchemical Body. Siddha Traditions in Medieval India* (Chicago: University of Chicago Press, 1996), 240–52.

36. Noble and Sankhyan ("Signs," 348 and nn. 18 and 19, 374–75) give a different interpretation of this motif: the moon would represent the womb and essence of femininity, whereas the sun would be the image of procreation. The origin of this symbolism would be found in Mesopotamia.

37. Madeleine Biardeau, *Hinduism, the Anthropology of a Civilization,* trans. Richard Nice (Delhi: Oxford University Press, 1989), 46–52.

38. Such is the translation I suggested in 1979. See Catherine Thomas, *L'Ashram de l'amour. Le gandhisme et l'imaginaire* (Paris: Editions de la Maison des sciences de l'homme, 1979), 128.

39. On the goddess Speech, see Charles Malamoud's contribution to the work edited by Marcel Detienne and G. Hamonic, *La Déesse Parole. Quatre figures de la langue des dieux* (Paris: Flammarion, 1995).

40. Eugène Burnouf, *Introduction à l'histoire du Buddhisme indien* (Paris: Maisonneuve, 1876), 443.

41. Thomas, *L'Ashram de l'amour.*

42. On speech as energy, see André Padoux, *L'Energie de la parole. Cosmogonies de la parole tantrique* (Paris: Le Soleil Noir, 1980; Paris: Fata Morgana, 1994); revised English translation *Vāc, The Concept of the Word in Selected Hindu Tantras,* trans. Jacques Gontier (Albany, N.Y.: SUNY Press, 1989).

43. Henry Yule and Arthur Coke Burnell, *Hobson-Jobson: A Glossary of Anglo-Indian Words and Phrases, and of Kindred Terms, Etymological, Historical, Geographical, and Discursive* (London: J. Murray, 1903; reprint Delhi: Munshiram Manoharlal, 1968), s.v. "Suttee," 878–83.

44. In Hindi and in other vernacular north Indian languages, the expression "to eat" is used for "to suffer, endure": one *eats* deceit, insult, blows, dizziness, etc.

45. On the semantic field of the word *bhāv,* see above, p. 19, and for its specific use as "possession by *sat,*" see below, p. 134.

46. In Hindi: *āveś, āveg.* The word *joś* will also be employed and is translated in this context as "excitation," "holy furor."

47. The word *karman,* from the root *kṛ* "to make, do," designates both action and ritual, because ritual is the act par excellence, whose model was given to men by the gods in primordial times.

48. N. K. Parik, *Sant Rām Singh aor unkī sūfī bhāvnā* (Jaipur: Ramasram Samsthan, 1987), 21.

49. One also says "to take away" or "destroy" the *sat.*

50. For a synthesis of the viewpoint of the *dharma* literature on the question, see the (thirteenth-century) *Smṛticandrikā of Devaṇṇabhaṭṭa,* 2 vols., trans. J. R. Gharpure (Poona: V. J. Gharpure, 1946), 1:92.

51. The brahmanic student is forbidden to wear any dyed garment (*Gautama Dharma Sūtra,* 1.17–18; *Vasiṣṭha Dharma Sūtra* 11.67).

52. The dyer figures in the list of those whose polluting contact requires as a rudimentary rite of atonement a purifying bath and the drinking of holy water, according to the *Smṛticandrikā* cited above, which refers to a multitude of sources from the *dharma* literature. In this quasi-surrealist enumeration, the dyer figures alongside (among others) the tanner, the hunter, the washerman, the actor, the dancer, "he who has his anus in his mouth," the dog, cock, and pig (*Smṛticandrikā* 1.199–201).

53. See C. G. H. Fawcett, *A Monograph on Dyes and Dyeing in the Bombay Presidency* (Bombay, 1896), 1–4; and Françoise Cousin, *Tissus imprimés du Rajasthan* (Paris: L'Harmattan, 1986), 34–37.

54. On the stages of life according to Hindu orthodoxy, see Patrick Olivelle, *The Āśrama System. The History and Hermeneutics of a Religious Institution* (New York:

Oxford University Press, 1994). For a brief overview of the subject, see Catherine Weinberger-Thomas, "Les stades de la vie selon l'idéal hindou," in *L'Etat du monde en 1492,* ed. G. Martinière and C. Varela (Paris: La Découverte, 1992), 83–85.

55. This is expressed in Hindi with a single word: *suhāgin* (from *suhāg:* the happy state of the married woman whose husband is still alive).

56. In Rajasthani, these pieces of clothing are called *pīliyā,* from *pīlā,* "yellow."

57. Sir John Malcolm, *A Memoir of Central India, Including Malwa and Adjoining Provinces,* 2 vols. (London and Calcutta: Thatcher & Spink, 1824–1832), 1:358; Sir James Tod, *Annals and Antiquities of Rajasthan,* 2 vols. (London: 1829–1832; reprint in 3 vols. Delhi: Low Price Publications, 1990), 1:226, 334; 2:793, 1044; 3:1471, 1483, 1491, 1522; Norman Ziegler, "Action, Power, and Service in Rajasthani Culture. A Social History of the Rajputs of Middle Period Rajasthan" (Ph.D. diss., University of Chicago, 1973), 69.

58. On the *khyāl*s, see Jean-Luc Chambard, "Les chansons à plaisanterie *(khyâl)* chantées par les femmes d'un village de l'Inde centrale (Madhya Pradesh)," *Cahiers de littérature orale* 6 (1981), 71–99.

59. Gananath Obeysekere, *Medusa's Hair. An Essay on Personal Symbols and Religious Experience* (Chicago: University of Chicago Press, 1981), 107–8; and idem, *The Cult of the Goddess Pattini* (Chicago: University of Chicago Press, 1984), 44–45.

60. Sylvain Lévi, "La transmigration des âmes dans les croyances hindoues," lecture delivered 20 March 1904, Paris.

61. The Rabaris are classified as camel herders, but in fact most often they raise water buffalo. On the Rabaris, see Sigrid Westphal-Hellbusch and Heinz Westphal, *Die Rabari,* vol. 1 of *Hinduistischer Viehzüchter im nord-westlichen Indien,* 2 vols. (Berlin: Duncker und Humblot, 1974); Sigrid Westphal-Hellbusch, "Changes in the Meaning of Ethnic Names as Exemplified by the Jat, Rabari, Bharwad and Charan in Northwestern India," in *Pastoralists and Nomads,* ed. Leshnik and Sontheimer, 124; and Judy Frater, *Threads of Identity: Embroidery and Adornment of the Nomadic Rabaris* (Ahmedabad: Mapin Publishing, 1995).

62. This protective thread is called *nazariyā,* from *nazar,* the "evil eye." Occasionally the maternal uncle offers an outfit, consisting of a tunic and a small hat in this color.

63. These marks are called *ḍiṭhaunā* in Rajasthani, from *ḍīṭh,* the "evil eye." Dalpat Ram Daya offered an extended discussion on the subject in an essay presented in 1849 to the Guzerat Vernacular Society. It was originally published under the title *Bhut Nibandh: An Essay, Descriptive of the Demonology and Other Popular Superstitions of Guzerat* (Bombay, 1850), and republished as Dalpat Ram Daya, *Demonology and Popular Superstitions of Gujarat* (Gurgaon: Vintage Books, 1990). According to this source, black is used throughout Gujarat to drive away the evil eye. Thus a black silken thread will be tied to any object being used for the first time, as well as to a newborn's cradle. A black flower will be embroidered on new clothing. People pour small amounts of coal into milk, a sacred product whose very whiteness marks

it as a prey to evil spirits (ibid., 76–79). Even today women in Rajasthan attach a black thread to ornaments worn for the first time, even if they be simple glass bangles; and a black pot is hung in a new home or apartment when one moves into it. See Mahendra Bhanavat, *Ajūbā Rājasthān* (Udaipur: Mudrak Prakasan, 1986), 128–32. For Tamil Nadu, see also Hélène Stork, "Mothering Rituals in Tamilnadu: Some Magico-Religious Beliefs," in *Roles and Rituals for Hindu Women,* ed. Julia Leslie (Rutherford, N.J.: Fairleigh Dickinson University Press, 1992), 101–3.

64. On this subject, see Charles Malamoud, *Le svādhyāya. Récitation personnelle du Veda. Taittirīya-Āraṇyaka, livre 2* (Paris: De Boccard, 1977).

65. *Āpastambasmṛti,* 6.2–3, in *Smṛtīnāṃ Samuccayaḥ,* ed. V. G. Apte (Poona: Anandasrama Sanskrit Series, 1929), 39.

66. Jamila Brij Bhushan, *The Costumes and Textiles of India* (Bombay: Taraporewala's Treasure House, 1958), 8.

67. Jacques Pouchepadass, *Planteurs et Paysans dans l'Inde coloniale: l'indigo du Bihar et le mouvement gandhien de Champaran, 1917–1918* (Paris: L'Harmattan, 1986), 64.

68. *Āpastambasmṛti,* 6.1b in *Smṛtīnāṃ Samuccayaḥ,* translated in Julia Leslie, *The Perfect Wife. The Orthodox Hindu Woman According to the* Strīdharmapaddhati *of Tryambakayajvan* (Delhi: Oxford University Press, 1989), 244–45.

69. *Nirṇayasindhu of Kamalākara Bhaṭṭa,* ed. with a Hindi translation by M. M. Vrajaratna Bhattacharya (Banaras: Chowkamba Vidyabhavan, 1991), 392.

70. In Hindi and in Rajasthani: *sat kā jos'.*

71. Rupkuar Mehta, *Rājasthān kī sant-śiromaṇi Bālā Satī* (Jodhpur: Rajasthani Granthakar, 1991). An ardent devotee of Bala, Rupkuar Mehta earlier published an exemplary life of the saintly woman—*Śrī Satī Mātā caritāmṛt* (Jodhpur: Susma Prakasan, 1986). We will return to Bala later in this book, pp. 145–52.

72. The expression "living satī" *(jīvit satī)* has an entirely different meaning in Sanskrit, particularly in the *dharma* literature, where it signifies "a widow who outlives her husband" (and who leads an ascetic life conforming to the ideal of widowhood) as opposed to one who burns on her husband's funeral pyre.

73. John Masters, *The Deceivers* (London: Michael Joseph, Ltd., 1952). See Catherine Weinberger-Thomas, "Pour l'amour de Kâlî. *The Deceivers* de John Masters," in *Rêver l'Asie. Exotisme et littérature coloniale aux Indes, en Indochine et en Insulinde,* ed. Denys Lombard (Paris: Editions de l'EHESS, 1993), 447–54.

74. It was inaugurated on March 31, 1986, by Kalyan Singh Kalvi (then head of the Janata Party for the State of Rajasthan); Gunvant Kanvar, the Maharani of Shahpura; and Gayatri Devi, the Maharani of Jaipur. His adherence to the movement for the defense of the "*dharma* of the satīs" in Rajasthan was a springboard for Kalvi's political career (he became Energy Minister in 1990).

75. Jasvant Kanvar's eldest son also officiates.

76. The *cūṇḍrī* can be a red cotton or silk veil *(oḍhnī)* or sari whose hem is frequently worked with gold or silver embroidery. Their tie-and-dye prints, patternwork, and sometimes the dimensions (1.8 by 3 meters) are unusual. Worn on her

wedding day, the *cūṇḍrī* symbolizes the condition of a married woman whose husband is alive *(suhāg).* A sister will receive a *cuṇḍrī* from her brother at the time of her children's weddings and at her death. This gift of the funeral *cūṇḍrī* is consecrated in the ceremony known as "the great *cūṇḍrī* festival" *(cūṇḍrī mahotsav),* which takes place on the twelfth day after death. On the symbolism of this piece of clothing and its ritual use (for example in the celebration of the Gangaur festival, which is connected to the divine marriage of Śiva and Gaurī), see Bhanavat, *Ajūbā Rājasthān,* 50–52. According to Komal Kothari, Rajasthan as a "subjective space" (in the terminology of geographers) would be the area in which the *cūṇḍrī* is used for ritual ends: cited in D. O. Lodrick, "Rajasthan as a Region: Myth or Reality," in Schomer, *Idea of Rajasthan,* 1:30.

77. Certain segments of this caste have nonetheless been integrated into the category of the "twice-born." On this subject, see R. V. Russell and Rai Bahadur Hira Lal, *Tribes and Castes of the Central Provinces of India,* 4 vols. (London: Macmillan, 1916; reprint Delhi: Cosmo, 1975), 4:517–34.

78. Sudesh Vaid and Kumkum Sangari, "Institutions, Beliefs, Ideologies. Widow Immolation in Contemporary Rajasthan," *Economic and Political Weekly* 26, no. 17 (27 April 1991), 16, note. Vaid and Sangari have indicated, with reference to the blue veil thrown over Bala, that in the Jodhpur region that color was associated with Muslims. Perhaps there is some memory of the fact that the Nilgar dyers were most often Muslims. This proves in any event that there continues to be an association between a substance representing the impure in its most tangible and concentrated form and a religious community that incarnates, for fundamentalist Hindus, the antithesis of the values of "Hindu-ness" *(hindutva).*

79. J. S. Stavorinus, *Voyages to the East-Indies,* trans. S. M. Wilcocke, 3 vols. (London: G. G. and J. Robinson, 1798; reprint London: Dawson's, 1969), 1:448. A French translation exists: *Voyage à Batavia, à Bantam et au Bengale, en 1768, 69, 70 et 71* (Paris, 1798).

80. François Bernier, *Voyages de F. Bernier (Angevin), contenant la description des Estats du Grand Mogol, de l'Indoustan, du royaume de Kachemire,* 2 vols. (Amsterdam: D.-P. Marrett, 1699), 1:117–18. (Translated here from the original French.)

81. Jules Verne, *Le Tour du monde en quatre-vingts jours* (Paris: J. Hetzel et Cie, 1873), 60–69. The novel is so stimulating and Bennett's illlustration so beautiful that Jules Verne will be forgiven the implausibility of the situation: by definition, Parsis are not Hindus and do not burn their dead, as is known. The fact that a Parsi woman was the spouse of an "independent Rajah of Bundelkund" may fit the logic of the narrative, which makes that woman, "as white as a European," the future Mrs. Phileas Fogg.

82. L. de Grandpré, *Voyage dans l'Inde et au Bengale, fait dans les années 1789 et 1790,* 2 vols. (Paris: Dentu, 1801), 2:68–75.

83. Alexander Hamilton, *A New Account of the East Indies,* 2 vols. (London: 1744), 2:6–7; J. Z. Holwell, *Interesting Historical Events Relative to the Provinces of Bengal &*

the Empire of Indostan (London: T. Becket & A. de Hondt, 1767), 100; and H. C. Biswas, "Job Charnock's Hindu Wife: A Rescued Satî," *Hindustan Review* 22, no. 133 (September 1910): 298–301.

84. See Komal Kothari, "Myths, Tales, and Folklore: Exploring the Substratum of Cinema," *India International Centre Quarterly* 8, no. 1 (March 1980); and especially idem, "Performers, Gods, and Heroes in the Oral Epics of Rajasthan," in *Oral Epics in India,* ed. Stuart H. Blackburn et al. (Berkeley: University of California Press, 1989), 102–17. The Epic of Pābū-jī has been translated, presented, and commented on by John D. Smith, *The Epic of Pābū-jī* (Cambridge: Cambridge University Press, 1991).

85. Puspa Bhati, *Rājasthān ke lok devtā evam lok sāhity* (Bikaner: Kavita Prakasan, 1991), 47–49. The oral epic of Ālhā contains two references (in Cantos 1 and 14) to a variant on the casting of indigo: a blue banner is waved in order to calm decapitated heroes' martial fury. See George Grierson, *The Lay of Alha. A Saga of Rajput Chivalry as Sung by Minstrels of Northern India* (London: Oxford University Press, 1923; reprinted Gurgaon: Vintage Books, 1990). Commenting on the episode in a short article, H. A. Ross has drawn a correlation (which he was unable to explain) between the blue of that banner and the blue-black color of the Devī of Hinduism: "Sacrifices of the Head to the Hindu Goddess," *Folklore. Transactions of the Folklore Society* 37, no. 1 (March 1926): 90–92.

86. See Lorenzen, *Kāpālikas,* 85–86.

87. Doshi, "Pāliyas," 163.

88. Harald Tambs-Lyche, "Power and Devotion. Religion and Society in Saurashtra," 3 vols. (Ph.D. diss., University of Bergen, 1992), 3:441, 463.

89. Quoted by Ziegler, *Action,* 96. On the *Chronicle of Naiṇsī,* see idem, "Marvari Historical Chronicles: Sources for the Social and Cultural History of Rajasthan," *The Indian Economic and Social History Review* 13, no. 2 (April-June 1976): 231, 245–48; and idem, "Evolution of the Rathor State of Marvar: Horses, Structural Change, and Warfare," in Schomer, *Idea of Rajasthan,* 2:211 n. 3. See also Smith, *Epic,* and idem, "The Story of Pābūjī: Bard versus Historian," in *Luigi Pio Tessitori. Atti del Convegno internazionale di Udine* (Brescia: Paideia Editrice, 1990), 177–93.

90. See Pramod Kumar, *Folk-Icons and Rituals in Tribal Life* (New Delhi: Abhinav, 1984), 33–35.

91. On this subject, see below, note 23 to "The Rite, the Law, and the Custom."

92. Rice, *Mysore and Coorg,* 187.

93. H. A. R. Gibb, ed., *The Travels of Ibn Baṭṭūṭa—A.D. 1325–1354,* 3 vols. (Cambridge: Cambridge University Press, 1971), 3:614–16. The Sumra formed the first Muslim dynasty of Sind.

94. See *Burning and Melting. Being the Sūz-U-Gudāz of Muhammad Rizā Nau'ī of Khabūshān,* trans. Mirza Y. Dawud and Ananda K. Coomaraswamy (London: Luzac, 1912). On the Muslim encounter with satīs, see S. Chaudhuri, "Sati as Social Institution, and the Mughals," in *Indian History Congress. Proceedings of the 37th Session,*

Calicut (New Delhi: Indian History Congress, 1976), 218–23. For an example of a Muslim princess dying on the funeral pyre of a Rajput hero, see M. Singh Gahlot and Lal Menariya, *A Muslim Princess Becomes Sati (A Historical Romance of Hindu-Muslim Unity)* (Jalore: Sri Mahavira Shodha Samsthan, 1981).

95. *Travels in India by Jean-Baptiste Tavernier Baron of Aubonne,* trans. V. Ball, 2d ed., ed. William Crooke, 2 vols. (London: Oxford University Press, 1925), 2:172.

96. Lutfullah, *Autobiography of Lutfullah, a Mohamedan gentlemen; & his Transactions with his Fellow-Creatures* (London: Smith, Elder Co., 1857), 221–27.

97. Sir William Jones, *Institutes of Hindu Law, or the Ordinances of Menu, According to the Gloss of Cullâla; Comprising the Indian System of Duties, Religious and Civil* (Calcutta, 1794). A French translation of the Sanksrit text is A. Loiseleur-Deslongchamps, *Lois de Manou* (Paris: Imprimerie de Craquelet, 1833). Wendy Doniger and Brian K. Smith have published the first unexpurgated translation of *Mānavadharmaśāstra: The Laws of Manu* (Harmondsworth: Penguin, 1991). On the subject of *dharma* literature, see Robert Lingat, *Les Sources du droit dans le système traditionnel de l'Inde* (Paris: Mouton, 1967).

98. This is the *Vivādabhaṅgārṇava* ("Ocean of Solutions to Legal Conflicts"), translated into English in 1797 by Henry T. Colebrooke, who was, like Jones, both a judge and a Sanskritist. On this point, see J. Duncan M. Derrett, "Sanskrit Legal Treatises Compiled at the Instance of the British," *Zeitschrift für vergleichende Rechtswissenschaft* (1961): 72–117.

99. Ram Mohan Roy, "A Conference between an Advocate for and an Opponent of the Practice of Burning Widows Alive," 30 November 1818; idem, "A Second Conference between an Advocate for and an Opponent of the Practice of Burning Widows Alive," 20 February 1820; and idem, *Modern Encroachments on the Ancient Rights of Female According to the Hindu Law of Inheritance* (Calcutta: By the author, 1822). The first two pamphlets (originally written in Bengali, then translated by the author) have been published in English in *Sati. A Writeup of Raja Ram Mohan Roy about Burning of Widows Alive,* ed. Mulk Raj Anand (Delhi: B. R. Publishing Corporation, 1989). There is a sizable bibliography on Roy's role in the anti-satī campaign. We limit ourselves here to S. D. Collet's major reference work, *The Life and Letters of Ram Mohun Roy* (1900), ed. D. K. Biswas and P. C. Ganguli (Calcutta: Sadharan Brahmo Samaj, 1962); Ashis Nandy's controversial study, "Sati. A Nineteenth-Century Tale of Woman, Violence, and Protest," in *At the Edge of Psychology. Essays in Politics and Culture* (Delhi: Oxford University Press, 1980), 1–31; and finally Benoy Bhusan Roy's well-documented *Socioeconomic Impact of Sati in Bengal and the Role of Raja Rammohun Roy* (Calcutta: Naya Prokash, 1987).

100. Charles Edward Buckland, *Bengal Under the Lieutenant-Governors. Being a Narrative of the Principal Events and Public Measures during their Periods of Office from 1854 to 1898* (Calcutta: S. K. Lahari, 1901; reprint New Delhi: Deep Publications, 1976), 160–61.

101. *Parliamentary Papers [=Papers Relating to East India Affairs, viz. Hindoo Wid-*

ows, and Voluntary Immolations] (London: House of Commons, 1830), 28:134. See, among other testimony: J. Z. Holwell, *Interesting Historical Events,* 169–70; William Ward, *A View of the History, Literature and Religion of the Hindoos* (Serampore: Mission Press, 1817; Madras: J. Higginbotham, 1863), 242 and 246; Quinten Crawfurd, *Researches Concerning the Laws, Theology, Learning, Commerce, etc. of Ancient and Modern India,* 2 vols. (London: T. Cadell and W. Davies, 1817), 2:19–25.

102. On this question, see below, p. 198.

103. On the act of truth, see E. W. Burlingame, "The Act of Truth *(Saccakiriya):* A Hindu Spell and its Employment as a Psychic Motif in Hindu Fiction," *Journal of the Royal Asiatic Society* (July 1917): 429–67; N. M. Penzer, "Note on the 'Act of Truth' Motif in Folk-lore," in *The Ocean of Story. Being C. H. Tawney's Translation of Somadeva's Kathā Sarit Sāgara,* 10 vols., ed. N. M. Penzer (London: Chas. J. Sawyer, Ltd., 1924–28), 3:179–82; W. Norman Brown, "The Metaphysics of the Truth Act *(Satyakriyā),*" in *Mélanges d'indianisme à la mémoire de Louis Renou,* ed. Charles Malamoud (Paris: De Boccard, 1968), 171–78; Charles Malamoud, "The Gods Have No Shadows," in idem, *Cooking the World: Ritual and Thought in Ancient India,* trans. David Gordon White (Delhi: Oxford University Press, 1996), 196. See also Mallison, *L'Epouse idéale,* 27–29.

104. Sir William Henry Sleeman, *Rambles and Recollections of an Indian Official* (London: J. Hatchard and Son, 1844); rev. ed. with annotations by Vincent A. Smith (London: Oxford University Press, 1915), 22. The italics are in Sleeman's text. A body bereft of its animating vital breath is called a "body of clay" *(miṭṭī kā tan);* the word *miṭṭī,* moreover, can have the sense of "mortal remains."

105. This word means "flag, banner, mark, insignia, emblem." It is not used to designate a turban. This may be a local or period usage, or a case of imprecision on the part of the author. It is nonetheless interesting to note that the word *dhvaja* appears in ancient medieval inscriptions in Rajasthan to designate funeral pillars commemorating the heroic sacrifice of warriors: they are in fact called *govardhana dhvaja.* On this subject, see Hermann Goetz, *The Art and Architecture of Bikaner State* (Oxford: B. Cassirer, 1950), 61–62.

106. Shib Chunder Bose, *The Hindoos as They Are. A Description of the Manners, Customs and Inner Life of Hindoo Society in Bengal* (London: Edward Stanford, 1881), 273–74.

107. B. Sarma Parik, *Mān Satī Sugan Kuñvari Caritr. Ūjolī kī satī* (Kishangarh: n.p., n.d.), 6.

108. On this practice, see for example John Campbell Oman, *The Mystics, Ascetics, and Saints of India. A Study of Sadhuism, with an Account of the Yogis, Sanyasis, Bairagis, and Other Strange Hindu Sectarians* (London: T. F. Unwin, 1903; reprint Delhi: Cosmo, 1973), 46–47.

109. This is, of course, also true of "saints."

110. The Rajasthani *parco* is a corruption of the Sanskrit *paricaya,* "the fact of being known or recognized, identified."

111. Lakshmi Kapani translates this word as "a prior residual impression, a disposition inherited from the past" in her book, *La Notion de saṃskāra dans l'Inde brahmanique et bouddhique,* 2 vols. (Paris: De Boccard, 1991–1993), 2:553.

112. Francis Zimmermann, *Le Discours des remèdes au pays des épices* (Paris: Payot, 1989), 127.

113. Surendranath Dasgupta, *A History of Indian Philosophy,* 5 vols. (Cambridge: Cambridge University Press,1922; reprint Delhi: Motilal Banarsidass, 1974), 2:275.

114. They were also frequently buried alive.

115. S. M. Edwardes, "A Note on a Case of Self-Immolation by Ten Persons at Vasad," *Journal of the Anthropological Society of Bombay* 7, no. 8 (1892): 603–7.

116. Anonymous, "Burning the Devil. Curious Case in Calcutta," *Journal of the Anthropological Society of Bombay* 7, no. 8 (1892), 647–51.

117. On this subject, see Filliozat, "L'abandon de la vie." On the Chinese Buddhist tradition, see Jacques Gernet, *L'Intelligence de la Chine. Le social et le mental* (Paris: Gallimard, 1993), 169–206.

118. N. Subrahmanian, ed., *Self-Immolation in Tamil Society* (Madurai: International Institute of Tamil Historical Studies, 1983).

119. On this subject, see Francis Zimmermann, "L'argument paresseux. Un problème grec dans un texte sanskrit," in *Différences, Valeurs, Hiérarchies. Textes offerts à Louis Dumont,* ed. Jean-Claude Galey (Paris: Editions de l'EHESS, 1984), 53–64.

120. David Dean Shulman, *The King and the Clown in South Indian Myths and Poetry* (Princeton: Princeton University Press, 1985), 110–29; and Jackie Assayag, *La Colère de la déesse décapitée. Traditions, cultes et pouvoir dans le sud de l'Inde* (Paris: Editions du CNRS, 1992).

121. Tulsī Dās, *Rāmcaritmānas,* book 3, canto 4. English translation: W. Douglas Hill, *The Holy Lake of the Acts of Rāma* (Delhi: Oxford University Press, 1952), 298. See bibliography for original editions consulted. On Tulsī Dās, see especially Charlotte Vaudeville, *Etude sur les sources et la composition du Rāmāyaṇa de Tulsī-Dās* (Paris: Maisonneuve, 1955); and Philip Lutgendorf, *The Life of a Text. Performing the Rāmcaritmānas of Tulsidas* (Berkeley: University of California Press, 1991). On the image of women in Tulsī Dās, see Linda Hess, "The Poet, the People, and the Western Scholar: Influence of a Sacred Drama and Text on Social Values in North India," *Theatre Journal* 40 (1988), 236–53.

122. See S. Gupta, *Vibhinn yugon men sītā kā caritr-citraṇ* (New Delhi: Prajna Prakasan, 1978), 101–3.

123. *Rāmāyaṇa* 6.103.17–6.104.26. Sītā's words to Rāma, quoted here, are in 6.103.17–20 and 6.104.24 (incuding insertion 3236* in the critical edition). On Sītā's ordeal by fire in Vālmīki's *Rāmāyaṇa,* see Anne-Marie Esnoul, *L'Hindouisme* (Paris: Fayard-Denoël, 1972), 273, 275.

124. In songs dedicated to satīs, the younger brother-in-law *(devar),* an emblematic figure, is the person the satī will charge with this task, which is essential to her sacrifice.

125. *Pradakṣiṇā,* the circumambulation of an object to be honored in worship—a sacrificial fire, divine image, or temple—is always effected from right to left. When rites are performed in honor of ancestors and in the rite of cremation, one moves in the opposite direction *(prasavya),* from left to right. Frequently, the chief mourner will circle the pyre in the inauspicious direction, but he will take the auspicious direction during his final turn in order to be liberated from the sway of death that he has so marked out. On *pradakṣiṇā,* see Richard Burghart, "The Regional Circumambulation of Janakpur Seen in the Light of Vaishnavite Tradition (Nepal)," in *L'espace du temple (Puruṣārtha 8 and 10),* ed. Jean-Claude Galey (Paris: Editions de l'EHESS, 1985), 8:139 n. 1.

126. On the notion of divine play *(līlā)* in Hinduism, see *The Gods at Play. Līlā in South Asia,* ed. William S. Sax (Oxford: Oxford University Press, 1995).

127. *Rāmcaritmānas* 6.108, canto 33, trans. in Hill, *Holy Lake,* 422.

128. On the "three functional sins of Rāma," see Daniel Dubuisson, *La Légende royale dans l'Inde ancienne. Rāma et le Rāmāyaṇa* (Paris: Economica, 1986), 139–40.

129. On Tulsī Dās's borrowing from the *Adhyātma Rāmāyaṇa* for this episode, see Vaudeville, *Etude sur les sources,* 191; on the body of popular variants on the *Rāmāyaṇa* in which the motif of Sītā's double appears, see Wendy Doniger O'Flaherty, *Dreams, Illusions, and Other Realities* (Chicago: University of Chicago Press, 1984), 92–98. For an evocation of the theme of the shadow *(chāyā)* in Vedic literature, see idem, *Women, Androgynes, and Other Mythical Beasts* (Chicago: University of Chicago Press, 1980), 175–78. See also David Dean Shulman, "Fire and Flood: The Testing of Sītā in Kampan's *Irāmāvatāram,*" in *Many Rāmāyaṇas. The Diversity of a Narrative Tradition in South Asia,* ed. Paula Richman (Berkeley: University of California Press, 1991), 285–90.

130. Ritual recitations of Tulsī Dās's *Rāmcaritmānas* during the festival celebration of the birth of Rāma, performances of the "Play of Rāma" (*Rām Līlā,* the word *līlā* here bearing its twofold sense of divine *māyā* and theatrical performance) during the festival of *Daśahrā,* women's songs, folktales and sayings. On these traditions, see Richman, *Many Rāmāyaṇas.* On the *Rām Līlā,* see Christiane Tourlet and Jacques Scherer, *Quand le dieu Rāma joue à Bénarès* (Louvain: Cahiers théâtre, 1990). See also Jean-Luc Chambard, "Le *Râmâyana* des femmes dans un village de l'Inde centrale," *Cahiers de littérature orale* 31 (1992): 101–24.

131. F. Vicenzo, *Il Viaggio all'Indie Orientali del padre F. Vicenzo* (Venice: Giacomo Zattoni, 1678), 344.

132. John Fryer, *A New Account of East-India and Persia* (London: Chiswell, 1698), 198. A *luṅgī* is a loincloth, worn by men, that falls to the ankles. The word is thus inadequate in this context. According to tradition, a widow no longer has a right to more than a single item of clothing.

133. For Karnataka, see S. Hanchett, *Coloured Rice. Symbolic Structure in Hindu Family Festivals* (Delhi: Hindustan Publishing, 1988), 287. Margaret Sinclair Stevenson *(The Rites of the Twice-Born* [London: Oxford University Press, 1920; reprint New Delhi: Oriental Books Reprint Corporation, 1971], 205) noted in 1920 that a widow,

in Kathiawar at least, is required to wear only black if she is of mature age, and dark red or dark blue if she is young.

134. See Cousin, *Tissus imprimés.*

135. *Kuṃkum* powder (also called *rolī*) is a mixture of turmeric and lime. It is generally used in the form of a paste.

Handprint, Dagger, and Lemon

1. The right hand is pure, linked to life-cycle rituals, whereas the left hand is impure and linked to death rituals. On this question, see especially Veena Das, *Structure of Cognition: Aspects of Hindu Caste and Ritual* (Delhi: Oxford University Press, 1977); and Francis Zimmermann, "Géométrie sociale traditionnelle. Castes de main gauche et castes de main droite en Inde du Sud," *Annales ESC* 29, no. 6 (November-December 1974). If the satī leaves an imprint of her right hand, it is also because her husband took that hand during the rite of the "taking of the hand" *(pāṇi-grahaṇa),* an essential moment of the marriage ceremony. Very few satī stones bear a representation of a left hand. On this subject, see Günther Sontheimer, "Some Memorial Monuments of Western India," in *German Scholars on India,* 2 vols. (Bombay: Nachiketa Publications, 1976), 2:264–65; idem, "On the Memorials to the Dead in the Tribal Area of Central India," 90; and idem, "Hero- and Sati-Stones," in *Memorial Stones,* ed. Settar and Sontheimer , 279. Sontheimer maintains that the right-left opposition would coincide with that between higher and lower castes. I do not believe he should be followed on this point, since a number of low-caste satīs—such as the Nārāyaṇī of the Alwar district (tenth century) who was born into the impure caste of Barbers—have been deified.

2. Rice, *Mysore and Coorg,* 185.

3. See Thapar, "Death and the Hero," 304. For an interpretation of the scotomization of widowhood, see Weinberger-Thomas, "Cendres d'immortalité," 23–24. For a thoroughly researched analysis of the symbolism of satī-stones in which the sacrifice of the woman is represented by a raised right arm, bent at the elbow, the forearm emerging from a capped post, see Alf Hiltebeitel, *The Cult of Draupadī, vol. 2, On Hindu Rituals and the Goddess* (Chicago: University of Chicago Press, 1991), 129, 131. Hiltebeitel makes a connection between this pole and the *yūpa,* the sacrificial post to which the victim was bound in ancient India, a connection I find to be well founded. I would add that a (material and no longer symbolic) pole planted in the middle of the pyre or inside the hut *(koṭhī)* is frequently attested to in west-central India: the satī was bound to it. See in particular Jean Thévenot, *Voyages de Monsieur de Thévenot, contenant la relation de l'Indostan, des nouveaux Mogols, & des autres Peuples et Pays des Indes* (Paris: Biestkins, 1684), 251–52.

4. "Of bread," the text says. I believe, however, that it was more likely rice.

5. Sarat Chandra Mitra, "On a Recent Instance of Human Sacrifice from the Central Provinces of India," *Journal of the Anthropological Society of Bombay* 13, no. 6 (1926): 599–605.

6. In his chapter on "suicides by fire among Chinese Buddhists from the Fifth to the Tenth Centuries" (in *L'intelligence de la Chine,* 172), Jacques Gernet notes that certain monks figure in biographies of heroic suicides, not for having given up their lives, but for having offered some part of their body (burning their fingers or arms, for example). He observes in this regard: "There did not exist in the mind of the authors [of these biographies] and their contemporaries a clear boundary between suicide properly speaking and the sacrifice of a portion of the body. What made these (which are so different for us) one and the same act in their eyes was undoubtedly the very fact of individual self-sacrifice: if the total gift of the 'body' is preeminent, it does not differ in nature from a partial gift." With regard to practices of self-mutilation in India (whose range, variety, and persistence appear to me to be of a different order than the Chinese examples—however interesting they may be in and of themselves and in a comparative perspective), I think one has to go still further: partial sacrifice is not only the equivalent of total sacrifice; it constitutes its essential phase.

7. Rice, *Mysore and Coorg,* 187.

8. Devi, *Religion,* 267–68.

9. Russell and Lal, *Tribes and Castes,* 2:255. See also Ziegler, *Action,* 28–30; and idem, "Marvari Historical Chronicles." For a perspective on Charan literature, see, among other works, H. L. Maheshwari, *History of Rajasthani Literature* (New Delhi: Sahitya Akademi, 1980); S. S. Manohar, *Cāraṇ-carjāen aor unkā adhyayan* (Jaipur: Vivek Publishing House, n.d.); and M. L. Jigyasu, *Cāraṇ sāhity kā itihās* (Jodhpur: Jain Brothers, 1992).

10. "Lines of generations" are kept in registers by the genealogist castes and are considered to be their own property, whereas "lines of descendants" are the property of the families themselves (families that are locally illustrious or powerful, it goes without saying). See Ziegler, *Action;* idem, "The Seventeenth Century Chronicles of Mārvāṛa: A Study in the Evolution and Use of Oral Traditions in Western India," in *History of Africa* 3 (1976): 127–53; and idem, "Marvari Historical Chronicles." For Central India, see Adrian C. Mayer, *Caste and Kinship in Central India. A Village and its Region* (Berkeley: University of California Press, 1966), 194–201. See also Romila Thapar, *Cultural Transaction and Early India: Tradition and Patronage* (Delhi: Oxford University Press, 1987), 9; and idem, *From Lineage to State. Social Formations in the Mid-First Millennium B.C. in the Ganga Valley* (Delhi: Oxford University Press, 1984, 1990), 131–32.

11. See A. M. Shah and R. G. Shroff, "The Vahīvancā Bāroṭs of Gujarat: A Caste of Genealogists and Mythographers," *Journal of American Folklore* 71 (1958): 248–76, as well as preliminary remarks by M. N. Srinivas, ibid., 246–48; and Smith, *Epic,* passim.

12. On the Charans, see: Tod, *Annals and Antiquitie,* 1:554, 2:500; Malcolm, *Memoir,* 2:137–38; Russell and Lal, *Tribes and Castes,* 2:256–58; Reginald E. Enthoven, *The Tribes and Castes of Bombay,* 3 vols. (Bombay: Government Central Press, 1920–22; reprint Delhi: Cosmo, 1975), 1:284–85; Westphal-Hellbusch and

Westphal, *Hinduistischer Viehzüchter*, vol. 2, *Die Bharvad und die Charan;* Tambs-Lyche, *Power and Devotion*, 2:193–204. In my opinion, one of the best sources on the Charans and the Bhats remains the Hindi version of the census of the kingdom of Marwar in 1891, by Munshi Devi Prasad: *Riporṭ Mardumśumārī Rāj Mārvāṛ bābat san 1891 īsvī, tīsrā hissā*, 2 parts (Jodhpur: Vidyasal, 1895), 2:327–63. A simplified English version of the report was published in 1894 by Munshi Hardyal Singh, *The Castes of Marwar* (Jodhpur: Books Treasure, 1990).

13. See for example Michael Kennedy, *The Criminal Classes in India* (Bombay: Government Central Press, 1907; reprint Delhi: Mittal, 1985). On this question, see Jacques Pouchepadass, "Délinquance de fonction et marginalisation sociale: les tribus 'criminelles' dans l'Inde britannique," in *Les Marginaux et les Exclus dans l'histoire* (Paris: UGE, 1979), 122–54.

14. In 1920, Reginald Enthoven (*Tribes and Castes*, 1:283) noted that lower castes in Kutch addressed Charan women with the honorific title *mātā*.

15. Shah and Shroff, "Vahīvancā Bāroṭs," 250.

16. C. U. Aitcheson, *A Collection of Treaties, Engagements and Sanads, Relating to India and Neighboring Countries* (Calcutta: Government of India Central Publications, 1932), 6: 2, 165, 167. See also Westphal-Hellbusch and Westphal, *Hinduistischer Viehzüchter*, 2:234.

17. Ziegler, *Action*, 156.

18. *Tiga* in Dingal, the classical language of the bards.

19. J. C. Heesterman, *The Broken World of Sacrifice. An Essay in Ancient Indian Ritual* (Chicago: University of Chicago Press, 1993), 17.

20. Regulation 21 of 1795, Regulation 8 of 1799, reimplemented in the Annexed Territories by Regulation 8 of 1803. The ethnographical literature has associated Bhats and Charans on this point. And yet *trāgā* was practiced above all by Charans, as my Charan informants confirmed to me on many occasions. In 1832, Sir John Malcolm observed that the Bhats "seldom sacrifice themselves; but, as chroniclers or bards, they share power, and sometimes office, with the Charans" (*Memoir*, 2:137).

21. Concerning stele representing *trāgā*, see Alexander Kinloch Forbes, *Rās Mālā, Hindoo Annals of the Province of Goozerat in Western India*, 2 vols. (London: Richardson, 1856; reprint New Delhi: Heritage Publishers, 1993), 2:428–29; and J. Jain, "Ethnic Background of Some Hero-Stones of Gujarat," in *Memorial Stones*, ed. Settar and Sontheimer, 83–86 and fig. 1 facing 128.

22. I wish to thank Inder Dan Detha, whose friendship with me goes back many years, as well as U. K. Ujjwal, both Charans, for their information on this delicate subject. The immolation by fire of women of this caste as a sign of protest has a specific name in Marwar: *jamaṛ* (a word deriving from Jamṛo, a Rajasthani corruption of Yama, the god of the dead).

23. The Barots (from *bārah-haṭ*) are royal bards. See Shah and Shroff, "Vahīvancā Bāroṭs."

24. It is customary to call on the drummer (Dholi) in such circumstances, to

give full force to the act and bring it to the attention of those who wish to be present at the spectacle.

25. *Riport,* 2:343–44.

26. See L. Panigraha, *British Social Policy and Female Infanticide in India* (New Delhi: Munshiram Manoharlal, 1972), 75; and R. Vyas, "Social and Religious Reform Movements in the Nineteenth and Twentieth Centuries in Western Rajasthan," in *Social and Religious Reform Movements in the Nineteenth and Twentieth Centuries,* ed. S. Sen (Calcutta: Institute of Historical Studies, 1979), 184.

27. John Macmurdo, "Journal of a Route through the Peninsula of Guzeraut in the Year 1809 and 1810," in *The Peninsula of Gujarat in the Early Nineteenth Century,* ed. S. C. Ghosh (New Delhi: Sterling Publishers, 1977), 61–62.

28. This essay, titled *Bhut Nibandh,* published in Bombay in 1850 in the English version produced by Forbes, had been written to obtain a prize awarded by the Guzerat Vernacular Society, for which Forbes served as secretary. For Daya's narrative, see *Demonology,* 34–37, and Forbes, *Rās Mālā,* 2:386–89.

29. Louis Renou, "Le jeûne du créancier dans l'Inde ancienne," in *L'Inde fondamentale. Etudes d'indianisme réunies et présentées par Ch. Malamoud* (Paris: Hermann, 1978), 164–74. Marcel Mauss had presented a note on the question in 1925: "Sur un texte de Posidonius. Le suicide, contre-prestation suprême," *Revue celtique* 42 (1925): 338 (the article has been reprinted in *Marcel Mauss, Oeuvres,* 3 vols. [Paris: Editions de Minuit, 1968–1969], 3:52–57). On *dharnā* (which too often tends to be reduced to mere fasting), see in particular Horace Hayman Wilson, "Dharnâ," in *A Glossary of Judicial and Revenue Terms, & of Useful Words Occurring in Official Documents relating to the Administration of the Government of British India* (London: W. H. Allen & Co., 1855); J. H. Nelson, *A Prospectus of the Scientific Study of the Hindû Law* (London: Kegan & Co., 1881), 165; and *Hobson-Jobson,* s.v. "Dhurna," 315–17.

30. See Colette Caillat, "Fasting unto Death According to the Jaina Tradition," *Acta Orientalia* 38 (1977): 43–66; Marie-Claude Mahias, *Délivrance et Convivialité. Le système culinaire des Jaina* (Paris: Editions de la Maison des sciences de l'homme, 1985); S. Settar, *Inviting Death. Indian Attitudes towards Ritual Death* (Leiden: Brill, 1989); and idem, *Pursuing Death. Philosophy and Practice of Voluntary Termination of Life* (Leiden: Brill, 1990).

31. Hiranmay Karlekar, *In the Mirror of Mandal: Social Justice, Caste, Class and the Individual* (Delhi: Ajanta Publications, 1992). For a recent case of revenge suicide in central India, see Jean-Luc Chambard, "Les Violences d'un village hindou. Suicide de femme chez les barbiers et 'violences légitimes' des dominants au Madhya Pradesh," in *Violences/non-violences en Inde (Puruṣārtha 16),* ed. Gilles Tarabout, Denis Vidal, and Eric Meyer (Paris: Editions de l'EHESS, 1993), 61–80.

32. See Macmurdo, "Journal," 62; Enthoven, *Castes and Tribes,* 284; Shah and Shroff, "Vahīvancā Bāroṭs," 250–51, and Westphal-Hellbusch and Westphal, *Hinduistischer Viehzüchter,* 2:234. See also Denis Vidal, *Violences et Vérités. Un royaume du Rajasthan face au pouvoir colonial* (Paris: Editions de l'EHESS, 1995).

33. Sarat Chandra Mitra, "Note on a Recent Instance of Self-Immolation for Propitiating a God," *Journal of the Anthropological Society of Bombay* 14, no. 2 (1928): 227–28.

34. Quoted by Mrs. Postans, *Cutch; or Random Sketches, Taken during a Residence in One of the Northern Provinces of Western India* (London: Smith, Elder & Co., 1839), n. 172. See also J. Macmurdo, "Remarks on the Province of Kattiawar, its Inhabitants, their Manners, and Customs," *Transactions of the Literary Society of Bombay* 1 (1819); and idem, "An Account of the Province of Cutch, and of the Countries Lying between Guzerat and the River Indus," *Transactions of the Literary Society of Bombay* 2 (1820).

35. See for example *Manusmṛti,* 5.135.

36. Initiates of the Kaula sects, which are famous for the "left-handed" practices *(vāmācāra)* characteristic of that school of Tantrism, absorb as an elixir of immortality sexual secretions obtained in ritual copulation *(maithuna).* The most highly valued beverage, which confers greatest efficacy on this secret rite, is a mixture of semen and menstrual blood: the ideal sexual partner, incarnating all possible figures of transgression, ought to have her "flowers": her period (being a *puṣpiṇī*). These practices must, of course, be situated within their own perspective, in a field of extremely complex religious representations in which tantra, yoga, and alchemy play a part, and in which the consumption of sexual fluids causes the adept to enter into the "lineage" or "clan" *(kula,* whence *kaula)* of the divinity, that filiation being simultaneously "biological" and sectarian. On this subject, see White, *Alchemical Body.* On the adept's absorption of the remains of ritual copulation, see in particular J. A. Schoterman, *The Yonitantra* (New Delhi: Manohar, 1980), who observes that the principal aim of *maithuna* is to obtain that substance, which is at once a source of miraculous powers and an essential ingredient of the cult (pp. 28–29); and Dominique-Sila Khan, "Deux rites tantriques dans une communauté d'intouchables au Rajasthan," *Revue de l'histoire des religions* 211, no. 4 (1994): 443–62.

37. See *Riporṭ,* 2:29.

38. On *dakṣiṇā,* see Charles Malamoud, "Terminer le sacrifice. Remarque sur les honoraires rituels dans le brahmanisme," in Madeleine Biardeau and Charles Malamoud, *Le Sacrifice dans l'Inde ancienne* (Paris: Presses Universitaires de France, 1976), 155–204.

39. Malcolm, *Memoir,* 2:136. See also Ziegler, "Marvari Historical Chronicles."

40. Panigraha, *British Social Policy,* 9 and 67–81; R. P. Vyas, "Social Changes in Rajasthan from the Middle of the 19th Century to the Middle of the 20th Century," in *Socio-Economic Study of Rajasthan,* ed. G. L. Devra (Jodhpur, 1986), 139–40.

41. *Jogī* (Sanskrit *yogin*) and *jati* (Sanskrit *yati*) designate two types of itinerant ascetic who live by begging. *Jogīs* are known for their supernatural powers, achieved through the practice of yoga. In Forbes's time, the term *jati* often designated Jaina ascetics. As for *fakīr* (whose primary meaning is "poor man"), the Arabic term was originally reserved for Muslim ascetics, but was subsequently used to designate

Hindu ascetics, particularly those who went naked and indulged in bodily mortifications (*Hobson-Jobson,* s.v. "Fakeer," 347–48).

42. Jonathan Parry, "Sacrificial Death and the Necrophagous Ascetic," in *Death and the Regeneration of Life,* ed. Maurice Bloch and Jonathan Parry (Cambridge: Cambridge University Press, 1982), 78. For Parry, the contradiction between the impurity and the sacredness of the corpse may be explained in terms of the noncoincidence between biological and ritual death: in the Hindu perspective, the body of the deceased remains animated by the vital breath until the moment when the chief mourner releases it by cracking open the skull, a rite that is performed midway through the cremation process. The act of cremation (rather than the corpse or the biological phenomenon of death) would thus be the source of pollution. It follows from this argument that the body abandoned to the flames of the crematory fire is not simply a corpse, but rather a being still endowed with life. Cremation might thus be viewed as a sacrifice in the fullest sense of the term: the offering of a live victim. The son's (or the deceased's nearest male relative's) breaking of the skull would be tantamount to a parricide—or a murder. See Jonathan Parry, "Death and Cosmogony in Kashi," *Contributions to Indian Sociology* 15 (1981): 356–62. See also idem, *Death in Banaras* (Cambridge: Cambridge University Press, 1994), 180–81. The wordplay between Śiva and *śava,* moreover, is embedded in another perspective, this time sectarian: Śiva is represented as a corpse in Śākta literature and iconography (especially in texts and images celebrating Chinnamastā, the decapitated Goddess). On this question, see Teun Goudriaan and Sanjukta Gupta, *Hindu Tantric and Śākta Literature* (Wiesbaden: Harrassowitz, 1981), 81, 86; Wendy Doniger O'Flaherty, *Women, Androgynes,* 80–87; and Charles Malamoud, "Spéculations indiennes sur le sexe du sacrifice," *L'Ecrit du temps* 16 (1987): 7–28.

43. Daya, *Demonology,* 56–57 and 77. For Sri Lanka, see Obeysekere, *Medusa's Hair,* 153.

44. See Smith, *Epic,* 249 of the text and 458 of the translation. On the symbolism of hair, see below, notes 22–27 of "Under the Spell of Sacrifice."

45. From *japnā,* the "muttering" of ritual formulae, incantations, or the name of one's chosen deity in continuous repetition.

46. James Burgess, *Report on the Antiquities of Kâṭhiâwâḍ and Kachh, Being the Result of the Second Season's Operations of the Archaeological Survey of Western India, 1874–75* (London: India Museum, 1876; reprint: Delhi: Indological Book House, 1971), 174.

47. For a review of the current state of the debate over the foundation of Vijayanagar, see Hermann Kulke, "Maharajas, Mahants and Historians. Reflections on the Historiography of Early Vijayanagara and Sringeri," in *Vijayanagara—City and Empire. New Currents of Research,* 2 vols., ed. A. L. Dallapiccola (Wiesbaden: Steiner, 1985), 1:120–43.

48. Duarte Barbosa, *Livro em que da relação de que viu o ouviu no Oriente,* compiled between 1517 and 1518. Editions consulted: *A Description of the Coasts of East Africa*

and Malabar in the Beginning of the 16th century (London: Hakluyt Society, 1866); and *Libro di Odoardo Barbosa,* in Ramusio, *Navigazioni e Viaggi,* 2:608–10. See E. Löschhorn, "Vijayanagar—as Seen by European Visitors," in *Vijayanagara,* ed. Dallapiccola, 1:345–46. For an illustration of the flaming pit, see in particular J. W. Massie, *Continental India. Travelling Sketches & Historical Recollections* (London: Thomas Ward & Co., 1840). A staircase from which the officiants in the ceremony would hurl the widow occasionally completed the tableau. A depiction may be found in Cesare de' Fedrici, *Viaggio de M. Cesare dei Fedrici nell'India Orientale, et oltra l'India: nelquale si contengono cose diletteuoli dei riti, di costumi di quei paesi* (Venice: Andrea Muschio, 1587). An illustration of this may be found in G. B. Ramusio, *Navigazioni e Viaggi,* vol. 6.

49. On emblems of royalty, see G. H. Khare, "Emblems of Royalty in Art and Literature," in *Annals of the Bhandarkar Oriental Research Institute, Diamond Jubilee Volume* (Poona: BORI, 1978), 682–89. On the parasol as royal emblem, see N. M. Penzer, "Umbrellas," in *Ocean,* 1:263–69.

50. On the protective symbolism of these objects and the ritual formula accompanying them, see Kapani, *Notion de saṃskāra,* 2:117. The husband traces the part separating the hair *(sīmantonnayana)* of his wife during the fourth, sixth, or eighth month of pregnancy with the quill of a porcupine. On the mirror, see S. S. Dange, *Hindu Domestic Rituals. A Critical Glance* (Delhi: Ajanta Publications, 1985), 31–34.

51. *The Travels of Pietro della Valle in India. From the Old English Translation of 1664, by G. Havers,* 2 vols., ed. Edward Grey, Hakluyt Society, first series, nos. 84–85 (New York: Burt Franklin, 1892), 2:266–67.

52. One finds another "colloquy" between a foreigner and a satī in the account of an Englishman present at the sacrifice of a Brahman woman in the village of Marud in southern Konkan. This highly moving dialogue takes place at the site of the cremation ground itself. See *Parliamentary Papers* 24 (1825): 211–13, which contains the anonymous "Letter" published in the *Bombay Courier* on October 16, 1824.

53. Gasparo Balbi, *Viaggio dell'Indie Orientali* (Venice: Camillo Borgominieri, 1590), 82. Other accounts: Abraham Rogerius, *Le Théâtre de l'idolâtrie, ou la Porte ouverte pour parvenir à la connoissance du Paganisme caché . . .* (Amsterdam: Jean Schipper, 1670), 130 (original edition: *De Open-Deure tot het Verborgen Heydendom . . .* [Leiden: F. Hackes, 1651]); Roberto de Nobili, in V. Cronin, *A Pearl to India. The Life of Roberto de Nobili* (London: Rupert Hart-Davis, 1959), 54; Nicolao Manucci, *Storia do Mogor or Mogul India. 1653–1708,* 4 vols. (London: J. Murray, 1907), 2:62. On the "impaled" lemon as a representation of sacrifice in the cult of the goddess Draupadī, see Hiltebeitel, *Cult of Draupadī,* vol. 2.

54. Jan Haafner, *Voyages dans la Péninsule occidentale de l'Inde et dans l'ile de Ceilan (1808),* 2 tomes. (Paris: Arthus-Bertrand, 1811), 2:61.

55. De' Fedrici, *Viaggio,* 37.

56. Robert Drummond, *Illustrations of the Grammatical Parts of the Guzerattee, Mahratta & English Languages* (Bombay: Courier Press, 1808), 37–38.

57. See Katherine Hansen, "The *Virangana* in North Indian History. Myth and Popular Culture," *Economic and Political Weekly* 13, no. 18 (30 April 1988): 25–33.

58. Malamoud, "Spéculations indiennes."

59. On the opposition (or rather the pair) "world"/"non-world" *(loka/aloka),* see Charles Malamoud, "Cosmologie prescriptive. Observations sur le monde et le non-monde dans l'Inde ancienne," *Le Temps de la réflexion* 10 (1989): 303–25.

60, Madeleine Biardeau, *Histoires de poteaux. Variations védiques autour de la Déesse hindoue* (Paris: École Française d'Extrême-Orient, 1989), 68.

61. On this subject, see Malamoud, "Return Action in the Sacrificial Mechanics of Brahmanic India," in idem, *Cooking the World,* 163–64.

62. *Manusmṛti,* 5.39.

63. Sylvain Lévi, *La Doctrine du sacrifice dans les Brâhmanas* (Paris: Presses Universitaires de France, 1966), 133.

64. "Extract from Sir John Malcolm's Report on Malwa, dated the 11th February 1821," *Parliamentary Papers* 20 (1826–1827): 42, note.

65. James Forsyth, *The Highlands of Central India: Notes on their Forests and Wild Tribes, Natural History, and Sports* (London: Chapman and Hall, 1872), 171–76.

66. When a sterile woman conceives for the first time, it is said that her womb is opening *(kokh khulnā),* which is regarded as a sign of divine favor.

67. "Extract from Sir John Malcolm's Report," 42.

68. On this subject, see John B. Carman and Fréderique Apffel Marglin, eds., *Purity and Auspiciousness in Indian Society (Journal of Developing Societies* 1 [1985]).

69. See Olivier Herrenschmidt, "Le sacrifice du buffle en Andhra côtier. Le 'culte de village' confronté aux notions de sacrifiant et d'unité de culte," in *Autour de la Déesse hindoue (Puruṣārtha 5),* ed. Madeleine Biardeau (Paris: Editions de l'EHESS, 1981), 137–77.

70. This ceremony has been described in Biardeau, *Histoires de poteaux,* 306–8. Although they have retained their title and prestige with the local population, the Maharajahs lost their power and privileges after independence. They nonetheless continue to play an important role in the religious and political life of western India. On this, see K. L. Kamal, *Party Politics in an Indian State. A Study of the Main Political Parties in Rajasthan* (Delhi: S. Chand & Co., 1971).

71. See Pandurang Vamana Kane, *History of Dharmaśāstra* (Poona: Bhandarkar Oriental Research Institute, 1930–1962), especially 4:427–28; Wilhelm Caland, *Die Altindischer Ahnencult. Das "śrāddha" nach den verschiedenen Schulen mit Benützung handschriftlicher Quellen dargestellt* (Leiden: Brill, 1893); and K. C. Vidyalankar, *Pitṛ-pūjā* (New Delhi: Bharatiy Granth Niketan, 1990). See also Kapani, *Notion de saṃskāra,* 1:129–37, which contains the translation of the *Piṇḍopaniṣad* (p. 133), a short Upaniṣad devoted to funeral *piṇḍas.* For a synoptical overview of the poly-

semy of the word *piṇḍa* and a penetrating analysis of the link between funeral rice-balls, the *śrāddha* rites, and karma, see Wendy Doniger O'Flaherty's editor's introduction to *Karma and Rebirth in Classical Indian Traditions* (Berkeley: University of California Press, 1980), 5–13.

72. This debt is truly settled only by procreating (a son)—that is, by becoming a "father" in turn. On the notion of the debt, see Louis Dumont, "La dette vis-à-vis des ancêtres et la catégorie de *sapiṇḍa*," in *La Dette (Puruṣārtha 4)*, ed. Charles Malamoud (Paris: Editions de l'EHESS, 1980), 15–37, and Charles Malamoud, "Dette et devoir dans le vocabulaire sanscrit et dans la pensée brahmanique," in *Lien de vie, Noeud mortel*, ed. Malamoud (Paris: Editions de l'EHESS, 1988), 187–205.

73. On the category of *sapiṇḍa* in mourning, inheritance, and marriage, see Dumont, "La dette," and Roland Lardinois, "L'ordre du monde et l'institution familiale en Inde," in André Burguière et al., *Histoire de la famille*, 2 vols. (Paris: Armand Colin, 1986), 1:519–55.

74. See David M. Knipe, "*Sapiṇḍīkaraṇa:* the Hindu Rite of Entry into Heaven," in Reynolds and Waugh, *Religious Encounters*, 111–24. There are all sorts of variants of this schema, which are reviewed by Kapani, *Notion de saṃskāra*, 1:133–35. Through the offering of the tenth funeral rice-ball, the *preta* gains the ability to digest and consequently to satisfy his hunger and thirst (or rather, the tenth rice-ball sates the hunger of the reconstructed body). This first group of post-mortem (or primary *śrāddha*) rites, which corresponds to the period of ritual impurity, lasts ten or twelve days.

75. See Kane, *History*, 4:334–551.

76. In other words, transforming him into a beneficiary of funerary rice-balls. See Michel Hulin, *La Face cachée du temps: l'imaginaire de l'au-delà* (Paris: Fayard, 1985), 393–94, n. 34. A description of the rite of *sapiṇḍīkaraṇa* from a textualist perspective may be found in Kane, *History*, 4:520–25); for remarks on the same from the field, see especially Stevenson, *Rites*, 185–87; Véronique Bouillier, *Naître renonçant. Une caste de sannyāsi villageois au Népal central* (Nanterre: Laboratoire d'ethnologie, 1979), 146–52; Ann Grodzins Gold, *Fruitful Journeys. The Ways of Rajasthani Pilgrims* (Delhi: Oxford University Press, 1989), 90–94; and Parry, *Death in Banaras*, especially 191–92. The rite of *sapiṇḍīkaraṇa* was traditionally observed in the twelfth month after death.

77. Hulin, *La face cachée*, 377–78.

78. Knipe, "*Sapiṇḍīkaraṇa*," 118.

79. *Nirṇayasindhu*, 1034.

80. On the scholastic debate, see ibid., 813–16.

81. *Garuḍa Purāṇa* 2.5.60–62, translated from the Sanskrit in *The Garuḍa Purāṇa* by a board of scholars, 2 vols. (Delhi: Motilal Banarsidass, 1979), 2:754.

82. On divergences of opinion among *dharma* commentators regarding the offering of *piṇḍas* to the wives of ancestors, see Kane, *History*, 4:474–76.

83. This duty falls to the son, who will keep the bones in a niche of the house

(sometimes he will carry them in a case around his neck) before immersing them at a pilgrimage site *(tīrtha)*. See Gold, *Fruitful Journeys*, 85–87. Pierre Dubois notes in his *Lettres* that the mortal remains of the Rajah of Badung and those of his wives and concubines were placed in separate funerary urns. See above, "A Burning in Bali," in "Funereal Prelude."

84. Dalpat Ram Daya (*Demonology*, 53–56) observes that the Bhuwo, a category of ecstatics who function as exorcists in Gujarat, are possessed by goddesses—like Bahucārā-jī or Khoḍīyār—born into the Charan caste.

85. Charles Malamoud, "Les morts sans visage: remarques sur l'idéologie funéraire dans le brâhmanisme," in *La Mort, les Morts dans les sociétés anciennes*, ed. Gherardo Gnoli and Jean-Pierre Vernant (Cambridge: Cambridge University Press, 1982), 441–53. In 1777, Nicolas Desvaulx gave a very precise account of the burial of ascetics in chapter 43 of his *Moeurs et Coutumes des Indiens*, edited by Sylvia Murr in *L'Inde philosophique entre Bossuet et Voltaire*, 2 vols. (Paris: École Française d'Extrême-Orient, 1987), 1:130.

86. Charles Malamoud, "Cooking the World," in *Cooking the World*, 47–48. On the renouncer's death to the world, see Patrick Olivelle, "Ritual Suicide and the Rite of Renunciation," *Wiener Zeitschrift für die Künde Südasiens* 22 (1978): 19–44; and idem, *Saṃnyāsa Upaniṣads. Hindu Scriptures on Asceticism and Renunciation* (New York: Oxford University Press, 1992), 89–94. See also Bouillier, *Naître renonçant*, 175–78.

87. The expression was coined by Louis Dumont in his study on "Renunciation in the Religions of India," *Archives de sociologie des religions* 7 (January–June 1959): 45–69.

88. This is a regional variant of the classical rite of "taking the hand" *(pāṇigrahaṇa)*, concerning which Lakshmi Kapani (*Notion de saṃskāra*, 1:116) has quite properly noted that it is common to both initiation and marriage. At present, the ball of henna is often replaced by a sweet cake (called *peṛā*), since the macabre connotation of the *piṇḍa* is frightening in such a circumstance.

89. *Naiṇsī rī khyāt*, 2:327–28, quoted in Ziegler, *Action*, 57. On the Marvari chronicles and the *khyāt* genre, see idem, "The Seventeenth Century Chronicles" and "Marvari Historical Chronicles."

90. Kapani, *Notion de saṃskāra*, 1:145.

91. I thank Wendy Doniger for this information, as well as Madeleine Biardeau, who informed me that Śiva's *liṅga (Śaṅkar-liṅg)* is commonly called *Śaṅkar-piṇḍ* in Marathi.

92. The medieval chronicles of Rajasthan provide us with another illustration of the homology between funerary rice-ball and sacrificed body: mortally wounded in combat, the Rajput warrior mixed his blood with earth, thereby making a *piṇḍa* which he offered to his ancestors. See Ziegler, *Action*, 76.

Death in the Telling

1. *De natura rerum,* 1:84–103, trans. Cyril Bailey, *Lucretius on the Nature of Things* (Oxford: Clarendon Press, 1910, 1950), 29–30.

2. *Parliamentary Papers* 18 (1821): 136.

3. See, for example, *Nirṇayasindhu,* 1054.

4. J. de Maistre, *Les Soirées de Saint-Pétersbourg, ou Entretiens sur le gouvernement temporel de la Providence,* 2 vols. (Paris: Cosson, 1821), 2:416. A new edition of de Maistre's *Eclaircissement sur les sacrifices* has recently come out, with an introduction and commentary by Jean-Louis Schefer (Paris: Agora, 1994).

5. Durkheim, *Suicide,* 221.

6. Ibid., 223.

7. This line of argument was at the heart of the rift between supporters of the rite and their adversaries in the regional and nationwide debate that followed the immolation of Rup Kanvar in Deorala in September 1987. On this question, see below, pp. 184–86.

8. Sattar, *Inviting Death;* and idem, *Pursuing Death.*

9. I will not repeat here the description of the ceremony, reconstituted from beginning to end, already given in my 1989 article "Cendres d'immortalité," which includes an analysis of the ritual sequences, types, and variants, as well as an interpretative overview of the rite's underlying symbol system.

10. This is a case of homonymy (see "Living Satīs" section of "Funereal Prelude"): Rup is an extremely common surname which is also especially auspicious for a woman, since a primary meaning of the term is "beauty." As for Kanvar, this is a title borne by married women from the Rajput or Charan castes. The satīs mentioned below who are designated by this honorific name were all Rajputs. One encounters numerous cases of homonymy among satīs of recent date; thus there are two Savitris (another very popular surname, since Sāvitrī was a paragon of conjugal virtue): the Savitri of Kothri, a woman from the Goldsmith caste, who died on April 1, 1973; and the Savitri of Golyana, a woman from the Potter caste, who burned herself on October 3 of the same year. There are also two Son Kanvars (from Khundraut and from Maunda Kala, who died in 1956 and 1975, respectively); two Sugan Kanvars (from Jodhpur and Ujoli, who died in 1954 and 1959). On the revival of the rite within the narrow boundaries of the Shekhavati, see below, "Shekhavati, an Endangered Region."

11. See Catherine Weinberger-Thomas, "Les yeux fertiles de la mémoire. Exotisme indien et représentations occidentales," in *L'Inde et l'imaginaire,* ed. Weinberger-Thomas, 9–31.

12. *Cakra-pūjā* is known by the name of *hook-swinging* in colonial historiography. On this practice, see especially Gilles Tarabout, *Sacrifier et Donner à voir en pays Malabar. Les fêtes de temple au Kerala (Inde du Sud): étude anthropologique* (Paris: École Française d'Extrême-Orient, 1986), 262–63; and Hiltebeitel, *Cult of Draupadī,* 2: 175–76, 195–97.

13. Rogerius, *Théâtre de l'idolâtrie.* On Rogerius's image of India, see Partha Mitter, *Much Maligned Monsters. History of European Reaction to Indian Art* (Oxford: Oxford University Press, 1977), 51–52; and Catherine Weinberger-Thomas, "Les chemins du paganisme. Images de l'Inde à l'âge classique," in *As Others See Us. Mutual Perceptions, East and West,* ed. Bernard Lewis, Edmund Leites, and Margaret Case (New York: International Society for the Comparative Study of Civilizations, 1986), 117–31.

14. Bernier, *Voyages,* 1:106, 119 (translated from the original French). On Bernier, see France Bhattacharya's introduction to *Voyage dans les Etats du Grand Mogol* (Paris: Fayard, 1981), 7–23; and Sylvia Murr, "Le politique 'au mogol' selon Bernier: appareil conceptuel, rhétorique stratégique, philosophie morale," in *De la royauté à l'Etat. Anthropologie et histoire du politique dans le monde indien (Puruṣārtha 13),* ed. Jacques Pouchepadass and Henri Stern (Paris: Editions de l'EHESS, 1991), 239–83.

15. Comte de Modave, *Voyage en Inde du Comte de Modave, 1773–1776 (Nouveaux mémoires sur l'état actuel de l'Indoustan),* ed. and annotated by Jean Deloche (Paris: École Française d'Extrême-Orient, 1971), 174.

16. *Parliamentary Papers* 17 (1823): 54–62, 65–66.

17. Bernier, *Voyages,* 1:116–17. Translated from the original French.

18. *Śuddhitattva,* 242–43 (see Kane, *History of Dharmaśāstra,* 2.1: 633, and 2.2: 1268); *Nirṇayasindhu,* 1053–55; and *Dharmasindhu* (Bombay: Venkatesvara, 1984), 766–69. I was unfortunately unable to consult the *Satīpurāṇa,* whose existence is indicated in G. N. Sharma, *Social Life in Medieval Rajasthan, 1500–1800 A.D.* (Agra: Lakshmi Narain Agarwal, 1968), 127. Sharma had access to a manuscript copy of this verse Purāṇa, which was in the private possession of a *paṇḍā* (a brahman serving as a priest for pilgrims) from Udaipur.

19. Stavorinus, *Voyages,* 1:441–48.

20. Gujurati *cūṛo,* Hindi *cūṛā:* a set of bracelets, serving as symbols of marriage (or rather of conjugal bliss) worn on the forearm (from the wrist to the elbow). This word can also designate more specifically the bracelet or bracelets worn above the elbow, whose symbolism is the same (*khānc* in Rajasthani).

21. This version of Durlabh Ram's account is the simplified prose given in S. C. Dixit, "An Account of Widow Immolation in Gujurat in 1741 A.D.," *Journal of the Anthropological Society of Bombay* 14, no. 7 (1931): 830–33. I have retained Dixit's transcription. Dixit had himself obtained the manuscript from the Gujerati Forbes Society.

22. See above, note 103 to "Funereal Prelude."

23. Catherine Clémentin-Ojha, *La divinité conquise. Carrière d'une sainte* (Nanterre: Société d'ethnologie, 1990), 49–50.

24. Smith, *Epic,* 244 of the text and 452 of the translation.

25. Emma Roberts, ed., *Views in India. Chiefly Among the Himalayan Mountains* (London: Fisher, Son & Co., 1845), 86–87.

26. *National Archives of India* (New Delhi), *Foreign Department, Political,* nos. 53–55.

27. See for example *Parliamentary Papers* 20 (1826–1827): 126.

28. Sleeman, *Rambles,* 27–28.

29. *Parliamentary Papers* 28 (1830): 12–13.

30. A dream during the first hour takes one year to become reality; a dream during the second hour, six months; a dream during the third hour, three months; a dream during the fourth hour, a month; a dream during the last two 48-minute timespans before awakening, ten days; finally, a dream at sunrise becomes reality instantaneously, according to Julius van Negelein, *Der Traumschlüssel des Jagaddeva,* 14–15, quoted in Penzer, *Ocean,* 8:100, note. The standard reference on this question is Wendy Doniger O'Flaherty, *Dreams, Illusion, and Other Realities* (Chicago: University of Chicago Press, 1984). See also Anne-Marie Esnoul, "Les songes et leur interprétation en Inde," in *Les Songes et leur interprétation,* Serge Sauneron et al. (Paris: Seuil, 1959), 209–47. For scholarly conceptualizations of dreams, see Kapani, *Notion de saṃskāra,* 288–91 and 387–421.

31. There is a booklet devoted to the subject of Savitri: M. D. Svarnkar, ed., *Satī Caritam (Koṭhrī-vāsinī-satī Sāvitrī caritr)* (Sri Dungargarh: Ratan Art Press, 1974).

32. This adjective is adequate only if one adopts the viewpoint of the great tradition. In popular Hinduism, these are the divinities who receive the special devotion of the faithful, whereas the great gods are relegated to the fringes of devotional space, or absorbed into local pantheons.

33. Ancestors who have died an evil death are often represented on Rajasthani stele in the form of a cobra (this is the case for Kallā-jī, Gātod-jī, or Tejā-jī). See Gold, *Fruitful Journeys,* 69. *Pitar* is a corruption of the Sanskrit *pitṛ* ("father," "ancestor"), from which *patrī* is derived. In Sanskrit, *pitṛ* is contrasted with *preta,* "departed" (the dead who have not yet received the sacraments enabling them to accede to ancestral status). But in popular Hindi, as in Rajasthani, *pitar* has rather the sense of "ghost" or "spirit" and designates above all the unhappy dead who died before marriage. To designate ancestors, one uses the term *buzurg,* of Persian origin, which means "of a venerable age."

34. Daya, *Demonology,* 15–16.

35. This tree is assimilated with the *śamī,* a tree and wood associated in the great tradition with sacrificial fire. See Madeleine Biardeau, "L'arbre *śamī* et le buffle sacrificiel," in idem, *Autour de la Déesse,* 215–43.

36. Obeysekere, *Medusa's Hair,* 76–77.

37. A fifth day of the dark fortnight of the month of *Caitra* in the year 2010 of the Vikrama era *(caitr kṛṣṇā pañcamī).*

38. Sudesh Vaid, "Politics of Widow Immolation," *Seminar* 342 (February 1988): 20–23.

39. In the exemplary Life of Tara Kunvari *(Tārā Kuñvari Caritr, arthāt Madho-Kā-Bās kī satī caritr)* published by B. Sarma Parik in Kishangarh, it is said that Jarav Kanvar was herself a *patibhaktā,* a wife entirely devoted to the service of her husband.

40. See above, nn. 119–120 to "Funereal Prelude."

41. The reference is to B. M. Malabari, author of *Infant Marriage and Enforced Widowhood in India,* published in Bombay in 1877.

42. Gustave Le Bon, *Les Civilisations de l'Inde* (Paris: Firmin-Didot, 1887), 650–51.

43. *Parliamentary Papers* 18 (1821): 227–29.

44. Ibid., 227.

45. The Court of Directors took up Ewer's argument. See *Parliamentary Papers* 20 (1826–1827): 30–31.

46. *Parliamentary Papers* 18 (1821): 229.

47. "Observations on the State of Society Among the Asiatic Subjects of Great Britain by Charles Grant," in *Parliamentary Papers* 20 (1826–1827): 33, italics in original. On the debate at the time between British judges and pundits on the Hindu woman as a legal subject, see especially Lata Mani, "Production of an Official Discourse on Sati in Early Nineteenth Century," and Vasudha Dalmia-Lüderitz, " 'Sati' as a Religious Rite. Parliamentary Papers on Widow Immolation, 1821–1830," *Economic and Political Weekly* 21, no. 17 (26 April 1986): 32–40 and 58–64, respectively.

48. *Parliamentary Papers* 20 (1826–1827): 41.

49. *Durgāṣṭamī* is the festival celebrated on the eighth night *(aṣṭamī)* of the cycle of the Nine Nights of the Goddess *(Navarātri).*

50. The rite of tying the turban *(pagṛī bāndhnā),* which closes the funeral cycle, underscores the identity between father and son that will be discussed below, 132 and note 104 to the present chapter. In this sense, the father is reborn a second time, or at least has his life extended through his son by this ritual act, which is perceived as auspicious *(śubh, māṅglik).* On this rite, see Mayer, *Castes,* 236–37.

51. *Parliamentary Papers* 20 (1826–1827): 100.

52. See above, pp. 43–44.

53. Sleeman, *Rambles,* 24 and 21.

54. On the different stages of the construction of the temple of Jhunjhunu and on the entire question, see Vaid and Sangari, "Institutions, Beliefs, Ideologies," 2–18.

55. *Voyage en Inde,* 174.

56. *Parliamentary Papers* 24 (1825): 74, 124. It is likely that the reference here is to 51 (rupees), an auspicious number, a detail that escaped the authors of the note.

57. On this subject, see below, "Cross-Examination of a District," in "Shekhavati, an Endangered Region."

58. Diana Eck, *Dársan: Seeing the Divine Image in India* (Chambersburg, Pa.: Anima, 1981); Lawrence A. Babb, "Glancing: Visual Interaction in Hinduism," *Journal of Anthropological Research* 37 (1982): 387–401.

59. A booklet commemorates the sacrifice of this particular Sugan Kanvar (who bears the same name as the sati of Ujoli, mentioned above). See Sri Acyut, ed., *Śrī Satī Sugan Kuñvari Caritr, arthāt Jodhpur kī satī kā hāl* (Kishangarh: Sri Syam Pustakalay, 1954).

60. On this phase of worship, see below, p. 171.

61. *Indian Express,* 8 August 1981. See also V. Subramaniam, in *Sati: The Burning Issue* (10 January 1988 issue of *Express Magazine).*

62. This does not mean it is not used in other circumstances, since the coconut is the universal symbol of sacrifice (of the person of the sacrificer), as we have seen above. In Rajasthan, the betrothal is sealed with a ritual exchange of coconuts: the father of the engaged girl offers her future husband a coconut, while the father of the boy gives the future bride a coconut to seal the engagement *(nārel jhelānā).*

63. Wood or bamboo are also commonly used, and it is sometimes said that the ascetic's (*yati*'s) skull should be broken with the "sacred fruit" (*śrīphal,* the coconut), and that of the householder (*gṛhasth:* man-in-the-world) with ordinary materials. This procedure, which constitutes the most dramatic moment of the ritual ceremony, and consists of staving in the fontanelle through which the "soul" or the "vital breaths" *(prāṇa)* escape, appears to be a source of constant guilt for the relative of the deceased performing it. It is as if violence perpetrated against one's dead father could not be neutralized in consciousness through the religious (impersonal, ritualized) dimension of the act, nor by the redemptive value attributed to it. On this final point, see Parry, *Death in Banaras,* 180–81.

64. The term *khopṛā* is also used to designate the embryo, the child, and ultimately the male sexual organ, since a man will speak of his organ by calling it "the little one" or "the child."

65. Bhanavat, *Ajūbā Rājasthān,* 109–12.

66. See above, n. 125 to "Funereal Prelude."

67. Which means: "All is but illusion in this world, except for the name of the Lord." Here Rām is referring not to an individualized divine figure but to the supreme Divinity, whose name alone is a source of salvation. See Charlotte Vaudeville, *Kabīr* (Oxford: Clarendon Press, 1974), 141.

68. The accounts of Arab, Italian, and Portuguese travelers all mention hundreds of women immolated in Vijayanagar during the funerals of Nayak warlords or sovereigns.

69. Cronin, *Pearl to India,* 53–55.

70. Garcia de Resende, *Miscelanea e Variedade de historias, costumes, casos e cousas que em seu tempo acontesceram* (Evora: A. de Burgos, 1554). I am grateful to Geneviève Bouchon for bringing this reference to my attention, and for translating Resende's text for me.

71. For a discussion of Kabīr's dates, see David N. Lorenzen, *Kabīr Legends and Ananta-Dās's "Kabīr Parachāī"* (Albany, N.Y.: SUNY Press, 1991), 9–18.

72. Vermilion paste, a symbol of marriage, which a woman applies to the part in her hair. See above, p. 51.

73. According to Charlotte Vaudeville, Masān is likely the horrible goddess Masānī, a form of Kālī, who dwells on the burning grounds (*śmaśāna,* in Sanskrit). See Vaudeville, *Kabīr,* 219 n. 4. In popular Hinduism, Masān designates a category of ghosts *(bhūt)* that haunt cremation grounds. It is frustration that renders these spirits malevolent: they died in childhood or before marriage and envy the earthly happiness of the living.

74. The mystic "Word."

75. Vaudeville, *Kabīr,* 219–26.

76. See Charlotte Vaudeville, "La conception de l'amour divin chez Muhammad Jāyasī: *virah* et *'ishq,"* *Journal Asiatique* 250 (1962): 350–67.

77. Tod, *Annals and Antiquities,* 1:213–15. Padminī probably never existed. A creation of the Sufi poet, she would have entered the realm of legend. Endorsed by the bards of Rajasthan, the myth of Padminī would acquire a cachet of authenticity through Tod's *Annals and Antiquities of Rajasthan* (originally published in 1829–1832). On the myth of Padminī, see Kalika Ranjan Qanungo, *Studies in Rajput History,* 2d ed. (New Delhi: S. Chand, 1971), 1–20. On Tod's impact on historiography, see Robert W. Stern, *The Cat and the Lion: Jaipur State in the British Raj* (Leiden: Brill, 1988); and Dirk Kolff, *Naukar, Rajput and Sepoy: The Ethnohistory of the Military Labour Market in Hindustan, 1450–1850* (Cambridge: Cambridge University Press, 1990), 72.

Albert Roussel wrote an opera based on Padminī: see Jackie Assayag, "L'aventurier divin et la bayadère immolée. L'Inde dans l'opéra," in C. Weinberger-Thomas, *L'Inde et l'imaginaire,* 197–227. A discussion of Padminī without broaching the question of her historicity is presented in Lindsey Harlan, *Religion and Rajput Women. The Ethic of Protection in Contemporary Narratives* (Berkeley: University of California Press, 1992), 182–204.

78. Rabindranath Tagore, *Rabīndra Racanābalī,* 15 vols. (Calcutta: Pascimbanga Sarkar, 1961), 1:666–68. Here we are referring to the poem titled "Vivāha" ("Marriage") in the collection of "Stories" *(Kathā)* dating from 1900: Tagore takes up a perennial theme of Rajasthani literature (and annals)—a wedding that is interrupted by a declaration of war. The groom is killed in combat and his bride immolates herself. See also, by Tagore: "Satī," a short dramatic poem that appeared the same year in a collection titled *Kāhinī* (ibid, 5:534–40), whose more complex action is borrowed from Marathi tradition (the poem was translated into English in the collection known as *The Fugitive* [London: Macmillan,1921]). I am grateful to France Bhattacharya for locating these texts for me.

79. Ananda Kentish Coomaraswamy, *The Dance of Shiva,* rev. ed. (New York: Noonday Press, 1957), 98–123.

80. Published under the title "Sati: A Vindication of the Hindu Woman," *Sociological Review* 6, no. 2 (1913): 117–35. Coomaraswamy defended the same ideas in the preface to his translation of the *Sūz-U-Gudāz* of Muhammad Riza Nau'i (*Burning and Melting:* see n. 94 to the "Funereal Prelude" chapter of the present volume).

81. *Nārī-Aṅk, Kalyāṇ* (Gorakhpur: Gita Press, n.d.), 96 and 144.

82. Since *Kalyāṇ* began appearing in 1926, it has been published by the Gita Press, which has also published such monuments of Hinduism as the *Rāmcaritmānas* of Tulsī Dās.

83. The *Satī Dharma Rakṣā Samiti* (whose convener was Narendra Singh Rajawat) was obliged to very quickly change its name to the "Committee for the Protection of *Dharma" (Dharma Rakṣā Samiti).* It thus retained a legal façade after the Rajasthan Sati (Prevention) Act of October 1, 1987, punishing any form of satī glorifica-

tion. In addition, by effecting a fusion between its defense of the cause of *dharma* and its vindication of the heroic sacrifice of satīs, the Committee sought to present itself, among its Rajput sympathizers, as the spearhead of Hindu nationalism.

84. There are, nevertheless, a few cases of men who have accompanied their wives in death. These are called *satā* or *satū,* in echo of *satī,* a term that also designates a man who follows his master in death. In his work on the wonders of Rajasthan, Mahendra Bhanavat (*Ajūbā Rājasthān,* 31) points out this curiosity.

85. This assertion, a veritable article of faith, is a matter of broad consensus, as I was able to ascertain in the course of my investigations. Moreover, it was forcefully argued in a propaganda sheet distributed among participants in the massive pro-satī demonstration that took place in Jaipur on October 8, 1987. This *Appeal to Hindus* emanated from the Committee for the Defense of *Dharma,* which makes an open display of its ties with the Hindu nationalist parties, the RSS, the BJP, and the *Vishva Hindu Parishad.* On the Hindu nationalist parties, see especially Christophe Jaffrelot, *Les Nationalistes hindous. Idéologie, implantation et mobilisation des années 1920 aux années 1990* (Paris: Presses de la FNSP, 1993).

86. To my knowledge, this document has never been published. Omkar Singh, whom I interviewed at length, spontaneously gave me a photocopy of it.

87. This passage is taken from p. 61 of *The Writ Petition Filed in the Supreme Court of India by Shri Jeevan Kulkarni to Challenge Constitutional Validity of the Commission of Sati (Prevention) Act 1987 (Act no. 3 of 1988), Being Numbered Writ Petition (Civil) 587 of 1989* (Bombay: By the Author, 1989), which was transmitted to me through the same channels. In January 1995, the joint petition of Omkar Singh and Jeevan Kulkarni was still awaiting a ruling from the Supreme Court. Kulkarni had presented the same argument in an article written in response to the immolation of Rup Kanvar in Deorala: "Sati—Pride or Shame," *Organizer* 24 (22 November 1987): 10–11. *Organizer* is the newspaper of militant Hindus affiliated with the RSS.

88. *Kāma Sūtra,* 5.1.3–5.

89. Zimmermann, *Discours des remèdes,* 195–96, and 260 n. 17; Obeysekere, *Medusa's Hair,* 107; and idem, "Depression, Buddhism, and the Work of Culture in Sri Lanka," in *Culture and Depression,* ed. Arthur Kleinman and Byron Good (Berkeley: University of California Press, 1985), 134–52.

90. Francis Zimmermann, "The Love-Lorn Consumptive: South Asian Ethnography and the Psychosomatic Paradigm," in Beatrix Pfleiderer and Gilles Bibeau, *Anthropologies of Medicine: A Colloquium on West European and North American Perspectives* (Braunschweig: Vieweg, 1991), 185–95. On the suicide of engaged women in south India, see Louis Dumont, *Une Sous-Caste de l'Inde du Sud. Organisation sociale et religion des Pramalai Kallar* (Paris: Mouton, 1957), 394.

91. On June 14, 1820, a Gujar woman from Jelalabad burned herself together with her paramour while her husband was still alive (*Parliamentary Papers* 17 [1823]: 49). Another case indicated in the same "DETAILED STATEMENT OF SUTTIES, OR HINDOO WIDOWS, WHO WERE BURNT, OR BURIED ALIVE, WITH THEIR DECEASED HUSBANDS, in the several Zillahs and Cities, during the Year

1820" was that of an Ahir woman whose husband had left her due to her lax behavior. She burned herself in the Kanpur region a year after the death of her lover, a Rajput farmer. Bernier (*Voyages,* 1:115–16) recounts an incident that caused a great stir in the Indies: a Hindu woman poisoned her husband in order to flee with her Muslim paramour, who was a tailor and drummer by profession. When the latter rejected her out of fear of reprisal, she decided to die as a satī. Her paramour played the role of drummer at the ceremony. While taking leave of her relatives and friends in a final farewell, she threw herself upon him and dragged him into the fiery pit where they burned together. A Hindu proverb affirms: "You never can tell with women: they can eat their husbands and still become satīs!" *(triyā caritr jānae nehīn koy, khasam mārke sattī hoy).*

92. The *Parliamentary Papers* (28 [1830]: 29) draw attention to the case of a very poor woman of the Hajjam caste who burned in Shajahanpur together with her young brother-in-law, with whom she had been sharing her existence since the death of her husband twenty years earlier. Secondary marriages with a younger brother-in-law *(nātā)* are commonly practiced in castes that do not make the prohibition of widow remarriage a mark of their social prestige. But this bond does not have the same religious sanction as holy matrimony, the sole form considered licit, according to *dharma. Nātā* allows the family-in-law to retain its daughter-in-law, who is considered to be their inalienable property *(sampatti),* even when the husband is gone. In Haryana and Punjab, this secondary marriage with a brother-in-law is punctuated by a rite: a sheet is thrown over the daughter-in-law—whence the expression "throwing the sheet" *(cādar ḍālnā)* to designate this type of union. On the entire subject, consult Pauline Kolenda, *Regional Differences in Family Structure in India* (Jaipur: Rawat, 1987), 289–354. See also Wendy Doniger, "Begetting on Margin: Adultery and Surrogate Pseudomarriage in Hinduism," in *From the Margins of Hindu Marriage. Essays on Gender, Religion and Culture,* ed. Lindsey Harlan and Paul B. Courtright (New York: Oxford University Press, 1995), 160–83. (On *niyoga,* see ibid., 172–80.)

93. *Parliamentary Papers* 28 (1830): 13.

94. See below in the present volume, pp. 131–33.

95. H. N. Singh, *Shekhawats and their Land* (Jaipur: Educational Printers, 1970), 102.

96. K. Singh Varhaspaty, *Karnī-Caritr* (Deshnok: Sri Hanuman Sarma Bookseller, 1938), 74–75.

97. Bhanavat, *Ajūbā Rājasthān,* 30.

98. The Jogis (whose name presumably stems from the Sanskrit *yogin,* a practitioner of yoga and, more generally, an ascetic) would formerly have been renouncers (*saṃnyāsins*) who broke their vow of celibacy, or the offspring of a Brahman widow and a fallen ascetic. Renouncers are buried and not burned, as noted earlier. On the debate over the burial of Jogi widows in Bengal, see below, n. 14 to "The Rite, the Law, and the Custom."

99. *Parliamentary Papers* 18 (1821): 114–15.

100. *Parliamentary Papers* 28 (1830): 10–11.

101. This designation is also employed for any satī, but in this case there is a deliberate emphasis.

102. *Parliamentary Papers* 17 (1823): 50.

103. *Parliamentary Papers* 24 (1825): 57.

104. The *Garuḍa Purāṇa* (1.95.20) thus teaches that if a woman voluntarily aborts, her act is equivalent to the murder of her husband "born in her womb in the shape of the fetus" (when the child is his). See *The Garuḍa-Purāṇam,* trans. M. N. Dutt Shastri (Banaras: Chowkhamba Sanskrit Series Office, 1968), 269. On the identity of father and son, see *Aitareya Upaniṣad* 4:1–3; *Manusmṛti* 9:8; *Yājñavalkyasmṛti* 1:56. On this subject, see J. C. Heesterman, *The Inner Conflict of Tradition: Essays in Indian Ritual, Kingship, and Society* (Chicago: University of Chicago Press, 1985), 134–35; Kapani, *Notion de saṃskāra,* 1:139–40 and 155–58; Parry, *Death in Banaras,* 151–52.

105. On *pīliyā,* see n. 56 to "Funereal Prelude."

106. *Beṭe kī mān ādhī suhāgin,* literally: "a woman who has a son is half a *suhāgin*" (a married woman whose husband is alive). The very word "widow" *(vidhvā)* is so negatively charged, so filled with imprecation that it is used only to describe an objective situation in which one is not implicated, or as an insult.

Under the Spell of Sacrifice

1. See above, pp. 19–20.

2. See above, p. 19.

3. See above, pp. 29–30. During the extended period during which I conducted field research in various regions of Rajasthan, I encountered only two cases of "living satīs": Bala and Jasvant Kanvar, with the prestige of the former, stemming from her miraculous twenty-three-year fast, elevating her considerably above the latter. My informants did not fail to indicate other cases to me, with a quite apparent desire to swell the number of India's heroic satīs in the eyes of a Western researcher; but their leads never led anywhere. I also heard on occasion of women whose *sat* could not stand up against the sprinkling of water stained with indigo. These were not, however, considered to be "living satīs."

4. George Devereux, *Basic Problems of Ethnopsychiatry,* trans. Basia Miller Gulati and George Devereux (Chicago: University of Chicago Press, 1980), 12. A booklet commemorates the failed sacrifice of Jasvant Kanvar: *Mahāmahim Mahāsatī Jasvant Kuñvar Candrāvat* (Devipura: n.p., n.d.).

5. On the importance of the numbers 108 and 1008, see D. C. Sirkar, *The Śākta Pīṭhas* (Delhi: Motilal Banarsidass, 1973), 24–25.

6. Modave (*Voyage en Inde,* 173), who saw a brahman woman burn herself in Faizabad on January 1, 1775, reports that "[t]he eldest son of the unfortunate

woman, a young boy of nine or ten, was led to a spot six feet from the pyre and he was made to perform a few ceremonies whose purpose I could not ascertain. . . . The child did not so much walk as let himself be dragged. He seemed beside himself. No doubt nature was speaking forcefully to him, drowning out the voice of superstition. He did not shed any tears, but his demeanor, his movements, all the features of his face bespoke the terror and anguish of his soul."

7. Tejā thus belongs to the category of ancestors called *bhomiyās* (see above, p. 34). On different versions of his story, see the DEA thesis by Isabelle Rémignon, "Les différentes versions de la geste de Tejājī" (Ecole Pratique des Hautes Etudes, 4è section, Paris, 1993).

8. On the Minas, see above, p. 26.

9. Tejā is said to have been a Dholiya Jat born in Kharnal, a village in Nagaur District. The tribal Minas, the Bhambhi Untouchables, but also, among the upper castes, the Rajputs as well as Brahmans worship Tejā-jī. Through their hagiographies, moreover, the Brahmans have attempted to raise this popular deity within the ranks of the divine hierarchy. See Rémignon, "Différentes versions."

10. As seen above, tears are an evil portent in the context of a sacrifice, even as they are a requirement of normal mourning. Nevertheless, even in cases of simple death (without the "accompaniment" of a wife), weeping over the deceased begins only after the mortuary laying out of the corpse.

11. On this red-edged yellow veil that is worn only by happy wives whose husbands are alive, see above, n. 76 to "Funereal Prelude."

12. Ramcandr Ary, *Śrī Satī-Mātā Hem Kanvar* (Byavar: R. Joshi, 1953).

13. See above, "The Dream as Proof," in "Death in the Telling."

14. *Riporṭ,* 1:61. The genealogist of Tejā-jī's lineage, the Bhat Bheru of Degana (Nagaur District), maintains that this transfer took place in 1734 (see Rémignon, "Différentes versions," 29–30). According to Puspa Bhati (*Rājasthān ke lok devtā,* 103), the chieftain of Parbatsar would have used this subterfuge to draw capital to his city through the cattle fair linked to the cult of the god.

15. "The hut of the *dīkṣita* is the womb of the *dīkṣita;* in truth, they [the officiants] thus lead him into his own womb" (*Aitareya Brāhmaṇa,* 1:3).

16. In general, women in labor are made to drink the divine image's "foot nectar" or water over which magical formulas *(pānīmantar)* have been pronounced; otherwise, mustard seeds (over which similar incantations have been pronounced) are thrown in their room.

17. *Aitareya Brāhmaṇa,* 1:3. On this subject, see Walter O. Kaelber, "Tapas, Birth, and Spiritual Rebirth in the Veda," *History of Religions* 15 (1976): 350–77; Jan Gonda, *Change and Continuity in Indian Religion* (The Hague: Mouton, 1965), 350–77.

18. On this subject, as it concerns other cultural areas, see in particular Benedict Anderson, *Imagined Communities: Reflections on the Origin and Spread of Nationalism* (London: Verso, 1983).

19. The aunt's account agrees with that of another female informant, who was also an eyewitness to the burning of Hem Kanvar.

20. *Śiva Purāṇa,* 7.25:1–48.

21. The girl is made to worship Gaurī before the wedding ceremony, in order to obtain marital happiness.

22. See in particular Charles H. Berg, *The Unconscious Significance of Hair* (London: G. Allen & Unwin, 1951); Edmund R. Leach, "Magical Hair," *Journal of the Royal Anthropological Institute* 88 (1958): 147–64; P. Herschman, "Hair, Sex, and Dirt," *Man* 9 (1974): 274–98; Daniel Dubuisson, "La Déesse chevelue et la reine coiffeuse. Recherches sur un thème épique de l'Inde ancienne," *Journal Asiatique* 166 (1978): 291–310; Alf Hiltebeitel, "Draupadī's Hair," in Biardeau, *Autour de la Déesse,* 179–214; Obeysekere, *Medusa's Hair;* Assayag, *Colère de la déesse;* and idem, "Le panier, les cheveux, la Déesse et le monde. Essai sur le symbolisme sud-indien," *Diogène* 142 (April-June 1988): 104–27.

23. It is thought that the "gift of the virgin" *(kanyādāna)* bears more fruit *(phala)* if the girl still has her baby hair *(janam keś);* even so, that hair is regarded as impure: the rite of the first cutting of the hair *(cūḍākarm)* is one of the "perfectionings" (*saṃskāras*) marking the birth of the "twice-born." The hair that is cut is buried (see Kapani, *Notion de saṃskāra,* 1:103–4). The importance attached to the girl's baby hair seems to me to be all the more significant. And yet a second set of beliefs comes into play here: the goddess of Lightning (Bijlī Mātā) is said to strike down with her jealousy girls whose hair has never been cut. Thus parents will, against their will, cut a fraction of an inch from their little girls' hair. Generally speaking, it is thought that malevolent spirits are attracted by unbound hair. This is why men bearing a long lock at the top of their skulls *(coṭī)* tie it in a knot.

24. Assayag, *La Colère de la déesse;* and idem, "Le panier, les cheveux."

25. The vermilion will be removed during the rite of entry into widowhood. See above, p. 51.

26. In the classical tradition, women whose husbands are far away and who suffer from the pangs of separation *(viraha)* will wear their hair in a single braid. Sītā refused any other hairstyle during her captivity in the palace of Rāvaṇa.

27. Obeysekere, *Medusa's Hair.*

28. See above, n. 10 to "Death in the Telling."

29. Mehta, *Rājasthān,* 114. An article by Paul Courtright in which the story of Bala is mentioned appeared in 1995, while the original French version of this book was in press. As will be seen, our respective data do not agree in all points and it seems to me that our interpretations, while not totally opposed to each other, are quite different. See Paul H. Courtright, "*Satī,* Sacrifice and Marriage: The Modernity of Tradition," in *From the Margins,* ed. Harlan and Courtright, 184–203 (especially 190–203, on Bala).

30. See above, pp. 29–31.

31. See above, pp. 44, 132–33.

32. See above, p. 83 and n. 88 to "Handprint, Dagger, and Lemon."

33. On this question, see R. Singh Vatsa, "The Remarriage and Rehabilitation of the Hindu Widows in India 1856–1914," *Journal of Indian History* 54 (December 1976), Part 3: 713–30.

34. See above, n. 92 to "Death in the Telling."

35. According to the orthodox standpoint, the widow is to remain behind closed doors until the observance of the commemorative rite of the first anniversary of her husband's death *(barsī),* which marks the end of mourning pollution (see Forbes, *Rās Mālā,* 2:363; and Stevenson, *Rites of the Twice-Born,* 204). After this ceremony, she must go to a pilgrimage site for a purifying bath, escorted by a man of the family or another widow. The very sight of her is so ill-omened that she may only leave the house in the very early morning hours, when it is still dark. The duration of her confinement may be shortened for practical reasons. For example, if a wedding is to be celebrated in the family, the date of the death-anniversary will be moved forward. Until that time, the widow is not only to remain in a corner, but she is to mourn the death of her husband *(pallā lenā)* every day before taking the single humble meal allotted to her, as well as each time a festival is celebrated in the house. There is an increasing tendency today to minimalize periods of impurity and the confinement associated with mourning: the pollution of mourning will now often come to an end with the thirteenth-day rite that concludes the cycle of funeral ceremonies, with the widow's confinement lifted the same day.

36. Even in families in which she is allowed to attend such celebrations, she may not fully participate in them: she is obliged to keep her distance, and not cross the threshold of the room where they are taking place.

37. Remains are impure. On this question, see Charles Malamoud, "Remarks on the Brahmanic Concept of the 'Remainder'," in idem, *Cooking the World,* 6–22.

38. On women in Tulsī Dās and the impact of that image upon Hindu traditionalists, see Hess, "The Poet, the People, and the Western Scholar."

39. See, for example, Mrs. Postans's account: *Cutch; or Random Sketches,* 66.

40. Stevenson, *Rites of the Twice-Born,* 207–8. On this subject, see below, p. 165 and n. 88 to the present chapter.

41. See Ramabai Sarasvati, *The High-Caste Hindu Woman* (Philadelphia: J. B. Rodgers, 1887), 69–93; Bose, *Hindoos as They Are,* 237–45; Moriz Winternitz, *Die Frau in den indischen Religionen* (Leipzig: Kabitzsch, 1920), 55–85; Johann Jakob Meyer, *Sexual Life in Ancient India: A Study in the Comparative History of Indian Culture* (New York: E. Dutton, 1930; reprint Delhi: Motilal Banarsidass, 1971), 406–41; Anant Sadashiv Altekar, *The Position of Women in Hindu Ciivilization from Prehistoric Times to the Present Day* (Banaras: Banaras Hindu University, 1938; reprint Delhi: Motilal Banarsidass, 1962), 168–95; Nita Kumar, "Widows, Education, and Social Change in Twentieth Century Banares," *Economic and Political Weekly* 26, no. 17 (27 April 1991): 19–25; Susan S. Wadley, "No Longer a Wife: Widows in Rural North India," in *From the Margins,* ed. Harlan and Courtright, 92–118. See also I. J. Badhwar et al., "Wrecks of Humanity," *India Today,* 15 November 1987, 69–75.

42. Kapani (*Notion de saṃskāra,* 1:98) describes the rite known as *cathurthī-karman* and has translated *Pāraskaragṛhyasūtra,* 1.2:4.

43. *Taittirīya Saṁhitā,* 2.5:1–2; *Mārkaṇḍeya Purāṇa,* 46:1–65; *Kūrma Purāṇa,* 1.28:15–40. See especially Wendy Doniger O'Flaherty, *The Origins of Evil in Hindu Mythology* (Berkeley: University of California Press, 1980), 27–28 and 153–60; and Frederick M. Smith, "Indra's Curse, Varuṇa's Noose, and the Suppression of the Woman in the Vedic Ritual" in *Roles and Rituals,* ed. J. Leslie, 17–45. In other variants of the myth, Indra's sin is divided among four (and not three) categories of beings: women, fire, trees, and cows; rivers, mountains, earth, and women; trees, women, earth, and water. Whatever the formula chosen, women are invariably present, as Julia Leslie (*Perfect Wife,* 251) has pointed out.

44. Norman Chevers, *Manual of Medical Jurisprudence for India, Including the Outline of a History of Crime against the Person in India* (Calcutta: Thacker, Spink & Co., 1870). Chevers's report dates from 1854.

45. For example, Cesare de' Fedrici, in Ramusio, *Navigazioni e Viaggi,* 6:1032.

46. *The Voyage of John Huyghen van Linschoten to the East Indies, from the Old English Translation of 1598,* 2 vols., ed. Arthur Coke Burnell and A. Tiele (New York: Burt Franklin, 1884), 1:250–51.

47. Weinberger-Thomas, "Les yeux fertiles de la mémoire."

48. Sudhir Kakar, *The Inner World: A Psychoanalytic Study of Childhood and Society in India* (Delhi: Oxford University Press, 1978). See also Obeysekere, *Cult of the Goddess Pattini,* 427–28.

49. For a critique of Kakar, see François Chenet and Lakshmi Kapani, "L'Inde au risque de la psychanalyse," *Diogène* 135 (October 1986): 65–80; Stanley N. Kurtz, *All the Mothers Are One. Hindu India and the Cultural Reshaping of Psychoanalysis* (New York: Columbia University Press, 1992), especially chap. 3.

50. Nicolo di Conti, quoted in Robert Sewell, *A Forgotten Empire (Vijayanagara), a Contribution to the History of India* (London, 1900; reprint Shannon: Irish University Press, 1972), 84. The original Italian may be found in Ramusio, *Navigazioni e Viaggi,* 2:791.

51. Rogerius, *Théâtre de l'idolâtrie,* 117.

52. *Pādukās* are the symbolic substitute for the husband with which certain codes and digests—that prescribe widow-burning—recommend that the wife burn herself when she ascends a separate pyre *(anugamana),* when the husband has died away from home. The husband's "lotus feet" are an object of adoration for the wife in the same way that the guru's feet are sacred for his disciple. The feet of satīs are occasionally represented on stele as "prints" (*thāpā*s). So it is that three miles from Amarsar, in the Toravati, such a stela commemorates the sacrifice of a young wife from the Barber caste who immolated herself for her savior, a Haritval Jat: when looters attempted to assault her virtue, this Jat had given up his life to save the woman after her cowardly husband had taken flight. Bushby notes the abundance of satī stele in Udaipur in which the motif of the sole of the foot appears in bas

relief: Henry Jeffreys Bushby, *Widow-Burning. A Narrative* (London: Parbury, Allen & Co., 1832), 5–6.

53. See for example *Parliamentary Papers* 23 (1828): 25–26.

54. According to Hindu belief, the gods send a celestial vehicle to earth when a faithful wife is to accompany her husband in death. See above, p. 24 and fig. 5.

55. Shah and Shroff, "Vahīvancā Bāroṭs," 249.

56. On the region and its *havelīs*, see Francis Wacziarg and Amar Nath, *Rajasthan: The Painted Walls of Shekhavati* (London: Croom Helm, 1982); and V. S. Pramar, *Haveli: Wooden Houses and Mansions of Gujarat* (Ahmedabad: Mapin, 1989).

57. The trident has become the symbol par excellence of militant Hinduism. According to one version of the legend, before ascending the pyre erected by her faithful servant Rāṇa, Nārāyaṇī Devī forbade her worshippers to portray her worship image in any way other than by the abstract form of the trident. She also asked to be celebrated thereafter under the name of Rāṇī Satī, in order to integrate the devotion of her servant into her divine personality (on which, see Vaid and Sangari, "Institutions, Beliefs, Ideologies," 10).

58. Generally speaking, new moon days *(amāvasyā)* are dedicated to the ancestors. On the negative aspect of new moon days, see John M. Stanley, "Special Time, Special Power: The Fluidity of Power in a Popular Hindu Festival," *Journal of Asian Studies* 38, no. 1 (November 1977): 27–43.

59. In the inner courtyard of many *havelīs* in Shekhavati one finds painted niches for ancestors, who have become household deities (*gṛh-devtās*). See Wacziarg and Nath, *Rajasthan,* 30.

60. On Santoṣī Mā, see A. L. Basham, "Santoshi Mata: A New Divinity in the Hindu Pantheon," *Proceedings of the 28th International Congress of Orientalists,* Canberra, 6–12 January 1971 (Wiesbaden: Harrassowitz, 1976); Veena Das, "Sati versus Shakti. A Reading of the Santoshi Ma Cult," *Manushi* 49 (1988): 26–30; and idem, "The Mythological Film and its Framework of Meaning: An Analysis of *Jai Santoshi Ma,*" *India International Centre Quarterly* 8, no. 1 (March 1980): 43–56; Kurtz, *Mothers.* See also Kathleen M. Erndl, *Victory to the Mother: The Hindu Goddess of Northwest India in Myth, Ritual and Symbol* (New York: Oxford University Press, 1993), 141–52.

61. Westphal-Hellbusch and Westphal, *Hinduistischer Viehzüchter,* 2:235.

62. Silk and wool are the two purest textiles.

63. Tod, *Annals and Antiquities,* 2:500. The bracelets referred to are the *cūṛās,* which are emblems of marriage. See above, n. 20 to "Death in the Telling."

64. *Aṃśa.* The term is used to designate a partial incarnation *(aṃśāvatāra).*

65. The Charans consider themselves "children of the Goddess" (*devīputras*), so much so that the word *suāsaṇī,* I believe, ought to be understood here as Mātā-jī's daughter rather than sister.

66. Varhaspaty, *Karnī-Caritr,* 20.

67. On this point, see Tambs-Lyche, *Power and Devotion.* In 1959, a woman from the village of Valvod in Saurashtra passed herself off as an incarnation of Mahākālī,

sacrificing a buffalo and drinking its blood to prove her divine nature. She had a group of devotees and established a cult which was, however, short-lived, since the government forbade it (Westphal-Hellbusch and Westphal, *Hinduistischer Viehzüchter,* 2:183).

68. *Asiatick Researches* 5 (1797): 371–91.

69. *Kālikā Purāṇa,* 67:3–6. I have slightly emended Shastri's translation of this passage *(Kālikāpurāṇa,* 3:1001–2).

70. See above, pp. 16, 74.

71. E. A. Gait, s.v. "Human Sacrifice (Indian)," in *Encyclopaedia of Religion and Ethics,* 12 vols., ed. James Hastings (New York: Scribner's, 1908–26), 6:849.

72. *Bhavabhūtis Mālatī-Mādhava, with the Commentary of Jagaddhara,* 3d ed., ed. M. R. Kale (Delhi: Motilal Banarsidass, 1967), 46–50.

73. The standard reference on the Kāpālikas is Lorenzen, *Kāpālikas and Kālāmukhas* (especially chapter 3, which links the use of human sacrifice among the Śāktas with that of the Kāpālikas). See also idem, "New Data on the Kāpālikas," in *Criminal Gods,* ed. A. Hiltebeitel, 231–38, which relies on Alexis Sanderson's discovery and publication of a group of Tantric texts from Kashmir, in which the rites and observances of the Kāpālikas are described.

74. Edward Albert Gait, *A History of Assam,* 3d rev. ed. (Calcutta: Thacker, Spink & Co., 1967), 59.

75. On this point, see David Kinsley, *Hindu Goddesses: Visions of the Divine Feminine in the Hindu Religious Traditions* (Berkeley: University of California Press, 1986), 178–96. On the *śākta pīṭhas*, see especially Sircar, *Śākta Pīṭhas.*

76. On the Hardwar temple, see Jaffrelot, *Nationalistes hindous,* 416.

77. On the temple of Kāmākhyā, see B. K. Barua and H. V. Sreenivasa Murthy, *Temples and Legends of Assam* (Bombay: Bharatiy Vidya Bhavan, 1988), and B. K. Kakati, *The Mother Goddess Kāmākhyā* (Guwahati: Publication Board Assam, 1989).

78. Tod, *Annals and Antiquities,* 1:503.

79. Heinrich Zimmer, *The King and the Corpse: Tales of the Soul's Conquest of Evil,* ed. J. Campbell, 2d ed. (Princeton: Bollingen, 1956), 296–306.

80. *Kālikā Purāṇa,* 18:40–50.

81. K. S. Varhaspaty (*Karnī-Caritr,* 20), for example, enumerates the four most important pilgrimage sites of Śākta tradition: Kāmākhyā to the east, Jvālāmukhī to the north, Hiṅglāj to the west, and Mīnākṣī to the south. Nevertheless, Hiṅglāj does not figure in the canonical lists of the four principal "seats" described in D. C. Sircar's work (*Śākta Pīṭhas,* 11–15), cited above, which remains the standard reference on the subject.

82. On variants of this mythic episode, see M. M. Pathak, "*Dakṣayajñavidhvaṃsa*-Episode in Comparative Studies," *Purāṇa* 20, no. 2 (July 1978): 204–23; and, among other authors, Wendy Doniger O'Flaherty, *Asceticism and Eroticism in the Mythology of Śiva* (London: Oxford University Press, 1973). This work was reprinted as a paperback under the title *Śiva, The Erotic Ascetic* (New York: Oxford University Press, 1981). See also idem, *Women, Androgynes.*

83. On the Saṃdhyā myth cycle (in which she occasionally appears as Uṣas, goddess of the Dawn), see O'Flaherty, *Asceticism and Eroticism.*, especially 64–65 and 118–19.

84. "Woman is inherently impure, but if she serves her husband faithfully, she wins to highest bliss" *(Sahaj apāvani nāri pati sevat subh gati lahai),* says Tulsī Dās in *Rāmcaritmānas,* 3 : 5 (in Hill, *Holy Lake,* 298). This verse has become a maxim throughout Hindi-speaking India.

85. Bhati, *Rājasthān ke lok devtā,* 61.

86. I have translated a number of Munshi Premchand's short stories—see Catherine Thomas, *Le Suaire. Récits d'une autre Inde* (Paris: Publications Orientalistes de France, 1975), where the reader will find a preface surveying his complete works, which is significant from a literary as well as a sociological standpoint. See also my *Ashram de l'amour* and, among the articles I have written on this author, "Le village dans la forêt. Sacrifice et renoncement dans le *Godān* de Premchand," *Puruṣārtha* 2 (1975): 205–58.

87. Munshi D. R. Premchand, *Mānsarovar,* 2 vols. (Allahabad: Sarasvati Press, 1965), 2 : 14 (the story dates from 1933).

88. On this practice, see, among other publications, D. N. Gautam and B. V. Trivedi, *Unnatural Deaths of Married Women with Special Reference to Dowry Deaths. A Sample Study of Delhi* (New Delhi: Bureau of Police Research and Development, Ministry of Home Affairs, Government of India, 1986); Jamila Verghese, *Her Gold and Her Body* (Delhi: Shakti Books, 1986); Ranjana Kumari, *Brides Are Not for Burning. Dowry Victims in India* (New Delhi: Radiant Publishers, 1989); and A. S. Garg, *Bride Burning: Social, Criminological and Legal Aspects* (New Delhi: Sandeep, 1990).

89. Zimmer, *King and the Corpse,* 291–92. The passage upon which he bases his translation is *Kālikā Purāṇa,* 16 : 32–47.

90. Ibid., 292 (*Kālikā Purāṇa,* 16 : 48–49). Zimmer follows the *Kālikā Purāṇa* quite closely, taking occasional liberties that give his narrative a poetic feel that is absent from the original. On different versions of Satī's "abandonment of the body," see Pathak, "*Dakṣayajñavidhvaṃsa*-Episode."

91. This adage has the sense of "ready to do anything to succeed."

92. On Joma, see Kothari, "Myths, Tales and Folklore," 40.

93. Cf. Westphal-Hellbusch and Westphal, *Hinduistischer Viehzüchter,* 2 : 107, 183, 202, 235.

94. See Dominique-Sila Khan, "L'origine ismaélienne du culte hindou de Rāmdeo Pīr," *Revue de l'historie des religions* 210, no. 1 (1993): 27–47. I am grateful to this author for providing me with this information concerning Kāḷal De. On the satīs who belong to the Nāth tradition, see Divakar Pandey, *Gorakhnāth evam unkī paramparā kā sāhity* (Gorakhpur: Gorakhpur University, 1980), especially 165, where Pandey mentions the "living *samādhi*" taken by Joje Kanvar following the death of her husband Ladunath in 1828. See also Ann Grodzins Gold, *A Carnival of Parting: The Tales of King Bharthari and King Gopi Chand as Sung and Told by Madhu Natisar of Ghatiyali, Rajasthan* (Berkeley: University of California Press, 1992), 106–7 and

320–22. This author quite rightly draws attention to the ambiguity with which satīs are regarded in Rajasthan.

95. Bhishan Singh died subsequent to the 1996 French publication of this book.

96. It is the fifth day of the dark fortnight of the month of *Vaiśākha (baesākh kṛṣṇā pañcamī).*

97. See above, p. 119.

98. An esoteric connection links the fire of the *sat* with the sun, which ignites the pyre, according to Hindu belief. Satīs consequently address a prayer to the sun, in the form of an invocation, before burning themselves. See above, final paragraph of "Speech as Instrument," in "Funereal Prelude"; and n. 21 to "Death in the Telling."

99. See above, p. 119.

100. This act is quite exceptional in itself: only men are authorized to perform sacrifices; thus, only male officiants may split coconuts. The satī cult transforms the female officiant into a repository of *śakti,* and it is in that capacity, reversing the order of the sexes, that the woman can proceed with the ritual act.

101. See above, p. 138.

102. Bhavānī is also a regional goddess of Rajasthan: her main temple is located about twelve miles from Mount Abu.

103. Only satīs, as emanations of *śakti,* and deities connected with the god Śiva (Bhairava or Hanumān) receive the form of worship known as *jot* in Rajasthani, in which the essential element is a flame that is burned for hours in front of the divine image. A devotee par excellence of Rāma, Hanumān, son of the god Vāyu, also sprang from the seed of Śiva according to one variant of his birth myth, which is given in special detail in the *Śiva Purāṇa.* On this subject, see Philip Lutgendorf, "My Hanuman is Bigger than Yours," *History of Religions* 33, no. 3 (February 1994): 225–26.

104. The reader will have guessed that I have not named her here in order not to betray her trust.

105. *Mahāsatī Oṃ Kanvar* (Jharli: Om Kanvar Trust, n.d.). The "Śrī Samiti Trust" has also published a booket on Om Kanvar titled *Mahāsatī Oṃ Kanvar Mā Bhajan-mālā,* 3d ed. (Jharli: Sri Samiti Trust, 1982).

106. Raghubir Singh Rathor, "Hamārī Saṃskṛti aor Mahāsatiyān," in ibid., 8–12.

Shekhavati, an Endangered Region

1. *"Bahū mare, uṛe rākh/ tabhī rahe kul kī sākh."* Shekhavati is a form of Marvari specific to this region, where (among the thirty-four vernaculars officially listed) Hindi, Marvari, Urdu, and Dhundhari are also spoken.

2. A title given to Rajput chiefs (who are also known by other more prestigious

designations) and to those members of the dominant classes with kṣatriya status. The word means "master," but it is also used to designate deities in popular Hindi.

3. This prince was Rao Rajah of Sikar. On this episode (which he characterizes as an "opera bouffe"), see Stern, *Cat and the Lion,* 42 and 264–65; and Barnett R. Rubin, *Feudal Revolt and State-Building. The 1938 Sikar Agitation in Jaipur* (New Delhi: South Asia Publishers, 1983).

4. On the history of Shekhavati, see Tod, *Annals and Antiquities,* 2:313–54; *The Imperial Gazetteer of India,* 24 vols. (Oxford: Clarendon Press, 1907–1909), 22:268–70; H. N. Singh, *Shekhawats;* S. Singh Shekhavat Jhajhar, *Śekhāvaṭī ke śilāekh. Ek adhyayan* (Jhunjhunu: Sri Sardul Education Trust, 1988); idem, *Śekhāvaṭī, pradeś kā prācīn itihās* (Jhunjhunu: Sri Sardul Education Trust, 1989); B. D. Agrawal, *Rajasthan District Gazetteers (Sikar)* (Jaipur: Government Central Press, 1978), 23–48 [the *Sikar District Gazetteer* is vol. 20 in this series]; and Wacziarg and Nath, *Rajasthan.* On Shardul Singh, see Devi Singh Mandawa, *Śārdul Singh-jī Śekhāvat* (Jhunjhunu: Sri Sardul Education Trust, 1970). A site from the Harappan period was excavated at Ganeshwar in 1977. On this question, see R. C. Agrawala and V. Kumar, "Ganeshwar-Jodhpura Culture: New Traits in Indian Archeology," in *Harappan Civilization: A Contemporary Perspective,* ed. G. L. Possehl (Warminster: Aris and Phillips, 1982), 125–34; and H.-P. Francfort, "The Frontier of Indus Civilization in Northern Rajasthan," in Schomer, *Idea of Rajasthan,* 1:177–202. In addition, inscriptions in Khandela attest to the region's being populated since the fourth century C.E.

5. For a critical analysis of this concept as applied to India, see Stern, *Cat and the Lion.*

6. See T. A. Timberg, *The Marwaris: From Traders to Industrialists* (New Delhi: Vikas, 1978), 41–42; and D. K. Taknet, *Marvāṛī Samāj* (Jaipur: Kumar Prakasan, 1989).

7. On all these points, see Timberg, *Marwaris,* 67–76.

8. The *jāgīrdārī* system was abolished by a 1952 law, the Rajasthan Land Reform and Resumption of Jagirs Act, which was amended in 1954 and followed in 1956 by a new law on the ownership of land (Rajasthan Land Revenue Act). On this question and on the Rajput agitation in the region, see especially Kamal, *Party Politics,* 83–84; *Report on Rajasthan Jagirdari Abolition* (Jaipur: Government of Rajasthan, 1953); and D. Singh, *Land Reforms in Rajasthan: A Report of a Survey* (Delhi: Government of India, 1964).

9. According to L. van den Bosch, who received his information from members of the board of trustees of the temple in Jhunjhunu, there are also temples dedicated to Rāṇī Satī in Rangoon, Bangkok, Singapore, and even in Japan and the United States. See "A Burning Question: Sati and Sati Temples as the Focus of Political Interest," *Numen* 37, no. 2 (1990): 174–94.

10. The Nārāyaṇī of Jhunjhunu is not to be confused with the Nārāyaṇī of Alwar, a Barber's wife thought to have lived at the end of the tenth century. See above, p. 104.

11. For the symbolism of the number 108, see above, p. 101 and n. 5 to "Under

the Spell of Sacrifice." This procession plainly recalls that of Dubois's account.

12. On the network of Bombay committees and associations propagating the worship of the satīs of Shekhavati, see C. Shahane, in *Sati: The Burning Issue* (10 January 1988 issue of *Express Magazine*), 6.

13. See, for example, Harish Chandra Upreti and Nandini Upreti, *The Myth of Sati (Some Dimensions of Widow Burning)* (Bombay: Himalaya, 1991), 37.

14. In 1861, since Svarup Singh, the Maharana of Udaipur, had expressly shown his disavowal of the custom, no rani followed him onto the pyre. A concubine, however, was persuaded to sacrifice herself. Between 1488 (the date of Shekha's death) and 1853 (date of the last immolation on record), there were only fifteen satīs who followed Shekhavat princes in death. Only two of Shekha's six wives burned with him; Keshri Singh departed for the next world escorted by his seven ranis in 1697, while in 1833 Lakshman Singh, abandoned by his seven wives, was accompanied by only one of his eight concubines. On the other hand, inscriptions at the Mahasati site in Bundi show that 237 women burned with nine of the kingdom's sovereigns: Sattra Sal was followed in death by 95 women; 84 satīs accompanied Kishan Singh. See Matthew Atmore Sherring, *Hindu Tribes and Castes as Represented in Benares,* 3 vols. (London: Trubner and Co., 1872–1881; reprint Delhi: Cosmo, 1974), 3:15–16.

15. Vaid and Sangari, "Institutions, Beliefs, Ideologies." See also Kumkum Sangari and Sudesh Vaid, "Sati in Modern India: A Report," *Economic and Political Weekly* 16, no. 31 (1 August 1981): 1284–88; idem, "The Politics of Widow Immolation," *Imprint* (October 1987): 27–31; Kumkum Sangari, "Perpetuating the Myth," *Seminar* 342 (February 1988): 24–30; and Sudesh Vaid, "Politics of Widow Immolation" (see above, n. 38 to "Death in the Telling").

16. See Jean Pouillon, *Le cru et le su* (Paris: Seuil, 1993).

17. The choice of the word "plot" is intentional. The authors' purpose is to show that the phenomenon was a total fabrication that took place in the 1950s in that region of Rajasthan where no tradition of widow sacrifice would ever have existed, in which case women are victims of a "plot." See Vaid and Sangari, "Institutions, Beliefs, Ideologies," 3.

18. The two feminist organizations that I had alerted in 1980 to the risk of a propagation of the practice in Rajasthan manifested an attitude which quite astonished me at first: a few widows burned in that particularly "backward" region of India were not worth the energy of their militants, who had other concerns. Were not 550 daughters-in-law per year burned in the region of Delhi alone for the sordid matter of dowry? Seven years later, when the "Deorala affair" had captured the headlines, those same organizations were on the front line of the pressure groups that forced the government of Rajasthan, and later the federal government, to pass a law banning the sacrifice and glorification of satīs.

19. On this case, see Noble and Sankhyan, "Signs of the Divine," 367 and the photograph on 382.

20. These lands are called *khālsā,* as opposed to those held by *jāgīrs*, which are called *jāgīrī.* For a historical overview of these different systems of land tenure, see Agarwal, *Rajasthan District Gazetteers (Sikar),* 233–34; and Kamal, *Party Politics,* 15–16.

21. The Bhumiyas possessed a right of hereditary and (theoretically) inalienable tenure over a piece of land *(bhūm),* which was obtained by their ancestors as recompense for services rendered, or through conquest or clearing. See Sharma, *Social Life,* 88 and 289. On the different types of tenancy rights and revenue administration in the Sikar District, see Agarwal, *Rajasthan District Gazetteers (Sikar),* 233–58; and Rubin, *Feudal Revolt,* 6–11. On the history of the Bhumiyas, see Singh, *Land Reforms.* The Bhumiyas are not to be confused with the ancestral category of the *bhomiyā* (which is derived from the same root). On this subject, see above, p. 34.

22. See Kamal, *Party Politics,* 233–34.

23. On the suppression of the rite in the Princely States of Rajputana, see Edward Thompson, *Suttee: A Historical and Philosophical Enquiry into the Hindu Rite of Widow-Burning* (London: Allen & Unwin, 1928), 82–116. The date of 1861 corresponds to the burning of the concubine of Svarup Singh of Udaipur. See also Vyas, "Social and Religious Reform Movements"; and B. L. Bishnoi, "Sati suppression in Rajput States," in Devra, *Socio-Economic Study,* 79–89. For the last authorized case of satī in Kutch (in 1852), see Sir George LeGrand Jacob, *Western India Before and During the Mutinies: Pictures Drawn from Life* (London: H. S. King & Co., 1871), 138–41. A great deal of ink has been spilled, within India and abroad, on the Deorala affair. The Indian media file in English, Hindi, and Rajasthani alone constitute a vast corpus. Sources include *Trial by Fire: A Report on Rup Kanwar's Death* (Women and Media Committee, Bombay, 11 December 1987); Madhu Kishwar and Ruth Vanita, "The Burning of Roop Kanvar," *Manushi* 43–44 (1987): 15–25; S. Narasimhan, *Sati: A Study of Widow Burning in India* (New Delhi: Viking Penguin Books, 1990); and Upreti and Upreti, *Myth of Sati.*

24. Ashis Nandy, "Sati as Profit versus Sati as Spectacle: The Public Debate on Roop Kanwar's Death," in Hawley, *Sati,* 141–42.

25. Ibid. See also idem, "The Sociology of Sati," *Indian Express,* 5 October 1987; and idem, "The Human Factor," *The Illustrated Weekly of India,* 17 January 1988, 20–23. The sociologist Veena Das offers a point of view close to Nandy's in an article in which she shows to what extent the current debate bears the imprint of colonial discourse on the sacrifice of widows ("Strange Response," *The Illustrated Weekly of India,* 8 February 1988). Finally, the sanskritist Sheldon Pollock has brought the debate back to earth, so to speak, by dismantling a (rather brilliant) article by the historian Lata Mani titled "Contentious Traditions: The Debate on Sati in Colonial India" (*Cultural Critique* 7 [Fall 1987]: 119–56). Pollock reminds us that the controversy over the rite, far from being a construction of colonial discourse, was initiated by the Mīmāṃsakas themselves, India's ritual exegetes, particularly by Lakṣmīdhara (twelfth century C.E.). See Sheldon Pollock, "Deep Orientalism? Notes

on Sanskrit and Power beyond the Raj," in Carol A. Breckenridge and Peter van der Veer, *Orientalism and the Postcolonial Predicament: Perspectives on South Asia* (Philadelphia: University of Pennsylvania Press, 1993), 76–133.

26. Altough he is a dominant figure in the Indian intelligentsia, Nandy keeps his distance from Indian intellectual circles, which he takes to task here. Although his current line of argument, like the positions he has taken in the past ("Sati. A Nineteenth Century Tale"), are remarkable for their acumen, one may wonder about the grounding of an interpretation in which the author simultaneously places himself in the position of a person who sees things from the inside (because he belongs to the culture) and who denounces the same (because he is an outsider). See, for example, "Sati as Profit," 147 n. 14. For a critique of Nandy on Rammohun Roy and on the epidemic of widow sacrifices that occured in Bengal in the last century, see Sanjukta Gupta and Richard Gombrich, "Another View of Widow-Burning and Womanliness in India," *Journal of Commonwealth and Comparative Politics* 12, no. 3 (November 1984): 252–58. For a critique of that same text (which provoked all sorts of reactions), see the position of the psychologist G. Morris Carstairs: "Ashis Nandy on the Inner World," *Journal of Commonwealth and Comparative Politics* 12, no. 3 (November 1984): 259–74.

27. The Rajputs constituted 5.6 percent of the population of Rajasthan according to the 1931 Census (the last census to register caste distinctions).

28. The female population of the State of Rajasthan was 6.6 million in 1941, 12.3 million in 1971, and 21 million at the last census (1991). The female population of the Indian Union was 407 million in 1991.

29. According to an informant, there is another "Blue Indigo Sati" who is still alive and well. This Rajput woman, some thirty years of age, purportedly lives in the village of Tarbini, near Neem-Ka-Thana.

30. These figures are provisional, since not all the data are in my possession, as noted above.

31. It is still common today not to register births and deaths, a fact that 1991 census procedures acknowledge. As for marriages and divorces, these are never registered.

32. Investigations carried out by feminist groups have arrived at opposite conclusions: see for example "Rural Women Speak," *Seminar* 342 (February 1988): 40–44. I would like to recall two matters in this context: first, as noted above (p. 88), the viewpoints expressed are never homogeneous nor stable; second, field investigations (those that are not perfunctory or carried out by pressure groups, but long-term and conducted by individuals) show that once a climate of trust has been established, many people who entrenched themselves behind a wall of denial when first questioned later made no mystery of their beliefs and practices. Jeanne Favret-Saada constructed an entire book around the interplay between denial and belief on the subject of witchcraft in the Mayenne region of France, in which she relates

a limit-experience in ethnological research: Jeanne Favret-Saada, *Les Mots, la Mort, les Sorts: La sorcellerie dans le Bocage* (Paris: Gallimard, 1977).

33. Vaid and Sangari, "Institutions, Beliefs, Ideologies," 13.

34. Romila Thapar does not distance herself from this view of things, when she notes that the rite was "originally limited to the kṣatriya caste": ("Romila Thapar talks to Madhu Kishwar and Ruth Vanita," *Manushi* 42–43 [September–December 1987]: 8). Elsewhere she is more nuanced, for instance when she writes that "Initially a ritual which ensured that a faithful wife accompanied her hero-husband to heaven, and therefore associated largely with *kṣatriya* castes and those dying heroic deaths, its practice by other castes in the second millennium A.D. involved a change in eschatology" (idem, *Interpreting Early India* [Delhi: Oxford University Press, 1994], 71). See also idem, "In History," *Seminar* 342 (February 1988); and idem, "Death and the Hero."

35. See above, n. 77 to "Death in the Telling."

36. The territory corresponding to the present district of Sikar also encompassed eleven villages belonging to the former fief *(ṭhikānā)* of Shyamgarh as well as the two former revenue-districts *(tehsīl)* of Danta Ramgarh (with the exception of forty-eight villages that had been attached to the Phulera *tehsīls*) and Neem-Ka-Thana. In 1951, it was divided into three administrative subdivisions (Sikar, Fatehpur, and Neem-Ka-Thana), which were subdivided into six *tehsīls*. On this question, see H. Singh Ary, *Śekhāvāṭī ke ṭhikānon kā itihās evam yogdān* (Jaipur: Pancsil Prakasan, 1987).

37. The figures are as follows: 964 women per 1,000 men in 1961; 961 in 1971; and 963 in 1981. The imbalance of the sex ratio is even clearer at the state level in Rajasthan: there were 908 women per 1,000 men in 1961; 911 in 1971; 919 in 1981; and 910 in 1991. The sex ratio for all of the Indian Union was 941 women per 1,000 men in 1961; 930 in 1971; 934 in 1981; and 929 in 1991. This fall of five percentage points was noted in the Indian government's official publication, *India 1992. A Reference Annual,* with the following commentary: "The reason for the general disparity in the sex ratio and the declining trend over the years need further examination" (p. 17). While female infanticide has disappeared, more sophisticated methods such as "foeticide" following amniocentesis, gross negligence resulting in high female infant mortality, and finally, a significant number of female suicides, tend to perpetuate this imbalance between the sexes. On women as an "endangered population," to use Roland Lardinois's expression, see K. Lynch and A. Sen, "Indian Women: Well-being and Survival," *Cambridge Journal of Economics* 7 (1983): 363–89; and Roland Lardinois, "Les usages sociaux de l'infanticide féminin en Inde," *Nervure* 3 (April 1988): 40–42. The statistical data are taken from various official documents, to wit: *Census of India 1971—Rajasthan—Population Statistics* (Jaipur: Directorate of Census Operations, 1972); Agarwal, *Rajasthan District Gazetteers (Sikar); Census of India 1981. Series 18, Rajasthan, Part XII* (Jaipur: Directorate of District

Gazetteers, Government of Rajasthan, 1983); *Census of India 1981. Series 18, Rajasthan, Parts XIII–A & B: Sikar District* (Delhi: Controller of Publications, 1983); *India 1992. A Reference Annual* (New Delhi: Government of India, 1993). I have also consulted B. Hunter, ed., *The Statesman's Year-Book, Statistical and Historical Annual of the States of the World for the Year 1994–1995* (New York: St. Martin's Press, 1994).

38. The rural population of the district was 83 percent in 1971 and 79.8 percent in 1981.

39. The literacy rate rose to 19.6 percent in 1971 and to 25.4 percent in 1981. A 2.5 percent rise in literacy for the female population of the district between 1971 and 1981 was noted (during the same period, the rise was 9 percent for the male population). The literacy rate for the entire State of Rajasthan (one of the least literate in the Indian Union) was 38.8 percent in 1991: 55.1 percent for men and 20.8 percent for women).

40. In 1981, the figures rose to 89 percent for Hindus and 10.4 percent for Muslims. By way of comparison, we offer the figures for the Indian Union: 82.7 percent for Hindus and 11.2 percent for Muslims in 1971; 82.6 percent and 11.4 percent in 1981.

41. With the exception of scheduled castes and tribes who are registered, since, according to the terms of the Indian Constitution, they have the right to benefit from quotas in public-sector employment as well as for all sorts of social advantages.

42. Agarwal, *Rajasthan District Gazetteers (Sikar),* 59.

43. This region is also called Battisa because it comprises thirty-two *(battīs)* villages. Those villages are presently divided between the two districts of Jaipur and Sikar. On the history of Toravati, see M. Sarma, *Toravāṭī kā itihās* (Kotputli: Lokbhasa Prakasan, 1980).

44. See Joseph E. Schwartzberg, "Folk Regions in Northwestern India," in *India: Culture, Society and Economy. Geographical Essays in Honor of Professor Asok Mitra,* ed. A. B. Mukerji and A. Ahmad (New Delhi: Inter-India Publications, 1985), 81–114; and Lodrick, "Rajasthan as a Region," 16–17.

45. Hathideh constitutes an administrative and survey unit together with Hardas-Ka-Bas, even though the two villages are two and a half miles apart.

46. On the myth of the birth of Shekha (whose very name derives from *śeikh*), see Wacziarg and Nath, *Rajasthan,* 13.

47. A religious fair used to bring her devotees together prior to the Rajasthan Sati (Prevention) Ordinance of 1987. She remains an object of worship today; newlyweds from the region come to ask for her blessing, as custom dictates. This Mother Satī is renowned for her powers as a healer of skin diseases.

48. Especially in Uttar Pradesh, Punjab, Delhi, and the former states of Bharatpur and Dholpur.

49. *India Today,* 31 October 1987, 41. As indicated above, Kalvi was one of the conveners of the October 8, 1987, mass demonstration in protest of the promulgation, on October 6, of the Rajasthan Sati (Prevention) Ordinance.

50. As I have had occasion to indicate, the Rajput population is paradoxically quite low in the state of Rajasthan (whereas their population is far more significant in other states of India).

51. On the village council *(pañcāyat samiti)* and on the Panchayat system in Rajasthan, see J. W. Björkman and H. R. Chaturvedi, "Panchayati Raj in Rajasthan: the Penalties of Success," in Schomer, *Idea of Rajasthan,* 2:132–58.

52. On the ceremony called *cūndṛī mahotsav,* see above, n. 76 to "Funereal Prelude."

53. On *ārtī,* see above, p. 116.

54. On the contagious spread of satī sacrifices through proximity, eyewitnessing, and word of mouth, see above, "The Transmission of the Deadly Vow," in "Death in the Telling."

55. Officially, between fourteen and eighteen for young women, and eighteen and twenty-five for men.

56. Reference is to the Hindu Marriage Act and the Hindu Succession Act. See K. Gill, *Hindu Women's Right to Property in India* (New Delhi: Deep & Deep Publications, 1986), 352–53.

57. Jean-Luc Chambard, "Mariages secondaires et foires aux femmes en Inde centrale," *L'Homme* 1, no. 2 (1961): 51–88. On *nātā,* see above, n. 92 to "Death in the Telling."

58. Nowadays, the cohabitation of spouses often coincides with marriage: young men and women now marry when cohabitation becomes possible. Formerly, several years might separate the wedding ceremony from that of the *gaunā,* the ceremony marking a daughter's departure to the home of her in-laws. For a general treatment of family structures in India, see Lardinois, "L'ordre du monde"; and idem, "En Inde, la famille, l'Etat, la femme," in Burguière, *Histoire de la famille,* 2:267–99.

The Rite, the Law, and the Custom

1. Like any other literate brahman, a *śāstrī* (a *Śāstra* master) will bear the honorific title of pundit. The British of the period nevertheless made a distinction between those they called "Pundits," who had a knowledge of the ancient brahmanic sacred texts, and "Shastrees," who were more versed in the literature of the *Śāstras* and who were experts in Indian jurisprudence.

2. The *Nizāmat Adālat* would be transferred to Calcutta in 1790.

3. On this question, see especially Benoy Bhusan Roy, *Socioeconomic Impact of Sati in Bengal and the Role of Raja Rammohun Roy* (Calcutta: Naya Prokash, 1987). Roy analyzed the statistical data pertaining to the distribution of widow sacrifices in the Bengal Presidency on regional, divisional, and district scales, and drew up district-level maps of the distribution of the phenomenon as a function of the caste and economic level of the families of satīs.

4. Domestic rites are divided into three broad categories: obligatory *(nitya);* occasional *(naimittika);* and votive *(kāmya),* motivated by the wish to obtain a specific "fruit" (*kāmya* is derived from *kāma,* desire). Occasional and votive rites are at times considered identical; in addition, it is sometimes the case that a votive rite takes place within the context of an occasional rite. On this subject, see Kapani, *Notion de saṃskāra,* 1:82. The question of knowing to which of these categories the rite of "dying with" (and *a fortiori* that of "dying after") belongs is obviously crucial, since it forms the basis of the religious legitimacy of widow sacrifice. Between the position of Medhātithi (whose commentary on Manu is believed to date from the ninth century C.E.)—who maintains that such a sacrifice is tantamount to suicide (that is, a "murder of the self"), that it is contrary to *dharma* and not prescribed in the *Śāstra*s, and who does not hesitate to compare it to a rite of black magic whose aim is to secure the death of one's enemy *(śyenayāga)*—and that of Aṅgiraṣ (quoted by Mitākṣara in his twelfth-century commentary on *Yājñavalkya Smṛti,* 1:96), who engages in the most radical apologetics on its behalf, one finds a wide range of perspectives on the rite. It is impossible to lead the uninitiated reader through the labyrinth of these scholastic debates concerning one of the most controversial questions in the history of the *dharma* literature and of Orientalism. One finds a summary of the literature in Lingat *(Les sources du droit,* 149) and Arvind Sharma, *Sati. Historical and Phenomenological Essays* (Delhi: Motilal Banarsidass, 1988), 31–33; a detailed discussion is contained in Kane's monumental *History of Dharmaśāstra,* 2.1:631–33. For an analysis of the polemical use currently being made of the controversy, see Pollock, "Deep Orientalism," 99–101.

5. There is another view on these matters: the wife guilty of sins redeems herself by burning herself. One must therefore encourage her to immolate herself, in which case "dying with" is considered a *prāyaścitta,* a form of expiation (see Leslie, *Perfect Wife,* 295–96). The criterion of being "ideal" required of a faithful wife for her to be fit to be sacrificed has been contradicted in the real world on numerous occasions, of which we have given a few examples. According to Jan Haafner, whose *Voyage en Orissa et sur la Côte de Coromandel* appeared in 1811, "there are examples of public dancers (*devedaschies,* commonly called nautch-girls) abandoning themselves to the flames with the body of their deceased lover" (p. 57). The term "public dancer" captures quite well the Western perception of the *devadāsī* as a temple dancer and "sacred prostitute."

6. There is a great diversity of opinion on this point (as on so many others concerning this particularly controversial rite). The fervent apologists of widow sacrifice (Aparārka, Viṣṇu, Hārita, Śaṇkha, Aṅgiras, etc.) prescribe it for women of all castes, from Brahmans to Caṇḍālas. But throughout the entire corpus of *dharma* literature on the subject, Brahman women are singled out, and there is more reticence than approbation toward their immolation (especially in the case of deferred cremations).

7. *Parliamentary Papers* 18 (1821): 103.

8. Robert Challe, *Journal d'un voyage fait aux Indes Orientales (1690–1691)* (Paris: Mercure de France, 1979), 292.

9. Another characteristic of the solemn rites is that they require the presence of specialized officiants.

10. *Parliamentary Papers* 18 (1821): 117. The so-called *smārta* implements are used in rites based in tradition *(smṛti).*

11. Ibid., 105. *Kumāra* would designate a child under four years of age, and *śiśu* between four and seven; *bāla* would refer to all children up to age five.

12. *Parliamentary Papers* 28 (1830): 223–28. A magistrate denied permission to burn herself to a Beid (Vaidya) woman from Dacca, arguing that she did not belong to a pure caste.

13. Ibid., 105–6 and 121–22.

14. On Yogis, see above, n. 98 to "Death in the Telling." George Weston Briggs established a connection between the Yogis and Nāths in *Gorakhnāth and the Kānphaṭa Yogis* (Calcutta: YMCA Press, 1938; reprint Delhi: Motilal Banarsidass, 1973), 4–5. For an opposing opinion, see Vaudeville, *Kabīr,* 87–89. We have mentioned the case of a satī following her husband, a guru belonging to the Jasnathi sect, in his living *samādhi* (ascetic suicide by burial): see above, pp. 168–69. We have also referred to the case of Bastari, a Jogi woman who had her husband exhumed in order to be able to burn with him without violating the newly enacted legislation (see above, p. 130). This form of the rite seems to have been particularly odious to Europeans. The *Parliamentary Papers* of 1821 (in which that question, submitted to the expert opinion of the pundits, arises on several occasions) affords additional detail on the alleged origins of this caste of Untouchables, who are traditionally weavers by profession—"[t]hey who from the tribe of jogees are born of a licentious sunyassee, cohabiting with a female of the brahmin tribe, during the period of her menstruation; among these, some adopt red clothing, wear shell-earrings, and travel about as jogees; others take to the trade of weaving, and lead the life of a householder. These are called jogee and nauth indiscriminately": such is the opinion of Sree Rajah Chundra Turkalunkar, Pundit to the Provincial Court of Appeal of the Province of Bengal for the Division of Dacca (*Parliamentary Papers* 18 [1821]: 112). The notion of a biological incompatibility between the Brahman woman's menses and the conception of the first Jogi never crossed this pundit's mind. No doubt the enigma is part and parcel of the repulsion he feels for that impure caste, which issued from the transgresssion of such powerful taboos.

15. Serge Bouez has observed that prestige would be a secularized form of status. See *La Déesse apaisée. Norme et transgression dans l'hindouisme au Bengale* (Paris: Cahiers de l'Homme, 1992), 49.

16. On this subject, see A. Mukherjee, *Reform and Regeneration in Bengal* (Calcutta: Rabindra Bharati University, 1968), 241; and Roy, *Socioeconomic Impact,* 19–20.

17. There was a mutiny of the Sepoys at Vellore in 1806, and another at Barrack-

pur in 1824. On the fear of reactions within the army, see for example *Parliamentary Papers* 20 (1826–27): 182; for an opposite view, see *Parliamentary Papers* 28 (1830): 32–33.

18. On the entire legal dossier, including (especially) Robertson's reports, the letters from the commissioner, and the depositions of various witnesses, see *Parliamentary Papers* 24 (1825), 162–204.

19. Ibid., 164–65.

20. Ibid., 202.

21. Ibid., 196.

22. On the Caṇḍāla as "the old prototype of the Untouchable," see Louis Dumont, *Homo hierarchus. An Essay on the Caste System,* trans. Mark Sainsbury (Chicago: University of Chicago Press, 1970), 52–53.

23. According to some commentators, the rite of atonement known as "proper to Prajāpati" consists of a series of dietary restrictions: taking only one meal in the morning during the first three days; then one at night on the three following days; eating exclusively food obtained from begging for the next three days; and finally, fasting during the last three days. According to other opinions, the rite consists of feeding twelve brahmans (as is done in normal cases of mourning during the funeral banquet on the twelfth day after death). Finally, still others prescribe for such occasions the gift of a cow or some other form of compensation to the officiating brahman.

24. *Parliamentary Papers* 20 (1826–1827): 151–53.

25. On the concept of ritual, the interpretations the etymology of the word *ritus* has spawned, and the deprecation of ritual as an object of study, see the entire January-March 1994 issue (no. 85) of the *Archives de sciences sociales des religions,* titled *Oubli et remémoration des rites. Histoire d'une répugnance,* especially the article by Jean-Louis Durand and John Scheid, "'Rites' et 'religions': Remarques sur certains préjugés des historiens de la religion des Grecs et des Romains" (pp. 23–42). See also François Héran, "Le rite et la croyance," *Revue française de sociologie* 27 (1986): 231–63.

26. *Parliamentary Papers* 20 (1826–1827): 151–52. On this occasion the Commissioner of the Deccan distanced himself from the Collector of Poona, whose efforts had not had the desired results, given the fact that a new case of widow-burning had occurred (ibid., 145–46). On the opinion voiced by the Judicial Department in London on the entire affair, see *Parliamentary Papers* 23 (1828): 28.

27. Ibid., 152–53.

28. 1,143 very closely printed sheets (corresponding to about two thousand normal printed pages).

29. "Extract from the Proceedings of the Nizamut Adawlut, under date the 4th July 1823," *Parliamentary Papers* 24 (1825): 75. The error in calculation was not noticed by the Court. The total number of satīs registered in 1821 was indeed 654, according to the document issued by the same source on May 24, 1824 ("654 in

1821 as opposed to 597 in 1820, or an increase of 57"). See *Parliamentary Papers* 23 (1824): 33.

30. The role of statistics in the colonial imagination is placed in perspective in Arjun Appadurai, "Number in the Colonial Imagination," in Breckenridge and Van der Veer, *Orientalism,* 314–39.

31. See above, pp. 40–41.

32. The short controversial writings of Raja Rammohun Roy are constructed after the model of the debates between ritualists (Mīmāṃsakas) in ancient India, where the advocates of two contrasting viewpoints form a structural pair.

33. Raja Rammohun Roy, in Anand, *Sati. A Writeup,* 27. Here Roy cites the *Chāndogya Upaniṣad* (8.1 : 6), taking a number of liberties with the text, which reads as follows in Robert E. Hume's translation (*The Thirteen Principal Upanishads,* 2d ed. [New York: Oxford University Press, 1971], 263): "As here on earth the world which is won by work becomes destroyed, even so there the world which is won by merit becomes destroyed." Patrick Olivelle (*Upaniṣads* [New York: Oxford University Press, 1996], 167) translates this passage as follows: "[A]s here in this world the possession of a territory won by action comes to an end, so in the hereafter a world won by merit comes to an end."

34. Raja Rammohun Roy in ibid., 25–35 and 39–44. The argument is taken up in *Parliamentary Papers* 24 (1825): 11.

35. This is the reason for which Desu—whose fatal heart attack in 1977, upon the death of her husband, was mentioned above—was considered a genuine satī. On her case, see above, p. 183.

36. "Extracts from a Summary of the Law and Custom of Hindoo Castes within the Dekhun Provinces Subject to the Presidency of Bombay, Compiled by Mr. Arthur Steele, and Printed at Bombay by Order of the Governor in Council, in 1827," *Parliamentary Papers* 28 (1830): 271–72.

37. See above, p. 118.

38. *Parliamentary Papers* 24 (1825): 198. This passage is a nearly verbatim translation of the Hindi-language commentary (pp. 1055–56) to the Sanskrit (p. 1053) of the *Nirṇayasindhu.*

39. See above, pp. 148–49.

40. Here I am quoting *Āpastambasmṛti,* 7 : 4, in *Smṛtīnāṃ Samuccayaḥ.*

41. On this question, see the authors cited in n. 72 to "Handprint, Dagger, and Lemon."

42. The spectacular increase in the number of satīs in Bengal during those years has been attributed, among other things, to this epidemic. In a sense, cholera concealed the government's own heavy responsibility. It was not until February 1824 that the Company's Court of Directors assessed its own shortcomings in the minutes of its annual meeting, in which each and every disastrous effect of the half measures taken out of humanitarian concern and political strategy was examined, and in which the shifts and reversals of British policy in the matter were de-

nounced (see *Parliamentary Papers* 20 [1826–1827]: 1–34). When one looks at the matter closely, particularly with reference to Benoy Bhusan Roy's maps charting the district-level distribution of widow-burning in Bengal, one can see that the districts most affected by the cholera epidemic did not always correspond to those where the highest number of satī sacrifices were registered.

43. *Parliamentary Papers* 24 (1825): 197, italics in original. Certain *dharma* commentators recommend that the woman wash herself with 60 clods of earth when taking her ritual bath on the fourth day, which marks the end of her menstrual period. If she is a widow, no fewer than 120 clods are necessary to produce the same effect (see Leslie, *Perfect Wife,* 286).

44. The expiatory rite called *cāndrāyaṇa* consists of regulating one's diet according to the phases of the moon *(candra):* during the dark fortnight of the lunar month, one progressively reduces one's intake of food from fifteen mouthfuls to one. One fasts on the full moon day. Then, during the bright fortnight, one increases one's ration from one mouthful to fifteen.

45. *Dharmasindhu,* 764–65. See also *Nirṇayasindhu,* 1058.

46. See above, n. 83 to "Handprint, Dagger, and Lemon."

47. The metaphor is taken from a text by Mahadevi Varma, the great poetess of the *Chāyāvādī* movement—who left a number of Sketches of her life story. In the first of those short reminiscent tales, she tells the story of her servant Lakshmi, a village woman from the Ahir caste, who suffers all manner of abuse and persecution at the hands of her in-laws because she has given birth only to girls. Her in-laws incite her husband to separate from this "counterfeiter." See Mahadevi Varma, *Smṛti kī rekhāen* (Allahabad: Leader Press, 1965), 7–8. The Hindi novelist Shanti Joshi dealt with the same theme in a novel titled *Śūny ki bānhon men* ("In the Arms of the Void") (Delhi: Rajkamal Prakasan, 1967).

48. See Fréderique Apffel Marglin, *Wives of the God-King: The Rituals of the Devadasis of Puri* (Delhi: Oxford University Press, 1989), 235.

49. Ibid. See also idem, "Types of Oppositions in Hindu Culture," as well as the contributions collected in *Purity and Auspiciousness,* ed. Carman and Marglin, vol. 1.

50. Marglin, *Wives,* 234–55.

51. See Christopher J. Fuller, "The Divine Couple's Relationship in a South Indian Temple: Mīnākṣī and Sundeśvara at Madurai," *History of Religions* 19 (1980): 334–37; and Tarabout, *Sacrifier et Donner à voir,* 437–38.

52. Barua and Murthy, *Temples and Legends,* 37–38. On Kāmākhyā, see above, p. 160.

53. See Schoterman, *Yonitantra,* 31.

54. See above, n. 36 to "Handprint, Dagger, and Lemon."

55. Werner F. Menski, "Marital Expectations as Dramatized in Hindu Marriage Rituals," in *Roles and Rituals,* ed. J. Leslie, 57–63.

A Foreword in Retrospect

1. Official statistics register 8,134 cases in the Bengal Presidency alone between 1815 and 1828. To be sure, we are dealing with an unusual period in which there was a veritable epidemic of widow sacrifices in the region. All the same those figures provide an incentive for gauging the extent of the phenomenon, particularly if one views them in the long-term perspective and over the entire subcontinent.

2. See above, p. 170.

3. The notion of *illusio,* introduced by Pierre Bourdieu as the "individual or collective, private or official, subjective illusion," issuing from a "belief effect" rather than from an effect of reality, corresponds exactly to what I am attempting to convey here. On *illusio* in Bourdieu, see especially *The Logic of Practice,* trans. Richard Nice (Stanford, Calif.: Stanford University Press, 1990), 107; idem, *Choses dites* (Paris: Editions de Minuit, 1987), 106, 111; and idem, *The Rules of Art. Genesis and Structure of the Literary Field,* trans. Susan Emanuel (Stanford, Calif.: Stanford University Press, 1995), 333–36.

4. See above, p. 200.

5. See above, pp. 83–84.

6. Parry, *Death in Banaras,* 180–81. On this subject, see above, n. 63 to "Death in the Telling."

7. Malamoud, "Dénégation de la violence," 41–42.

8. Ibid., 41 n. 24. The author is quoting *Kāṭhaka Saṁhitā,* 30:9. The other references will be found in the footnote cited here.

9. See above, p. 188.

10. Here I am quoting Raghubir Singh Rathor, in his preface to the religious booklet dedicated to Om Kanvar. See above, pp. 173–74.

GLOSSARY

Ādiśakti: primal form of the divine energy, whose emanations are the incarnate *Śakti*s.

Agni: the god of fire in the Indian tradition.

agni-snān ("fire-bath"): a euphemism for the sacrifice of satīs.

agni-parīkṣā ("trial by fire"): the episode of Sītā's trial by fire in the *Rāmāyaṇa.*

āhitāgni: the "twice-born" who is qualified to perform the solemn *(śrauta)* rites, and who possesses the three sacrificial fires needed for such.

amāvasyā: last day of the dark lunar fortnight (consecrated to ancestor worship).

antyeṣṭi ("final oblation"): the rite of cremation in ancient Brahmanism and Hinduism.

anugamana ("going after") / **anumaraṇa** ("dying after"): deferred cremation, in which the wife is burned after her husband, on a separate pyre.

anvārohaṇa ("ascending" the pyre): widow sacrifice.

ārtī: a phase of worship in which the officiant waves an earthen lamp *(dīpa)* in front of the divine image, in the auspicious (clockwise) direction. This act is carried out to the accompaniment of the muttered recitation of *mantra*s or songs of praise, as well as by the ringing of bells.

āśrama: the successive stages (theoretically four in number) in the life of a "twice-born," according to Hindu ideals.

ātma-hatyā ("murder of the self"): suicide or voluntary death.

ātman: the self conceived as an eternal principle that animates empirical beings from rebirth to rebirth.

avatāra ("descent"): the incarnation of a *bhakti* deity (especially Viṣṇu) on earth in order to restore order to an imperilled world.

ayonija: term used for deities not born from a human womb.

bahī (Gujarati: *vahī*): registers in which genealogists keep records of "generational lines" or "lines of descent."

baniyā (from the Sanskrit *vaṇij*): a (frequently pejorative) term used to designate merchants.

bela (in Old Javanese: "to sacrifice oneself, to be prepared to die for, to follow in death"): in Bali, those servants or wives who follow their deceased master in death. Women who burn in a pit separate from that of their husband or master, as opposed to *satia*s.

bhādon badī amāvasyā: the last day of the dark fortnight of the sixth month of the lunar calendar (August-September), on which a festival in honor of all satīs is celebrated.

bhakti: devotion, the predominant form of Hinduism, which emphasizes the personal relationship uniting the devotee with his chosen deity, as well as the concept of divine grace.

bhāva (in Sanskrit, "disposition or propensity to"): an orientation of those affects that characterize a particular moment in one's emotional life and are disclosive of one's inner nature *(svabhāva)*. In Hindi and in Rajasthani, the term *bhāv* refers to an inner disposition (a feeling or emotion), or else to possession by a deity, spirit, or supernatural force.

bhomiyā (from *bhūmi:* earth): in Rajasthan, this term refers to an ancestor who died fighting to protect cows or territory, and who has thereby become the guardian deity of the territory.

bhūta ("being"): malevolent spirit, ghost, or one of the dead who has not been appeased by the funerary rites and who therefore torments the living. Feminine form: *bhūtnī*.

bhūtāveśa: possession by a spirit.

brahmarandhra ("cleft of *brahman*"): the fontanelle bone through which the vital breaths *(prāṇa)* or *ātman* escape during the cracking open of the skull, a crucial moment in the cremation ritual. This act is performed by the son or closest male relative of the deceased.

buzurg ("of venerable age"): a popular term for ancestors.

caṇḍāla: the prototype of the Untouchable, said to arise from the union of a Brahman woman with a Śūdra man.

carṇāmṛt ("foot nectar"): the consecrated water with which a disciple or devotee has washed the feet of a guru, saint, or divine image, and which the disciple drinks.

cūndṛī: in Rajasthan, a red cotton or silk sari or veil *(oḍhnī)*, cut to a specific length and printed with particular decorative patterns. Worn by a woman on her wedding day, it symbolizes her status as a married woman whose husband is still alive *(suhāg)*.

cūndṛī mahotsav ("the great *cūndṛī* festival"): in Rajasthan, the ceremony occurring on the twelfth day after death, in which a brother gives his deceased sister a funeral *cūndṛī*.

cūṛo / cūṛā: set of bracelets, symbolizing marriage (or the marital bliss of the wife whose husband is alive: *suhāg*), worn on the forearm (between the wrist and elbow); bracelet[s] worn above the elbow that have the same symbolic value.

dakṣiṇā: sacrificial fee paid to Brahman officiants.

ḍamaru: the hourglass-shaped drum that is an emblem of Śiva, Bhairava, and the Goddess.

darśan: sanctifying vision of the object of adoration, the simplest form of worship.

deha-tyāga ("abandonment of the body"): a metaphor for voluntary death.

devadāsī: female temple servant of a Hindu god, of whom she is considered to be the wife (the "sacred dancer," "temple prostitute," or "nautch-girl" of Western depictions).

devar: a husband's younger brother.

devḷī: in Rajasthan, the funerary pillar commemorating the death of a hero or satī; today the term refers to the small shrine of a satī.

dharma: at the universal level, the cosmic order that upholds the "Triple World"; at the individual level, behavior appropriate to one's birth *(jāti)* into a particular social group and gender.

dharmaśāstra: lawbooks on *dharma,* which expound on the rules of Hindu theology and jurisprudence.

dharmasūtra: aphorisms on *dharma.*

dharnā ("to be placed"): a modern form of protest suicide (as known by tradition) consisting of sitting on the threshold of the house of the person who has given offense, and vowing not to move until one's grievances have been redressed (with the implicit threat of suicide).

dīkṣā ("Consecration"): a preliminary phase of Vedic sacrifice, the initiation of the prospective sacrificer. In Hinduism: initiation into a sect.

dīkṣita ("the Consecrated"): one who undergoes *dīkṣā;* an intitiate.

doṣa ("flaw," "fault"): humoral disorder caused by the passions.

Durgāṣṭamī: the night falling between the eighth and ninth days of the *Navarātri* festival cycle, which celebrates the victory of the goddess Durgā over Mahiṣa, the Buffalo-Demon.

gaunā: the ceremony that marks the beginning of actual spousal cohabitation; the husband comes to fetch his wife from her parental home, and brings her into her new home.

ghāghro: the ankle-length broad pleated skirt worn by women in Rajasthan and Gujarat. Term used for the wife's family line as opposed to that of her husband, which is said to be "of the turban."

gusti: title given to the Vesias (Sanskrit: *vaiśya*s), who constitute the third order of Balinese society.

havelī: palatial residences found in certain regions of western India (Rajasthan and Gujarat), characterized by a distinctive architecture style and decorative painted murals.

hindū (a Persian word, from the Sanskrit *sindhu*): the Indus River; India as it is known to us (the Indus River region, the Indo-Gangetic plain, the Indian subcontinent); its inhabitants; the Hindus.

hindutva (from the Persian *hindū*): the sense and essence of being a Hindu; the feeling of belonging to that religious community; the "Hindu-ness" claimed by militant Hindu nationalists.

iṣṭ satī ("chosen satī"): one's personal or preferred satī, who need not be a lineage satī *(kul-satī)*.

jauhar: in Rajasthan, the mass immolation of women, the elderly, and children that took place when the Rajput citadels were under Muslim siege.

jośś: "frenzy," "holy furor"; *sat ka jośś:* the "madness of the sat," possession by that supernatural force.

jot (from the Sanskrit *jyotis:* "light," "brilliance"): worship rite of adoration offered to Śiva, Bhairava, Hanumān (as the son of Śiva), the *Śakti*s, and the satīs.

jhūjhār (from the Sanskrit *yuddhakārin,* "warrior"): in Rajasthan, a deified hero who was decapitated while fighting against cattle thieves. Like the *bhomiyā*s, these deities are territorial guardians.

kaliyuga: according to the cosmogonies of the Purāṇas, the fourth and final age of the world, during which *dharma* stands on but one leg instead of four; the Hindu Iron Age, in which humanity is presently living.

karmadoṣa ("flaw in or of one's *karma*"): sins committed in past births or the present life that explain a person's destiny (for both Hindus and Buddhists).

karman ("act"): applies to both acts in general and sacrificial acts; the principle of universal causality that governs acts and their—immediate and deferred—effects (their "fruit": *phala*); acts committed in prior lives; the doctrine of retribution for acts, in Buddhism and Hinduism.

kesariyā bānā: in Rajasthan, clothes dyed in a decoction of saffron extract worn by Rajput warriors as a sign of world renunciation when they departed for a final battle with their enemy.

khasam khānī ("husband eater"): an insult addressed to widows, the term is also used as a general designation for them.

kul-devī: the tutelary goddess of a lineage or clan.

kuṃkum (also called *rolī*): a mixture of powdered turmeric and lime, usually used in the form of a paste.

kuṇḍa: a pool; the depression that houses the sacrificial fire; the flaming pit into which satīs leap.

kuśa (or *darbha*): sacrificial grass: the sacrificial ground is strewn with bunches of this grass.

līlā ("play"): God's Play; the phenomenal world conceived of as the *māyā* of the gods, the supreme deity's playful creation, which is consequently viewed in that perspective and thereby relativized.

liṅga: phallic representation of Śiva, the supreme form of the god for his devotees. Usually, the *liṅga* is inserted in a *yoni,* the symbolic representation of the female sexual organ.

luṅgī: a loincloth worn by men which hangs down to the ankles.

maḍhulī: a canopy of dry branches and twigs forming a sort of hut in which women burned themselves in Gujarat and certain regions of north India. In the Deccan, the hut was called a *koṭhī*.

mahāsatī (or *māsti*): literally "great satī"; a woman who dies for a son, as opposed to a husband; an honorific title reserved for certain satīs.

mandir: a temple for the worship of Hindu gods.

mantra: a ritual formula; the formula given to the initiand into a sect during his initiation ceremony.

mātā ("mother"): in popular Hinduism, a female divinity and territorial guardian, considered to be an incarnation of the Goddess in her "terrifying" aspect.

māyā: the illusory forms created by the gods in order to deceive their enemies; the phenomenal world conceived of as a cosmic illusion for any Hindu whose goal is liberation from the cycle of rebirths.

melā: a religious fair in honor of a god, saint, or satī.

mokṣa/mukti: deliverance; liberation from the cycle of rebirths and the "flow" of transmigration (*saṃsāra*, another term designating the phenomenal world).

mūrti: any representation or abstract (sometimes aniconic) image of a god in a temple, worship site, or domestic shrine.

nātā ("bond"): a secondary marriage (generally with one's husband's younger brother) without religious value or sacramental sanction.

nath: a nose ring symbolizing marriage.

Navarātri (the "Nine Nights of the Goddess"): a festive cycle celebrating the victory of the goddess Durgā over Mahiṣa, the Buffalo-Demon.

nazariyā (from *nazar*, "evil eye"): a black silk protective thread worn by infants.

niyoga: the practice of levirate in ancient India.

Nizāmat Adālat: the Court of Criminal Justice under the East India Company, and subsequently under the Crown during the colonial era.

pāliyā (Rajasthani/Gujarati *pāḷiyo:* territorial "guardian"): in western India, funerary stela erected to a hero, satī, or deified ancestor.

pañcagavya: the "five products" of the cow—milk, clarified butter, curd, urine, and dung—which are absorbed during expiatory rites to restore ritual purity to sinners.

pañcamī: a worship rite observed on the fifth day of the (light or dark) fortnight of a lunar month.

paṇḍit: a title given to brahmans, who are learned by definition; and, in modern India, to any brahman, including those who are illiterate. In the nineteenth century, the British distinguished between "pundits," who knew the sacred texts of ancient Brahmanism, and "Shastrees," who were versed in the *Śāstra* literature.

parco (from the Sanskrit *paricaya:* "the fact of being known, recognized, or identified"): in Rajasthan, the miracles performed by a woman who declares herself a satī, and which allow her to be identified as such.

pardā ("curtain" in Persian): a customary rule requiring the confinement of women within the *zenana* (women's apartments) or house, and the wearing of the veil. It varies according to time, place, and caste.

pativrata: a wife's marital vow, which entails absolute faithfulness, obedience, and devotion, as well as the observance of fasts and rites intended to ensure the husband's protection and survival.

pativratā ("one who observes the marital vow"): the chaste and faithful wife who serves her husband as she would a god.

patrī (from *pitar*): an amulet in effigy of an ancestor, worn to appease him and obtain his protection.

pherā ("turn"): during the wedding ceremony, the set of seven (or three) sacramental circumambulations of the sacrificial fire that seal the bond of marriage between bride and groom.

piḍhiāvalī ("generational lines"): genealogies kept by the genealogist caste.

pīliyā (from *pīlā:* "yellow"): in Rajasthan, the *bandhani* patterned veil or sari worn by a woman whose husband is alive and who has offspring.

piṇḍa: a round mass; a ball of flesh, dough, clay, etc.; an embryo; a body; a ball of cooked rice, the essential ingredient of funerary rites and the cult of the dead. In Śaiva literature the term may be applied to Śiva's *liṅga.*

pitar (from the Sanskrit *pitṛ*): in Rajasthani, an unhappy ancestor who died prior to marriage (a *bāla-pitar* is an ancestor who died in childhood).

pitṛ: in ancient India, the deceased who has acceded to the status of lineage ancestor through the funerary rites (especially that of *sapiṇḍīkaraṇa).*

pitrāṇī: a female ancestor.

pitṛ-loka ("World of the Fathers"): the dwelling-place of the ancestors in Indian traditions. It is also depicted as the kingdom of Yama, god of the dead *(Yama-loka).*

pradakṣiṇā: ritual circumambulation in the auspicious direction (in which the god or object one is worshipping is kept to one's right).

prasād (literally divine "grace"): the food offerings that the god "eats" in the course of the rite and whose leftovers are consumed by devotees.

prasavya: ritual circumambulation in the inauspicious direction, required in funerary rites and ancestor worship.

prem: in devotional literature and in the sphere of the emotions, mystical or sublimated Love.

preta: "the departed," as opposed to *pitṛ,* "ancestor." In ancient India, this term was applied to the dead for the period between biological death and the celebration of the rite of *sapiṇḍīkaraṇa,* which transformed him into an ancestor. In popular Hinduism, *bhūta*s and *preta*s are linked together, as malevolent spirits or ghosts.

pūjā: the ritual of worship of Hindu deities, in temples or domestic shrines.

pūjāpā: in Rajasthan, the set of ingredients used in *pūjā* or in the rite known as *jot.*

puruṣārtha ("goal of man"): one of the four basic aims of human activity—*dharma, kāma, artha,* and *mokṣa.*

pūrvaj ("predecessor"): in Hindi and Rajasthani, a popular term for ancestor.

rajasvalā: a menstruating woman.

rātījagā ("being awake at night"): in Rajasthan, ritual night vigils in which, in principle, only women and children take part.

ṛtudoṣa (literally, "the seasonal fault or flaw"): menstruation, a manifestation of women's sin.

sadgati ("the way of good [people]"): a good death, granting access to the world of the ancestors or gods through the performance of funerary rites.

Sadr (or *Saddar*) **Divānī Adālat**: the Court of Appeals under the East India Company, subsequently under the Crown during the colonial era.

sagat (from *śakti*): in western India, the protest suicide practiced by Charan women.

sahagamana ("going with") / **sahamaraṇa** ("dying with"): joint cremation, in which the woman burns on the funeral pyre of her husband; in a more general sense, the sacrifice of widows.

sākā (from *śakti*): in Rajasthan, the heroic death of a Rajput warrior viewed as a supreme form of sacrifice.

Śākta: a devotee of the Goddess as energy *(śakti).*

śakti: divine energy or power; the Goddess (or her incarnations) as divine energy.

Śāktism: Hinduism as practiced by the Śāktas.

sallekhana (or *niśidhi*): voluntary death by fasting in Jainism.

samādhi: seated posture of yogic meditation; ecstatic trance; a tumulus erected over the interred body of a renouncer (whose burial site may become a place of worship); the rite and site of live burial for ascetics *(jīvit samādhi),* Nāths, and satīs who are wives of Nāths.

saṃkalpa ("determination"): sacrificer's declaration of intention, a necessary preliminary to any sacrificial act or religious observance; a widow's solemn declaration of intention to accompany her husband in death.

saṃskāra ("perfecting"): the life-cycle rituals of a "twice-born"; an acquired disposition; *pūrvasaṃskāra:* a psychological construction whose origin is to be sought in past lives.

sapiṇḍa ("those who have [the offering of] sacrificial rice-balls in common"): a kinship group of varying extension according to whether it refers to marriage, mourning, or inheritance.

sapiṇḍīkaraṇa ("making the dead *sapiṇḍa*"): rite of the tenth or twelfth day after death by means of which the deceased as *preta* is transformed into an ancestor *(pitṛ).*

sarvapitṛ amāvasyā: festival of the dead in Hinduism which, falling at the close of the "Fortnight of the Fathers" *(pitṛpakṣa),* is traditionally celebrated on the last day of the dark fortnight of the seventh month of the lunar calendar *(āśvin kṛṣṇā amāvasyā).*

śāstrī ("*Śāstra* Master"): a Brahman *Śāstra*-expert, and specialist in religious jurisprudence.

sat: in the context of widow sacrifice, the essence of "satī-hood"; the supernatural power that possesses a satī; the inner fire that consumes her.

satia (or *mesatia,* from the Sanskrit *satī*): in Bali, a woman who burns in her husband's or master's cremation fire, or who first stabs herself with a kris.

satī-caritr: narrative of the exemplary life of a satī, commited to writing in a religious booklet containing a brief (occasionally versified) biography, invocations, and prayers used in her worship.

satīdāha ("burning of the satī"): the sacrifice of a satī.

satī-sthal: site of a satī's cremation, transformed into a sacred place.

satītva ("satī-hood"): the virtue that is specific to satīs: the principle of absolute chastity and fidelity from which the sacrifice of widows follows. In common parlance: feminine chastity.

satya: truth; the word of truth that brings what is into being.

saubhāgyavatī ("a lucky one" or one having a "happy fate"): a woman whose husband is alive.

savāmaṇī: an offering made to the gods in gratitude for the boons they have granted.

siddhis: the eight supernatural powers realized through *sādhanā* (religious or spiritual practice).

snāna: a ritual bath of purification.

śrāddha (from *śraddhā,* "faith, trust"): ancestor worship rituals.

sthān (or *thān,* "place"): small shrine or movable temple of painted cloth *(paṛ)* for the worship of Pābū-jī.

suhāg (or *sohāg*): the felicitous state of a married woman whose husband is alive.

suhāgin (or *sohāgin*): a wife whose husband is still alive.

svabhāva: the inherent nature of a being.

tej (from the Sanskrit *tejas:* "brilliant energy"): the imperishable entity that transmigrates from rebirth to rebirth and is characterized by its luminosity; the soul viewed as an aura or fiery principle; a satī's supernatural power or sacred furor.

ṭhākur ("master"): a title given to Rajput chiefs and superordinates possessed of kṣatriya status; in vernacular Hindi, *ṭhākur-jī* means "deity."

thāpā: a satī's right handprint found on the doors of a house, palace, or city gates, and depicted on stele dedicated to satīs.

tyāg (*trāgā* in Gujarati): the set of practices involving self-mutilation or voluntary death as a sign of protest formerly in use among the Charans; ritual compensation the father of the groom was required to give to Bhats and Charans, bards and genealogists, on the occasion of marriages.

tyāga ("abandonment," "giving up"): in Vedic ritual, a dedicatory formula employed by the sacrificer while pouring an oblation into the fire. By extension, "sacrifice."

vaṃśāvalī ("lines of descendants"): genealogies kept by royal or illustrious families.

vardān: boon accorded by a deity to the devotee who requested it.

veḷevāḷi (in the Kannada language): one who has taken a vow to accompany his master in death; a heroic warrior.

vibhūti: the sacred ashes of Śivaites, Śāktas, and Nāths; the miraculous ashes remaining after the cremation of a satī.

vīra: a heroic warrior; one who dies in combat.

Yama: god of death and the dead (more precisely, of the Manes) in Brahmanism and Hinduism.

yogāgni ("fire of yoga"): the fire generated in one's own body through the practice of yoga.

yogī / jogī (Sanskrit *yogin*): a practitioner of yoga; an ascetic.

yoginī (Hindi *joginī*): a hypostasis of *Śakti;* a woman possessed of supernatural powers.

yoni: symbolic representation of the female sexual organ, into which the *liṅga* of the god Śiva is inserted; divine womb.

yonija ("womb-born"): said of gods who take incarnation in a human form in order to undertake some earthly venture. *Yoni-jā:* deified human heroines, considered to be partial incarnations of the primal *Śakti.*

BIBLIOGRAPHY

"Acyut," Sri. *Śrī Satī Sugan Kuñvari Caritr, arthāt Jodhpur kī satī kā hāl.* Kishangarh: Sri Syam Pustakalay, 1954.

Agrawal, B. D. *Rajasthan District Gazetteers (Sikar).* Jaipur, Directorate of District Gazetteers, Government of Rajasthan, 1978.

Agrawala, R. C., and V. Kumar. "Ganeshwar-Jodhpura Culture: New Traits in Indian Archaeology." In *Harappan Civilization: A Contemporary Perspective,* edited by G. L. Possehl, 125–34. Warminster: Aris and Phillips, 1982.

Aitareya-Brāhmaṇa. Edited by V. G. Apte. Anandasrama Sanskrit Series, no. 32. Poona: Anandasrama, 1930.

Aitcheson, C. U. *A Collection of Treaties, Engagements, and Sanads, Relating to India and Neighbouring Countries.* Calcutta: Government of India, Central Publication Branch, 1932.

Altekar, Anant Sadashiv. *The Position of Women in Hindu Civilization. From Prehistoric Times to the Present Day.* Delhi: Motilal Banarsidass, 1962. First edition 1938.

Anand, Mulk Raj, ed. *Sati. A Writeup of Raja Ram Mohan Roy about Burning of Widows Alive.* Delhi: B. R. Publishing Corporation, 1989.

Anderson, Benedict. *Imagined Communities. Reflections on the Origin and Spread of Nationalism.* London: Verso, 1983.

Anonymous. "Burning the Devil. Curious Case in Calcutta." *Journal of the Anthropological Society of Bombay* 7, no. 8 (1892): 647–51.

Appadurai, Arjun. "Number in the Colonial Imagination." In *Orientalism,* edited by C. A. Breckenridge and P. Van der Veer, 314–39.

Ary, H. Singh. *Śekhāvāṭī ke ṭhikānon kā itihās evam yogdān.* Jaipur: Pancsil Prakasan, 1987.

Ary, Ramcandr. *Śrī Satī-Mātā Hem Kanvar.* Byavar: R. Joshi, 1953.

Assayag, Jackie. "L'aventurier divin et la bayadère immolée. L'Inde dans l'opéra." In *L'Inde et l'Imaginaire,* edited by C. Weinberger-Thomas, 197–227.

———. "Le panier, les cheveux, la Déesse et le monde. Essai sur le symbolisme sud-indien." *Diogène* 142 (April–June 1988): 104–27.

———. *La Colère de la déesse décapitée. Traditions, cultes et pouvoir dans le sud de l'Inde.* Paris: Editions du CNRS, 1992.

Babb, Lawrence. "Glancing: Visual Interaction in Hinduism." *Journal of Anthropological Research* 37 (1982): 387–401.

Badhwar, I. J., et al. "Wrecks of Humanity." *India Today,* 15 November 1987, 69–75.

Balbi, Gasparo. *Viaggio dell'Indie Orientali.* Venice: Camillo Borgominieri, 1590.

Barbosa, Duarte. *Livro em que da relação de que viu o ouviu no Oriente.* Written between 1517 and 1518. English translation: *A Description of the Coasts of East Africa and Malabar in the Beginning of the 16th Century.* London: Hakluyt Society, 1866. Italian translation: *Libro di Odoardo Barbosa.* In Ramusio, *Navigazioni e Viaggi,* 2:608–10.

Barua, B. K., and H. V. Sreenivasa Murthy. *Temples and Legends of Assam.* Bombay: Bharatiy Vidya Bhavan, 1988. First edition 1964.

Basham, A. L. "Santoshi Mata: A New Divinity in the Hindu Pantheon." In *Proceedings of the 28th International Congress of Orientalists.* Canberra, 6–12 January 1971. Wiesbaden: Otto Harrassowitz, 1976.

Berg, Charles. *The Unconscious Significance of Hair.* London: G. Allen & Unwin, 1951.

Bernier, François. *Voyages de F. Bernier (Angevin), contenant la description des Estats du Grand Mogol, de l'Indoustan, du royaume de Kachemire.* Amsterdam: D.-P. Marret, 1699.

Bhanavat, Mahendra. *Ajūbā Rājasthān.* Udaipur: Mudrak Prakasan, 1986.

Bhati, Puspa. *Rājasthān ke lok devtā evam lok sāhity.* Bikaner: Kavita Prakasan, 1991.

Bhattacharya, France. Introduction. In François Bernier, *Voyages dans les Estats du Grand Mogol.* Paris: Fayard, 1981.

Biardeau, Madeleine, ed. "L'arbre *śami* et le buffle sacrificiel." In *Autour de la Déesse hindoue,* ed. M. Biardeau, 215–43.

———, ed. *Autour de la Déesse hindoue (Puruṣārtha 5).* Paris: Editions de l'EHESS, 1981.

———. *L'Hindouisme. Anthropologie d'une civilisation.* Paris: Flammarion, 1981, 1995. English translation: *Hinduism, The Anthropology of a Civilization.* Trans. Richard Nice. Delhi: Oxford University Press, 1989.

———. *Histoires de poteaux. Variations védiques autour de la Déesse hindoue.* Paris: École Française d'Extrême-Orient, 1989.

Bishnoi, B. L. "Sati Suppression in Rajput States." In *Socio-Economic Study of Rajastha,* edited by G. L. Devra, 79–89.

Biswas, H. C. "Job Charnock's Hindu Wife: A Rescued Satî." *Hindustan Review* 22, no. 133 (September 1910): 298–301.

Björkman, J. W., and H. R. Chaturvedi. "Panchayati Raj in Rajasthan: The Penalties of Success." In *The Idea of Rajasthan,* edited by Karine Schomer et al., 2:132–58.

Blackburn, Stuart H. et al., eds. *Oral Epics in India.* Berkeley: University of California Press, 1989.

Boon, James A. *Affinities and Extremes: Crisscrossing the Bittersweet Ethnology of East India Studies, Hindu-Balinese Culture, and Indo-European Allure.* Chicago: University of Chicago Press, 1990.

Bose, Shib Chunder. *The Hindoos as They Are. A Description of the Manners, Customs, and Inner Life of Hindoo Society in Bengal.* London: Edward Stanford, 1881.

Bouchon, Geneviève. "L'Image de l'Inde dans l'Europe de la Renaissance." In *L'Inde et l'imaginaire,* edited by C. Weinberger-Thomas, 69–90.

Bouez, Serge. *La Déesse apaisée. Norme et transgression dans l'hindouisme au Bengale.* Paris: Cahiers de l'Homme, 1992.

Bouillier, Véronique. *Naître renonçant. Une caste de sannyasi villageois au Népal central.* Nanterre: Laboratoire d'ethnologie, 1979.

Bourdieu, Pierre. *Le Sens pratique.* Paris: Editions de Minuit, 1980. English translation: *The Logic of Practice.* Trans. Richard Nice. Stanford, Calif.: Stanford University Press, 1990.

———. *Choses dites.* Paris: Editions de Minuit, 1987.

———. *Les Règles de l'art. Genèse et structure du champ littéraire.* Paris: Seuil, 1992. English translation: *The Rules of Art. Genesis and Structure of the Literary Field.* Trans. Susan Emanuel. Stanford, Calif.: Stanford University Press, 1995.

Breckenridge, Carol A., and Peter van der Veer. *Orientalism and the Postcolonial Predicament. Perspectives on South Asia.* Philadelphia: University of Pennsylvania Press, 1993.

Briggs, George Weston. *Gorakhnāth and the Kānphaṭā Yogis.* Calcutta: YMCA Press, 1938; reprint Delhi: Motilal Banarsidass, 1973.

Brij Bḥushan, Jamila. *The Costumes and Textiles of India.* Bombay: Taraporevala's Treasure House, 1958.

Brown, W. Norman. "The Metaphysics of the Truth Act *(Satyakriyā).*" In *Mélanges d'indianisme à la mémoire de Louis Renou,* 171–78. Paris: De Boccard, 1968.

Buckland, Charles Edward. *Bengal under the Lieutenant-Governors, Being a Narrative of the Principal Events and Public Measures during their Periods of Office, from 1854 to 1898.* Calcutta: S. K. Lahari, 1901; reprint New Delhi: Deep Publications, 1976.

Burgess, James. *Report on the Antiquities of Kâṭhiâwâḍ and Kachh, Being the Result of the Second Season's Operations of the Archaeological Survey of Western India, 1874–75.* London: India Museum, 1876; reprint Delhi: Indological Book House, 1971.

Burghart, Richard. "The Regional Circumambulation of Janakpur Seen in the Light of Vaishnavite Tradition (Nepal)." In *L'espace du temple,* edited by Jean-Claude Galey, 2:121–47.

Burlingame, E. W. "The Act of Truth *(Saccakiriya)*: A Hindu Spell and Its Employment as a Psychic Motif in Hindu Fiction." *Journal of the Royal Asiatic Society* (July 1917): 429–67.

Burning and Melting. Being the Sūz-U-Gudāz of Muhammad Rizā Nau'ī of Khabūshān. Trans. Mirza Y. Dawud and Ananda K. Coomaraswamy. London: Luzac, 1912.

Burnouf, Eugène. *Introduction à l'histoire du Buddhisme indien.* Paris: Maisonneuve, 1876.

Bushby, Henry Jeffreys. *Widow-Burning. A Narrative.* London: Parbury, Allen & Co., 1832.

Caillat, Colette. "Fasting unto Death According to the Jaina Tradition." *Acta Orientalia* 38 (1977): 43–66.

Caland, Wilhelm. *Die Altindischer Ahnencult. Das "śrāddha" nach den verschiedenen Schulen mit Benützung handschriftlicher Quellen dargestellt.* Leiden: Brill, 1893.

Carman, John B., and Fréderique Apffel Marglin, eds. *Purity and Auspiciousness in Indian Society* (*Journal of Developing Societies* 1). 1985.

Carstairs, G. Morris. "Ashis Nandy on the Inner World." *Journal of Commonwealth and Comparative Politics* 12, no. 3 (November 1984): 259–74.

Census of India 1971—Rajasthan—Population Statistics. Jaipur: Directorate of Census Operations, 1972.

Census of India 1981. Series 18, Rajasthan, Part XII. Jaipur: Directorate of District Gazetteers, Government of Rajasthan, 1983.

Census of India 1981. Series 18, Rajasthan, Parts XIII-A & B: Sikar District. Delhi: Controller of Publications, 1983.

Challe, Robert. *Journal d'un voyage fait aux Indes Orientales (1690–1691).* Paris: Mercure de France, 1979.

Chambard, Jean-Luc. "Mariages secondaires et foires aux femmes en Inde centrale." *L'Homme* 1, no. 2 (1961): 51–88.

———. "Les chansons à plaisanterie *(khyâl)* chantées par les femmes d'un village de l'Inde centrale (Madhya Pradesh)." *Cahiers de littérature orale* 6 (1981): 71–99.

———. "Le *Râmâyana* des femmes dans un village de l'Inde centrale." *Cahiers de littérature orale* 31 (1992): 101–24.

———. "Les violences d'un village hindou. Suicide de femme chez les barbiers et 'violences légitimes' des dominants au Madhya Pradesh." In *Violences/non-violences en Inde,* ed. Tarabout, Vidal, and Meyer, 61–80.

Chāndogya Upaniṣad. In *The Thirteen Principal Upanishads.* Trans. Robert E. Hume. 2d ed. New York: Oxford University Press, 1971.

———. In *Upaniṣads.* Trans. Patrick Olivelle. New York: Oxford University Press, 1996.

Chaudhuri, S. "Sati as Social Institution, and the Mughals." In *Indian History Congess. Proceedings of the 37th Session, Calicut,* 218–23. New Delhi: Indian History Congress, 1976.

Chenet, François, and Lakshmi Kapani. "L'Inde au risque de la psychanalyse." *Diogène* 135 (October 1986): 65–80.

Chevers, Norman. *Manual of Medical Jurisprudence for India, Including the Outline of a History of Crime against the Person in India.* Calcutta: Thacker, Spink & Co., 1870.

Clémentin-Ojha, Catherine. *La divinité conquise. Carrière d'une sainte.* Nanterre: Société d'ethnologie, 1990.

Collet, S. D. *The Life and Letters of Ram Mohun Roy* (1900). Edited by D. K. Biswas and P. C. Ganguli. Calcutta: Sadharan Brahmo Samaj, 1962.

Conti, Nicolo di. *Viaggio di Nicolo di Conti Veneziano, scritto per messer Poggio Fiorentino.* In G. B. Ramusio, *Navigazioni e Viaggi,* vol. 2.

Coomaraswamy, Ananda Kentish. "Sati: A Vindication of the Hindu Woman." *Sociological Review* 6, no. 2 (1913): 117–35.

———. *The Dance of Shiva.* New York: Noonday Press, 1957. First edition 1924.

Courtright, Paul B. "The Iconographies of Sati." In *Sati, the Blessing and the Curse. The Burning of Wives in India,* edited by John Stratton Hawley. New York: Oxford University Press, 1994.

———. "*Satī,* Sacrifice and Marriage: The Modernity of Tradition." In *From the Margins of Hindu Marriage,* edited by Lindsey Harlan and Paul B. Courtright, 184–203.

Cousin, Françoise. *Tissus imprimés du Rajasthan.* Paris: L'Harmattan, 1986.

Crawfurd, J. *History of the Indian Archipelago.* 2 vols. Edinburgh, 1820.

Crawfurd, Quinten. *Researches Concerning the Laws, Theology, Learning, Commerce, etc., of Ancient and Modern India.* 2 vols. London: T. Cadell and W. Davies, 1817.

Cronin, V. *A Pearl to India. The Life of Roberto de Nobili.* London: Rupert Hart-Davis, 1959.

Dallapiccola, A. L., ed. *Vijayanagara—City and Empire. New Currents of Research.* 2 vols. Stuttgart: Steiner Verlag, 1985.

Dalmia-Lüderitz, Vasudha. "Sati' as a Religious Rite. Parliamentary Papers on Widow Immolation, 1821–1830." *Economic and Political Weekly* 21, no. 17 (26 April 1986): 58–64.

Dange, S. S. *Hindu Domestic Rituals. A Critical Glance.* Delhi: Ajanta Publications, 1985.

Das, Veena. *Structure of Cognition: Aspects of Hindu Caste and Ritual.* Delhi: Oxford University Press, 1977.

———. "The Mythological Film and Its Framework of Meaning: An Analysis of *Jai Santoshi Ma.*" *India International Centre Quarterly* 8, no. 1 (March 1980): 43–56.

———. "Sati versus Shakti. A Reading of the Santoshi Ma Cult." *Manushi* 49 (1988): 26–30.

———. "Strange Response." *The Illustrated Weekly of Indi,* 8 February 1988.

Dasgupta, Surendranath. *A History of Indian Philosophy.* 5 vols. Cambridge: Cambridge University Press, 1922; reprint Delhi: Motilal Banarsidass, 1951–55.

Daya, Dalpat Ram. *Demonology and Popular Superstitions of Gujarat.* Trans. Alexander Kinloch Forbes. Gurgaon: Vintage Books, 1990. Originally published as *Bhut Nibandh: An Essay Descriptive of the Demonology and Other Popular Superstitions of Guzerat, Being the Prize Essay of the Guzerati Vernacular Society for the Year 1849.* Bombay, 1850.

De Grandpré, L. *Voyage dans l'Inde et au Bengale, fait dans les années 1789 et 1790.* 2 vols. Paris: Dentu, 1801.

De natura rerum of Lucretius. Trans. Cyril Bailey, *Lucretius on the Nature of Things.* Oxford: Clarendon Press, 1910, 1950.

Della Valle, Pietro. *The Travels of Pietro della Valle in India. From the Old English Translation of 1664, by G. Havers.* 2 vols. Edited by Edward Grey. Hakluyt Society, first series, nos. 84–85. New York: Burt Franklin, 1892.

Derrett, J. Duncan M. "Sanskrit Legal Treatises Compiled at the Instance of the British." *Zeitschrift für vergleichende Rechtswissenschaft* 1961: 72–117.

Desvaulx, Nicolas. *Moeurs et coutumes des Indiens* (1777). In Sylvia Murr, *L'Inde philosophique entre Bossuet et Voltaire,* vol. 1.

Detienne, Marcel, and G. Hamonic. *La Déesse Parole. Quatre figures de la langue des dieux.* Series of interviews between G. Charachidzé, M. Detienne, G. Hamonic, Ch. Malamoud, and C. Severi. Paris: Flammarion, 1995.

Devereux, George. *Basic Problems of Ethnopsychiatry.* Trans. Basia Miller Gulati and George Devereux. Chicago: University of Chicago Press, 1980.

Devi, Konduri Sarojini. *Religion in Vijayanagara Empire.* New Delhi: Sterling Publishers, 1990.

Devra, G. L., ed. *Socio-Economic Study of Rajasthan.* Jodhpur: Rajasthani Granthakar, 1986.

Dharmasindhu. Śrīmadanantopādhyāyasūnukāśināthopādhyāyaviracita Dharmasindhuḥ. Bombay: K. Srikrsndas, 1984. Original *Dharmasindhu:* 1790.

Dixit, S. C. "An Account of Widow Immolation in Gujarat in 1741 A.D." *Journal of the Anthropological Society of Bombay* 14, no. 7 (1931): 830–33.

Doniger, Wendy [see also O'Flaherty, Wendy Doniger]. "Begetting on Margin: Adultery and Surrogate Pseudomarriage in Hinduism." In *From the Margins of Hindu Marriage,* edited by Lindsay Harlan and Paul B. Courtright, 160–83.

Doniger, Wendy, and Brian K. Smith. *The Laws of Manu.* Harmondsworth: Penguin, 1991.

Doshi, S. "Pāliyas of Saurashtra." In *Memorial Stones. A Study of their Origin, Significance and Variety,* edited by S. Settar and Günther Sontheimer, 157–73. Dharwad: Institute of Indian Art History, 1982.

Drummond, Robert. *Illustrations of the Grammatical Parts of the Guzerattee, Mahratta & English Languages.* Bombay: Courier Press, 1808.

Dubois, Pierre. *Légère idée de Balie, 1830 (Lettres adressées à Monsieur H. Y., demeurant à Z.).* The Hague: Algemeen Rijksarchief. Collection no. 3087.

Dubuisson, Daniel. "La Déesse chevelue et la reine coiffeuse. Recherches sur un thème épique de l'Inde ancienne." *Journal Asiatique* 166 (1978): 291–310.

———. *La Légende royale dans l'Inde ancienne. Rāma et le Rāmāyaṇa.* Paris: Economica, 1986.

Dumont, Louis. *Une Sous-Caste de l'Inde du Sud. Organisation sociale et religion des Pramalai Kallar.* Paris and The Hague: Mouton, 1957.

———. "Le renoncement dans les religions de l'Inde." *Archives de sociologie des religions* 7 (January–June 1959): 45–69.

———. *Homo hierarchicus. An Essay on the Caste System.* Trans. Mark Sainsbury. Chicago: University of Chicago Press, 1970.

———. "La dette vis-à-vis des ancêtres et la catégorie de *sapiṇḍa*." In *La Dette*, edited by Ch. Malamoud, 15–37.

Durand, Jean-Louis, and John Scheid. "'Rites et 'religion': Remarques sur certains préjugés des historiens de la religion des Grecs et des Romains." In *Oubli et remémoration des rites. Histoire d'une répugnance (Archives de sciences sociales des religions)* 85 (January–March 1994): 23–42.

Durkheim, Emile. *Suicide, A Study in Sociology*. Trans. John A. Spaulding and George Simpson. Glencoe, N.Y.: Free Press, 1951. First edition 1876.

Eck, Diana. *Darśan: Seeing the Divine Image in India*. Chambersburg, Pa.: Anima Books, 1981.

Edwardes, S. M. "A Note on a Case of Self-Immolation by Ten Persons at Vasad." *Journal of the Anthropological Society of Bombay* 7, no. 8 (n.d.): 603–7.

Encyclopaedia of Religion and Ethics. 12 vols. Edited by James Hastings. New York: Scribners, 1908–26.

Enthoven, Reginald E. *The Tribes and Castes of Bombay*. 3 vols. Bombay: Government Central Press, 1920–22; reprint Delhi: Cosmo, 1975.

Erndl, Kathleen M. *Victory to the Mother. The Hindu Goddess of Northwest India in Myth, Ritual, and Symbol*. New York: Oxford University Press, 1993.

Esnoul, Anne-Marie. "Les songes et leur interprétation en Inde." In *Les Songes et leur interprétation*. Paris: Seuil, 1959.

———, ed. *L'Hindouisme*. Paris: Fayard-Denoël, 1972.

"Extract from the Proceedings of the Nizamut Adalwut, under date the 4th July 1823." In *Parliamentary Papers, Hindoo Widows* 24 (1825): 75.

"Extract from Sir John Malcolm's Report on Malwa, dated the 11th February 1821." In *Parliamentary Papers, Hindoo Widows* 20 (1826–1827): 40–42.

"Extracts from a Summary of the Law and Custom of Hindoo Castes within the Dekhun Provinces Subject to the Presidency of Bombay, Compiled by Mr Arthur Steele, and Printed at Bombay by Order of the Governor in Council, in 1827." In *Parliamentary Papers, Hindoo Widows* 28 (1830): 271–72.

Favret-Saada, Jeanne. *Les Mots, la Mort, les Sorts. La sorcellerie dans le Bocage*. Paris: Gallimard, 1977.

Fawcett, C. G. H. *A Monograph on Dyes and Dyeing in the Bombay Presidency*. Bombay, 1896.

Fedrici, Cesare de'. *Viaggio de M. Cesare dei Fedrici nell'India Orientale, e oltra l'India: nelquale si contengono cose diletteuoli dei riti, di costumi di quei paesi*. Venice: Andrea Muschio, 1587. Reprinted as *Viaggio di messer Cesare de' Fedrici nell'India Orientale*. In G. B. Ramusio, *Navigazioni e Viaggi*, vol. 6.

Filliozat, Jean. "L'abandon de la vie par le sage et les suicides du criminel et du héros dans la tradition indienne." *Arts asiatiques* 15 (1968): 74–88.

Forbes, Alexander Kinloch. *Râs Mâlâ, Hindoo Annals of the Province of Goozerat in Western India*. 2 vols. London: Richardson, 1856; reprint New Delhi: Heritage Publishers, 1993.

Forsyth, James. *The Highlands of Central India: Notes on their Forests and Wild Tribes, Natural History, and Sports.* London: Chapman & Hall, 1872.

Francfort, H.-P. "The Frontier of Indus Civilization in Northern Rajasthan." In *The Idea of Rajasthan,* edited by Karine Schomer et al., 1 : 177–202.

Frater, Judy. *Threads of Identity: Embroidery and Adornment of the Nomadic Rabaris.* Ahmedabad: Mapin Publishing, 1995.

Friederich, R. T. *Voorloopig Verslag van het Eiland Bali.* In *Verhandelingen van het Bataviaasch Genootschap voor Kunsten en Wetenschappen* 22 (1849) and 23 (1850). English translation: *The Civilization and Culture of Bali.* Calcutta: Sushil Gupta, 1959.

Fryer, John. *A New Account of the East-India and Persia.* London: R. Chiswell, 1698.

Fuller, Christopher J. "The Divine Couple's Relationship in a South Indian Temple: Mīnākṣī and Sundeśvara at Madurai." *History of Religions* 19 (1980): 321–48.

Gahlot, M. Singh, and P. Lal Menariya. *A Muslim Princess Becomes Sati (A Historical Romance of Hindu-Muslim Unity).* Jalore: Shri Mahavir Shodha Samsthan, 1981.

Gait, Edward Albert. *A History of Assam.* 3d rev. ed. Calcutta: Thacker Spink & Co,, 1967. First edition 1906.

———."Human Sacrifice (Indian)." In *Encyclopaedia of Religion and Ethics,* vol. 6, p. 849.

Galey, Jean-Claude, ed. *L'espace du temple (Puruṣārtha 8, 10).* 2 vols. Paris: Editions de l' EHESS, 1985, 1986.

Gandhi, R. S. "*Sati* as Altruistic Suicide. Beyond Durkheim's Interpretation." *Contributions to Asian Studies* 10 (1977): 141–57.

Garg, A. S. *Bride Burning. Social, Criminological and Legal Aspects.* New Delhi: Sandeep Publications, 1990.

Garuḍa Purāṇa. Garuḍa Purāṇam of Maharṣi Vedavyāsa. Edited by R. S. Bhattacharya. Varanasi: Chowkhamba Sanskrit Series Office, 1964.

———. *The Garuḍa-Purāṇam.* 2d ed. Trans. M. N. Dutt Shastri. Varanasi: Chowkhamba Sanskrit Series Office, 1968.

———. *The Garuḍa Purāṇa.* 2 vols. Trans. by a board of scholars. Delhi: Motilal Banarsidass, 1979.

Gautam, D. M., and B. V. Trivedi. *Unnatural Deaths of Married Women with Special Reference to Dowry Deaths. A Sample Study of Delhi.* New Delhi: Bureau of Police Research and Development, Ministry of Home Affairs, Government of India, 1986.

Gericke, J. F. C., and T. Roorda. *Javaansch-Nederlandsch Handwoordenboek.* Edited by A. C. Vreede. Amsterdam and Leyden: Johannes Müller, 1901.

Gernet, Jacques. *L'intelligence de la Chine. Le social et le mental.* Paris: Gallimard, 1993.

Gibb, H. A. R., ed. *The Travels of Ibn Baṭṭūṭa*—A.D. 1325–1354. 3 vols. Cambridge: Cambridge University Press, 1971.

Gill, K. *Hindu Women's Right to Property in India.* New Delhi: Deep & Deep Publications, 1986.

Goetz, Hermann. *The Art and Architecture of Bikaner State.* Oxford: B. Cassirer, 1950.

Gonda, Jan. *Change and Continuity in Indian Religion.* The Hague: Mouton, 1965.

Goudriaan, Teun, and Sanjukta Gupta. *Hindu Tantric and Śākta Literature.* Wiesbaden: Harrassowitz, 1981.

Grierson, George. *The Lay of Alha. A Saga of Rajput Chivalry as Sung by Minstrels of Northern India.* London: Oxford University Press, 1923; reprint Gurgaon: Vintage Books, 1990.

Gold, Ann Grodzins. *Fruitful Journeys. The Ways of Rajasthani Pilgrims.* Delhi: Oxford University Press, 1989.

———. *A Carnival of Parting. The Tales of King Bharthari and King Gopi Chand as Sung and Told by Madhu Natisar of Ghatiyali, Rajasthan.* Berkeley: University of California Press, 1992.

Gros, François. "La littérature du Sangam et son public." In *Inde et Littératures,* edited by M.-C. Porcher, 77–107.

Gupta, S. *Vibhinn yugon men Sītā kā caritr-citraṇ.* New Delhi: Prajna Prakasan, 1978.

Gupta, Sanjuka, and Richard Gombrich. "Another View of Widow-Burning and Womanliness in India." *Journal of Commonwealth & Comparative Politics* 12, no. 3 (November 1984): 252–58.

Gurumurthy, S. "Self-Immolation in South India." *Bulletin of the Institute of Traditional Cultures Madras* 1 (1969): 44–49.

Haafner, Jan. *Voyages dans la péninsule occidentale de l'Inde et dans l'île de Ceilan.* 2 tomes. Paris: Arthus-Bertrand, 1811. First edition 1808.

Hamilton, Alexander. *A New Account of the East Indies.* 2 vols. London, 1744.

Hanchett, S. *Coloured Rice. Symbolic Structure in Hindu Family Festivals.* Delhi: Hindustan Publishing Corporation, 1988.

Hansen, Katherine. "The *Virangana* in North Indian History, Myth, and Popular Culture." *Economic and Political Weekly* 13, no. 18 (30 April 1988): 25–33.

Harlan, Lindsay. *Religion and Rajput Women. The Ethic of Protection in Contemporary Narratives.* Berkeley: University of California Press, 1992.

Harlan, Lindsay, and Paul B. Courtright, eds. *From the Margins of Hindu Marriage. Essays on Gender, Religion and Culture.* New York: Oxford University Press, 1995.

Hart, George L. *The Poems of Ancient Tamils. Their Milieu and their Sanskrit Counterparts.* Berkeley: University of California Press, 1975.

Hawley, John Stratton. *Sati, the Blessing and the Curse. The Burning of Wives in India.* New York: Oxford University Press, 1994.

Hazra, R. C. *Studies in the Upapurāṇas.* 2 vols. Calcutta: Calcutta Sanskrit College Research Series, 1963.

Heesterman, J. C. *The Inner Conflict of Tradition. Essays in Indian Ritual, Kinship, and Society.* Chicago: University of Chicago Press, 1985.

———. *The Broken World of Sacrifice. An Essay in Ancient Indian Ritual.* Chicago: University of Chicago Press, 1993.

Helffer, Mireille, and Marc Gaborieau. "A propos d'un tambour du Kumaon et de l'ouest du Népal: remarques sur l'utilisation des tambours-sabliers dans le monde indien, le Népal et le Tibet." In *Studia instrumentorum musicae popularis. Festschrift to E. Emsheimer on the occasion of his 70th birthday.* Stockholm: Musikhistorika Museet, 1974.

Héran, François. "Le rite et la croyance." *Revue française de sociologie* 27 (1986): 231–63.

Herrenschmidt, Olivier. "Le sacrifice du buffle en Andhra côtier. Le 'culte de village' confronté aux notions de sacrifiant et d'unité de culte." In *Autour de la Déesse,* edited by M. Biardeau, 137–77.

Herschman, P. "Hair, Sex and Dirt." *Man* 9 (1974): 274–98.

Hess, Linda. "The Poet, the People, and the Western Scholar: Influence of a Sacred Drama and Text on Social Values in North India." *Theatre Journal* 40 (1988): 236–53.

Hiltebeitel, Alf, ed. *Criminal Gods and Demon Devotees. Essays on the Guardians of Popular Hinduism.* Albany, N.Y.: SUNY Press, 1989; New Delhi: Manohar, 1990 .

———. *The Cult of Draupadī.* 2 vols. Chicago: University of Chicago Press, 1988, 1991.

———. "Draupadī's Hair." In *Autour de la Déesse,* edited by M. Biardeau, 179–214.

Hodges, William. *Travels in India during the Years 1780, 1781, 1782, and 1783.* London: J. Edwards, 1793.

Holwell, J. Z. *Interesting Historical Events Relative to the Province of Bengal and the Empire of Indostan.* London: T. Becket & P. A. de Hondt, 1767.

Hudson, D. Dennis. "Violent and Fanatical Devotion among the Nayanars: A Study in the *Periya Purāṇam* of Cekkilār." In *Criminal Gods and Demon Devotees,* edited by A. Hiltebeitel, 373–404.

Hulin, Michel. *La Face cachée du temps: l'imaginaire de l'au-delà.* Paris: Fayard, 1985.

Hunter, B., ed. *The Statesman's Year-Book, Statistical and Historical Annual of the States of the World for the Year 1994–1995.* New York: St. Martin's Press, 1994.

India 1992. A Reference Annual. New Delhi: Government of India, 1993.

Jacob, Sir George LeGrand. *Western India Before and During the Mutinies: Pictures Drawn from Life.* London: H. S. King & Co., 1871.

Jaffrelot, Christophe. *Les Nationalistes hindous. Idéologie, implantation, et mobilisation des années 1920 aux années 1990.* Paris: Presses de la FNSP, 1993.

Jain, J. "Ethnic Background of Some Hero-Stones of Gujarat." In *Memorial Stones,* edited by S. Settar and Günther Sontheimer, 83–86.

Jhajhar, S. Singh Shekhavat. *Śekhāvaṭī ke śilālekh. Ek adhyayan.* Jhunjhunu: Sri Sardul Education Trust, 1988.

———. *Śekhāvāṭī, prades kā prācīn itihās.* Jhunjhunu: Sri Sardul Education Trust, 1989.

Jigyasu, M. L. *Cāraṇ sāhity kā itihās.* Jodhpur: Jain Brothers, 1992.

Jones, Sir William. *Institutes of Hindu Law, or the Ordinances of Menu, According to the Gloss of Cullûca; Comprising the Indian System of Duties, Religious and Civil.* Calcutta, 1794.

Joshi, Shanti. *Śūny kī bānhon men.* Delhi: Rajkamal Prakasan, 1967.

Kaelber, Walter O. "Tapas, Birth, and Spiritual Rebirth in the Veda." *History of Religions* 15 (1976): 343–86.

Kakar, Sudhir. *The Inner World: A Psycho-Analytic Study of Childhood and Society in India.* Delhi: Oxford University Press, 1978, 1991.

Kakati, B. K. *The Mother Goddess Kāmākhyā.* Guwahati: Publication Board Assam, 1989.

Kālikā Purāṇa. Kālikāpurāṇam. Edited by B. N. Sastri. Varanasi: Chowkhamba Sanskrit Series Office, 1972.

———. *The Kālikāpurāṇa (Text, Introduction & Translation in English).* Edited by B. N. Sastri. Delhi: Nag Publishers, 1992.

Kalyāṇ Nārī-Aṅk. Gorakhpur: Gita Press, 1987.

Kamal, K. L. *Party Politics in an Indian State. A Study of the Main Political Parties in Rajasthan.* Delhi: S. Chand & Co., 1971.

Kane, Vaman Pandurang. *History of Dharmaśāstra.* 5 vols. Poona: Bhandarkar Research Institute, 1930–1962.

Kapani, Lakshmi. *La Notion de saṃskāra dans l'Inde brahmanique et bouddhique.* 2 vols. Paris: De Boccard, 1992, 1993.

Karlekar, Hiranmay. *In the Mirror of Mandal: Social Justice, Caste, Class and the Individual.* Delhi: Ajanta Publications, 1992.

Kennedy, Michael. *The Criminal Classes in India.* Bombay: Government Central Press, 1907; reprint Delhi: Mittal, 1985.

Khan, Dominique-Sila. "Miracle à Sedya." *Ulysse* 20 (September–October 1991): 4–7.

———. "L'origine ismaélienne du culte hindou de Rāmdeo Pīr." *Revue de l'histoire des religions* 210:1 (1993): 27–47.

———. "Deux rites tantriques dans une communauté d'intouchables au Rajasthan." *Revue de l'histoire des religions* 211 (1994): 443–62.

Khare, G. H. "Emblems of Royalty in Art and Literature." In *Annals of the Bhandarkar Oriental Research Institute, Diamond Jubilee Volume,* 682–89. Poona: BORI, 1978.

Kinsley, David R. "'The Death That Conquers Death': Dying to the World in Medieval Hinduism." In *Religious Encounters with Death,* edited by Reynolds and Waugh, 97–108.

———. *Hindu Goddesses. Visions of the Divine Feminine in the Hindu Religious Traditions.* Berkeley: University of California Press, 1986.

Kishwar, Madhu, and Ruth Vanita. "The Burning of Roop Kanwar." *Manushi* 42–43 (September–December 1987): 15–25.

Knipe, David M. "Night of the Growing Dead: A Cult of Vīrabhadra in Coastal Andhra." In *Criminal Gods and Demon Devotees,* edited by A. Hiltebeitel, 123–51.

———. "*Sapiṇḍīkaraṇa*: the Hindu Rite of Entry into Heaven." In *Religious Encounters with Death,* edited by Reynolds and Waugh, 111–24.

Kolenda, Pauline. *Regional Differences in Family Structure in India.* Jaipur: Rawat Publications, 1987.

Kolff, Dirk. *Naukar, Rajput and Sepoy: The Ethnohistory of the Military Labour Market in Hindustan, 1450–1850.* Cambridge: Cambridge University Press, 1990.

Kothari, Komal. "Myths, Tales and Folklore: Exploring the Substratum of Cinema." *India International Centre Quarterly* 8, no. 1 (March 1980).

———. "Performers, Gods, and Heroes in the Oral Epics of Rajasthan." In *Oral Epics in India,* edited by Blackburn et al., 102–17.

Kṛtyakalpataru of Bhaṭṭa Lakṣmīdhara, Tīrthavivecanakāṇḍa. Edited by K. V. Rangaswami Aiyangar. Baroda: Oriental Institute, 1942.

Kulkarni, Jeevan M. "Sati—Shame or Pride." *Organiser* 24 (22 November 1987): 10–11.

———. *The Writ Petition Filed in the Supreme Court of India by Shri Jeevan Kulkarni to Challenge Constitutional Validity of the Commission of Sati (Prevention) Act 1987 (Act no. III of 1988), Being Numbered Writ Petition (Civil) 587 of 1989.* Bombay: The author, 1989.

Kulke, Hermann. "Maharajas, Mahants and Historians. Reflections on the Historiography of Early Vijayanagara and Sringeri." In *Vijayanagara—City and Empire,* edited by A. L. Dallapiccola, 1:120–43.

Kumar, Nita. "Widows, Education and Social Change in Twentieth Century Banaras." *Economic and Political Weekly* 26, no. 17 (27 April 1991): 19–25.

Kumar, P. *Folk-Icons and Rituals in Tribal Life.* New Delhi: Abhinav, 1984.

Kumari, Ranjana. *Brides Are Not for Burning. Dowry Victims in India.* New Delhi: Radiant Publishers, 1989.

Kurtz, Stanley N. *All the Mothers Are One: Hindu India and the Cultural Reshaping of Psychoanalysis.* New York: Columbia University Press, 1992.

Lardinois, Roland. "En Inde, la famille, l'Etat, la femme." In André Burguière et al., *Histoire de la famille.* 2 vols. 2:267–99. Paris: Armand Colin, 1986.

———. "L'ordre du monde et l'institution familiale en Inde." In André Burguière et al. *Histoire de la famille.* 2 vols. 1:519–55. Paris: Armand Colin, 1986.

———. "Les usages sociaux de l'infanticide féminin en Inde." *Nervure* 3 (April 1988): 40–42.

Leach, Edmund R. "Magical Hair." *Journal of the Royal Anthropological Institute* 88 (1958): 147–64.

Le Bon, Gustave. *Les Civilisations de l'Inde.* Paris: Firmin-Didot, 1987.

Leshnik, L. S. "Nomads and Burials in South India." In *Pastoralists and Nomads in South Asia,* edited by L. S. Leshnik and G. Sontheimer, 62.

Leshnik, L. S., and Günther Sontheimer, eds. *Pastoralists and Nomads in South Asia.* 2 vols. Wiesbaden: Harrassowitz, 1975.

Leslie, Julia. *The Perfect Wife. The Orthodox Hindu Woman According to the Strīdharmapaddhati of Tryambakayajvan.* Delhi: Oxford University Press, 1989.

———, ed. *Roles and Rituals for Hindu Women.* Rutherford, N. J.: Fairleigh Dickinson University Press, 1991, 1992.

Lévi, Sylvain. *La Doctrine du sacrifice dans les Brâhmanas.* Paris: Presses Universitaires de France, 1966. First edition 1898.

———. "La transmigration des âmes dans les croyances hindoues." Lecture delivered 20 March 1904, Paris.

Lincoln, Bruce. *Death, War and Sacrifice.* Chicago: University of Chicago Press, 1991.

Lingat, Robert. *Les Sources du Droit dans le système traditionnel de l'Inde.* Paris: Mouton, 1967.

Lodrick, D. O. "Rajasthan as a Region: Myth or Reality." In *The Idea of Rajasthan,* edited by Karine Schomer et al., 1:1–44.

Loiseleur-Deslongchamps, A. *Lois de Manou.* Paris: Imprimerie de Craquelet, 1833.

Lorenzen, David N. *The Kāpālikas and Kālāmukhas. Two Lost Śaivite Sects.* New Delhi: Thomson Press, 1972.

———. *Kabir Legends and Ananta-Das's "Kabir Parachai."* Albany, N.Y.: SUNY Press, 1991.

———. "New Data on the Kāpālikas." In *Criminal Gods and Demon Devotees,* edited by A. Hiltebeitel, 231–38.

Löschhorn, E. "Vijayanagar—as Seen by European Visitors." In *Vijayanagara—City and Empire,* edited by A. L. Dallapiccola, 1:345–46.

Lutfullah. *Autobiography of Lutfullah, a Mahomedan Gentleman; & his Transactions with his Fellow-Creatures.* London: Smith, Elder & Co., 1857.

Lutgendorf, Philip. *The Life of a Text. Performing the Rāmcaritmānas of Tulsidas.* Berkeley: University of California Press, 1991.

———. "My Hanuman is Bigger than Yours." *History of Religions* 33, no. 4 (February 1994): 213–45.

Lynch, K., and A. Sen. "Indian Women: Well-Being and Survival." *Cambridge Journal of Economics* 7 (1983): 363–89.

Macmurdo, John. "An Account of the Province of Cutch and of the Countries Lying between Guzerat and the River Indus." *Transactions of the Literary Society of Bombay* [London] 2 (1820).

———. "Remarks on the Province of Kattiawar, its Inhabitants, their Manners and Customs." *Transactions of the Literary Society of Bombay* [London] 2 (1820).

———. "Journal of a Route through the Peninsula of Guzerat in the Year 1809 and 1810." In *The Peninsula of Gujarat in the Early Nineteenth Century,* edited by S. C. Ghosh. New Delhi: Sterling Publishers, 1977.

Mahāmahim Mahāsatī Jasvant Kuñvar Candrāvat. Devipura: n.p., n.d.

Mahāsatī Oṃ Kanvar Mān Bhajanmālā. 3d ed. Jharli: Sri Samiti Trust, 1982.

Maheshwari, H. L. *History of Rajasthani Literature.* New Delhi: Sahitya Akademi, 1980.

Mahias, Marie-Claude. *Délivrance et Convivialité. Le système culinaire des Jaina.* Paris: Editions de la Maison des sciences de l'homme, 1985.

Maistre, J. de. *Les Soirées de Saint-Pétersbourg, ou Entretiens sur le gouvernement temporel de la Providence.* 2 vols. Paris: Cosson, 1821. New edition of the second and ninth *Entretiens: Eclaircissement sur les sacrifices.* Introduction and notes by Jean-Louis Schefer. Paris: Agora, 1994.

Malabari, B. M. *Infant Marriage and Enforced Widowhood in India.* Bombay, 1877.

Malamoud, Charles. "Observations sur la notion de 'reste' dans le brâhmanisme." *Wiener Zeitschrift für die Kunde Südasiens* 17 (1972): 6–26. English translation: "Remarks on the Brahmanic Concept of the 'Remainder'." In idem, *Cooking the World,* 6–22.

———. "Cuire le monde." *Puruṣārtha* 1 (1975): 91–135. English translation: "Cooking the World." In idem, *Cooking the World,* 23–53.

———. "Terminer le sacrifice. Remarque sur les honoraires rituels dans le brahmanisme." In Madeleine Biardeau and Charles Malamoud, *Le Sacrifice dans l'Inde ancienne,* 155–204. Paris: Presses Universitaires de France, 1976.

———. *Le svādhyāya. Récitation personnelle du Veda. Taittirīya-Āraṇyaka, livre II. Texte traduit et commenté.* Paris: De Boccard, 1977.

———, ed. *La dette (Puruṣārtha 4).* Paris: Editions de l'EHESS, 1980.

———. "Les morts sans visage. Remarques sur l'idéologie funéraire dans le brâhmanisme." In *La Mort, les Morts dans les sociétés anciennes,* edited by Gherardo Gnoli and Jean-PierreVernant, 441–53. Cambridge: Cambridge University Press, 1982.

———. "Les dieux n'ont pas d'ombre. Remarques sur la langue secrète des dieux dans l'Inde ancienne." *Traverses* 30–31 (March 1984): 86–94. English translation: "The Gods Have No Shadows." In idem, *Cooking the World: Ritual and Thought in Ancient India,* 195–206.

———. "Spéculations indiennes sur le sexe du sacrifice." *L'Ecrit du temps* 16 (1987): 7–28.

———. "Dette et devoir dans le vocabulaire sanscrit et dans la pensée brahmanique." In *Lien de vie, Noeud mortel,* edited by Charles Malamoud, 187–205. Paris: Editions de l'EHESS, 1988.

———. "Action en retour et mécanisme du sacrifice dans l'Inde brahmanique." In idem, *Cuire le monde. Rite et Pensée dans l'Inde ancienne.* Paris: La Découverte, 1989. English translation: "Return Action in the Sacrificial Mechanics of Brahmanic India." In idem, *Cooking the World,* 156–68.

———. "Cosmologie prescriptive. Observations sur le monde et le non-monde dans l'Inde ancienne." *Le Temps de la réflexion* 10 (1989): 303–25.

———. "La dénégation de la violence dans le sacrifice védique" *Gradhiva* 15 (1994): 35–41.

———. *Cooking the World: Ritual and Thought in Ancient India.* Trans. David Gordon White. Delhi: Oxford University Press, 1996.

Mālatī-Mādhava of Bhavabhūti. *Bhavabhūti's Mālatī-Mādhava, with the Commentary of Jagaddhara.* 3d ed. Edited by M. R. Kale. Delhi: Motilal Banarsidass, 1983. First edition 1908.

Malcolm, Sir John. *A Memoir of Central India, Including Malwa, and Adjoining Provinces.* London and Calcutta: Thatcher & Spink, 1824, 1832.

Mallison, Françoise. *L'Epouse idéale. La Satī-Gītā de Muktānand.* Paris: Institut de civilisation indienne, 1973.

———. “A Note on the Holiness Allowed to Women: *Pativratā* and *Satī*.” In *Ludwick Sternbach Felicitation Volume.* Lucknow: Akhil Bharatiy Sanskrit Parisad, 1979.

Mandawa, Devi Singh. *Śārdul Singh-jī Śekhāvat.* Jhunjhunu: Sardul Educational Trust, 1970.

Mani, Lata. “Production of an Official Discourse on Sati in Early Nineteenth Century.” *Economic and Political Weekly* 21, no. 17 (26 April 1986): 32–40.

———. “Contentious Traditions: The Debate on Sati in Colonial India.” *Cultural Critique* 7 (Fall 1987): 119–56.

Manimekhalaï (The Dancer with the Magic Bowl) by Merchant-Prince Shattan. Trans. Alain Daniélou with the collaboration of T. V. Gopala Iyer. Delhi: Penguin Books India, 1993.

Manohar, S. S. *Cāraṇ-carjāen aor unkā adhyayan.* Jaipur: Vivek Publishing House, n.d.

Manucci, Nicolao. *Storia do Mogor or Mogul India. 1653–1708.* London: J. Murray, 1907.

Marco Polo. *La Description du monde.* Edited by L. Hambis. Paris: Klincksieck, 1955.

Marglin, Fréderique Apffel. “Types of Oppositions in Hindu Culture.” In *Purity and Auspiciousness,* edited by J. Carman and F. Apffel Marglin, 1:65–83.

———. *Wives of the God-King. The Rituals of the Devadasis of Puri.* Delhi: Oxford University Press, 1989.

Massie, J. W. *Continental India. Travelling Sketches & Historical Recollections.* London: Thomas Ward & Co., 1840.

Masters, John. *The Deceivers.* London: Michael Joseph Ltd., 1952.

Mauss, Marcel. “Sur un texte de Posidonius. Le suicide, contre-prestation suprême.” In *Marcel Mauss, Oeuvres,* 3 vols., 3:52–57. Paris: Editions de Minuit, 1968–1969.

Mayer, Adrien C. *Caste and Kinship in Central Asia. A Village and its Region.* Berkeley: University of California Press, 1966.

Medhurst, W. H. “Short Account of the Island Bali.” *Singapore Chronicle,* June 1830.

Mehta, Rupkuar. *Śrī Satī Mātā caritāmṛt.* Jodhpur: Susma Prakasan, 1986.

———. *Rājasthān kī sant-śiromaṇi Bālā Satī.* Jodhpur: Rajasthani Granthakar, 1991.

Menski, Werner F. “Marital Expectations as Dramatized in Hindu Marriage Rituals.” In *Roles and Rituals,* edited by J. Leslie, 47–67.

Meyer, Johann Jakob. *Sexual Life in Ancient India. A Study of the Comparative History of Indian Culture.* New York: E. P. Dutton, 1930; reprint Delhi: Motilal Banarsidass, 1971.

Mitra, Sarat Chandra. “On a Recent Instance of Human Sacrifice from the Central Provinces of India.” *Journal of the Anthropological Society of Bombay* 8, no. 6 (1926): 599–605.

———. “Note on a Recent Instance of Self-Immolation for Propitiating a God.” *Journal of the Anthropological Society of Bombay* 14, no. 2 (1928): 227–28.

Mitter, Partha. *Much Maligned Monsters. History of European Reactions to Indian Art.* Oxford: Clarendon Press, 1977.

Modave, Comte de. *Voyage en Inde du Comte de Modave, 1773–1776 (Nouveaux Mé-*

moires sur l'état actuel de l'Indoustan). Edited by J. Deloche. Paris: École Française d'Extrême-Orient, 1971.

Mukherjee, Amitabha. *Reform and Regeneration in Bengal.* Calcutta: Rabindra Bharati University, 1968.

Murphy, H. B. M. "History of the Evolution of Syndromes: The Striking Case of *Latah* and *Amok.*" In *Psychopathology, Contributions from the Social, Behavioral and Biological Sciences,* edited by M. Hammer, K. Salzinger, and S. Sutton, 33–55. New York: John Wiley & Sons, 1973.

Murr, Sylvia. *L'Inde philosophique entre Bossuet et Voltaire.* 2 vols. Paris: École Française d'Extrême-Orient, 1987.

———. "Le politique 'au mogol' selon Bernier: appareil conceptuel, rhétorique stratégique, philosophie morale." In *De la royauté à l'Etat,* edited by J. Pouchepadass and H. Stern, 239–83.

Murthy, M. L. K. "Memorial Stones in Andhra Pradesh." In *Memorial Stones,* edited by S. Settar and G. Sontheimer, 209–18.

Nandy, Ashis. "Sati. A Nineteenth Century Tale of Woman, Violence and Protest." In *At the Edge of Psychology. Essays on Politics and Culture,* 1–31. Delhi: Oxford University Press, 1980.

———. "The Sociology of Sati." *Indian Express,* 5 October 1987.

———. "The Human Factor." *The Illustrated Weekly of India,* 17 January 1988, 20–23.

———. "Sati as Profit versus Sati as a Spectacle: The Public Debate on Roop Kanwar's Death." In *Sati, the Bleessing and the Curse,* edited by J. S. Hawley, 131–49.

Narasimhan, Sakuntala. *Sati. A Study of Widow Burning in India.* New Delhi: Viking Penguin Books, 1990.

Nelson, J. H. *A Prospectus of the Scientific Study of the Hindû Law.* London: Kegan & Co., 1881.

Nirṇayasindhu of Kamalākara Bhaṭṭa. *Śrīkamalākarabhaṭṭapranitaḥ Nirṇayasindhu.* Edited with a Hindi translation by M. M. Vrajaratna Bhattacharya. Varanasi: Caukhamba Vidyabhavan, 1991. First edition 1612.

Nobili, Roberto de. In V. Cronin, *A Pearl to India. The Life of Roberto de Nobili.* London: Rupert Hart-Davis, 1959.

Noble, W. A., and Sankhyan, A. R. "Signs of the Divine: *Satī* Memorials and *Satī* Worship in Rajasthan." In *The Idea of Rajasthan,* edited by Karine Schomer et al., 1:343–89.

Obeysekere, Gananath. *Medusa's Hair. An Essay on Personal Symbols and Religious Experience.* Chicago: University of Chicago Press, 1981.

———. *The Cult of the Goddess Pattini.* Chicago and London: University of Chicago Press, 1984.

———. "Depression, Buddhism, and the Work of Culture in Sri Lanka." In *Culture and Depression,* edited by A. Kleinman and B. Good, 134–52. Berkeley: University of California Press, 1985.

"Observations on the State of Society among the Asiatic Subjects of Great Britain, by Charles Grant." In *Parliamentary Papers* 20 (1826–1827): 33–34.

O'Flaherty, Wendy Doniger [see also Doniger, Wendy]. *Asceticism and Eroticism in the Mythology of Śiva.* London: Oxford University Press, 1973. New edition: *Śiva, the Erotic Ascetic.* New York: Oxford University Press, 1981.

———. *The Origins of Evil in Hindu Mythology.* Berkeley: University of California Press, 1976, 1980.

———. *Women, Androgynes and Other Mythical Beasts.* Chicago: University of Chicago Press, 1980.

———. "Karma and Rebirth in the Vedas and Purāṇas." In idem, *Karma and Rebirth in Classical Indian Traditions,* 3–37. Delhi: Motilal Banarsidass, 1983.

———. *Dreams, Illusion and Other Realities.* Chicago: University of Chicago Press, 1984.

Olivelle, Patrick. "Ritual Suicide and the Rite of Renunciation." *Wiener Zeitschrift für die Kunde Südasiens* 22 (1978): 19–44.

———. *Samnyāsa Upaniṣads. Hindu Scriptures on Asceticism and Renunciation.* New York: Oxford University Press, 1992.

———. *The Āśrama System. The History and Hermeneutics of a Religious Institution.* New York: Oxford University Press, 1994.

———. *Upaniṣads.* New York: Oxford University Press, 1996.

Oman, John Campbell. *The Mystics, Ascetics, and Saints of India. A Study of Sadhuism, with an Account of the Yogis, Sanyasis, Bairagis, and Other Strange Hindu Sectarians.* London: T. F. Unwin, 1903; reprint Delhi: Oriental Publishers, 1973.

Padoux, André. *L'Énergie de la parole. Cosmogonies de la parole tantrique.* Paris: Le Soleil noir, 1980; Paris: Fata Morgana, 1994. Revised English translation: *Vāc, The Concept of the Word in Selected Hindu Tantras.* Trans. Jacques Gontier. Albany, N.Y.: SUNY Press, 1990.

Pandey, Divakar. *Gorakhnāth evam unkī paramparā kā sāhity.* Gorakhpur: Gorakhpur University, 1980.

Panigraha, L. *British Social Policy and Female Infanticide in India.* New Delhi: Munshiram Manoharlal, 1972.

Parik, Nand Kiśor. *Sant Rām Singh aor unkī sūfī bhāvnā.* Jaipur: Ramasram Sansthan, 1987.

Parliamentary Papers [Papers Relating to East India Affairs, viz. Hindoo Widows, and Voluntary Immolations]. London: House of Commons. 1821, vol. 18; 1823, vol. 17; 1824, vol. 23; 1825, vol. 24; 1826–1827, vol. 20; 1828, vol. 23; 1830, vol. 28.

Parry, Jonathan P. "Death and Cosmogony in Kashi." *Contributions to Indian Sociology* 15 (1981): 356–62.

———. "Sacrificial Death and the Necrophagous Ascetic." In *Death and the Regeneration of Life,* edited by Maurice Bloch and Jonathan P. Parry. Cambridge: Cambridge University Press, 1982.

———. *Death in Banaras.* Cambridge: Cambridge University Press, 1994.

Pathak, M. M. "*Dakṣayajñavidhvaṃsa*-Episode in Comparative Studies." *Purāṇa* 20, no. 2 (July 1978): 204–23.

Peggs, James. *India's Cries to British Humanity, Relative to Suttee, Infanticide British Connexion with Idolatry, Ghaut Murders and Slavery in India.* London: Seely & Son, 1830. First edition 1828.

Penzer, N. M. "Note on the 'Act of Truth' Motif in Folk-Lore." In *The Ocean of Story. Being C. H. Tawney's Translation of Somadeva's Kathā Sarit Sāgara (or Ocean of Streams of Story),* 10 vols., edited by N. M. Penzer, 3: 179–82. Delhi: Motilal Banarsidass, 1921–28.

———. "Umbrellas." In ibid., 1: 263–69.

Perec, Georges. *Life, A User's Manual.* Trans. David Bellos. Boston: David R. Godine, 1987.

Pollock, Sheldon. "Deep Orientalism? Note on Sanskrit and Power beyond the Raj." In *Orientalism,* edited by C. A. Breckenridge and P. Van der Veer, 76–133.

Porcher, Marie-Claude, ed. *Inde et littératures (Puruṣārtha 7).* Paris: Editions de l'EHESS, 1983.

Postans, Mrs. *Cutch: Or Random Sketches, Taken during a Residence in One of the Northern Provinces of Western India.* London: Smith, Elder & Co., 1839.

Pouchepadass, Jacques. "Délinquance de fonction et marginalisation sociale: les tribus 'criminelles' dans l'Inde britannique." In *Les Marginaux et les Exclus dans l'histoire,* 122–54. Paris: UGE, 1979.

———. *Planteurs et Paysans dans l'Inde coloniale: l'indigo du Bihar et le mouvement gandhien de Champaran, 1917–1918.* Paris: L'Harmattan, 1986.

Pouchepadass, Jacques, and Henri Stern, eds. *De la royauté à l'Etat. Anthropologie et histoire du politique dans le monde indien (Puruṣārtha 13).* Paris: Editions de l'EHESS, 1991.

Pouillon, Jean. *Le cru et le su.* Paris: Seuil, 1993.

Pramar, V. S. *Haveli. Wooden Houses and Mansions of Gujarat.* Ahmedabad: Mapin Publishing,, 1989.

Premchand, Munshi D. R. *Mānsarovar.* Allahabad: Sarasvati Press, 1965.

Qanungo, Kalika Ranjan. *Studies in Rajput History.* 2d ed. New Delhi: S. Chand & Co., 1971.

Rāmāyaṇa of Vālmīki. 7 vols. Edited by G. H. Bhatt et al. Baroda: Oriental Institute, 1960–75.

Rāmcaritmānas of Tulsī Dās. *The Holy Lake of the Acts of Rāma, A Translation of Tulasī Dās's Rāmacaritamānasa.* Trans. W. Douglas P. Hill. Delhi: Oxford University Press, 1952.

———. *Śrī Rāmcaritmānas: vijayā ṭīkā.* Edited with a Hindi commentary by V. A. Tripathi. Calcutta: Indian Development Trust, 1955, 1980.

———. Edited by V. P. Misra. Ramnagar: All-India Kashiraj Trust, 1962.

Ramusio, G. B. *Navigazioni e Viaggi.* 6 vols. Turin: Einaudi, 1979. First edition 1550.

Rathor, R. Singh. "Hamārī Saṃskṛti aor Mahāsatiyān." In *Mahāsatī Oṃ Kanvar,* 6–12. Jharli: Om Kanvar Trust, n.d.

Rémignon, Isabelle. "Les différentes versions de la geste de Tejājī." DEA diss., Ecole Pratique des Hautes Etudes, 4e section. Paris: 1993.

Renou, Louis. "Le jeûne du créancier dans l'Inde ancienne." In *L'Inde fondamentale. Etudes d'indianisme,* collected with an introduction by Charles Malamoud, 164–74. Paris: Hermann, 1978.

———. *Prolégomènes au Vedānta.* Paris: Maisonneuve, 71951.

Report on Rajasthan Jagirdari Abolition. Jaipur: Government of Rajasthan, 1953.

Resende, Garcia de. *Miscelanea e Variedade de historias, costumes, casos e cousas que em seu tempo acontesceram.* Evora: A. de Burgos, 1554.

Reynolds, Frank E., and Earle H. Waugh, eds. *Religious Encounters with Death, Insights from the History and Anthropology of Religions.* University Park: Pennsylvania State University Press, 1977.

Rice, B. Lewis. *Mysore and Coorg from the Inscriptions.* London: A. Constable & Co., 1909; New Delhi: Asian Publishing Services, 1986.

Richman, Paula, ed. *Many Rāmāyaṇas. The Diversity of a Narrative Tradition in South Asia.* Berkeley: University of California Press, 1991.

Riporṭ Mardumśumārī Rāj Mārvāṛ bābat san 1891 īsvī, tīsrā hissā. Jodhpur: Vidyasal, 1895. Partial English translation: Munshi Hardyal Singh. *The Castes of Marwar.* 1894; reprint Jodhpur: Books Treasure, 1990.

Roberts, Emma, ed. *Views on India. Chiefly among the Himalayan Mountains.* London: Fisher, Son & Co., 1845.

Rogerius, Abraham. *De Open-Deure tot het Verborgen Heydendom ofte Waerachtigh vertoog von het Leven ende Zeden, mitsgaders de Religie ende Godsdienst der Bramines op de cust Chormandel.* Leyden: F. Hackes, 1651. French translation: *Le Théâtre de l'idolâtrie, ou La Porte ouverte pour parvenir à la connoissance du Paganisme caché.* Amsterdam: Jean Schipper, 1670.

Ross, H. A. "Sacrifices of the Head to the Hindu Goddess." *Folk-Lore. Transactions of the Folk-Lore Society* 37, no. 1 (March 1926): 90–92.

Roy, Benoy Bhusan. *Socioeconomic Impact of Sati in Bengal and the Role of Raja Rammohun Roy.* Calcutta: Naya Prokash, 1987.

Roy, Raja Rammohun. "A Conference between an Advocate for and an Opponent of the Practice of Burning Widows Alive." 30 November 1818. In *Sati. A Writeup,* edited by M. R. Anand, 20–30.

———. "A Second Conference between an Advocate for and an Opponent of the Practice of Burning Widows Alive." 20 February 1820. In *Sati. A Writeup,* edited by M. R. Anand, 31–57.

———. *Modern Encroachments on the Ancient Rights of Females According to the Hindu Law of Inheritance.* Calcutta: The author, 1822.

Rubin, Barnett R. *Feudal Revolt and State-Building. The 1938 Sikar Agitation in Jaipur.* New Delhi and Madras: South Asian Publishers, 1983.

"Rural Women Speak." *Seminar* 342 (February 1988): 40–44.

Russell, R. V., and Rai Bahadur Hira Lal. *Tribes and Castes of the Central Provinces of India.* London: Macmillan, 1916; reprint Delhi: Cosmo, 1975.

Sangari, Kumkum. "Perpetuating the Myth." *Seminar* 342 (February 1988): 24–30.

Sangari, Kumkum, and Sudesh Vaid. "The Politics of Widow Immolation." *Imprint.* October 1987: 27–31.

———. "Sati in Modern India: A Report." *Economic and Political Weekly* 16, no. 31 (August 1981): 1284–88.

Sarasvati, Pandita R. *The High-Caste Hindu Woman.* Philadelphia: J. B. Rodgers, 1887.

Sarma, M. P. *Toravāṭī kā itihās.* Kotputli: Lokbhasa Prakasan, 1980.

Sarma Parik, Pandit B., ed. *Mān Satī Sugan Kuñvari Caritr. Ūjolī kī satī.* Kishangarh: n.p., n.d.

———, ed. *Tārā Kuñvari Caritr, arthāt Madho-Kā-Bās kī satī caritr.* Kishangarh: n.p., n.d.

Sax, William S., ed. *The Gods at Play. Līlā in South Asia.* New York: Oxford University Press, 1995.

Schomer, Karine et al., eds. *The Idea of Rajasthan. Explorations in Regional Identity.* 2 vols. New Delhi: Manohar, 1994.

Schoterman, J. A. *The Yonitantra.* New Delhi: Manohar, 1980.

Schwartzberg, Joseph E. "Folk Regions in Northwestern India." In *India: Culture, Society and Economy. Geographical Essays in Honor of Professor Asok Mitra,* edited by A. B. Mukerji and A. Ahmed, 81–114. New Delhi: Inter-India Publications, 1985.

———, ed. *A Historical Atlas of South Asia.* Chicago: University of Chicago Press, 1978; revised edition New York: Oxford University Press, 1992.

Settar, S. *Inviting Death. Indian Attitude towards the Ritual Death.* Leiden: Brill, 1989.

———. "Memorial Stones in South India." In *Memorial Stones,* edited by S. Settar and G. Sontheimer, 183–97.

———. *Pursuing Death. Philosophy and Practice of Voluntary Termination of Life.* Leiden: Brill, 1990.

Settar, S., and Günther Sontheimer, eds. . *Memorial Stones: A Study of their Origin, Significance, and Variety.* Dharwad: Institute of Indian Art History, 1982.

Settar, S., and M. M. Kalaburgi. "The Hero Cult. A Study of Kannaḍa Literature from 9th to 13th century." In *Memorial Stones,* edited by S. Settar and G. Sontheimer, 31–35.

Sewell, Robert. *A Forgotten Empire (Vijayanagara), a Contribution to the History of India.* London, 1900; reprint Shannon: Irish University Press, 1972.

Shah, A. M., and Shroff, R. G. "The Vahīvancā Baroṭs of Gujarat: A Caste of Genealogists and Mythographers." *Journal of American Folklore* 7 (1958): 248–76.

Shahane, C. In *Sati: The Burning Issue. Express Magazine,* 10 January 1988.

Sharma, Arvind. *Sati. Historical and Phenomenological Essays.* Delhi: Motilal Banarsidass, 1988.

Sharma, G. N. *Social Life in Medieval Rajasthan, 1500–1800* A.D. Agra: Lakshmi Narain Agarwal, 1968.

Sherring, Matthew Atmore. *Hindu Tribes and Castes as Represented in Benares.* 3 vols. London: Trubner and Co., 1872–1881; reprint Delhi: Cosmo, 1974.

Shulman, David Dean. "Fire and Flood: The Testing of Sitā in Kampan's Irāmāvatāram." In *Many Rāmāyaṇas,* edited by P. Richman, 285–90.

———. *The King and the Clown in South Indian Myths and Poetry.* Princeton: Princeton University Press, 1985.

Singh, D. *Land Reforms in Rajasthan: A Report of a Survey.* Delhi: Government of India, 1964.

Singh, H. N. *Shekhawats and their Land.* Jaipur: Educational Printers, 1970.

Singh, Omkar. "Writ Petition (Civil) no. 699 of 1988 in the Matter of Omkar Singh, Petitioner, versus Union of India, Respondent." Typescript, 42 pp.

Singh, S. *A Passion for Flames.* Jaipur: RBSA Publishers, 1989.

Sirkar, D. C. *The Śākta Pīṭhas.* 2d rev. ed. Delhi: Motilal Banarsidass, 1973.

Sleeman, William Henry. *Rambles and Recollections of an Indian Official.* London: J. Hatchard and Son, 1844; rev. ed. with annotations by Vincent A. Smith, London: Oxford University Press, 1915; reprint 1980.

Smith, Frederick M. "Indra's Curse, Varuna's Noose, and the Suppression of the Woman in the Vedic Ritual." In *Roles and Rituals,* edited by J. Leslie, 17–45.

Smith, John D. "The Story of Pābūjī: Bard versus Historian." In *Luigi Pio Tessitori. Atti del Convegno internazionale di Udine,* 177–93. Brescia: Paideia Editrice, 1990.

———. *The Epic of Pābūjī.* Cambridge: Cambridge University Press, 1991.

Smṛticandrikā of Devaṇṇabhaṭṭa. 2 vols. Trans. J. R. Gharpure. Poona: Aryabhusan Press, 1946–1952.

Smṛtīnāṃ Samuccayaḥ. Edited by V. G. Apte. Poona: Anandasrama Sanskrit Series, 1929.

Sonnerat, P. *Voyage aux Indes orientales et à la Chine, fait par ordre du Roi, depuis 1774 jusqu'en 1781.* Paris: Dentu, 1806. First edition 1782.

Sontheimer, Günther-Dietz. "Between Ghost and God: A Folk Deity of the Deccan." In *Criminal Gods,* edited by A. Hiltebeitel, 299–337.

———. "Hero and Satī-Stones of Maharashtra." In *Memorial Stones,* edited by S. Settar and G. Sontheimer, 261–81.

———. "On the Memorials to the Dead in the Tribal Area of Central India" In *Memorial Stones,* edited by S. Settar and G. Sontheimer, 87–99.

———. "Some Memorial Monuments of Western India." In *German Scholars on India,* 2 vols., 2:264–75. Bombay: Nachiketa Publications, 1976.

Srinivas, M. N. Foreword to A. M. Shah and R. G. Shroff, "The Vahīvancā Baroṭs of Gujarat: A Caste of Genealogists and Mythographers." *Journal of American Folklore* 7 (1958): 246–48.

Stanley, John M. "Special Time, Special Power: The Fluidity of Power in a Popular Hindu Festival." *Journal of Asian Studies* 37, no. 1 (November 1977): 27–43.

Stavorinus, J. S. *Voyages to the East-Indies.* Trans. S. M. Wilcocke, 3 vols. London: G. G. and J. Robinson, 1798; reprint London: Dawson's, 1969.

Stern, Robert W. *The Cat and the Lion. Jaipur State in the British Raj.* Leiden: Brill, 1988.

Stevenson, Margaret Sinclair. *The Rites of the Twice-Born.* London: Oxford University Press, 1920; reprint New Delhi: Oriental Book Reprint Corporation, 1971.

Stork, Hélène. "Mothering Rituals in Tamilnadu: Some Magico-Religious Beliefs." In *Roles and Rituals,* edited by J. Leslie, 101–3.

Subrahmanian, N., ed. *Self-Immolation in Tamil Society.* Madurai: International Institute of Tamil Historical Studies, 1983.

Subramaniam, V. In *Sati: The Burning Issue. Express Magazine,* 10 January 1988.

Svarnkar, M. R., ed. *Satī Caritam (Koṭhrī-vāsinī-satī Sāvitrī caritr).* Sri Dungargarh: Ratan Art Press, 1974.

Swaminathan, A. "Self Immolation and Human Sacrifice in the History of South India." *Journal of Tamil Studies* 16 (December 1979): 10–18.

Tagore, Rabindranath. *Rabīndra Racanābalī.* 15 vols. Calcutta: Pascimbanga Sarkar, 1961.

Taknet, D. K. *Marvāṛī Samāj.* Jaipur: Kumar Prakasan, 1989.

Tambs-Lyche, Harald. *Power and Devotion. Religion and Society in Saurashtra.* 3 vols. Ph.D. diss., University of Bergen (Norway), 1992. This thesis has been published under the title *Power, Profit and Poetry. Traditional Society in Kathiawar, Western India.* New Delhi: Manohar, 1997.

Tarabout, Gilles. *Sacrifier et Donner à voir en pays Malabar. Les fêtes de temple au Kerala (Inde du Sud): étude anthropologique.* Paris: École Française d'Extrême-Orient, 1986.

Tarabout, Gilles, Denis Vidal, and Eric Meyer, eds. *Violences/non-violences en Inde (Puruṣārtha 16).* Paris: Editions de l'EHESS, 1993.

Tavernier, Jean-Baptiste. *Les Six voyages de Jean-Baptiste Tavernier, chevalier d'Aubonne, qu'il a faits en Turquie, en Perse et aux Indes.* Paris: Gervais Clouzier, 1681. First edition 1677. English translation: *Travels in India by Jean-Baptiste Tavernier Baron of Aubonne.* Trans. V. Ball. 2d ed., edited by William Crooke, 2 vols. London: Oxford University Press, 1925.

Thakur, U. N. *The History of Suicide in India.* Delhi: Munshiram Manoharlal, 1963.

Thapar, Romila. "Death and the Hero." In *Mortality and Immortality. The Archeology and Anthropology of Death,* edited by S. C. Humphries and H. King, 293–315. London: Academic Press, 1982.

———. "Elegy in Stone, In Memory of the Sati and the Hero." *The India Magazine.* April 1982, 12–15.

———. *From Lineage to State. Social Formations in the Mid-First Millenium* B.C. in the Ganga Valley. Delhi: Oxford University Press, 1984, 1990.

———. *Cultural Transaction and Early India: Tradition and Patronage.* Delhi: Oxford University Press, 1987.

———. "Romila Thapar talks to Madhu Kishwar and Ruth Vanita." *Manushi* 42–43 (September–December 1987): 3–14.

———. "In History." *Seminar* 342 (February 1988): 14–19.

———. *Interpreting Early India.* Delhi: Oxford University Press, 1994.

The Commission of Sati (Prevention) Bill, 1987. Act no. 3 of 1988. New Delhi: Government of India, 1988.

The Imperial Gazetteer of India. 24 vols. Oxford: Clarendon Press, 1908.

Thévenot, Jean de. *Voyages de Monsieur de Thévenot, contenant la relation de l'Indoustan, des nouveaux Mogols, & des autres Peuples et Pays des Indes.* Paris: Biestkins, 1684.

Thomas, Catherine [see also Weinberger-Thomas, Catherine]. *Le Suaire. Récits d'une autre Inde.* Paris: Publications Orientalistes de France, 1975.

———. "Le village dans la forêt. Sacrifice et renoncement dans le *Godān* de Premchand." In *Puruṣārtha* 2, 205–52. Paris: Editions de l' EHESS, 1975.

———. *L'Ashram de l'amour. Le gandhisme et l'imaginaire.* Paris: Editions de la Maison des sciences de l'homme, 1979.

Thompson, Edward. *Suttee. A Historical and Philosophical Enquiry into the Hindu Rite of Widow-Burning.* London: Allen & Unwin, 1928.

Timberg, T. A. *The Marwaris: From Traders to Industrialists.* New Delhi: Vikas Publishing House, 1978.

Tod, James. *Annals and Antiquities of Rajasthan.* 2 vols. London: Routledge & Kegan Paul, 1972. Reprinted in 3 vols., Delhi: Low Price Publications, 1990. First edition 1829–1832.

Tourlet, Christiane, and Jacques Scherer. *Quand le dieu Rama joue à Bénarès.* Louvain: Cahiers théâtre, 1990.

Trial by Fire. A Report on Roop Kanvar's Death. Women and Media Committee, Bombay Union of Journalists. Bombay, 11 December 1987.

Upreti, Harish Chandra, and Nandini. *The Myth of Sati (Some Dimensions of Widow Burning).* Bombay: Himalaya Publishing House, 1991.

Vaid, Sudesh. "Politics of Widow Immolation." *Seminar* 342 (February 1988): 20–23.

Vaid, Sudesh, and Kumkum Sangari. "Institutions, Beliefs, Ideologies. Widow Immolation in Contemporary Rajasthan." *Economic and Political Weekly* 26, no. 17 (27 April 1991): 2–17.

Van den Bosch, L. P. "A Burning Question. Sati and Sati Temples as the Focus of Political Interest." *Numen* 37, no. 2 (1990): 174–94.

Van der Kraan, Alfons. "Human Sacrifice in Bali: Sources, Notes and Commentary." *Indonesia* 40 (October 1985).

Van Kol, H. *Driemaal Dwars door Sumatra en Zwerftochten door Bali.* Rotterdam: Brusse, 1914.

Van Kooij, Karel R. *Worship of the Goddess According to the Kālikāpurāṇa.* Leiden: Brill, 1972.

Van Linschoten, John Huyghen. *Histoire de la navigation de Jean Hughes de Linscot.* Amsterdam: T. Pierre, 1610. First edition 1596. English translation, *The Voyage of John Huyghen van Linschoten to the East Indies, from the Old English Translation of 1598,* 2 vols. Edited by Arthur Coke Burnell and P. A. Tiele. New York: Burt Franklin, 1884.

Varhaspaty, K. Singh. *Karnī-Caritr.* Deshnok: Sri Hanuman Sarma Bookseller, 1938.

Varma, Mahadevi. *Smṛti kī rekhāen.* Allahabad: Leader Press, 1965.

Vatsa, R. Singh. "The Remarriage and Rehabilitation of the Hindu Widows in India, 1856–1914." *Journal of Indian History* (Decamber 1976): Part 3, 713–30.

Vaudeville, Charlotte. "La conception de l'amour divin chez Muhammad Jāyasī: *virah* et *'ishq*." *Journal Asiatique* (1962): 351–67.

———. *Étude sur les sources et la composition du Rāmāyaṇa de Tulsī-Dās.* Paris: Maisonneuve, 1955.

———. *Kabīr.* Oxford: Clarendon Press, 1974.

Verghese, Jamila. *Her Gold and her Body.* Delhi: Shakti Books, 1986.

Verne, Jules. *Le Tour du monde en quatre-vingts jours.* Paris: J. Hetzel, 1873.

Vidyalankar, K. C. *Pitṛ-pūjā.* New Delhi: Bharatiy Granth Niketan, 1990.

Vincenzo, F. *Il Viaggio all'Indie Orientali del padre F. Vincenzo.* Venice: Giacomo Zattoni, 1678.

Vogel, Jean-Philippe. "The Head-Offering to the Goddess in Pallava Sculpture." *Bulletin of the School of Oriental Studies* 6 (1930–1932): 539–43.

Vyas, R. P. "Social and Religious Reform Movements in the Nineteenth and Twentieth Centuries in Western Rajasthan." In *Social and Religious Reform Movements in the Nineteenth and Twentieth Centuries,* edited by S. P. Sen, 177–96. Calcutta: Institute of Historical Studies, 1979.

———. "Social Change in Rajasthan from the Middle of the 19th Century to the Middle of the 20th Century." In *Socio-Economic Study of Rajasthan,* edited by G. L. Devra, 130–48.

Wacziarg, Francis, and Amar Nath. *Rajasthan: The Painted Walls of Shekhavati.* London: Croom Helm, 1982.

Wadley, Susan S. "No Longer a Wife: Widows in Rural North India." In *From the Margins of Hindu Marriage,* edited by L. Harlan and P. B. Courtright, 92–118.

Ward, William A. *A View of the History, Literature, and Religion of the Hindoos.* Serampore: Mission Press, 1817; Madras: J. Higginbotham, 1863.

Weinberger-Thomas, Catherine [see also Thomas, Catherine]. "Les chemins du paganisme. Images de l'Inde à l'âge classique." In *As Others See Us. Mutual Perceptions, East and West,* edited by Bernard Lewis, Edmund Leites, and Margaret Case, 117–31. New York: International Society for the Comparative Study of Civilizations, 1986.

———, ed. *L'Inde et l'imaginaire (Puruṣārtha 11).* Paris: Editions de l'EHESS, 1988.

———. "Les yeux fertiles de la mémoire. Exotisme indien et représentations occidentales." In *L'Inde et l'imaginaire,* edited by C. Weinberger-Thomas, 9–31.

———. "Cendres d'immortalité. La crémation des veuves en Inde." *Archives de sciences sociales des religion* 67, no. 1 (1989): 9–51.

———. "Les stades de la vie selon l'idéal hindou." In *L'Etat du monde en 1992,* edited by G. Martinière and C. Varela, 83–85. Paris: La Découverte, 1992.

———. "Pour l'amour de Kâlî. *The Deceivers* de John Masters." In *Rêver l'Asie. Exotisme et littérature coloniale aux Indes, en Indochine et en Insulinde,* edited by Denys Lombard, 447–54. Paris: Editions de l' EHESS, 1993.

Westphal-Hellbusch, Sigrid. "Changes in the Meaning of Ethnic Names as Exemplified by the Jat, Rabari, Bharwad and Charan in Northwestern India." In *Pastoralists and Nomads in South Asia,* edited by L. S. Leshnik and G. Sontheimer, 124–28.

Westphal-Hellbusch, Sigrid, and Heinz Westphal. *Hinduistische Viehzüchter im nordwestlichen Indien.*
2 vols. Berlin: Duncker & Humblot, 1974, 1976.

White, David Gordon. *The Alchemical Body. Siddha Traditions in Medieval India.* Chicago: University of Chicago Press, 1996.

Wilson, Horace Hayman. *A Glossary of Judicial and Revenue Terms, & of Useful Words Occurring in Official Documents Relating to the Administration of the Government of British India.* London: W. H. Allen & Co., 1855.

Winternitz, Moriz. *Die Frau in den indischen Religionen.* Leipzig: Kabitzsch, 1920.

Yule, Henry, and Arthur Coke Burnell. *Hobson-Jobson: A Glossary of Anglo-Indian Words and Phrases, and of Kindred Terms, Etymological, Historical, Geographical, and Discursive.* London: J. Murray, 1903; reprint Delhi: Munshiram Manoharlal, 1968.

Ziegler, Norman P. *Action, Power and Service in Rajasthani Culture. A Social History of the Rajputs of Middle Period Rajasthan.* Ph.D diss., University of Chicago, 1973.

———. "Marvari Historical Chronicles: Sources for the Social and Cultural History of Rajasthan." *The Indian Economic and Social History Review* 13, no. 2 (April–June 1976): 219–50.

———. "The Seventeenth Century Chronicles of Mārvāṛa: A Study in the Evolution and Use of Oral Traditions in Western India." *History of Africa* 3 (1976): 127–53.

———. "Evolution of the Rathor State of Marvar: Horses, Structural Change and Warfare." In *The Idea of Rajasthan,* edited by Karine Schomer et al., 2:192–216.

Zimmer, Heinrich. *The King and the Corpse. Tales of the Soul's Conquest of Evil.* 2d ed. Edited by Joseph Campbell. New York: Pantheon Books, 1956. First edition 1948.

Zimmermann, Francis. "Géométrie sociale traditionnelle. Castes de main droite et castes de main gauche." *Annales ESC* 29, no. 6 (November–December 1974): 1381–1401.

———. "L'argument paresseux. Un problème grec dans un texte sanskrit." In *Différences, Valeurs, Hiérarchie. Textes offerts à Louis Dumont,* edited by Jean-Claude Galey, 53–64. Paris: Editions de l'EHESS, 1984.

———. *Le Discours des remèdes au pays des épices.* Paris: Payot, 1989.

———. "The Love-Lorn Consumptive: South Asian Ethnography and the Psychosomatic Paradigm." In *Anthropologies of Medicine. Colloquium on West European and North American Perspectives,* edited by Beatrix Pfleiderer and Gilles Bibeau, 185–95. Braunschweig: Vieweg, 1991.

Zollinger, Heinrich. "Het Eiland Lombok." *Tijdschrift voor Nederlandsch Indie* 9, no. 2 (1847): 345–49.

INDEX